Does God Exist?

Does God Exist?

A BELIEVER AND AN ATHEIST DEBATE

Terry L. Miethe and *Antony G. N. Flew*

HarperSanFrancisco

A Division of HarperCollins*Publishers*

FIRST EDITION

Library of Congress Cataloging-in-Publication Data

Miethe, Terry L., 1948–
    Does God exist? : a believer and an atheist debate / Terry Miethe and
    Antony Flew.—1st ed.
        p.   cm.
    Includes bibliographical references.
    ISBN 0-06-065579-8 (alk. paper)
    1. God—Proof.   2. God—Proof—Controversial literature.
    3. Disputations, Religious.   I. Flew, Antony, 1923–   . II. Title.
    BT102.M49   1991
    212'.1—dc20   91-70040
                                                                                      CIP

91   92   93   94   95   RRD(H)   10   9   8   7   6   5   4   3   2   1

Dedicated to

Leonard James Eslick (1914–1991)

Master Teacher and true Philosopher among men,
who patiently, lovingly taught students for almost five decades.

Contents

Foreword

Does God exist? If there is one thing on which Antony Flew and Terry Miethe agree, it is the enduring importance of this question. It is the most fundamental question that we questioning beings can ask. We all wish to know the source of this mysterious and uncertain reality into which we are thrown. We wish to know: where do we come from? Where are we going? What is the origin of morality, love, and meaning? Why is there evil in the world? As finite beings in a finite world we know, however, that this world is not in itself God, and so we are impelled, even compelled, to ask: Does God exist at all?

This vigorous and probing debate between two friends—the atheistic, analytical philosopher Antony Flew and the Christian metaphysician Terry Miethe—provides us with two radically different answers to this great question. Readers will follow with interest the intricate development of arguments and counterarguments in a series of presentations and critical engagements. The Humean empiricism of Professor Flew challenges the theist to account for his claims for God given the limits of human experience but is itself criticized as limited and empirically inadequate by the broader notion of experience offered by Terry Miethe. Dr. Miethe's spirited defence of the classical arguments for the existence of God, such as the cosmological argument, come under the sharp blade of Ockham's razor wielded by Antony Flew for postulating more than is necessary to explain causality. Terry Miethe's critique of Christian Neoplatonism and Antony Flew's reminder of the abiding questions raised by his early essay "Theology and Falsification" bring us back to the issues underlying the central topic. The question of free will, the nature of religious experience, the value of metaphysical arguments, and the fundamental issue of where the burden of proof lies are among the many other interesting points of dispute in this debate.

Fortunately, I do not have to act as an *arbiter elegantiarum* in this dispute, even less as an *arbiter veritatis*. My own position, developed at length in my book *Does God Exist? An Answer for Today* (German edition 1978), has not been treated in this dialogue. Therefore I am grateful that the two authors invited me, nevertheless, to present my own position in this book. Due to an engagement in a long-term research project on the situation of the world religions today, it was not possible for me to present my own position personally in this context. I therefore asked my colleague Hermann Häring, Professor of Systematic Theology at the University of Nijmegen, to replace me. During his time as my collaborator at the Institute for Ecumenical Research at the University of Tübingen, Hermann Häring supported me in my work on *Does God Exist?*. One could hardly find another person who could do such an excellent job in presenting my position on the question of God. Professor Häring did this with utmost care and fairness, and I can approve his essay wholeheartedly. I am especially in agreement with his hermeneutical observations. Hermann Häring was able to present my position in the light of the contemporary debate on hermeneutics and philosophy of language. In such a way my arguments have been presented even more convincingly and readers who are familiar with such debate in hermeneutics and philosophy will profit from this essay.

If I understand the debate correctly, my own position on the problem of God is identical neither with the position of Professor Flew nor that of Dr. Miethe. For me neither the position of the agnostic nor the position of the Christian metaphysican is convincing. I try to hold a third position. And it would be of utmost interest to see how my position could be brought into the dialogue, if the debate on the existence of God continues. But even in this phase of the debate, readers will be able to decide for themselves which arguments are the most convincing ones.

For German theologians it is certainly of great importance to be present in such an in-depth debate, which grew out of the tradition of the English-speaking world. Mutual exchange is possible, and as theologians and philosophers we do need more international cooperation. All these reasons make me very grateful to be present in a debate where so much is at stake. The question of God is not closed, but open again thanks at least to this important and thorough debate.

Hans Küng
Professor of Ecumenical Theology
and Director of the Institute for Ecumenical Research
at the University of Tübingen
Tübingen, January 1991

Introduction

Since the beginning of philosophical inquiry, the question "Does God exist?" has been of prime importance. The question of God's existence and what we can "know" of it has motivated philosophers for well over two millennia. There is no more important question either theoretically or practically. No question could have more vital importance to everyday life than the question of the existence of God. Professor Antony G. N. Flew and I are in full agreement about this.

Except for the period of the last two hundred years, the history of philosophy as a record of thought was motivated by much the same type of question that motivated theology. It seems that almost everyone in the history of thought would agree that the most important question one can ask is "Is there a God?" Everyone agrees on the question, but obviously not on the answer. The whole history of philosophical thought speaks out in support of the importance of metaphysical inquiry.

Logical positivism, a twentieth-century philosophical movement that grew out of the Vienna Circle founded by Moritz Schlick in 1924,[1] practically changed all of this. It maintained that a synthetic statement is meaningful only if there is a set of sense data that would verify or falsify it. Logical positivism (many of its adherents prefer the term logical empiricism") tends to restrict meaningfulness to analytical statements and empirical observations.[2] Thus, according to this view, metaphysical statements or statements about "God" are meaningless or all but meaningless (such statements may have some limited cultural, sociological, or psychological significance).

Philosophers who adhere to this view have been in control of the philosophy departments at most universities for the better part of this century. But the philosophical bankruptcy of this school of thought has now been clearly shown. Thus Bruce Reichenbach says: "The era is past when all metaphysical statements or arguments can simply be dismissed as silly or senseless, since they do not meet a preestablished criterion of verifiability" (1972). Yet, these developments from the early twentieth century are essential to an understanding of much of atheistic thought to this day and make this debate of particular importance.

A word is also appropriate here about the importance of debate in general. Many people do not think debate is important or valid. "Why waste your time debating," they say, "when debating never changes anyone's mind?" Sir Henry Wotton once wrote, *"disputandi pruritus ecclesiarum scabies,"* which has become translated as "the theologian's urge to debate is an incurable disease."[3] It is certainly true that modern debate often has more to do with style than content. Debaters learn to "make points," to make fun of the opponent, to use any tactic that will help win. If, along the way, they happen to have the better information, facts, "truth" to support their "performance," fine, but *winning* is everything. But this is not what debate should be about.

Since the time of Socrates, dialogue has been a powerful means of philosophical exploration and exposition. In the eighteenth century a great tradition of real debate developed. Debate was an honored method for "getting all the facts on the table," for pursuing the breadth and depth of a subject to discern the truth of a matter. Proponents and opponents alike honestly presented the very best evidence for what they believed to be true. Such debates were important events in shaping thought, the course of future discussions, and eventually public opinion. They were published not as an end, but as a means of carrying on discussion and advancing the pursuit of truth. Debate can produce the same results today, if practiced with intelligence and integrity.

There are several ways one could proceed in this debate: (1) As I have often seen done, we could have a "popular discussion," a lighthearted exchange in which more emphasis was put on "scoring points" and being "entertaining" than in searching for truth. In such an exchange, there would be much rhetoric, little substance, and ultimately little value. (2) We could simply go back and forth in answering claims and counterclaims. In this case my atheist "opponent" will have set the stage by starting the discussion. If all I did was answer him, I would be constantly following his lead and not really advancing the theistic argument. Or, (3) we could admit the extreme seriousness and complexity of the subject and try (while answering issues raised) to at least introduce the important historical metaphysical issues, shed some light on them, and in the process—at least in my case—attempt to build a philosophy of God. This is the method that should be followed. It may not be as "entertaining," but I hope it will challenge some to see the real important of the question and encourage them to commit themselves to the hard pursuit of the truth wherever the trail leads.

I am indeed pleased to have four such renowned scholars contribute essays to this volume. Sir Alfred Ayer (1910–1989) for more than half a century was considered the most famous living atheist philosopher. One of the last letters Sir Alfred read—about ten days before his death—was mine asking him to contribute to this volume. Ms. Guida Crowley, Sir

Alfred's secretarial assistant (and the person to whom *The Central Questions of Philosophy* is dedicated), wrote: "You will by now have heard the very sad news that Professor Sir Alfred Ayer died on 27 June. He was, however, well enough to read your letter. . . . He wasn't able to speak at the time but he wrote a note at the bottom of your letter. . . . " Though he was near death, Sir Alfred wrote that he would like for us to use his essay "The Claims of Theology" in our book. His death was sad news indeed. I am grateful to Ms. Crowley for her dedication to Sir Alfred and for her efforts on my behalf.

I am also very grateful to Hans Küng, a German scholar who is one of the world's best-known theologians, for his willingness to read this volume, write the Foreword, and read the article about his own thought written by Prof. Dr. Hermann Häring. Richard Swinburne, Professor of Philosophy at Oriel College, Oxford, and one of the best-known theistic scholars in the world, has very graciously contributed the essay "Evidence for God." Finally, I would like to thank Prof. Dr. Häring, Edward Schillebeeckx's successor at the University of Nijmegen, for contributing his essay on Hans Küng's argument for God's existence. Prof. Häring shouldered the burden of this essay during a time of great loss in his family and also of extremely demanding professional duties. I am indeed grateful to each one of these scholars for their willingness to enrich this debate.

Finally, by way of acknowledgment, I would like to thank Elizabeth M. Bischoff for her valuable help in translation and correspondence connected with this project. Ms. Bischoff was my son John Hayden's German teacher for three years and "labored in the vineyards" lovingly teaching students for forty-three years.

In *Agency and Necessity*, Professors Flew and Vesey write: "There will normally be more than two sides to any argument, and for any two 'opponents' there will be points of agreement as well as points of disagreement. The debate will not, therefore, necessarily cover every aspect of the chosen topic. . ." (Flew and Vesey 1987, p. vii). The decisions Prof. Flew and I reach regarding this debate should not—really cannot—take the place of a decision by you, the reader. Each person should study the arguments, sift the evidence, decide which case best fits the facts, and construct a worldview with which he or she can live. "Does God exist?" is what this debate is all about. Ultimately, the decision—and the responsibility for it—is yours. On with the debate!

Terry L. Miethe
Oxford, England
Trinity Term 1991

Does God Exist?

CHAPTER I

The Presumption of Atheism

Antony G. N. Flew

1. What Has the Atheist Not to Believe?

Let us begin by putting our present discussion into historical perspective. Although the publishers present *A History of Atheism in Britain: From Hobbes to Russell* as "the first history of British atheism," the author's preface is more modest: "There is still much field-work to be done. . . . The study of early atheism is still at the archaeological or natural history stage" (Berman 1988, p. viii). One kind of trophy brought back from Berman's own fieldwork consists in cases for identifying Hobbes, various "foundling followers of Hobbes," and Anthony Collins as covert atheists, their atheism "disguised by esoteric presentation, confined . . . to 'the private study and select conversation,' or condemned retrospectively" by themselves after their own apostate returns to religion (Berman 1988, p. 110). Of another kind is Berman's discovery, or perhaps it should be rediscovery, of the first overtly and avowedly atheist book to be published in Britain. This, appearing in 1782, was the anonymous *Answer to Dr. Priestley's Letters to a Philosophical Unbeliever.*

Berman is right to make much of the remarkable lateness of this first public avowal. Deafened by the clamor of accusations of atheism, historians of ideas have been tempted to overlook the lack of confessions. Even after what now appears to have been the first breaking of the ice, it was a further fourteen years before "the *Watson refuted*," which J. M. Robertson's *History of Free Thought* had credited with "the first explicit avowal of atheism in English controversy" (quoted in Berman 1988, p. 120). Simultaneous with the clamor of accusations we find abundant authorities, including some of the accusers, who question or

outright deny the possibility of any sincere theoretical commitment to
atheism—as opposed, that is, to a practical refusal to allow the (nevertheless still asserted) existence of God to affect everyday living.

Understandably enough, Berman devotes the whole of his first and
longest chapter to this threat to the reality of his subject matter. Since no
one has ever wanted to deny the possibility of either practical or
unthinking atheists, Berman suggests that such doubting of the possibility of sincere and thinking atheism should be construed as an
exercise in repression, repression (unconscious) here being contrasted
with suppression (conscious). He also indicates an inverse relationship
between the two: insofar as repression is effective there is less occasion
for what Leninists in power call "administrative measures."

This bumper chapter on "The Repression of Atheism" has, it would
seem, taken the place of an essential preliminary—a philosophical
discussion establishing the relevant criteria for the application of the
term "atheism." Precisely what does anyone have to do or not do, to
believe or disbelieve or simply not believe, if he or she is to be legitimately admitted into the company of British atheists?

i. That qualifying adjective is crucial, for disbelief and nonbelief are
necessarily relative to belief. Thus, in the early Roman Empire, on the
perfectly true grounds that they did indeed reject the whole theology of
Mount Olympus, even the most orthodox Christians could be, and
sometimes were, put down as atheists. Hence, in the present context of
discussion in the United States or Britain, the atheist will presumably be
required either to outright deny or at least not to positively believe that
the conception of God shared by the "peoples of the Book"—the
conception common to traditional forms of Judaism, of Christianity, and
of Islam—is a concept which possesses or corresponds to some actually
existing object.

(a) We have to move carefully in phrasing any account of the concept
or concepts in question. For instance, to speak of Mosaic theism without
reservation might be assumed to prejudice questions about how early
the ideas of an original ex nihilo creation and of a subsequent total
ontological dependence entered that tradition. Again, to omit the
qualification "traditional" would be to open the door to all manner of
indisputably heterodox substitutes for the God of the fathers and the
saints, of the councils and the popes.

It is notorious that ours is a period in which prominent clerics may
be heard to profess almost any variety of belief or unbelief, with perhaps
the sole exception of non–Third World opposition to the Leninist

totalitarian aspirations of the (South) African National Congress (Campbell 1986). Could it be—this sometime vice president of the Rationalist Press Association is tempted to ask—that, when our politicized priests contemplate Mrs. Winnie Mandela's gloatings over the potentialities of "our matches and our necklaces," they hanker for the days when their predecessors too could have dissidents burned alive, albeit then in the name of the Christ rather than of Communism?

(b) Let us here and now cite just one example of a heterodox substitution effected by someone who was in his day an influential professional theologian. We can then forthwith dismiss as irrelevant to our present discussion his obscurantist verbal acrobatics:

> The question of the existence of God can be neither asked nor answered. If asked it is a question about that which by its very nature is above existence, and therefore the answer—whether negative or affirmative—implicitly denies the nature of God. It is as atheistic to affirm the existence of God as it is to deny it. God is being-itself, not *a* being. (Tillich 1967, vol. 1, pp. 236–37; emphasis here, and everywhere else save the due notice given, as in original)

Elsewhere and earlier the same once widely respected and professedly Protestant theologian had offered a characteristic exercise in "conversion by definition" (Kaufman 1963, p. 90). Perhaps unbeknown to themselves converts were to be definitionally conveyed to a position that, though in name theist, was in fact, in our present understanding, atheist. Since "God is depth" it appears that "you cannot call yourself an atheist or an unbeliever":

> For you cannot think or say: Life has no depth! Life itself is shallow. . . .
> If you could say this in complete seriousness, you would be an atheist; but otherwise you are not. He who knows about depth knows about God. (Tillich 1948, p. 57)

ii. It might at first blush appear that the question of the existence of the God of Abraham, Isaac, and Jacob was on all fours with [equal to] the question of the existence of Loch Ness monsters, of unicorns, and of Abominable Snowpersons. In all cases of this sort the difficulty, if there is a difficulty, is the shortage of evidence. There is no dispute about what sort of evidence is or would be relevant and of which we perhaps need more and better. In such cases a neat tripartite division of the disputants is both possible and convenient. Some believe, and perhaps claim to know, that there do exist objects of these concepts; others believe, and perhaps claim to know, that there do not; while yet others—more cautious or simply indifferent—are put down by the pollsters as "Don't Knows."

It is tempting to attempt a similar tripartite division with respect to this or indeed any other concept of God. Here the committed believers will be called theists, the committed unbelievers atheists, while the "Don't Knows" will be dignified with the Greek title "agnostics," here employed simply in its etymological meaning, rather than in the more sophisticated sense given to it by T. H. Huxley (Huxley 1904, vol. 5, p. 239). Consider, as an example of such pure and unsophisticated nescience, aboriginals of the northern territories of Australia singing:

> The God-men say when die go sky
> Through pearly gates where river flow,
> The God-men say when die we fly
> Just like eagle, hawk and crow—
> Might be, might be; I don't know.
>   (Quoted in Flew 1984a, p. 36)

(a) Whereas, however, we have in all these other cases descriptions that would enable us decisively to identify a member of the class hypothesized were we so fortunate as to be directly confronted with such an actual specimen, this is not true of the present, or perhaps any, concept of God. Richard Swinburne, whose theological trilogy constitutes the most philosophically formidable of all contemporary defenses of traditional Christian theism (Swinburne 1977, 1979, and 1981), offers at the very beginning of the first of these three works what he considers to be an undisputatious definition: "By a 'God' he [the traditional, Mosaic theist] understands something like a person without a body (i.e., a spirit) who is eternal, free, able to do anything, knows everything, is perfectly good, is the proper object of human worship and obedience, the creator and sustainer of the Universe."

Swinburne's assumption that such a definition would be generally acceptable to theists is certainly sound. But, equally certainly, that is not to say that it is unproblematic. Take, for instance, that first phrase "a person without a body (i.e., a spirit)." Later we are told that "Human persons have bodies: he [God] does not" (Swinburne 1977, p. 51). Again, in the course of a discussion of "what it is for a body to be mine" Swinburne, having first listed various peculiarly personal characteristics, tells us that "we learn to apply the term 'person' to various individuals around us in virtue of their possession of the characteristics which I have outlined" (Swinburne 1977, p. 102).

This, surely, is all wrong? If persons really were creatures *possessing* bodies, rather than—as in fact we are—creatures who just essentially *are* members of one special sort of creatures of flesh and blood, then it would make sense to speak of a whole body amputation. Who is it, too, who is presupposed to be able sensibly to ask which of various bodies is his or hers? How is such a puzzled person to be identified or to self-identify, save by reference to the living organism that he or she actually is?

As for Swinburne's suggestion that we could, and even do, learn to apply the word "person" to "various individuals around us" by first learning how to pick out certain peculiarly personal characteristics and then identifying persons as creatures of the kind that possess these characteristics—this constitutes a perfect paradigm of the literally pre-posterous. The manifest truth is that our only experience of any peculiarly personal characteristics is, and indeed has to be, of these as characteristics peculiar to that particular kind of creatures that we have first learned to identify as mature and normal human beings. The identification of such peculiarly personal characteristics therefore is and must be posterior rather than prior to the identification of members of the particular kind of creatures to which alone these characteristics can be and are normally attributed.

It should certainly be seen as at least very far from obvious that talk of "a person without a body (i.e., a spirit)" is coherent and intelligible. In their ordinary everyday understanding, person words—the personal pronouns, personal names, words for persons playing particular roles (such as "spokesperson," "official," "premier," "aviator," etc.), and so on—are all employed to name or otherwise to refer to members of a very special class of creatures of flesh and blood.

In this ordinary, everyday understanding—what other do we have?—incorporeal persons are no more a sort of persons than are imaginary, fictitious, or otherwise nonexistent persons. "Incorporeal" is here, like those others, an aliens' adjective. To put the point less technically but more harshly and thus to provide an always welcome occasion for quoting "the Monster of Malmesbury," to assert in that ordinary everyday understanding that somebody survived death, but disembodied, is to contradict yourself. Hence, in chapter 5 of his *Leviathan*, the incorrigible Thomas Hobbes was so rude as to say that, "if a man talks to me of 'a round quadrangle'; or 'accidents of bread in cheese'; or 'inmaterial substances'; . . . I should not say that he was in error, but that his words were without meaning: that is to say, absurd."[1]

Swinburne thought to deflect the ferocity of such critical onslaughts by making the emollient point that no one has any business to argue, just because all the so-and-sos with which they happen themselves to have been acquainted were such-and-such, that therefore such-and-suchness must be an essential characteristic of anything that is to be properly rated a so-and-so (Swinburne 1977, p. 54). This is indeed perfectly correct. Certainly it would be intellectually and perhaps also morally scandalous to argue that, because all the human beings with whom you had so far become acquainted had had black skins, therefore anyone with any other skin pigmentation must be disqualified from being rated as a human being.

Incorporeality, however, is a very different kettle of fish—or more like no kettle and no fish—for to characterize something as incorporeal is to make an assertion that is at one and the same time both extremely comprehensive and wholly negative. Those proposing to do this surely owe it both to themselves and to others not only to indicate what positive characteristics might significantly be attributed to their putative incorporeal entities, but also to specify how such entities could, if only in principle, be identified and reidentified. It is not exclusively, or even primarily, a question of what predicates these putative spiritual subjects might take, but of how they themselves might be identified in the first place, and only after that reidentified as numerically the same through an effluxion of time.

(b) Paralleling the recognition of this and similar difficulties with the concept of God—difficulties that raise the question whether we have here a concept of a kind that could have a proper object—have been the developments that led John Wisdom to begin his famous article "Gods" with the sentence: *The existence of God is not an experimental issue in the way it was* (Wisdom 1953, p. 149). He went on: ". . . disagreement about whether there are gods is now less of this experimental or betting sort than it used to be. This is due in part, if not wholly, to our better knowledge of why things happen as they do" (Wisdom 1953, p. 149). As a reminder of the days when such disputed questions were, as Wisdom elsewhere so happily had it, "betting issues," let us, for a change, quote not from the biblical account of the contest between the priests of Baal and the priests of Jehovah but from the story of the conversion of Iceland in "The Sage of Burnt Njal." Some nowadays will sigh for the robust, confident, and forthright approach of the missionary, Thangbrand:

> "You heathens are to hallow one of the fires. I shall hallow the second.
> If the berserk is afraid of the fire I hallow, but walks unscathed through
> your fire, then you must accept the new faith."

He was, he did, and they did.

Thangbrand asked if they would now take the new faith. Gest replied that he never made promises which he did not intend to keep. So Thangbrand baptized Gest and all his household and many others. (Magnusson and Palsson 1960, sec. 103)

In the years immediately after World War II it used sometimes to be mischievously said that Oxford philosophers had invented a new cure for atheism. (I certainly said this myself often, even if I cannot be equally certain that I invented the phrase.) Young people coming up as shining-eyed atheists found after a term or two that they no longer knew in what atheists are essentially required to disbelieve. This current of opinion was epitomized in a much reprinted note entitled "Theology and Falsification."[2] Beginning with an acknowledged borrowing from John Wisdom's "Gods," this note concluded with a challenge:

> Just what would have to happen not merely (morally and wrongly) to tempt but also (logically and rightly) to entitle us to say "God does not love us" or even "God does not exist"? I therefore put to the succeeding symposiasts the simple central question: "What would have to occur or to have occurred to constitute for you a disproof of the love of, or of the existence of, God?" (Flew 1984a, p. 74)

In *A History of Atheism in Britain: From Hobbes to Russell*, David Berman's quotations from Charles Bradlaugh and others make it clear that I and my contemporaries were wrong in our brash assurance that we were members of the first generation to think such thoughts. For in *A Plea for Atheism* Bradlaugh wrote: "The atheist does not say 'there is no God' but he says: 'I know not what you mean by God; I am without an idea of God. . . . I do not deny, because I cannot deny that of which I have no conception'" (quoted in Berman 1988, p. 204).

iii. The upshot of this whole first section on "What has the atheist not to believe?" is that we need to give a new and much more comprehensive meaning to the term "atheist." Whereas it is currently construed as referring to a person who positively disbelieves that there is an object corresponding to what is thus tacitly taken to be a or the legitimate concept of God, I would now urge that the word be hereafter understood not positively but negatively. Let the originally Greek prefix "a" be read in the same way in "atheist" as it customarily is read in such other Greco-English words as "amoral," "atypical," and "asymmetrical." In this interpretation an atheist becomes not someone who positively asserts the nonexistence of God, but someone who is simply not a theist. Let us, for future ready reference, introduce the labels "positive atheist" for the former and "negative atheist" for the latter.

(a) Berman, operating with a version of the established positive conception that he appears never to make fully explicit, does contrive to draw more big fish into his net than many predecessors have done. This is achieved by scooping up those who, while still pretending a commitment to something to be called God, have nevertheless denied some essential of Mosaic theism. In that traditional conception, shared by all the "people of the Book," God not only first is "creator and sustainer of the Universe," but also, under the rubric "perfectly good," intervenes within the creation—by (sometimes) performing miracles, by (sometimes) answering prayer, and by favoring or disfavoring and eventually rewarding or punishing different kinds of conduct.

There can be no dispute but that both Hume, the gently mocking Scottish skeptic, upon at least the second of these two counts, and Spinoza, "the God-intoxicated man," upon both counts together, are, under the corresponding positive conception, correctly put down as atheists. Since the word "Universe" (with an initial capital) has here to be defined as including (with the exception only of a possible artificer or creator God) everything there is, Spinoza's pantheist identification of God with the Universe—"Deus sive Natura"—leaves no room for any external and additional Being. And both Spinoza and Hume refused to admit either divine interventions in the order of nature or a future life rewarding favored or punishing disfavored kinds of conduct.

While we are about it and before going on to consider the more extensive embrace of negative atheism, it is perhaps just worth noticing something to which we shall later need to return most emphatically. Much too little is usually made of the fact that there is a tension between the two contentions specified at the end of the last paragraph but one. Once this tension is recognized it becomes pretty clear that, in the history of ideas, the notion of a god or gods that either normally is or are committed to supporting, or that can at least sometimes be recruited to support, one side against another in conflicts internal to the Universe must have preceded that of a single God constituting both the originating and the sustaining cause of everything, including necessarily all the activities and all the inactivities of every party in every dispute.

No one, surely, who was approaching the suggestion of an infinite creator God without any prior commitment to some god or gods of powers more limited would be tempted to attribute such partisan interventions and such restricted sympathies to a Being stipulated to be an omniscient and omnipotent Creator. Revelation apart, the natural, the inevitable, the obvious assumption is that everything in such a creation must at all times both be and become exactly as its Creator wishes. If some features of that creation and some developments therein strike us as profoundly unsatisfactory, as indeed they do, then it must be in the last degree unrealistic—again revelation apart—to expect that the Creator—who, by the hypothesis, makes everything to be and to become as it is and as it is to be—will now take some satisfactory if belated corrective action. A priori the reasonable assumption must be— as, I am told, some Indian theistic thinkers have maintained—that such a Creator would be "beyond good and evil."

Anyone who is seeking—in the words of Matthew Arnold's description of the object of his religious quest—"something, not ourselves, which makes for righteousness" will be best advised to follow J. S. Mill in exploring the case for the existence of an extremely powerful yet still very far from omnipotent Being (see the essay "Theism" in Mill 1874). As Mill himself was well aware, the combination of the idea of an omnipotent and omniscient Creator God with the idea that that God somehow takes sides in conflicts within the creation generates intractable difficulties both moral and intellectual.

For a start, the introduction of the first element in that combination draws the teeth of what has always been the most persuasive argument of natural theology, for intelligent design is a matter of finding effective means to achieve intended ends by exploiting both the intractabilities and the potentialities of recalcitrant materials. But for such a Creator there can be no preexistent and recalcitrant materials, while all ends willed by Omnipotence must be achievable even if not actually achieved directly and without intervening means.

Again, if a Creator is hypothesized as being "perfectly good," as knowing everything, and as "able to do anything," then how come there is so much, indeed any, evil in the creation? And, furthermore, if we are all creatures of this Creator, then how can it be anything but monstrously unjust to arrange to punish any of us at all, much less some of us inordinately and eternally, for doing or failing to do precisely and only what—upon these embarrassing traditional assumptions—that Creator inexorably determines that we shall do or fail to do? These, of course, are the reasons why the theologically sophisticated Milton, who wanted *Paradise Lost* both to present epic conflicts and "to justify the ways of God to man," found the task to which he had set himself so impossibly difficult (see, for instance, Empson 1965).

(b) In the negative sense proposed the term "atheist" becomes correctly applicable to far more people. It applies, immediately, to all those who are atheists in the positive sense, to all those, that is, who "positively disbelieve that there is an object corresponding to what is thus tacitly taken to be a or the legitimate concept of God." But then it must also embrace all those who, for whatever reason, would echo Bradlaugh: "I know not what you mean by God; I am without idea of God. . . . I do not deny, because I cannot deny that of which I have no conception." Perhaps too we should include, as a third subclass of negative atheists, those who refuse "to allow the (nevertheless still asserted) existence of God to affect their everyday living," for, when the God thus still persistently asserted is stipulated to be the supreme partisan within the creation, then it becomes very hard to accept such assertions as sincere.

In many contexts this would certainly not be the right meaning to give to the word "atheism." The reason for suggesting that here it is is that its introduction is calculated to shift the emphasis toward the conceptual problems. Traditionally, issues that should be seen as concerning the legitimacy or otherwise of a proposed or supposed concept have by philosophical theologians been discussed either as surely disposable difficulties in reconciling one particular feature of the Divine nature with another or else as aspects of an equally surely soluble general problem of saying something about the infinite Creator in language intelligible to finite creatures. These traditional and still almost universally accepted forms of presentation are fundamentally prejudicial, for they assume that there is a Divine Being with an actual nature the features of which we can proceed to investigate.

All this is, no doubt, all very well when and insofar as the existence of God can be taken for granted. But when, as now, the question before us is whether a or the concept of God does or does not in fact have an object, then any such approach must be literally preposterous.[3] If we are inquiring whether there in fact is an object corresponding to some putative definite description or whether some supposed class does possess any actual members, then the obvious first steps are, in the one case, to make sure that the description is indeed both coherent and truly definite and, in the other, to ask how any members of that supposed class are to be decisively identified as such. It is only when, and if, and insofar as such logically prior conceptual problems have been satisfactorily solved that it can become sensible to move on to the substantial and much more exciting but logically secondary question or questions of fact.

2. The Burden of Proof

I have argued at some length elsewhere (Flew 1984a, chap. 1) that fundamental discussions of the present kind should start from what I like to label, with bold initial capitals, **The Presumption of Atheism**. In this coinage the word "presumption" is not—as on other lips it might be—a synonym for "presumptuousness." Instead it is intended to be construed as it is when we speak of the presumption of innocence in common law. The word "atheism" too has here to be understood in the negative rather than the positive sense.

i. Both these two presumptions are, of course, defeasible; and for that reason they are not to be identified with assumptions. The presumption of innocence indicates where the court should start and how it must proceed. Yet the prosecution is still able, more often than not, to bring forward what is in the end accepted as sufficient reason to warrant the verdict of "Guilty," which appropriate sufficient reason is properly characterized as a proof of guilt. The defeasible presumption of innocence is thus in this majority of cases in fact defeated. Were the indefeasible innocence of all accused persons an assumption of any legal system, then there could not be within that system any provision for any verdict other than "Not Guilty." To the extent that it is, for instance, an assumption of English common law that every citizen is cognizant of all that the law requires of him or her, that law cannot admit the fact that this assumption is, as in fact it is, false.

The presumption of atheism is similarly defeasible. It lays it down that thorough and systematic inquiry must start from a position of negative atheism and that the burden of proof lies on the theist proposition. Yet this is not at all the same thing as demanding that the debate should proceed on either a positive or a negative atheist assumption. That would indeed preclude a theist conclusion. But counsel for theism no more betrays the client by accepting the framework determined by this general presumption than counsel for the prosecution betrays the state by conceding the legal presumption of innocence. The latter is perhaps at heart unshakably convinced of the guilt of the particular defendant. Yet counsel for the prosecution must, and with complete consistency and perfect sincerity may, insist that the proceedings of the court should respect the presumption of innocence. The former is even more likely to be persuaded of the soundness of the theistic brief. Yet that counsel too can with a good conscience allow that a thorough and complete apologetic must start from, meet, and go on to defeat the presumption of atheism.

Although the presumption of atheism is as much impartial between rival disputants as the presumption of innocence, it is fair and proper for me to state now and in so many words that I do nevertheless believe that, in the fresh perspective proved by this proposed presumption, the whole enterprise of theism appears even more difficult and precarious than it did before. In part this is a corollary of what I have just been suggesting in Section 1: that certain difficulties and objections that may previously have seemed peripheral or even factitious are made to stand out as fundamental and unavoidable. But it is also in part a consequence of the emphasis it places on the imperative need to produce some sort of sufficient reason in order to justify theist belief.

(a) One thing that helps to conceal this need is confusion about the possible varieties of proof. Nowadays too it is frequently asserted, even by professing Roman Catholics, that everyone knows that it is impossible to prove the existence of God. The first objection to this putative truism is, as my reference to Roman Catholics should have suggested, that it is not true, for it is an essential dogma of Roman Catholicism, defined as such by the First Vatican Council, that "the one and true God our creator and lord can be known for certain through the creation by the natural light of human reason" (Denzinger 1953, sec. 1806). So even if this dogma is, as I myself believe, false, it is certainly not known to be false by those many Roman Catholics who remain, despite all the disturbances consequent upon the Second Vatican Council, committed to the full traditional faith.

To this sophisticated objectors might reply that the definition of the First Vatican Council speaks of knowing for certain rather than of proving or demonstrating, adding perhaps, if they were very sophisticated indeed, that the word *demonstrari* in an earlier draft was eventually replaced by the expression *certo cognosci*. But, allowing that this is correct, it is certainly not enough to vindicate the conventional wisdom, for the word "proof" is not ordinarily restricted in its application to demonstratively valid arguments, arguments, that is, in which the conclusion cannot be denied without thereby contradicting the premises. So it is too flattering to suggest that most of those who make this facile claim, that everyone knows that it is impossible to prove the existence of God, are intending only the strictly limited assertion that one special sort of proof is impossible, namely, demonstrative proof.

The truth, and the danger, is that wherever there is any awareness of such a limited and specialized interpretation, there will be a quick and illegitimate move to the much wider general conclusion that it is impossible and, furthermore, unnecessary to provide any sufficient reason for believing. It is, therefore, worth underlining that when the presumption of atheism is explained as insisting that the onus of proof must be on the theist, the word "proof" is being used in the ordinary wide sense in which it can embrace any and every variety of sufficient reason. It is, of course, in this and only this same sense that the word is interpreted when the presumption of innocence is explained as laying the onus of proof on the prosecution.

(b) Even if it is false to assert that everyone knows it to be impossible to prove the existence of God, it might nevertheless be true to say that it is. Those believing that any attempt at any kind of proof is fundamentally misconceived often go on to suggest that the territory that reason cannot inhabit may nevertheless be freely colonized by faith: "Faith alone will carry you forward," it is sometimes said, "when reason has gone as far as it can go"; and so on.

Perhaps it is indeed ultimately impossible to establish the existence of God or even to show that it is more or less probable. But, if so, the suggested moral is not correct: rational persons do not thereby become in this area free to believe or not to believe just as their fancy takes them. Faith, as my preacher father used sometimes to proclaim in sermons, should be not a leap in the dark but a leap toward the light. Arbitrarily to plump for some particular conviction and then stubbornly to cleave to it would be—to borrow the term Thomas Aquinas employed in discussing faith, reason and revelation in the *Summa Contra Gentiles*—"frivolous" (I (vi); his Latin word is *levis*). If your venture of faith is not to be arbitrary, irrational, and in the deepest sense frivolous, then you must have presentable reasons: first, for making any such commitment in this area, an area in which by hypothesis the available grounds are insufficient to warrant any firm conclusion; and, second, for opting for one particular possibility rather than any of the other available alternatives.

To most such offerings of reasons the presumption of atheism remains relevant, for though, again by the hypothesis, these cannot aspire to prove their conclusions, they will usually embrace some estimation of their probability. If the onus of proof lies on those who hope definitively to establish the existence of God, it must also by the same token rest on those who plan to make out only that this conclusion is more or less probable.

The qualifications "most" and "usually" have to be inserted in order to make room for apologetic in the tradition of Pascal's wager. In that famous—or should it be notorious?—argument Pascal makes no attempt to show that his Roman Catholicism is certainly or even probably true, while the reasons he suggests for putting the recommended bet on his particular preferred faith are motivating rather than evidencing (Flew 1989, chap. 6, sec. 7).

ii. In societies such as ours, in which professing positive atheists constitute a minute minority, it comes more easily to ask why one is not a theist than why one is. Construed as a biographical question this is no doubt methodologically inoffensive. But our concern here is not with questions of why people come to hold whatever opinions they do hold. Rather it is with the need for opinions to be suitably grounded if they are to be rated as items of knowledge or even of rational belief. The issue is not what does or does not need to be explained biographically, but where the burden of theological proof should rest.

A more sophisticated objection of fundamentally the same sort would urge that our whole discussion has been too artificial and too general, and that one's inquiries have to begin from wherever one happens to be: "We cannot begin with complete doubt. We must begin with all the prejudices which we actually have. . . . These prejudices are not to be dispelled by a maxim" (Peirce 1934, vol. 1, pp. 156–57). The paragraph concludes, however, with the concession: "A person may, it is true, find reason to doubt what he began by believing; but in that case he doubts because he has a positive reason for it, and not on account of the Cartesian maxim."

(a) The maxim Peirce had in his sights was indeed Cartesian. The first three parts of the *Discourse on the Method* are largely autobiographical and deceptively unexciting. But in the first paragraph of the fourth part Descartes opens up with what has a strong claim to constitute the most shattering single-sentence salvo in the entire literature of philosophy.

> So, because our senses sometimes play us false, I decided to suppose that there was nothing at all which was such as they cause us to imagine it; and, because there are men who make mistakes in reasoning, even with the simplest geometrical matters, and construct paralogisms, judging that I was as liable to error as anyone else, I rejected as unsound all the reasonings I had hitherto accepted as proofs.

For us the interest of this project for systematic doubt lies in the unheralded, sustained, and no doubt prudent refusal of Descartes to challenge precisely those beliefs that, upon his own previously stated principles, he had the strongest of positive reasons for doubting. In the first part, while reviewing the progress of his education, he contrasts philosophy with theology, rather waspishly: "Theology teaches how to gain heaven . . . philosophy gives the means by which one can speak plausibly on all matters and win the admiration of the less learned." He then takes his own somewhat enigmatic personal stand:

> I revered our theology, and aspired as much as anyone else to gain heaven; but . . . the revealed truths which lead to it are beyond our understanding. . . . To undertake the examination of them, and succeed, one would need some special grace from heaven, and to be more than a man.

Considered by itself this may be all very well. Yet it is certainly not consistent with one very pertinent remark made later in the same part:

> For it seemed to me that I might find much more truth in the reasonings which someone makes in matters that affect him closely, the results of which must be detrimental to him if his judgment is faulty, than from the speculations of a man of letters in his study; which produces no concrete effect, and which are of no other consequence to him except perhaps that the further they are away from common sense, the more vanity he will derive from them, because he will have had to use that much more skill and subtlety in order to make them seem dialectically probable.

We may expect everyday and practically oriented perceptual judgments to be, typically, correct. But, at least initially, speculations either about another world or about the operations of unobservables in this world must be legitimately suspect. The reason is obvious. Whereas the price of failing to perceive, say, advancing traffic will likely be immediate injury or death, the incomparably more appalling penalty of eternal damnation is too often felt to be—understandably even if falsely—both remote and unsure.

In the second part Descartes proceeds to provide a second and more decisive general reason for doubting all theological claims:

> Having learned from the time I was at school that there is nothing one can imagine so strange or so unbelievable that it has not been said by one or other of the philosophers; and since then, while traveling, having recognized that all those who hold opinions quite opposed to ours are not on that account barbarians or savages, but that many exercise as much as reason as we do, or more; and, having considered how a given man, with his given mind, being brought up from childhood among the French or Germans becomes different from what he would be if he had always lived among the Chinese or among

cannibals . . . I was convinced that our beliefs are based much more on custom and example than on any certain knowledge.

(b) Pierce was writing about doubt in general. A more particular objection to the presumption of atheism has been developed by John Hick, originally in *Theology Today*, April 1967:

> The right question is whether it is rational for the religious man himself, given that his religious experience is coherent, persistent, and compelling, to affirm the reality of God. What is in question is not the rationality of an inference from certain psychological events to God as their cause; for the religious man no more infers the existence of God than we infer the existence of the visible world around us. What is in question is the rationality of the one who has the religious experiences. If we regard him as a rational person we must acknowledge that he is rational in believing what, given his experiences, he cannot help believing. (pp. 86–87)

It must at once be conceded that it is one thing to say that a belief is unfounded or well founded and quite another to say that it is irrational or rational for particular persons, in their own particular times and circumstances and with their particular experience and lack of experience, to hold or to reject that belief. Granted that his usually reliable intelligence were sure that the enemy tank brigade was in town, it was entirely reasonable for the general also to believe this. But the enemy tanks had in fact pulled back. Yet it was still unexceptionably sensible for the general on his part to refuse to expose his flank to those tanks which were in fact not there. That genuine and important distinction cannot, however, save the day for Hick.

It might seem that, granted this concession, those for whom he was speaking could rest perfectly content, for, by the hypothesis, they consider that they have the very best of grounds for their belief. They regard their "coherent, consistent, and compelling" religious experience as analogous to perception; and these who can see something with their own eyes and feel it in their own hands are in a perfect position to know that it exists. Their position is indeed so perfect that, as Hick says, it is wrong to speak here of evidence and inference. If a man saw his wife in the act of intercourse with a lover then he no longer needs to infer her infidelity from bits and pieces of evidence. He has now what is better than inference, although for the rest of us, who missed this display, his testimony still constitutes an important part of the evidence in the case. The idiomatic expression "the evidence of my own eyes" derives its paradoxical piquancy precisely and only from the fact that to see for oneself is better than to have evidence (Austin 1962, pp. 115–16).

All this is true. Certainly, too, those who think that they can, as it were, see, hear, or otherwise perceive God must reject the suggestion that in so doing they infer "from certain psychological events to God as their cause." To accept this account would be to call down upon their heads all the insoluble difficulties that fall to the lot of all those who maintain that what we see, and all we ever really and directly see, is visual sense data. And, furthermore, it is useful to be reminded that when we insist that knowledge as opposed to mere belief has to be adequately warranted, this grounding may be a matter either of having sufficient evidence or of being in a position to know directly and without evidence. So far, therefore, it might seem that Hick's objection was completely at cross-purposes and that, anyway, his protégés have no need to appeal to the distinction between actual knowledge and what one may rationally and properly claim to know.

Wait a minute. The passage under discussion formed part of an attempt to rebut criticism of an argument from religious experience. The contention criticized was that enjoying religious experience is a kind of perceiving and hence a sort of being in a position to have knowledge of its putative object. The criticism was that those pushing this contention collapse the crucial distinctions between merely "seeing" (in disclaimer quotes) and truly seeing; between experience in the peculiar private sense of the philosopher and experience in the ordinary, everyday, plainpersons' public understanding.

If someone believes that he saw a cow, but if there was in fact no cow present and available to be seen, then the most that we can allow is, not that he truly saw the cow he thought he saw, but that he merely (in disclaimer quotes) "saw" it. It is clear that, in talking about the true believer's experience of God, Hick wants us to construe the word "experience" in its ordinary, public sense. This is the sense in which farmers, wanting to hire cowpersons, advertise for "hands with experience of cows." Such advertisers would, surely, be more surprised than pleased to find themselves interviewing candidates who confessed only to having enjoyed dreams or visions of cows or to having had some (possibly "wild" or hallucinatory) cowish sense data, but who disclaimed all confident physical or cognitive contact with real, external world, cud-chewing, flesh-and-blood cows (Flew 1989, chap. 6, sec. 6)?

The existence of mind-independent objects of experience, in the ordinary understanding of "experience," cannot be directly inferred either from the mere occurrence of experience or from claims about the mere occurrence of experience in the peculiar philosophers' interpretation of "experience." Yet just this, surely, is what Hick's believers are trying to do when they claim in their experience to be, as it were, directly perceiving their God? They must all know, just as well as everyone else knows, that whenever and wherever they themselves claim to be enjoying their brand of supposedly cognitive religious experience, there is nothing available to be ordinarily perceived other than what is ordinarily perceptible equally by all the rest of us and, hence, that they themselves are to all appearance engaged in nothing more or other than exercises of the imagination.

They know too, presumably, that adherents of other and often incompatible systems of religion are also persuaded that they have had experience, in the ordinary sense of that word, of the very different objects of their own religious devotions—experience, that is, of Apollo and Athena, of Siva and Ganesh, just as much as of Jesus bar Joseph and of his virgin mother. So how can it be reasonable of Hick's cobelievers to rest so confidently upon their conviction that they alone allegedly have in fact been privileged to enjoy genuinely informative religious experience? How can it be reasonable, that is, until and unless they have, by first meeting and defeating the presumption of atheism, maneuvered themselves into a position to maintain that it is through their prior knowledge of the existence and activities of its ostensible objects that they have become qualified to pick out their own brand of religious experience as uniquely and authentically cognitive and revelatory?

Hick supports the pretensions to rationality of his flock and tells us that "one who has the religious experience . . . cannot help believing." But until and unless these people produce good reason for their conviction that what they call their experience of God is something more than an exercise of their own imaginations, the proper response to such professions of incapacity must be a blunt: "Try harder!"

A growing awareness of the aptness and force of this sort of response is perhaps one of the reasons why Hick himself seems over the years to have become increasingly inclined to abandon long-distinguishing ideas of the unique and exclusive authority of the historic Christian revelation in favor of some more fashionably equalizing "antiracist," "multicultural" syncretism. So much for what, in a now ancient era of robuster faith, was proudly embraced as "the scandal of particularity"!

3. The Religious Hypothesis and the Stratonician Atheism

There have been times and places in which unbelievers were challenged to meet and to try to defeat some standard rational apologetic. In the

United Kingdom of the eighteenth century it seems to have been generally accepted that such a challenge must have two parts. In the first, natural theology aspired to provide a proof or proofs of the bare existence of God. Here the candidate most favored argued from particular features of the observable Universe to unobservable Design. In the second the exiguous and undemanding "religion of nature," resulting from the first, was supplemented by an abundant and uncomfortably demanding revelation. Here the claims of the Christian to constitute a uniquely authentic revelation of and from the true God were enforced primarily by appealing to what was supposed to be the historically established occurrence of endorsing and constitutive miracles, the crucial, constitutive miracle being the alleged physical resurrection of Jesus bar Joseph (Stephen 1876, vol. 1).[4]

Belief in the possibility of completing such a compelling two-stage apologetic was made for Roman Catholics *de fide* under two canons of the First Vatican Council. The first has been quoted already: that "the one and true God our creator and lord can be known for certain through the creation by the natural light of human reason" (Denzinger 1953, sec. 1806). The second reads: "If anyone shall say, that miracles cannot happen . . . or that miracles can never be known for certain, or that the divine origin of the Christian religion cannot be proved by them: let him be anathema" (Denzinger 1953, sec. 1813).

But when, now all of twenty-five years ago, I started work upon the book later reissued as *God: A Philosophical Critique* (Flew 1984b) I asked several Christian friends to refer me to the work or works they saw as presenting the most formidable intellectual challenge to my unbelief, they all admitted to great difficulty in thinking of anything they could recommend as adequate, and there was little if any overlap between the various lists eventually provided. Noting this in my preface to the first edition, I went on to suggest that if there were any who felt that the arguments actually examined did not represent the full strength of the case for Christian theism, then they should ask themselves where in print those more adequate arguments were to be found. Perhaps someone who had asked that question and found no satisfactory answer would respond by meeting the apparently long unfelt need for a systematic and progressive apologetic really beginning from the beginning: a rational apologetic, that is to say, one that would meet and labor to defeat the presumption of atheism.

So far as I know, and although the suggestion was repeated in the preface to the reissue, no one has ever accepted my challenge. So perhaps the most useful thing for me to do at this stage in the present discussion is to redeploy Hume's refutation of the standard eighteenth-century natural theology. Such redeployment is the more relevant since the centerprice of that natural theology was an argument of the kind that has always had the widest popular appeal.

Hume presented this refutation most forcibly, and yet with a necessary discretion and reserve, as section 11 of *An Enquiry Concerning Human Understanding* (Hume 1988). The whole book is interesting for its presentation of argued and aggressive agnosticism (Flew 1961). Whereas the agnosticism of the aboriginal quoted in Section I, ii, above, was a confession of helpless and despairing individual nescience—"Might be, might be; I don't know"—Hume is contending that the whole subject lies altogether beyond the limits of all human understanding:

> These are mysteries, which mere natural and unassisted reason is very unfit to handle; and whatever system she embraces, she must find herself involved in inextricable difficulties, and even contradictions, at every step which she takes with regard to such subjects. . . . Happy, if she be thence sensible of her temerity, when she pries into these sublime mysteries; and, leaving a scene so full of obscurities and perplexities, return, with suitable modesty, to her true and proper province, the examination of common life. . . . (Hume 1988, p. 138)

i. Hume was, and needed to be, discreet in his presentation. Whereas in the preceding section 10, "Of Miracles," he was attacking assumptions at which Deist writers had been sniping for some time, here he was attempting to undermine a citadel never previously subject to direct attack. Thus in *The Analogy of Religion*, a classic work by one of the two greatest philosophical talents ever to adorn the bench of British bishops, we read:

> There is no need of abstruse reasonings and distinctions, to convince an unprejudiced understanding, that there is a God who made and governs the world . . . to an unprejudiced mind ten thousand thousand instances of design cannot but prove a designer. (Butler 1896, vol. 1, p. 371)

Hume, therefore, in denying the validity of this pretended proof puts his objections into the mouth of Epicurus; the imagined setting is a heresy trial in ancient Athens. In connection with the subsequent claim never to have questioned the divine existence, it is worth mentioning that in his posthumous masterpiece, the *Dialogues Concerning Natural Religion*, Hume puts into the mouth of Philo—generally allowed to be speaking, more often than not, for the author himself—the insistence

"that the question is not concerning the *being* but the *nature* of *God*."
Since Philo proceeds immediately to assert that that nature is "altogether
incomprehensible and unknown to us" (Hume 1947, vol. 2, p. 141), it is
worth reflecting how far the content of this agreement upon "the
being . . . of *God*" differs from that involved in Tillich's "conversions by
definition" (sec. 1, i, b, above). By defining "the religious hypothesis"
Epicurus marks out the precise nature and limits of the proposed
discussion:

> You, then, who are my accusers, have acknowledged, that the chief or
> sole argument for a divine existence (which I never questioned) is
> derived from the order of nature; where there appear such marks of
> intelligence and design, that you think it extravagant to assign for its
> cause, either chance, or the blind and unguided force of matter. You
> allow, that this is an argument drawn from effects to causes. From the
> order of the work, you infer, that there must have been project and
> forethought in the workman. If you cannot make out this point, you
> allow that your conclusion fails; and you pretend not to establish the
> conclusion with a greater latitude than the phenomena of nature will
> justify. These are your concessions. I desire you to mark the con-
> sequences. (Hume 1988, p. 170)

(a) These consequences are all those pointed out in Section 1, iii, a,
above, in connection with J. S. Mill's exploration of the idea of a
superpowerful yet still finite God. It will not do—notwithstanding that it
is all too often done, even by a thinker of the caliber of Bishop Butler—
first, in order to account for the existence of the Universe and for the
order and integration to be observed therein, to postulate an extremely
intelligent and knowledgeable Superpower and then forthwith—without any further reason given—to insist that that hypothetical Being must
be, not just sufficiently powerful and sufficiently intelligent to produce
the Universe, but in sober truth both strictly omnipotent and strictly
omniscient—as well as, for full measure, perfectly good.

Again, as was also pointed out in the same place, evidences of
design could not of their very nature point to a conclusion so extreme,
for design is essentially a matter of finding within whatever are the given
limitations the best available means to whatever are the proposed ends,
a matter of exploiting the various strengths and weaknesses of inher-
ently recalcitrant materials, and so on. But a Being that really is both
omnipotent and omniscient cannot by definition be subject to any
limitations, unless, of course, that Being has itself chosen to become so
subject. An appeal to such a choice could render a design hypothesis

consistent with the attribution of that design to such a Being. But evidences of design can by themselves point only to a different God, and a much smaller one than the God of mainstream traditional theism.

Things are, if anything, even worse with such evaluative, side-taking characteristics as benevolence or justice, for here it is not only that the evidence is insufficient to warrant, but that it appears actually to refute the desired conclusion. Since "the simplest and most psychologically satisfying explanation of any observed phenomenon is that it happened that way because someone wanted it to happen that way" (Sowell 1980, p. 97), the idea of a personal God possesses an enormous initial appeal. It is also easy to see how it could seem to Bishop Butler that it must be easy, by appealing to an argument of the present sort, "to convince an unprejudiced mind that there is a God who made and governs the world."

We have, however, to suspect prejudice in someone—indeed in anyone—failing to recognize how very far from obvious it should be that the Creator thus inferred would be a partisan within the creation, that, as Butler goes on at once to say, the "God who made and governs the world . . . will judge it in righteousness." Consider, by contrast, the first of the two fundamental objections to any proposed proof suggested in the *Summa Theologica*:

> If of two contrary things one were to exist without limit the other would be totally eliminated. But what is meant by this word "God" is something good without limit. So if God were to have existed no evil would have been encountered. But evil is encountered in the world. Therefore, God does not exist. (I. q.2, a.3)

Hume puts the point in a nutshell, again through the mouth of Epicurus:

> If the cause be known only by effect, we never ought to ascribe to it any qualities, beyond what are precisely requisite to produce the effect: Nor can we by any rules of just reasoning, return back from the cause, and infer other effects from it, beyond those by which alone it is known to us. . . . Allowing, therefore, the gods to be the authors of the existence or order of the universe; it follows that they possess that precise degree of power, intelligence, and benevolence, which appears in their work-manship; but nothing farther can ever be proved, except as we call in the assistance of exaggeration and flattery to supply the defects of argument and reasoning. (Hume 1988, p. 171)

(b) The next move Hume makes in his own person:

If you saw, for instance, a half-finished building surrounded with heaps of brick and stone and mortar and all the instruments of masonry, could you not infer from the effect, that it was the work of design and contrivance? And could you not return again, from this inferred cause, to infer new additions to the effect, and conclude, that the building would soon be finished, and receive all the further improvements which art could bestow upon it? If you saw upon the seashore the print of one human foot, you could conclude that a man had passed that way, and that he had also left the traces of the other foot. . . . Why then do you refuse to admit the same method of reasoning with regard to the order of nature? (Hume 1988, pp. 176–77)[5]

This was indeed the sixty-four-thousand-guinea question. Hume has allowed, would indeed insist, that experience must be "the only standard of our judgment concerning this, and all other questions of fact" (Hume 1988, p. 175). He has also urged that "the religious hypothesis . . . must be considered only as a particular method of accounting for the . . . phenomena of the Universe" (Hume 1988, p. 173). Surely it could be as legitimate to frame some hypothesis about a god and to attempt with its aid to explain and predict further phenomena, as it is to postulate the existence of atoms and to try to explain and predict in terms of "the attributes which you so fondly ascribe" to these invisible entities?

Hume has his answer. The crux, he argues, lies in:

The infinite difference of the subjects. . . . In works of human art and contrivance, it is allowable to advance from the effect to the cause, and returning back from the cause, to form new inferences concerning the effect. . . . The case is not the same with our reasonings from the works of nature. (Hume 1988, pp. 176–77)

There are, Hume insists, two crucial differences. In the first place:

The Deity is known to us only by his productions, and is a single being in the Universe, not comprehended under any species or genus, from whose experienced attributes or qualities, we can, by analogy, infer any attribute or quality in him. . . . The great source of our mistake in this subject . . . is that we tacitly consider ourselves as in the place of the Supreme Being. . . . But besides that the ordinary course of nature may convince us, that almost everything is regulated by principles and maxims very different from ours . . . it must evidently appear contrary to all rules of analogy to reason from the intentions and projects of men, to those of a Being so different, and so much superior. (Hume 1988, pp. 177–78)

The first crucial difference, which disrupts the putative parity of reasoning, is thus that the hypothetical entity in the present peculiar case is one from whose postulated existence no determinate consequences could validly be derived. So the first part of Hume's response is as elegant as it is decisive, for he is simply drawing out—with the simplicity of genius—a necessary but unnoticed consequence of an accepted defining characteristic of a theist God. *The Analogy* itself had argued that:

> Upon supposition that God exercises a moral government over the world, the analogy of this natural government suggests and makes it credible that this moral government must be a scheme quite beyond our comprehension; and this affords a general answer to all objections against the justice and goodness of it. (Butler 1896, vol. 1, p. 161)

To appreciate the full force of this first objection it will help to compare and contrast the entirely different case of a straightforwardly finite and anthropomorphic god conjured up in an attempt to account for some but not all the phenomena of the Universe. Let us postulate, for instance, a sea god Poseidon, with the familiar attributes of arbitrary human despots and deduce that he will protect his votaries and afflict those who defy him. We then organize some experiments to test our hypothesis. Members of the experimental group are asked to make vows to Poseidon, promising to erect commemorative tablets and other votive offerings if they are returned home safely from their voyages, while the members of the control group are required to express incredulity about the existence of Poseidon or otherwise to blaspheme against Poseidon's name.

Certainly we do have a religious hypothesis of a sort here, and certainly it could be tested. But of course this is not at all what Hume meant by "the religious hypothesis," nor yet what his opponents, the theist natural theologians, are supposed to have in mind. There is a world of difference between any such hypothetical god and God.

The second crucial difference is one Hume points out in his own person, almost as if it were an afterthought:

> There occurs to me . . . a difficulty, which I shall just propose to you without insisting upon it. . . . It is only when two *species* of objects are found to be constantly conjoined, that we can infer the one from the other. . . . If experience and observation and analogy be, indeed, the only guides which we can reasonably follow in inferences of this nature; both the effect and cause must bear a similarity. . . to other effects and causes, which we know, and which we have found, in many instances,

to be conjoined with each other. I leave it to your own reflection to pursue the consequences of this principle. I shall just observe, that, . . . the antagonists of Epicurus always suppose the Universe, an effect quite singular and unparalleled, to be a proof of a Deity, a cause no less singular and unparalleled. (Hume 1988, p. 180)

Not only is the hypothetical cause thus unique by definition, but the supposed effect is also unique, again by definition. Although there is a regrettable sense in which the Andromeda nebula might be spoken of as "an island universe," the Universe whose existence and regularities the religious hypothesis might be thought to explain is specified as including everything there is (with the exception of its putative Creator). But this second essential uniqueness also carries its own devastating consequence. However far back we may be able to trace the, so to speak, internal history of the Universe, there can be no question of arguing that this or that external origin is either probable or improbable. We do not have, and we necessarily could not have, experience of other Universes to tell us that Universe or Universes with these particular features are the works of God or of gods of this or that particular sort. To improve slightly on a famous remark by C. S. Peirce: "Universes, unlike universes, are not as plentiful as blackberries."

Again, it may help to compare and contrast the religious hypothesis with a factitious hypothesis concerning not the Universe but universes. Suppose that someone far more ancient than Methuselah is in a spaceship approaching some still unexplored "island universe." He might well, to the exasperated distress of his younger colleagues, refer to the wealth of his experience: "Mark my words. Man and boy these million million years I have . . . ," and so on, and no doubt on and on and on. But the unique Universe is and must be itself all we have. How it is, is just how it is; and that's that.

ii. The conclusion, which I believe but cannot prove that Hume himself eventually drew, is that we should take the Universe itself and whatever our scientists discover to be its most fundamental laws as the ultimates in explanation. This is a version of what Pierre Bayle taught Hume to call the Stratonician atheism.

To appreciate the strength of such a position, we need to be seized of the point that every system of explanation must include at least some fundamentals that are not themselves explained. However far you rise in a hierarchy of explanations—particular events in terms of general laws, laws in terms of theories, theories in terms of wider and more comprehensive theories, and maybe even further—still there has to be at every stage, including the last stage, some element or elements in terms of which whatever is explained at that stage is explained. Nor is this inevitability of logic escaped by theists, for whatever else they may think to explain by reference to the existence and nature of their God, they cannot thereby avoid taking that existence and that nature as itself ultimate and beyond explanation.

This necessity is common to all systems. It is no fault in any and certainly not a competitive weakness of one as against another. The Principle of Sufficient Reason—that there has to be a sufficient reason for anything and everything being as it is and will be—is not, as has often been thought, necessarily true. It is instead demonstrably false. Granted this insight, how can we fail to see that there is no possible explanatory point in hypothesizing an uncaused Divine Cause to which all but only those powers and inclinations necessary and sufficient to guarantee the production of the Universe as it is are then gratuitously attributed? In what are always said to be the words of William of Occam but are not in fact to be found within his extant works: "Entities are not to be multiplied beyond necessity."

4. Other Evidencing Reasons, and Motivating

In his first *Enquiry* Hume directs most of his fire against arguments to Design, arguments that proceed from the existence and characteristics of the observable Universe to an inferred but unobservable Design. These are the only arguments in natural theology for which Hume has any respect, since they alone appeal to what he contends must be the ultimate authority in "matters of fact and real existence," namely, the supreme court of experience. And, of course, the experience he has in mind is experience of observable phenomena, which may be interpreted as pointing to further but unobservable realities behind rather than the specifically religious experience of believers.

By the way, in view of what was said in Section 2, ii, b, above, it becomes to the point to inquire, are those who enjoy such experience and ground their belief thereon truly claiming direct acquaintance with God? If so, how is this claim to be squared with such defining characteristics as incorporeality? If not, why is it thought to possess any independent evidencing authority? As so often, the most crushing comment was made by the incorrigible Hobbes. In chapter 32 of his *Leviathan* we read:

> If a man pretend to me that God hath spoken to him supernaturally, and immediately, and I make doubt of it, I cannot easily perceive what argument he can produce, to oblige me to believe it. . . . To say that

God . . . hath spoken to him in a dream, is no more than to say he
dreamed that God spake to him.

i. After giving a posteriori arguments the full treatment in section 11
Hume proceeds in the third part of section 12 to deal with a priori
alternatives. Rarely can the notorious ontological argument have been
seen off in such short order:

> It seems to me, that the only objects of the abstract sciences or of
> demonstration are quantity and number, and that all attempts to extend
> this more perfect species of knowledge beyond these bounds are mere
> sophistry and illusion. . . . All other enquiries of men regard only
> matter of fact and existence; and these are evidently incapable of
> demonstration. Whatever *is* may *not be*. No negation of a fact can
> involve a contradiction. The non-existence of any being, without
> exception, is as clear and distinct an idea as its existence. The proposi-
> tion, which affirms it not to be, however false, is no less conceivable and
> intelligible, than that which affirms it to be. . . . But that Caesar, or the
> angel Gabriel, or any being never existed, may be a false proposition,
> but still is perfectly conceivable, and implies no contradiction. (Hume
> 1988, pp. 193–94)

What Hume elsewhere characterizes as "matters of fact and real
existence" have to be established by appeals to experience:

> The existence, therefore, of any being can only be proved by arguments
> from its cause or its effect; and these arguments are founded entirely on
> experience. If we reason *a priori*, anything may appear able to produce
> anything. The falling of a pebble may, for aught we know, extinguish
> the sun; or the wish of a man control the planets in their orbits. It is
> only experience, which teaches us the nature and bounds of cause and
> effect, and enables us to infer the existence of one object from that of
> another. (Hume 1988, p. 194)

Furthermore, and finally, not only is it impossible to know, antecedent to empirical inquiry, that any particular thing or sort of thing either
must be or cannot be the cause of any other thing or sort of thing, but it is
also impossible similarly to know that everything or anything must have
any cause at all. This subversive implication is by Hume mischievously
and altogether characteristically presented as falsifying the "impious
maxim" that from nothing nothing comes:

> That impious maxim of the ancient philosophy, *Ex nihilo, nihil fit*, by
> which the creation of matter was excluded, ceases to be a maxim,
> according to this philosophy. Not only the will of the supreme Being

may create matter; but, for aught we know *a priori*, the will of any other being might create it, or any other cause, that the most whimsical imagination can assign. (Hume 1988, p. 194)

ii. Hume, it appears, never attended to the wager argument. It is nevertheless something that has to be noticed somewhere in our present discussion. Pascal's own presentation is in his posthumous *Pensées*, in section 343 in the Lafuma arrangement. He begins: "Let us examine this point then, and say, 'God is, or he is not.' But to which side shall we incline?" Understandably unaware that, more than two centuries after his own death, the First Vatican Council would rule that it is *de fide* for Roman Catholics to believe the contrary, Pascal insists in the very next sentence that "reason can decide nothing here . . ."

He therefore urges that our predicament is one in which we cannot by any means avoid staking our entire futures upon one of the available betting options. He also assumes that there are only two runners in the field: either we opt to devote our lives to Roman Catholicism or we do not. Suppose that we do. Then either that is the true religion or it is not. If it is, then we have won an eternity of bliss. If it is not, then our losses are at worst merely finite, for what are the three score years and ten compared with all eternity? Suppose that we make the other choice. If Roman Catholicism is true, then we are now doomed to an eternity of torment. Yet, if it is not, what have we gained? Our little life will have been rounded in not even a (never-awakening) sleep but annihilation.

Given all the assumptions as stated, Pascal is absolutely right. It would indeed be madly imprudent not to place your bet on Roman Catholicism. To the objection that "I am the sort of person who is so made that I cannot believe. So what would you have me do?" Pascal provides a psychologically sophisticated response:

> You want to go to the Faith, and you do not know the route . . . learn from those who have been bound like you and who are now wagering all they have; these are people who know the road which you want to follow. . . . Follow the way in which they began; by acting as if they believed, by taking the holy water, by having masses said, and so on. In the natural course of things, that will make you believe . . .

Certainly, given all the assumptions as stated, this wager argument does go through. But if we allow that first assumption of total ignorance—"Reason can decide nothing here"—then one of the other crucial assumptions—"that there are only two runners in the field"—cannot be conceded. For upon that first basic assumption of total nescience the list of runners must be allowed to contain not two names only but an infinity; and every single one of these is no more likely to turn out the winner than any other. In particular, for every conceivable option promising eternal bliss for one way of life (and perhaps, correspondingly, eternal torment for all outsiders), there is another conceivable option promising the diametric opposite; the in-group of the one becomes the out-group of the other, and the other way about; and so on.

I confess to myself entertaining, with some relish, the thought of the conceivable Creator who will hereafter punish—though I refrain from even supposing, savagely, that the sentences are to be endless—not all but only those prepared to persuade themselves that it would be perfectly just and proper for a Creator to sustain disfavored creatures in eternal torment.

Once, however, we have appreciated that and why the wager argument, as presented by Pascal, cannot go through, it becomes possible to point to the sort of predicament in which such an argument might reasonably be accepted as decisive. Suppose that you had good reason to believe that only one of all the infinity of heaven-promising and hell-threatening systems possessed any degree of plausibility. Then, surely, the path of prudence would be, for Pascalian reasons, to set yourself to satisfy the requirements of that particular conceivable heaven-promising and hell-threatening creator. (For a fuller treatment of the wager argument, compare Flew 1984a, chap. 5.)

iii. In the second part of section 8 of the first *Enquiry*—a part the full force and true direction of which seems to have been recognized by philosophical standards only rather recently (Flew 1961, pp. 159–65)—Hume argues from the impossibility of explaining "distinctly, how the Deity can be the mediate [ultimate?—A. F.] cause of all the actions of men, without being the author of sin and moral turpitude" to the conclusion (already quoted at the beginning of Section 3, above) that "mere natural and unassisted reason" should become "sensible of her temerity . . . and return . . . to her true and proper province, the examination of common life."

Back in Section 1, iii, a, above, it was suggested that there is a tension between the two contentions: first, that there is a "creator and sustainer of the Universe"; and, second, that this creator "intervenes within the creation . . . rewarding or punishing different kinds of conduct." That was putting it gently, for there is in this area not only tension but also contradiction.

(a) The tension has two aspects. In the first place, at least to "mere natural and unassisted reason," it must appear in the last degree gratuitous and perverse to insist upon attributing to the hypothesized external Cause of the existence of the Universe as we know it not just whatever powers and other attributes would be sufficient to produce that Universe, but instead several powers and other attributes defined as being of their kinds unlimited. In the second place, and again to "mere natural and unassisted reason," it is bound to seem equally perverse and factitious to attribute to that same hypothesized external and Creator cause deep dissatisfaction with aspects of the creation and a resolution to reward or to punish creatures for contrasting kinds of favored or disfavored conduct.

In both cases—as Hume was surely suggesting by his smirking reference to "mere natural and unassisted reason"—there needs to be an appeal to some rich revelation. But the revelation required—a revelation of an unobservable Cause, the *Deus absconditus* (hidden God) of Pascal—is one disconfirmed rather than confirmed by *The Analogy of Nature*, for the observable order of nature may or may not be sufficient "to convince an unprejudiced understanding, that there is a God who made and governs the world." But what unaided by revelation it most certainly ought not to do is, as in completing that sentence Butler himself claimed, "to convince an unprejudiced understanding" that the "God who made and governs the world . . . *will judge it in righteousness*" [emphasis added].

This unwarranted assurance is in any case rendered worthless by the assertion that, according to Butler, "affords a general answer to all objections against the justice and goodness" of God's government, for if and insofar as "his moral government must be a scheme, quite beyond our comprehension," then we ourselves certainly cannot be properly positioned to maintain that that scheme truly is, in our ordinary everyday understanding of those terms, just as good.

(b) That conclusion again puts it gently, for it ought to be inescapably clear that to describe a Creator—who as such cannot but be ultimately responsible for every creature's every action and passion—as perfectly just and good must be, if that Creator is also said in any way to punish any creatures for any of their perceived deficiencies, flatly contradictory. And of course, if the punishments are in their duration or intensity themselves infinite, the case is—in the strictest and most literal understanding—infinitely worse.

The least inadequate earthly analogue to the relation between creatures and their ever-sustaining Creator has to be that of puppets to their puppet-master. Apparent conflicts between individual puppets or puppet factions are always and necessarily bogus, their course and outcomes being determined by the (offstage) puppet-master rather than by the pretendedly independent (onstage) puppets. For such a puppet-master to hold the puppets whose very move he himself manipulates responsible for those moves would be absurd, escaping further condemnation as a moral outrage only because objects of wood and cloth are necessarily impassable.

The introduction of this unlovely picture is bound to provoke indignation and protest. It constitutes, it will be said, the most monstrous misrepresentation of the way in which Christians think, for Christians believe that the Creator gave free will to those creatures who are made in his image. Therefore the least inappropriate picture, and it is the picture that certainly remains most widely preferred, is that of a father and his children.

Such protests miss the present point, for the contention is not that theists in the Mosaic tradition do always, or even often, think in this way, but that these are in truth, albeit widely unrecognized, necessary consequences of doctrines to which they are as such explicitly and categorically committed. Indeed it is doubtful whether those who regularly and consistently thought of themselves as the puppet creatures of a Creator could preserve their sanity. So, to support the actual contention about necessary consequences, consider what Aquinas said in the *Summa Contra Gentiles:*

> Just as God not only gave being to things when they first began, but is also—as the conserving cause of being—the cause of their being as long as they last . . . ; so he also not only gave things their operative powers when they were first created, but is also always the cause of these things. Hence, if this divine influence stopped every operation would stop. Every operation, therefore, of anything is traced back to him as its cause. (3. 67)

The relevant, uncomfortable implications of that final statement are spelled out fully in two later chapters:

> God alone can move the will, as an agent, without doing violence to it. . . . Some people . . . not understanding how God can cause a movement of our will in us without prejudicing the freedom of the will, have tried to explain . . . authoritative texts wrongly; that is, they would say that God "works in us, to wish and to accomplish" means that he causes in us the power of willing, but not in such a way that he makes us will this or that. . . . These people are, of course, opposed quite plainly by authoritative texts of Holy Writ. For it says in *Isaiah* (xxvi, 2), "Lord, you have worked all our work in us." Hence we receive from God not only the power of willing but its employment also. (3. 88–89)

For further, parallel texts from Holy Writ, compare Edwards 1756, a powerful Calvinist polemic by the first major philosophico-theological talent to emerge within what were to become the territories of the United States. Luther too maintains substantially the same position. We need, however, to take special note of his insistence that this total divine control abolishes none of the familiar, humanly crucial differences. Luther's statement here displays his customary vigor:

> I did not say "of compulsion". . . a man without the Spirit of God does not do evil against his will, under pressure, as though he were taken by the scruff of his neck and dragged into it, like a thief or a footpad being dragged off against his will to punishment; but he does it spontaneously and voluntarily. (Luther 1957, II 8)

To his great credit, and in this respect altogether unlike Aquinas, the Reformer is appalled by the so pellucidly perceived implications:

> The highest degree of faith is to believe He is just, though of His own will he makes us . . . proper subjects for damnation, and seems (in the words of Erasmus) "to delight in the torments of poor wretches and to be a fitter object for hate than for love." If I could by any means understand how this same God . . . can yet be merciful and just, there would be no need for faith. (Luther 1957, II 7)

Asking, "Why then does He not alter those evil wills which He moves?" Luther concludes, understandably if unsatisfactorily:

> It is not for us to inquire into these mysteries, but to adore them. If flesh and blood take offence here and grumble, well, let them grumble; they will achieve nothing; grumbling will not change God! And however many of the ungodly stumble and depart, the elect will remain. (Luther 1957, II 6)

Had we been able to press Luther further, he would doubtless have referred us to a key passage from Romans, one that was perhaps also in the mind of Hobbes when he wrote in *Leviathan*, chapter 31: "And Job, how earnestly does he expostulate with God, for the many afflictions he suffered, notwithstanding his righteousness. The question in the case of Job, is decided by God himself, not by arguments derived from Job's sin, but his own power." The Authorized Version of Romans 9:18–24 reads:

> Therefore hath he mercy on whom he will have mercy, and whom he will be hardeneth. Thou wilt say then unto me, "Why doth he yet find fault? for who hath resisted his will?" Nay but, O man, who art thou that repliest against God? Shall the thing formed say to him that formed

it, "Why hast thou made me thus?" . . . What if God, willing to show his wrath, and to make his power known, endured with much longsuffering the vessels of wrath fitted to destruction: And that he might make known the riches of his glory on the vessels of mercy, which he had afore prepared unto glory, even us, whom he hath called . . . ?

CHAPTER II

A First Engagement

Terry L. Miethe

Introduction

Before I begin my formal reply to Antony Flew's "The Presumption of Atheism," some introductory comments are in order here about the importance of the question "Does God exist?".

Since the beginning of philosophical inquiry, whether one starts with the pre-Socratics, Socrates, or Plato and moves down through the ages to modern times via Aristotle, Augustine, Aquinas, Descartes, Hume, Kant, Bergson, and Whitehead, questions of metaphysical thought have been of prime importance. "Metaphysics" has sought to discern the existence of extraphysical reality by asking, for example, "What is the starting point of metaphysics?" and "Can we ground the so-called negative judgment of separation (that is, the judgment that to be is not the same as to be material)?" The question of God's existence and what we can "know" of it has motivated philosophers for centuries. As my old philosophy professor, Leonard James Eslick, was fond of saying:

> Metaphysics is almost essentially the philosophy of God. It is identical with it really. There are metaphysics perhaps which are atheistic or even agnostic which might claim, at least pretend in some way, to arrive at first principles; first principles inferior to God. But at least traditionally western metaphysics is the study of reality as such, being as such. It must be consummated by some kind of theory of God. (Miethe 1976, p. 1)

Without God's existence there is no possibility of "doing metaphysics." Thus a central question in this debate is whether there is evidence for a type of existence that is not irreducibly physical, that is, that cannot be reduced to the purely physical as such. A second important question that closely follows the first (but one that cannot really be treated here) is what we can know of such "existence."

Godfrey Vesey, in *Agency and Necessity*, writes:

> Some of the great debates in philosophy are on metaphysical issues that are far removed from everyday concerns. These issues are debated only by professional philosophers, not by psychologists, sociologists or social workers. Conclusions of these debates would have no bearing on how we should manage our lives, or deal with our fellow human beings. In short, such issues are academic, in the modern sense of "academic." (Flew and Vesey 1987, p. 3)

I am not sure which "great debates in philosophy . . . on metaphysical issues that are far removed from everyday concerns" Vesey had in mind. One could strongly argue Vesey underestimates (or misunderstands) the importance of metaphysical questions as foundational to all of life. But whatever "metaphysical issues" he had in mind, I know this question certainly *cannot* be one of them. No question could have more vital importance to everyday life than the question of the existence of God! As a university freshman, I realized that this is the most important question a person can ask. I also realized that—if a person has integrity—how this question is answered must affect, must have great "bearing on how we should manage our lives, or deal with our fellow human beings."

Vesey is certainly correct that all too often this question is "not [debated] by psychologists, sociologists or social workers." Yet, very often they simply make "pronouncements" (often negative) about the question or *act* as if they have answered it. They act, counsel, and work as if God does not exist, even if they have not availed themselves of the evidence, pro or con, from the great debates in the history of philosophy. Such practitioners may ignore the question of God's existence and, in fact, be so blind to its importance that they do not even realize that many of their most important pronouncements, analyses of behavior, and responsibilities to their clients *depend* on just how they *have* dealt with this most important question. To make fun of or to ignore the question of God's existence is to show great ignorance of the centrality of the question in all of history, not just the history of thought, and to be ignorant of the practical implications of the question for everyday living.

On the other hand, I know many who would say that what most of the psychologists, sociologists, and social workers are "debating" does not have much bearing on everyday life and our relationships either. To the extent that this is true, it may be precisely because they so often do not realize the importance of metaphysical questions like the existence of God. It is my strong contention that *this* "metaphysical debate" has vital importance to psychologists, sociologists, and social workers, to the everyday lives of every one of us as individuals, to our interpersonal relationships, and to our society as a whole.

Flew and I agree that the question we are debating has practical importance. After he distinguishes between "positive atheists" and "negative atheists" (and then lumps the two kinds together again), Flew asserts: "Perhaps too we should include, as a third subclass of negative atheists, those who refuse 'to allow the (nevertheless still asserted) existence of God to affect their everyday living'" (I, p. 10). *How telling an insight!* Perhaps we *should* call people who "assert" the existence of God, but "who refuse to allow the existence of God to affect their everyday living" atheists, for isn't that what they really are?

The question of whether God exists or does not exist is the most important question in the history of philosophy, as almost everyone will admit. In this, I know my friend and fellow philosopher Antony G. N. Flew agrees. This is the reason for this debate! Even Nietzsche prophetically envisages himself as a madman: to have lost God equals madness (Kaufmann 1966; the parable of the madman can be found on page 81). When humankind will discover that it has lost God, universal madness will break out. Much of Nietzsche's philosophy is involved with a forceful denial of what philosophy had for thousands of years considered Truth (Miethe 1981, pp. 130–60). Within the past three decades or so there has been a gradual renewal of interest in metaphysics in general and in the theistic arguments in particular (see Miethe 1976).

The existence of God is one of those questions of eternal importance to every human being. It cannot, must not, be ignored either on a theoretical or practical level. To ignore this question does indeed say more about the individual, the profession, or the society than it does about the importance of the question.

1. "What Has the Atheist Not to Believe?"—Response

Antony Flew starts "The Presumption of Atheism" by putting atheism into "historical perspective" in Britain. Flew makes frequent reference to Berman's *A History of Atheism in Britain: From Hobbes to Russell* and notes Berman's "rediscovery, of the first overtly and avowedly atheist book to be published in Britain," which "was the anonymous *Answer to Dr. Priestley's Letters to a Philosophical Unbeliever*" in 1782 (I, p. 1). It is important to note that—by Flew's own admission—atheism has a rather short history in Britain. Let me help my friend with his "historical context" to British atheism. In this connection, it is interesting that our own university (Oxford) expelled P. B. Shelley[1] in 1811 for publishing *The Necessity of Atheism*.[2]

In the grand scheme of the many hundreds of years of tradition (of which the British are so rightfully proud), a "century or so of atheism" is hardly more than a moment in time. I shall not name the dozens of famous British Christian scholars and defenders of the faith (not to mention the hundreds of thousands of "ordinary" believers) in the centuries before this outbreak of atheism. It is important—to put these claims in historical perspective—to mention that this "period of atheism" was by no means totally atheistic. There were even during this period many notable British believers and defenders of the Christian faith. Of course, John Wesley (1703–1791) was still alive when the anonymous answer to Dr. Priestley was published; and John Keble, E. B. Pusey, John Henry Newman, C. S. Lewis, J. R. R. Tolkien, and many others were yet to come. Even today there are many very well-known theistic scholars in England (or who are British by birth and education) such as F. F. Bruce, J. I. Packer, Oliver O'Donovan, N. T. Wright, Alister McGrath, and Richard Swinburne (who has contributed to this volume), to mention only a very few.

Flew believes: "Berman is right to make much of the remarkable lateness of this first public avowal [of atheism]." Flew goes on to say "historians of ideas have been tempted to overlook the lack of confessions" because they have been "deafened by the clamor of accusations of atheism" (I, p. 1) and that the "doubting of the possibility of sincere and thinking atheism should be construed as an exercise in (unconscious) repression" (I, p. 2). I agree. I also think this most regrettable. Historians (or other thinkers) should *never* fear in revealing the truth. Repression of this sort is very unhealthy, for it shows a real inadequacy in such a society. If that society claims (even broadly) to be Christian, it is all the more reprehensible.

Let me state categorically that I do not doubt the possibility of sincere and thinking atheists.[3] As David Elton Trueblood says:

Atheism tends to be a term of disrepute in the Western world, but we ought to do all that we can to change this situation. The honest atheist is simply a person who has looked out upon the world and has come to believe either that there is no adequate evidence that God is or that there is good evidence that God is not. Very seldom does this make a man happy or popular. (Trueblood 1957, p. 82)

I could not agree more. Part of what can be done "to change this situation" is to open serious and gracious dialogue with our atheist brothers, to treat them as we would like to be treated.

Trueblood goes on to write:

> A man who has no practical belief in God may nevertheless be a good man. [Such a man is often more of a "good man" than many of the fundamentalist Christians I have met—T. M.] Sometimes it is the very goodness of a man which makes him an unbeliever; he is so superlatively honest, so eager not to accept anything without adequate evidence, so sensitive to the danger of believing what is comforting, merely *because* it is comforting, that he rejects the very conception which alone could make reasonable his intense effort to be honest. Such a man we can only honor, and trust that he will go on loyally following the evidence wherever it leads. (Trueblood, 1957, p. 82)

So well said! We can only respect, even admire, such a one who claims to be an atheist.

Flew then says we need a: "philosophical discussion [of] . . . the relevant criteria for the application of the term 'atheism.' Precisely what does anyone have to . . . believe or disbelieve or simply not believe . . . to be legitimately admitted into the company of British atheists?" (I, p. 2). I must add here that Tony Flew has told me in personal conversation that he is really an "agnostic"[4]—what he now wants to call a "positive atheist" (which on the face of it is *seemingly* more open and, by definition, should be less dogmatic than the so-called negative atheist). In some very important ways, I too am an "agnostic" and so should we all be. Any individual so convinced of his or her position as to have cut off questioning, dialogue, and debate is *too convinced*. This is not intellectually honest or healthy. If God exists and the Christian faith is true,[5] then Christians should be constantly willing to reexamine their position and put forth its rationality in the marketplace. In short, an "unthinking" theist (though I have met many) is just as bad as—really worse than—an "unthinking atheist."[6]

Now as I turn to a critical analysis of Flew's paper and begin to construct my own argument, it is important to make four points: (1) I am not responsible for (nor do I believe) every tradition in church history, "off-the-wall" position from however brilliant a theistic philosopher or theologian, or offhand statement made by some unthinking fundamentalist. I will not defend what I do not believe. (2) The case for theism must be built carefully and with integrity. No one argument, book, or experience will ever bear the weight of a total foundation but will serve only as a building block. (3) Many arguments will need to be seriously examined that cannot be developed in the limited space here,[7] for example, the ontological argument, the moral argument, and the teleological argument (which is becoming very popular again with many scientists), as well as arguments from historical events, revelation, and personal experience—and all of this in the context of a worldview. (4) Perhaps new arguments will have to be developed where old ones only point. For example, Augustine (354–430) began so long ago an argument for the existence of God on the basis of the existence of truth (Miethe 1982).

i. A brief statement of what I am defending is appropriate at this point. It can be simply stated as in contrast to Flew's language: ". . . the atheist will presumably be required . . . to deny . . . that the conception of God . . . common to traditional forms of Judaism, of Christianity, and of Islam . . . possesses or corresponds to some actually existing object" (I, p. 2). I believe, affirm, and contend that there is a "Being," an "actually existing object," that is properly called "God."

Many concepts could be used in definition or characteristics given to describe this "actually existing object." It is enough here to say that I affirm the existence of "the Supreme Being, or the Ultimate Reality, whose nature is to exist. God is the living, personal, loving, and merciful Creator and Sustainer of all that exists. In every way that He exists, He exists in perfection, without limit" (Miethe 1988a, p. 98). Perhaps I should add God is "Spirit," does not have a physical body, and that there can be only one such Being.[8] He is the only proper object of worship.

Further, I believe this Being is identical with the God of Christianity. And, though I cannot defend it within the limits of this debate, I affirm that Jesus of Nazareth was God incarnate, fully God and fully man. This is important, for if the evidence supports that Jesus was God, then we obviously have very crucial historical evidence of the existence of God (see Miethe, Habermas, and Flew 1987).

(a) It is interesting to note here that Flew—though a "positive atheist"—realizes and acknowledges what many Christian thinkers today seem to have difficulty seeing—that there must be specific content to a "variety of belief" to in fact classify it as x and not y, as essential to what is "Christianity." Flew is not a cultural, social, or ideological relativist. He writes: "We have to move carefully in phrasing any account of the concept or concepts in question" and says, ". . . to omit the qualification 'traditional' would be to open the door to all manner of indisputably heterodox substitutes for the God of the fathers and the saints, of the councils and the popes." Later Flew tells us, "It is notorious that ours is a period in which prominent clerics may be heard to profess almost any variety of belief or unbelief . . ." (I, p. 2). In fact, I received a personal letter very recently from Flew in which he wrote:

> I look forward to hearing when next we meet about your exasperation with Fundamentalist Christians. The Archbishop of Canterbury recently attacked what he called Christian, Jewish, and Muslim Fundamentalists very much in the Style of Paul Kurtz and *Free Inquiry*. But from some other recent actions and inactions, I don't think he was girding against what you and I would call Fundamentalist Christians so much as against Christians. For he supported the elevation of Jenkins to the See of Durham (despite his contemptuous rejection of the Resurrection) and various political interventions which he never attempts to derive from any traditional source of Christian authority.

(b) Flew then goes on to "cite just one example of a heterodox substitution effected by someone who was in his day an influential professional theologian." He quotes Paul Tillich, who wrote: "The question of the existence of God can be neither asked nor answered." Flew writes: "Perhaps unbeknown to themselves converts were to be definitionally conveyed to a position that, though in name theist, was in fact, in our present understanding, atheist" (I, p. 3).

Part of the problem here—and I think this may be foundational to our present discussion—is that Tillich seems to have misunderstood the Christian concept of God. He says: "If asked it [the question of God's existence] is a question about that which *by its very nature is above existence*, and therefore the answer—whether negative or affirmative—implicitly denies the nature of God. It is as atheistic to affirm the existence of God as it is to deny it" [emphasis added].

I have long contended that most of the rather devastating errors in the history of theology can be traced to an uncritical acceptance of the concept of God from the Neoplatonic[9] philosophy of Plotinus (204/5–270). Neoplatonic theologies all identify the ultimate God or Godhead with the One or the Good. This is a principle that not only transcends the physical world, as Aristotle's God did, but transcends being itself. It is beyond being, essence, and knowledge (see Plotinus 1956).

While a complete discussion of Plato's philosophy regarding this point is not possible here, a few words are important. Plato does have a principle he calls the One or the Good that is the Form of all the Forms and is the first principle of the whole of reality, but Plato never identified this with God. Such a principle could hardly be an efficient cause of the sort that Plato needs in order to account for the motions of the world. Plato's divinity is the World Soul and is immanent in the world. It is a self-moving mover that causes all moved movers (see Miethe 1976, pp. 36–47).

Neoplatonic theology is based on an interpretation of the first hypothesis of the second part of the *Parmenides* of Plato. But in this hypothesis for Plato what follows is that nothing whatever can be predicated about the Good or the One. He intended this as a failure of the hypothesis. Plato is looking for a world of being that is intelligible. What Plato intended by his first hypothesis was to point out that even his earlier theory of Forms, in which each Form is a simple unity, is a failure if one is going to try to account for knowledge of any kind of a relationship of participation between the Forms and physical things. It is also a failure if one is going to try to account for interrelationship between the Forms themselves. This is to remove the power of the relatedness (*dynamis;* see Miethe 1976, pp. 191–93), that is, of one thing to make a difference to another existent and of the other to make a difference to the first.

There is a factor of simple unity in the being of the Forms. Every Form has a self-identity. It exists in its own right, in and of itself. It also must be capable of existing in relation to others. It is quite certain that Plato was attempting to point out that his own theory of the Forms required readjustment. Yet this simple unity becomes the basis of a new kind of theology in Neoplatonism—a theology of utter and absolute transcendence of the Divine. This Divine is identified with the ineffable One that is beyond being, essence, and knowledge.

The Neoplatonists use a second text to support their interpretation from the *Republic* where Plato is talking about the Good. He says that the Good is beyond being, essence, and knowledge (Plato 1961, p. 740). It is the cause of these things. Plato was not a mystic. It would be a contradiction of everything Plato thought to say that the Good was capable of being an object of intellectual vision. The Neoplatonic tradition is mystical throughout.[10] The ultimate encounter with the Good, the Divine, is a completely mystical experience. Thus the keystone of Neoplatonic theology is the utterly transcendent One which is beyond being itself. It is beyond Aristotle's divinity of the unmoved mover and even the perfect intellectual activity of contemplation. It is beyond any activity of any kind, even will or creation, which involves some kind of multiplicity that is a failure of perfect unity. The Neoplatonists want a "God" who is completely simple and beyond all distinctions whatever.

The One is beyond being, essence, and knowledge; but this is not to say for Plotinus that it is nonexistent (Plotinus 1956, pp. 239 ff., "Eighth Tractate: Nature, Contemplation, and the One"). It is nonbeing in the sense that it is beyond being. It is not less than being but more than being. But I think that what can be said of this "more" is a great problem. The One cannot even be identified with the sum total of all individual things. Moreover if the One were to be identified with each individual thing taken separately, then each thing would be identical with every other thing and the distinction of things in the world would become an illusion. Therefore the One cannot be any existing thing. It is prior to all existence. It is not the One of the historical Parmenides. The One is a monistic principle in Parmenides.

The One of Plotinus transcends all being of which we have any experience. It is a unity without any multiplicity, division, or distinction. There cannot be in the One the Aristotelian distinction of substance and accident. Plotinus's One is, strictly speaking, beyond anything that can be predicated of it. And herein lies the problem: it would be a principle that is utterly unknown. We cannot know that such a principle even exists in the sense of utterly and completely transcending being (see Miethe 1976, pp. 64–70).

Plotinus's divinity can only be spoken about negatively. He is the Good in terms of effects he produces. He is called the One in terms negatively of not having any plurality or multiplicity whatever. One wonders how we can account for the plurality of finite things from a principle of this sort. One cannot assume that this divinity produces the world out of itself. There will always be a tension for Christian Neoplatonism in accounting for a Trinity. The only process that Plotinus can use to account for plurality is a mysterious one called emanation. Much of what Plotinus says about the process of emanation is metaphorical.

Not only will later Christian theological tradition, under the influence of a Neoplatonic interpretation of Plato, think of God as utter and simple oneness, it will also think of God as not really related to the world at all. This will be regarded as part of the divine perfection. But creatures, for Thomas Aquinas, must stand in a real relation to God as being dependent upon him for their very existence. This is well and good. But the orthodox supposition has all too often been that God himself is not really related to his creatures, because a real relatedness would involve some kind of dependence and God's divinity demands that he be absolutely independent. Whether or not there is a created world would make no difference to the Being of God. The world can produce no effect upon God. This notion of divinity clearly has a Greek philosophical origin and is untenable.

Simple unity may not be a perfection at all as Leonard Eslick has said:

> Questions of this type of thing should be raised at the very outset. It is much too easy to take for granted such attributes of Godhead as absolutely unmoved, not really related to His creatures at all, though they are absolutely dependent upon Him. What for example is so perfect about the utterly simple? Why is the simple better, more perfect, than the complex? This question is never really answered. Why is an absolute mode of existence which is exclusive of relativity to the world better than a mode of divine existence which would combine both? (Miethe 1976, p. 185)

The true nature of God is such that he must have both an absolute character and be the prime example of perfect relativity. God must be in perfect relatedness to everything else. God must exist both in himself as indivisibly and incommunicably one and also must have the power to make a difference to other things and other things must have the power to make a difference to him.

Most problems in the history of theology are a result of this adoption of the Greek view of the nature of God. (1) The Christian doctrine of the Trinity clearly indicates some kind of distinction of persons. This is not consistent with the absolute unity of Godhead, that is, a unity that seemingly admits of no distinction whatever. In Neoplatonic tradition any kind of multiplicity or distinction involves a falling away or privation of perfect unity of God. Any kind of procession of persons is always a procession in inequality. Thus the dogma of the Trinity becomes extremely difficult to fit into the absolute unity of God.[11] Therefore the Holy Spirit and the Son become inferior to the ultimate Godhead, or all three are inferior to an absolute unity beyond all being whatever.

(2) Even worse than the problem of assimilating the Trinity is that of the doctrine of the incarnation. How can there be a union of two natures in a single person? How can God become man when he is by nature not really related to his creatures at all? Christ's incarnation becomes metaphysically impossible. (3) The problem of religious language also stems from this Greek view of God. If God is beyond "being, essence, and knowledge," then there is obviously no meaningful way to talk about his existence. Human language becomes separated from God and God from it by an insurmountable barrier.

Thus if one accepts Plotinus's view of the One, or the Good, as beyond being, essence, or knowledge, as it has generally been accepted in Western thought, then we have the great impenetrable gulf of the Kantian phenomena/noumena (see Miethe 1976, pp. 102–113; 1988a, pp. 123–24) and paradoxically every major problem in the history of theology. If Plotinus was correct (and we have already seen that his position is not really representative of Plato), and God is truly *beyond* being, essence, and knowledge, then how can we have such a thing as an incarnation, or talk meaningfully about prayer or religious language, or even have any knowledge whatsoever of this "God"? Sounds quite a bit like what modern atheists are saying, doesn't it?

For me, God is the God of the Judeo-Christian Scriptures. He must be a God that is immanent in and really related to the world in which we, his creatures, exist. He must be all-powerful in an absolute sense and be the "prime example of perfect relativity." God must make a difference to us, his creatures, but we must also make a difference to him. The One of Plotinus would scarcely make a covenant with "its" people Israel. For me, as for Plato, an atheist is one who is in effect holding that everything in the world is mechanical and a result of chance. This is, I think, untenable (see Miethe 1976, pp. 181–87).

ii. Flew starts this section (I, pp. 3–7) by relating: "It might at first blush appear that the question of the existence of the God of Abraham, Isaac, and Jacob was on all fours with the question of the existence of Loch Ness monsters, of unicorns, and of Abominable Snowpersons." (No sexist here!) Flew goes on: "In all cases of this sort the difficulty, if there is a difficulty, is the shortage of evidence. There is no dispute about what sort of evidence is or would be relevant. . ." (I, p. 3).

(a) I know where my friend is going. I can see it coming even without reading further in his presentation—the famous "death of a thousand qualifications" parable. So let us deal with it "posthaste." Flew is going most certainly for the theistic throat by way of his old, old essay "Theology and Falsification" (which he does indeed make reference to on page 7 of Chapter I and in note 2: "At the last count, which was no doubt not completely comprehensive, this short and slight piece . . . had reappeared no less than thirty-three times.") Pardon me for saying so, but this little piece long ago outlived its usefulness. In fact, we would have been better served if it had been limited to the "ephemeral undergraduate journal" for which it was "originally commissioned."

I am certainly not going to take the time or space to recount the whole piece, since we have already established that it can be found in a "multitude" of places. The piece starts with a parable told by Flew (taken from John Wisdom) that supposedly illustrates how meaningless are religious assertions that are incapable of being tested objectively. Of course, "objectively" here means by way of the five senses, or strictly physical/empirical means. It is also quite clear that (for the parable's presenter) *all* religious assertions fit into this category of "meaningless."

Flew ends his parable with the sentence: "Just how does what you call an invisible, intangible, eternally elusive gardener differ from an imaginary gardener or even from no gardener at all?" (Flew 1955, pp. 96–99). Flew thinks—as many other atheists have thought—this question shows the *caput mortuum*[12] of Christianity as well as all religious truth claims. According to Flew, "Someone may dissipate his assertion completely without noticing that he has done so. [Interesting, since this is exactly what I think Flew himself has done here—T. M.] A fine brash hypothesis may thus be killed by inches, the death by a thousand qualifications" (Flew 1955, p. 97). Flew finishes the short piece with the question: "What would have to occur or to have occurred to constitute for you a disproof of the love of, or of the existence of, God?" (Flew 1955, p. 99).

There are several points which must be made in answer to this "parable." (1) The parable itself is guilty of making a very big and unprovable assumption—the assumption of "truth" that all analytic philosophers (and British empiricists who stand in that tradition) have made. It assumes (really rather uncritically) that the analytic "Principle of Verification" is true in an unqualified sense. This Principle of Verification in analytic philosophy claims we can only know that a thing is true if it meets one of two tests. The "thing" claimed to be true must be either empirically verifiable or a tautology.[13] But as many recent philosophers have pointed out, the analytic "Principle of Verification" does not meet its own criterion (which, again, according to it is the only criterion by which a claim can be judged as true of reality). This principle cannot be "proven" (verified) because neither can it be "empirically verified" nor is it a "tautology."

(2) What Flew, and others who follow this line of reasoning, are really doing is committing a logical fallacy. They are simply committing the fallacy of *petitio principii*, or "begging the question." What they are really saying is: "God is defined as 'Spirit' and we have never seen [heard, felt, smelled, or tasted] a spirit; therefore, God cannot possibly exist." How can we tell that God does not exist? Because *we* [they] have no "empirical" evidence of such. The conclusion states only what has already been asserted and does not establish the truth of the conclusion

(Miethe 1988a, p. 45). Hans Küng's penetrating analysis also indicates that this is really begging the question:

> If God did not really exist and religious language was consequently unrelated to anything (as some early logical positivists assumed as a result of their partly understandable negative attitude to religion), it could be very difficult, even impossible, to justify religious language as an autonomous, irreducible language game. For there is also an atheistic language game . . . , which is not justified merely because (likewise after long use) it is a *fait accompli*. (Küng 1980, p. 505)

If we look closely, we see clearly that the logical positivists, or atheists, have really done nothing more than "assumed as a result of their . . . negative attitude to religion" that God does not exist. It is on this basis that the atheist can put forth his test and make the pronouncement that God is found nowhere in experience because he has really already been defined out of existence.

(3) While it looks (on the surface) like they are open to the evidence, they are really rather arbitrarily stating that only a certain kind of evidence (empirical) is acceptable and that because they have never seen any such evidence none exists. In the parable, the believer is the one who seems to be making the qualifications. But in reality, it is Flew who has set up the "qualifications" beforehand, because the proposition "God exists" can only be verified on the basis of a very limited type of evidence. Then because he (Flew), in his limited experience, has never seen such evidence, it is assumed that in all history there never has been nor is there any such evidence.

Thus, in reality, what Flew has done here is to limit the evidence and to limit what would be acceptable as evidence to recurring physical phenomena, to things that can be seen (experienced via the five senses) physically. But it is still an open question as to whether this is the only kind of evidence possible or acceptable. (And, further, there is real question as to whether Flew's analysis of experience itself is adequate.) Is Flew really only ruling other types of evidence arbitrarily out of court without examining them? To answer that question, one is going to have to be willing to examine basic historical questions like: "What is the starting point of metaphysics?" "Are there any empirical foundations for metaphysics?" "Can we ground the so-called negative judgment of separation?" "Is there a metaphysics of creation?" "Is the 'real distinction' valid?" "Is the rationally inescapable the real?"; as well as look at all philosophical, historical, and personal arguments and evidence *before* simply arbitrarily ruling vast ranges of thought out of court. Not everything we claim to know as truth can be proven via the five senses.

Perhaps we need to engage in a *more rigorous empiricism* than either Hume or Flew. What if it turns out that Hume did not go to the "supreme court of experience," as Flew thinks (I, p. 26), but was remiss in accepting the verdict of a much lower court when he should have appealed the decision! I am reminded of the rather intriguing French phrase: *au pays des aveugles les borgnes sont rois*, or "in the country of the blind the one-eyed men are kings." This is exactly what Hume and Flew (and the other analytical philosophers) are doing in this case, using only one eye.

(4) If it turns out (as I think it does) that Flew is the one who has arbitrarily limited—by definition—the evidence or has not even examined all the important empirical evidence, then we can give two very distinct (but different) answers to the last question in his famous essay, "Theology and Falsification," that is, "What would have to occur or to have occurred to constitute for you disproof of the love of, or of the existence of, God?"

First we would make clear (what we have really argued above) that the use of Flew's very language already prejudices the case, because it puts the discussion under the limited rules of a strict atheistic empiricism. Such an atheistic empiricism, by arbitrary definition, excludes vast ranges of reality (that we do in fact claim to know) that also cannot be "proven" via the principle of verification. We need to be open to all evidence and not try to arbitrarily rule out of hand any before it is adequately examined, whether the evidence be historical, revelational, or personal. We need to reexamine the claims implicit in this atheist empiricism in the context of a complete worldview. Perhaps what is needed is a more rigorous empiricism than Hume and Flew when it comes to issues involving metaphysical questions. Basically, I am saying that the parable not only prejudices the point, it really misses it completely.

Second, using Flew's language (game), we could answer by saying it is only fair that we should require the exact same kind of evidence to disprove the assertion "God exists" that he demands to prove it, that is, empirically verifiable evidence. "Present us your *positive* case against God, Prof. Flew!" Remember, Christianity claims to have positive empirical evidence. As many Christian scholars have indicated (using an often quoted statement of John Warwick Montgomery's), in commenting on Flew's parable:

This parable is a damning judgment on all religious truth claims save that of the Christian faith. [I am not sure I would want to grant Flew this much.—T. M.] For in Christianity we do not have merely an allegation that the garden of this world is tended by a loving Gardener; we have the actual, empirical entrance of the Gardener into the human scene in the person of Christ (cf. John 20:14, 15), and this entrance is verifiable by way of His resurrection. (Montgomery 1965, pp. 45–75)

While a student of Prof. Montgomery's (in a class on analytical philosophy), I remember asking Montgomery Prof. Flew's very question: "Dr. Montgomery, you agree that empirical evidence should be allowed to count for or against claims to truth in religious matters. What would be for you damning evidence against the Christian faith?" Montgomery answered: "If they produced the body of Jesus." In fact, this (or something very like it) would be necessary—using Flew's own cannon of acceptable evidence—to disprove the historical evidence supporting the resurrection of Jesus. While the resurrection cannot be adequately argued in the context of this book on the existence of God as a general question, it has been argued in many other places.[14] (See the seminal debate: Miethe, Habermas, and Flew 1987.)

(b) We certainly know Flew has trouble with the idea of "a person without a body (i.e., a spirit)." He writes: "Swinburne's assumption that such a definition would be generally acceptable to theists is certainly sound. But, equally certainly, that is not to say that it is unproblematic" (I, p. 4). I agree that it is not "unproblematic." But this is not to say that therefore it can just be ruled out of court with the wave of a hand or a simple statement in opposition.

Flew goes on to say: "This, surely, is all wrong? If persons really were creatures *possessing* bodies, rather than—as in fact we are—creatures who just essentially *are* members of one special sort of creatures of flesh and blood, then it would make sense to speak of a whole body amputation" (I, p. 5). Flew is, again, simply begging the question here. He is simply asserting his position when this is really the question at hand. Isn't this exactly what Christians and others affirm in believing in life after death, for which there is strong mounting evidence? (See Kübler-Ross 1969; Moody 1975; Küng 1984; see also the article recounting the near death experience of Sir Alfred Ayer in Appendix B.[15]) It is not good enough to dismiss Swinburne's statement simply because you don't like the idea, especially in light of the fact that there is a good deal of "empirical" evidence to indicate that human beings *do* survive "whole body amputation."

Again, Flew is *assuming* that there is nothing more to a human being than flesh and blood, that the human body—and hence thought and all that constitutes a human being—is reducible to a psychochemical machine (see Jaki 1969; Pannenberg 1976). But the question is, does the evidence—all the evidence—warrant such a conclusion? I think not! If one holds to a mechanistic worldview, reality is a great and complicated machine, like a tractor or airplane though much more intricate. All that we experience in the world can be explained in terms of how this physical/chemical machine works. Such a view reduces all physical and living processes to the natural functioning of this intricate machine. In Flew's view, "spirit"—which gives purpose and meaning to life and exists in nature—is just a concept imposed by some human minds on the structure of reality. Anything not strictly material is either said to be reducible to the merely material or is arbitrarily defined out of existence by naturalists who reject the supernatural out of hand, as a matter of course.

A theist thinks that while a mechanistic process can explain part of reality, it cannot explain all. There are laws of nature, but these have purpose behind them. As my friend Flew so aptly pointed out:

> Both [atheists and theists alike] have a vested interest in insisting on strong notions of natural necessity and natural impossibility, because only if you have a strong idea of a natural order can you suggest that this natural order, if it's overridden, is in this overriding evidence of a supernatural power at work. (Miethe, Habermas, and Flew 1987, p. 34)

Theists believe reality has a purposeful end and that the processes in the universe are grounded in an Eternal Being. It is only this Eternal Being (God) who can account for life, intelligence, and the creative powers of humankind. As we shall see, it is the theist who is consistent here, not the atheist. *It is the atheist who must present a very convincing case that all life, intelligence, and creativity can be explained on and by naturalistic principles alone.*

(1) The Existence of Life. The first question which must be discussed (and can really only be raised here) is: "Can we account for life on the basis of matter alone?" Currently accepted scenarios concerning the origin of life are based on the Darwin-Oparin-Haldane 'warm little pond' concept in which nucleotides, amino acids, and the basic compounds necessary to life are thought to have been formed by chemical and physical processes during a period of chemical evolution.[16] As early as 1977, at the end of a twenty-one-page article on information theory and

spontaneous biogenesis, Hubert P. Yockey said of this "warm little pond":

> The "warm little pond" scenario was invented *ad hoc* as a materialistic reductionist explanation of the origin of life. It is unsupported by any other evidence and it will remain *ad hoc* until such evidence is found. Even if it existed, as described in the scenario, it nevertheless falls very short indeed of achieving the purpose of its authors even with the aid of a *deus ex machina*. One must conclude that, contrary to the established and current wisdom a scenario describing the genesis of life on earth by chance and natural causes which can be accepted on the basis of fact and not faith has not yet been written. (Yockey 1977, p. 396)

Life is to some extent dependent on matter but not reducible to it. Even a *deus ex machina*[17] (any unconvincing character or event brought artificially into the plot of a story to settle an involved situation) cannot account for life.

When students study chemistry at the university they find the field divided into two parts: *inorganic*, dealing with nonliving matter, matter other than plant or animal; and *organic*, of, related to, or derived from, living organisms. Why is this? Because there is a fundamental difference between the two. You see, the general theory of evolution[18] has not one but *seven* basic assumptions in it: (i) that nonliving things gave rise to living material, that is, that spontaneous generation occurred; (ii) that spontaneous generation occurred only once; (iii) that viruses, bacteria, plants, and animals are all interrelated; (iv) that the protozoa gave rise to the metazoa; (v) that the various invertebrate phyla are interrelated; (vi) that the invertebrates gave rise to the vertebrates; and (vii) that the vertebrates and fish gave rise to the amphibia, the amphibia to the reptiles, and the reptiles to the birds and mammals. In the past many evolutionists ignored the first six and considered only the seventh. These are all assumptions that cannot be proven. Instead of there being one "missing link" on the evolutionary trail, there are actually thousands upon thousands of missing links.[19] G. A. Kerkut, an evolutionist, says regarding these seven assumptions that form the general theory of evolution: "The first point that I should like to make is that the seven assumptions by their nature are not capable of experimental verification. [The exact kind of verification atheists like Flew require in every other case, but evidently not in this one.—T. M.] They assume that a certain series of events has occurred in the past" (Kerkut 1960, vol. 4, p. 3). These seven assumptions are not capable of the very kind of proof that Flew and the rest of the analytic philosophers require!

But for our discussion here it is the first two assumptions that are most important. It is pure conjecture that nonliving things gave rise to living things. We accept it so readily because we have a high-sounding scientific term (for this supposed fact), which we are taught as proven "beyond a shadow of a doubt" from late grade school or early high school on—"spontaneous generation."[20]

What is "spontaneous generation?" The idea that matter, which had no life or living properties, came into being spontaneously, that is, immediately and without cause, self-acting, developed without apparent external influence, force, cause, or treatment. "Spontaneous generation" is the theory that matter, having none of the properties of life, all of a sudden on its own without any outside influence of any kind developed the properties of life, in fact became alive. Now who is making the bigger "leap of faith"? Surely it is the atheist. Certainly the theist who says that living things must come from living things is the one being truly "scientific" here. (For the philosophical discussion see pp. 66–68 of this chapter.)

But listen to what prominent evolutionists, nontheists, say about so-called evolution and/or spontaneous generation. Charles Darwin (1809–1882) himself said on the eve of the publication of his *Origin of Species* in a letter to Charles Lyell, a geologist: "Often a cold shudder runs through me, and I have asked myself whether I may not have devoted my life to a phantasy." George Wald, then a Harvard professor of biology, said: "One has only to contemplate the magnitude of this task of bringing together complex organisms in this manner to concede that spontaneous generation of a living organism is impossible. Yet, here we are, as a result, I believe, of spontaneous generation." Sir Arthur Keith, a famous anthropologist, has said: "Evolution is unproved and unprovable. We believe it because the only alternative is special creation, and that is clearly unthinkable."

The second assumption is that "spontaneous generation" has occurred only once. Why do we say that it happened only once? It must have happened at least once, that is, if one is going to accept the explanation given in atheistic evolutionary theory, for this is the only way one can account for life. But there is absolutely *no evidence* that it has ever happened, certainly not since recorded history.

Also, as we will see later, life is far too complicated to have come about by accident. For example:

If we see a tossed coin come up heads ten times, either we have witnessed a very rare event (probability $2^{-10} = 1/1024$), or the event is expected because the coin is two headed. If the test is successful 32 times we may be the ecstatic witnesses of an event whose probability is 2.33×10^{-9}. All scientists and other practical men, except for a set of very small probability, would, however, be virtually certain that the coin is two headed even without examining it. By the same token the conclusion that life arose by a very lucky accident only once in the universe, on earth about 4×10^9 years ago (Monod 1971) begs the question and must be rejected as a scientific explanation of the origin of life. A rationalist will hardly use standards of credibility for scenarios dealing with the origin of life less critical than those used to test other scientific hypotheses. (Yockey 1977, pp. 378–79)

There are just too many factors that would have to have come into being by chance evolution to believe this, for example, the world is in just the right relation to the sun; the crust of the earth is just the right thickness to support life; the depth of the ocean is just right for the presence of oxygen; the rotation of the earth at just the right speed; the size, density, and temperature of the sun and our distance from it are just right for life, and so on.[21]

In quoting Morrison, Warren C. Young says the following:

A. Cressy Morrison in his . . . book, *Man Does Not Stand Alone,* . . . says: "so many essential conditions are necessary for life to exist on our earth that it is mathematically impossible that all of them could exist in proper relationship by chance on any one earth at one time. Therefore, there must be in nature some form of intelligent direction." . . . The chance of any one of these factors (and others not mentioned) occurring would be one in a million; the chance that they would all occur is too great to be calculated. The evidence, then, says Dr. Morrison, is conclusively in favor of the existence of a Supreme Intelligence. (Young 1954, p. 146; Morrison 1944, p. 13)

Another example: water just happened. This is extremely hard to accept as water is the universal solvent. Water dissolves acids, bases, and salts. There are numerous other arguments, for example, the complexity of the human body, and so on.

(2) The Existence of Intelligent Life. One not only has to account for life itself on the basis of matter alone, but also for intelligent life. Perhaps they are not the same thing. Humor aside, certainly intelligent life is more than just life. The question is, can the more complex come from the less complex? Can we believe that simple living things over millions of years simply developed intelligence? Are humans merely the most sophisticated of machines, or are they essentially different from any conceivable feedback mechanism? Does our knowledge of the brain

support the claim that human reasoning corresponds to mechanical processes?[22]

There are many aspects of the mind, or intelligence, that are very hard to account for on the basis of a pure mechanism. I would argue that: (i) Our minds can work with the material world without being controlled by it. We have free will (Miethe 1987, pp. 42–47). (ii) Morals must be integrated with a material world as well. We act as if some things are right and some are wrong. (iii) Human beings have values that are not man-made. (iv) Humans have aesthetic experiences, which also separate us from the animal world. (v) Humans have religious experience that confirms meaning and purpose in the universe. God makes himself known both in the natural order and in human experience.

To just explain these away as a result of a mechanistic evolutionary process is to reduce these experiences to much less than they are in reality. How does a purely naturalistic, mechanistic system develop "purpose" or design or such complicated order, let alone the intricacies of freedom, morality, aesthetics, or religion? We are reminded of the scholar who admitted that the alternative to a mechanistic atheism is special creation [God] "and that is clearly unthinkable." What prejudice! A simple materialistic explanation for all that humankind is and does will not fit with human experience or with what is known about the human brain.

(3) The Existence of Creativity. There is yet another level, qualitatively different from the first two, that—according to the atheist—we can account for as the sole product of a naturalistic or mechanistic universe, for life and intelligence are not all that we experience in this "material" world. If intelligence is not reducible to life, then certainly creativity is not reducible to mere intelligence. We have to somehow be able to account for creativity in this (atheist) mechanistic model.

Philosophers sometimes refer to creativity as "radical novelty." For the totality of the universe—all that exists within it—to be a product of pure chance and mechanistic evolution, as the atheist claims, creativity must be explained on and by naturalistic principles alone. What is creativity, this "radical novelty" of the philosopher? It is the bringing about of something entirely new, something that never existed before. This is certainly a possibility in the realm of ideas. Yet, because we are limited by physical existence, our freedom and creativity are qualified. If we look only at the physical laws of nature, it seems that all are "perishing." The universe is running down.[23] Energy is being lost. The perishing is inseparable from physical time and change.

If this is true, then one cannot account for radical novelty on the basis of a mechanistic universe that is constantly losing energy. Creativity can only be accounted for if there is something outside of the physical process, a spiritual "motion" or "energy." It is the "spirit" that endures and creates. The mind must be different from the brain. Ultimately, the mind must be seated in the spirit of the human, not in the material part. The mental pole has to have priority over the physical pole for humans and this mental pole cannot be derived from the physical. This is the root of creative freedom. I argue that creativity cannot have any real meaning in a deterministic, mechanistic, naturalistic universe. And yet, we *do* experience creativity.

How can one preserve a vital and continuing selfhood, a continuing and growing self-identity, in terms of a merely static formal content that never changes in which accidental forms come to exist and perish. Only a spiritual reality can account for a continuing and growing self. But it is true that our creativity is qualified and subject always to material conditions, so that it cannot be a creativity precisely of existence itself. An absolute creativity can only be found in a Being whose very essence is existence and, as such, is unique and transcendent as well as really related to human beings.

(c) The essence of God is existence that is unlimited and unreceived. His perfection is not a matter of any measurement by finite capacity. It is only in God that creativity is not limited.

> The life of God is eternity in the famous formula of Boethius, "the simultaneous and total possession of life everlasting without beginning or end." Such a life is neither static nor inefficacious. God wills us, His creatures, from eternity and He has known us from eternity. In this sense we make a difference to God, because of God's creative power and not because of ours. (Miethe 1976, p. 161)

Thus, it would seem that the only way to account for creativity in the world of our experience is to ground that creativity in the Being of God whose essence is existence itself. Only a Being such as this can be totally creative and delegate freedom, that is, creativity, to the beings created in his image.

There are two analogies from experience of the creative power of God: (1) In literary art writers have always been thought of as creating a fictional world of their own. But there are two kinds of literary creativity: bad literary craftspeople who manipulate lifeless puppets in a predetermined pattern with no room for surprise; and writers like Shakespeare or Cervantes, whose creatures like Falstaff or Don Quixote exhibit a mysterious life and freedom of their own. I suspect that even their creators could not always have predicted in advance what these two would do. (2) In the relationship of teacher and student I believe that these teachers who only produce carbon copies of themselves and of their opinions have the least "power" or ability to teach. Their students are not given any independent power of judgment. Teaching as indoctrination is a betrayal or failure of the true power of the art. Plato was at his height in producing an Aristotle who so disagreed with his teacher.

God by unlimited authentic power can produce independently existing creatures who share in the liberty of deity and can become co-creators with him in their own measure. This is true *power* for God! Thus God's divine creative power is synonymous with the Divine Names of Freedom and Love. God is Freedom and Love and he imparts these to his creatures because it is his very nature to do so. The existence of freedom is itself the gift of Divine Power. (It rather amazes me that Flew cannot see this.) And, God is "really related" to his creatures. Power in its active dimension is self-relating. God wills us and knows us from eternity as persons made in his own image. "We do make a difference to God, because of God's creative power which has given us an authentic share in creativity" (Miethe 1976, p. 292).

> Then God said, "Let us make man in our image, according to our likeness; . . ." And God created man in His own image, in the image of God he created him; male and female He created them. (Gen. 1:26–27)

(d) Flew goes on to say: "It should certainly be seen as at least very far from obvious that talk of 'a person without a body (i.e., a spirit') is coherent and intelligible" (I, p. 5). While I would grant this here (at least for the sake of argument), is it really any more obvious to talk as if a person is reducible to "flesh and blood," to a psychochemical machine, as if this were obviously coherent and intelligible. I think not!

Further, Flew writes: "In this ordinary, everyday understanding—what other do we have?—incorporeal persons are no more a sort of persons that are imaginary, fictitious, or otherwise nonexistent persons" (I, p. 5). And, again: "Incorporeality, however, is a very different kettle of fish—or more like no kettle and no fish" (I, p. 6).[24] Of course, as we have seen, Flew puts God in this category. He quotes "the Monster of Malmesbury," Thomas Hobbes (1588–1679), who said, in what Flew calls "so rude" a way: "to assert . . . that somebody survived death, but disembodied, is to contradict yourself." Flew further quotes Hobbes to say that talk of incorporeal persons, or life after death, is akin to talk of "a round quadrangle" (I, p. 5). But, again, he is begging the question, not to mention ignoring all the current evidence.

Flew is right back to his "Parable of the Gardener" again, only this time, in this case, it is we human beings, at least our "spirits," that are "invisible, intangible, eternally elusive." This argument is fraught (filled, charged, or loaded) with all the problems I mentioned in the treatment of his parable above, and perhaps, some additional ones. But, as we have seen, this assumption is far from "obvious," empirically or otherwise. Flew is here really doing nothing other than stating the "shortcomings" of dogmatic British (atheistic) empiricism of the analytic philosophy variety.

This whole discussion, which I have claimed is largely begging the question (and which really misses the point altogether), needs to address the discipline of metaphysics and discuss there (as I have indicated above) just such classic questions as: the starting point of metaphysics, the empirical foundations of metaphysics, a metaphysics of creation, the real distinction, and so on, instead of defining them out of existence or refusing to look at them seriously in the history of thought. Thus, instead of simply arguing point by point with Flew's presentation, which is largely just a restatement of the British (atheist) empiricist view, I will (at the end of this my first engagement) briefly introduce—because they are really essential to any discussion of the possibility of metaphysics and foundational to arguments for God's existence—the metaphysical issues and answers to the issues Flew raises. As with all discussions of a metaphysical nature (this one being no different), it must be an open-ended one that points to an open-ended system.

(e) Now (as one might guess) Flew states that he has a problem with the very "concept of God." He says he has "difficulties with the concept of God—difficulties that raise the question whether we have here a concept of a kind that could have a proper object . . ." (see I, ii, b, pp. 6–7, which is relevant here). He even admits by quoting John Wisdom ("The existence of God is not an experimental issue in the way it was.") that he is limiting the "evidence" for God to the realm of empirical verification or what he considers modern science. Wisdom is quoted by Flew as saying: "This is due in part, if not wholly, to *our better knowledge of why things happen as they do*" [emphasis added] (I, p. 6). It turns out that Wisdom and Flew are using an old scientific worldview (the science of the Newtonian closed mechanical universe) to illuminate the possibility of the "extraphysical" in the physical.[25] It also turns out that Prof. Flew knows better. He would do well to remember a much earlier debate he had with Prof. Warren on the existence of God (see Flew and Warren 1977).

Of course, one would have "difficulties" with the concept of God if the possibility of "extraphysical" reality had already been defined out of court, out of existence, if all human experience—and therefore reality as we know it—had been defined as reducible to a mechanical/physical process. Again, the question is: "Is experience or reality as defined by the materialistic atheist the sum and substance of what we *actually* experience in the world in which we live?" I think the evidence indicates that the answer to this question is an overwhelming "No!"

Flew now writes: "In the years immediately after World War II it used sometimes to be mischievously said that Oxford philosophers had invented a new cure for atheism" (I, p. 7). Flew finally gets to his famous "Theology and Falsification" article with which we have already dealt. Flew then admits that:

> "I and my contemporaries were wrong in our brash assurance that we were members of the first generation to think such thoughts. For in *A Plea for Atheism* Bradlaugh wrote: "The atheist does not say 'there is no God' but he says: 'I know not what you mean by God; I am without idea of God. . . . I do not deny, because I cannot deny that of which I have no conception.'"(I, p. 7)

This is a curious statement, as we will later see, in light of Charles Hartshorne's great modern defense of Anselm's argument in *Proslogium* III. (Though I will not be defending the ontological argument per se in this book, modern developments of this grand old argument must be examined carefully and not just dismissed out of hand.)

A few more words here regarding this problem with "the concept of God." It is interesting to note that large numbers of great thinkers and hundreds of thousands of others have not had any trouble with such a concept over the centuries. Hans Küng says it very well:

> After all that we have heard, it may seem a little odd (not only to theologians) that, up to the present time, in certain philosophical schools and especially in analytical philosophy or linguistic analysis, discussion has centered, with a great display of erudition, not on whether God exists or does not exist but on whether "God" is a meaningful or meaningless term. How is this possible after the great minds of world history have wrestled for a lifetime particularly with the question of God, after the history of philosophy through two and a half millennia has turned mainly on this term, when even today there can be no doubt about the relevance of the term for the greater part of

mankind? *The riddle is quickly solved if we recall the fact that these discussions are the consequence of that positivistic theory of knowledge that had to be corrected in the course of its history. We heard about this at an earlier stage. If we do not accept the empiricist verification principle of logical positivism, then from the very outset there is no basis for asserting the meaninglessness of all "metaphysical" terms and thus particularly of the term "God."* (Küng 1980, p. 502 [emphasis added])

Küng's excellent analysis goes on as he writes:

Here, too, lies the reason why the aggressive book *Language, Truth and Logic* (1936), produced by the then twenty-five-year-old Oxford lecturer A. J. Ayer, which became the antitheological catechism of the logical analysts, is out of date. Out of date too is Anthony [sic] Flew's *Theology and Falsification* (1950), along with John Wisdom's frequently reprinted parable of God as a gardener, nowhere palpable, nowhere visible, in the dim light of the primeval forest and consequently not verifiable. All this is as out of date as the antimetaphysical positions of the Vienna Circle, on which it depends. Are ethical propositions merely "emotional expressions"? Is God a "nonsense"? This position is as unsound as it is radical. Discussion on Carnap's theories as early as the thirties showed the *untenability of the empiricist verification principle*. And Ayer himself had to admit that ethical statements at least can be meaningful without being empirically verifiable, an admission that makes the empiricist criterion of meaning thoroughly questionable. (Küng 1980, pp. 502–503)

Again, I contend that the whole discussion in Flew's "Theology and Falsification" is already stated in a way as to prejudge the answer via atheistic British empiricism. And, further, if what I will argue is correct, then when a more rigorous empiricism is applied it becomes clear that there is a God.

iii. Flew starts this section (I, iii, pp. 7–8) "sounding" very open, for example, "we need to give a new and much more comprehensive meaning to the term 'atheist.'" He opts for using the term "negative atheist" when "positive atheism" refers "to a person who positively disbelieves that there is an object corresponding to . . . the . . . concept of God." Flew says: "In this interpretation an atheist becomes not someone who positively asserts the nonexistence of God, but someone who is simply not a theist" (I, pp. 7–8). This definition of an atheist, on the face of it, is much more open and acceptable, for it seems to define the atheist as "simply not a theist," yet one who is totally open to examining the evidence in a comprehensive and fair manner.

But then Prof. Flew goes on to "show his true colors," to "draw in the circle" as it were:

(b) In the negative sense proposed the term "atheist" becomes correctly applicable to far more people. It applies, immediately, to *all those who are atheists in the positive sense*, to all those, that is, who "positively disbelieve that there is an object corresponding to what is thus tacitly taken to be a or the legitimate concept of God." But then it must also embrace all those who, for whatever reason, would echo Bradlaugh: "I know not what you mean by God; I am without idea of God. . . ." (I, pp. 9–10 [emphasis added]).

There goes the "openness," for here we are right back at the "outdated" (remember Küng's perceptive comments) analytical philosophy/linguistic analysis/British empirical atheism of the first half of this century. Yet, Flew will want to tell us, I am sure, that this is a new idea or argument!

Flew's argument (I, pp. 8–10) is really not so much an argument against the existence of God as it is against the possibility of "free will" given the existence of God, an argument from the problem of evil, and against the justification of divine punishment (see also Chapter I, pp. 30–33).

Revelation apart, the natural, the inevitable, the obvious assumption is that everything in such a creation must at all times both be and become exactly as its Creator wishes. If some features of that creation and some developments therein strike us as profoundly unsatisfactory, as indeed they do, then it must be in the last degree unrealistic—again revelation apart—to expect that the Creator—who, by the hypothesis, makes everything to be and to become as it is and as it is to be—will now take some to us satisfactory if belated corrective action. A priori the reasonable assumption must be . . . that such a Creator would be "beyond good and evil." (I, pp. 8–9)

Flew goes on to say "upon these embarrassing traditional assumptions—that Creator inexorably determines that we shall do or fail to do?" Not in my theology! Flew's view of the Christian concept of God is clearly not consistent with what a majority of Christians think the Bible teaches. It is important to note here that ultimately one can no more separate truth claims made in "revelation," from such claims made in philosophy, or any truth claims into totally separate unrelated categories. I think a close examination of Flew's whole presentation shows this very clearly. All truth claims have to be examined in the context of reality as a whole—in the context of a worldview.

Flew makes an interesting statement here regarding John Milton: "These [the embarrassing traditional assumptions mentioned above], of course, are the reason why the theologically sophisticated Milton, who wanted *Paradise Lost* both to present epic conflicts and 'to justify the ways of God to man,' found the task to which he had set himself so impossibly difficult." It should first be noted that Milton is not considered to have been a systematic theologian by scholars or historians. Second, perhaps this is why later in life Milton's belief in the freedom of the human will made him take a stand against the Calvinist doctrine of predestination. Milton started out as an Anglican with moderate Puritan leanings, then turned Presbyterian, and finally independent.

I will not argue here against the problem of evil or for the justification of divine punishment for three reasons: (1) I do not have the space (in printed pages) to do so. (2) I have argued most of this elsewhere, as have others (see Miethe 1987, pp. 42–48; Miethe 1984, pp. 127–32; as well as many items in the Bibliography.) And (3) these issues, as interesting and important as they are, bear only secondarily on the question of God's existence. I will, however, comment on Flew's material as space allows.

Flew says he wants to "shift the emphasis toward the *conceptual problems*" [emphasis added]. But this is precisely what he never does, certainly not in the rest of this essay.[26] To shift the argument toward the "conceptual problems" is exactly what I want to do in Section 5 of this chapter! Flew writes:

> These traditional and still almost universally accepted forms of presentation are fundamentally prejudicial, for they assume that there is a Divine Being with an actual nature the features of which we can proceed to investigate. All this is, no doubt, all very well when and insofar as the existence of God can be taken for granted" [I would add "or can be proven"—T. M.] (I, p. 10)

I have tried to show, at least indicate, that it is really Flew who is being "prejudicial" in argument.

Here Flew has made an interesting admission though I do not propose he intended to make it or even knows he made it. If there is evidence that God exists, then there isn't much of a problem with the concept ("All this is, no doubt, all very well . . ."). Is he admitting that the fundamental question of the evidence for the existence of God (from an examination of all reality) must come *before* rather than after an arbitrary defining of God out of existence and on the basis of that "defining" asserting a problem with the very concept? Two interesting questions arise from this statement. First, what about the evidence (most of which of necessity cannot be examined here) for God from philosophical argument, historical event (see Miethe, Habermas, and Flew 1987), revelation, and human experience. And, second, what of the millions and millions of people who haven't had or who have no problem with maintaining a positive concept of God (as mentioned earlier). I think Flew is simply wrong in stating that conceptual problems are "logically prior" to "questions of fact," (i, p. 10). If this is so, he is abandoning his own empirical canons! But, then, as we have seen—and will see—such atheists are only playing at empiricism. What they are really doing is playing an analytical language game.

2. "The Burden of Proof"—Response

Flew starts this section: "The presumption of atheism is similarly defeasible. [1.] It lays down that thorough and systematic inquiry must start from a position of negative atheism and [2.] that the burden of proof lies on the theist proposition." I really have little problem here (even with the second [2.] part), provided that we mean by "negative atheist" simply "one who is not a theist," provided that the atheist is not allowed to pontificate on what constitutes "evidence," and provided he or she is not allowed to simply define certain things out of existence. But it *is* very important that: "counsel too [in this case referring to Flew] . . . with a good conscience allow . . . a thorough and complete apologetic . . ." (I, p. 11–12).[27] I do fail to see how this "new" "presumption of atheism" has made the old arguments more valid, as Flew claims (p. 12).

Flew says (and I do not question it) that: "Nowadays too it is frequently asserted, even by professing Roman Catholics, that everyone knows that it is impossible to prove the existence of God." If this is true it is certainly unfortunate—no horrible—that these Roman Catholics (whoever they may be; Flew has not named them) have so misunderstood or forsaken their intellectual heritage. Flew correctly relates the history of Catholic thought when he quotes the First Vatican Council that "the one and true God our creator and lord can be known for certain through the creation by the natural light of human reason" (I, p. 12). It is also very unfortunate that many Protestants are also in the camp of "those believing that any attempt at any kind of proof is fundamentally misconceived . . ." and that they "often go on to suggest that the territory that reason cannot inhabit may nevertheless be freely colonized by faith" (I, p. 13). This is certainly not my position!

"Faith," Flew writes, "as my preacher father used sometimes to proclaim in sermons, should be not a leap in the dark but a leap toward

the light." I can only wish at this point that Tony had listened to his
father in these and other areas. Flew so very correctly states: "If your
venture of faith is not to be arbitrary, irrational, and in the deepest sense
frivolous, then you must have presentable reasons." To this I say: Amen!
I am almost surprised to see Antony Flew realize this so clearly when so
many of my evangelical colleagues cannot![28] I have tried to argue exactly
this point in my book on faith and reason (Miethe 1987, pp. 15–33). I
quote (among others) Richard L. Purtill, who shows "that the Christian
faith is not nonsensical and that none of the common arguments against
it is successful." In the second part of his book, Purtill says:

> Thus we showed that it is not unreasonable to believe in Christianity.
> Some Christians seem to feel that this is all reason can be expected to do
> in this area, and that then faith must take over. That this is not the
> biblical view nor the traditional Christian view is, I think, clear from a
> study of the scriptures and a study of history. It is also, I believe, based
> on a misunderstanding of the nature of faith. *Faith must be based on
> reasons, and the reasons must be good ones.* (Miethe 1987, p. 21; Purtill 1974,
> pp. 71–75 [emphasis added])

Here at least some atheists and theists agree, for example, Purtill, Flew,
and Miethe. Purtill thinks, and I agree, that C. S. Lewis's formula is the
best when Lewis says that faith is "assent to a proposition which we
think so overwhelmingly probable that there is a psychological exclusion
of doubt although not a logical exclusion of dispute" (Lewis 1955, p. 16).

Next Flew departs on a somewhat lengthy discussion of Descartes (I,
pp. 14–16) which I find largely irrelevant to the question at hand. Flew
does, however, quote from Descartes a statement I find quite interesting:
"the revealed truths which lead to it [understanding our theology to
'gain heaven'] are beyond our understanding. . . . To undertake the
examination of them, and succeed, one would need some special grace
from heaven, and to be more than a man" (p. 15). Not so! If this was
Descartes' position, then he not only misunderstood the whole purpose
of the Christian revelation but did not realize that if true, this would
render the revelation useless or at best unnecessary.[29]

Flew makes some important distinctions and "concessions" (pp. 16).
He says of the man who caught his wife "in the act," that he "no longer
needs to infer her infidelity from bits and pieces of evidence. He has
now what is better than inference, *although for the rest of us . . . his
testimony still constitutes an important part of the evidence in the case*"
[emphasis added]. Flew goes on: "The idiomatic expression 'the evidence of my own eyes' derives its paradoxical piquancy precisely and

only from the fact that to see for oneself *is better than to have evidence"* (p. 16–17 [emphasis added]). This is in some ways a curious statement. Thus, it seems, Flew does not deny either the possibility of (another's) eyewitness testimony as being important evidence or (one would presume) that such testimony having been recorded accurately in history, however long ago, is presently important to claims made for which it is relevant evidence. If this is indeed true, as I believe it to be, then Flew should have paid much closer attention to the teachings of his old Oxford ancient history professor A. N. Sherwin-White regarding history and the Christian faith (see Miethe, Habermas, and Flew 1987, pp. 40, 58–60, etc.).

I basically agree with Flew regarding his demands upon those who claim validity for their "religious experience" (I, pp. 16–18),[30] though this does not invalidate all claims to experience that supports theological truth, nor justify dismissing such claims without "a thorough and complete" examination of them.

3. "The Religious Hypothesis and the Stratonician Atheism"—Response

Section 3 of Chapter I is precious little more than a restatement of David Hume's very worn arguments. It is also interesting to note, *by Flew's own admission,* that it has been "now all of twenty-five years ago" (I, p. 19) since he started work on *God and Philosophy* published in 1966. In our bibliography, Flew references this book under its reissued title in 1984 of *God: A Philosophical Critique.* What is interesting to note is that (1) there is no indication of any revision of the 1966 book. And (2) it is quite amazing with the myriad of writing on Christian evidences and Christian apologetics in the last twenty-five years that there is no indication whatsoever that Flew has interacted with this important literature.

In fact, Flew indicates that he is unaware of such literature when he says: "So far as I know, and although the suggestion was repeated in the preface to the reissue, no one has ever accepted my challenge." Flew goes on to say: "So perhaps the most useful thing for me to do at this state in the present discussion is to redeploy Hume's refutation of the standard eighteenth-century natural theology" (I, p. 19–20), which is to both ignore his own debates over the last twenty-five years and the volumes of material written in both of the two areas of "natural theology" he mentioned.

Flew is totally ignoring vast ranges of literature that defend (both earlier and more modern) arguments that either withstand Hume's criticisms or on which Hume did not speak.[31] It should also be mentioned that there are many good critiques of Hume's position available (see, e.g., in Nash 1988 "David Hume's Attack on Miracles"; in Geisler 1982 "Are Miracles Incredible?"[32]; in Copleston 1964 "For and Against Hume"; Purtill 1976; Dietl 1968; Holland 1965). In his own lifetime, George Campbell (1762) wrote a very good reply to Hume on miracles.

While I am not as skeptical as Flew's other Christian friends evidently were about either the possibility of providing a "work or works" that present an "adequate" or "formidable intellectual challenge" to Flew's "unbelief," nor am I as skeptical about the existence of a work or works that *represent the full strength of the case for Christian theism,*"[33] [emphasis added]. I do, however, readily admit there is a need today "for a systematic and progressive apologetic really beginning from the beginning: a rational apologetic," (I, p. 20). I must also admit that, given the present state of the publishing world (of which I have rather intimate knowledge, having recently been the managing editor of a publishing house and having close friends in many publishing houses), I fear such will not be coming soon.

This dark prediction regarding this "systematic and progressive apologetic, rational apologetic" not coming in the near future is *not* because there is a lack of Christian scholars to produce this much needed joint effort, nor of the ability of such to be produced. I was recently sent a copy of a letter written to a Christian friend of mine who has written a book on faith and reason that bears directly on the problem.[34] The letter said in part:

> After carefully looking at the material we have come to the conclusion that this is not a proposal that we should pursue for publication. . . . However, we did take a careful look at your materials.
>
> I want you to understand this does not necessarily imply that your material is unworthy of publication. In your particular case, the fact is that we have tried publishing similar kinds of books, but with little or no success. *Our market simply does not seem to be interested in books defending the rationality of the Christian faith.* [emphasis added][35]

The above letter was written by the publisher of a major Christian press,[36] (and a person whom I consider a friend). First, I must say that if this is true, then we might as well "fold up our tents and go home," for the atheists have won the day simply by default! If this is true, no wonder the Church is powerless!

Flew's challenge for a "systematic and progressive apologetic, a rational apologetic" makes this letter very germane to this present discussion. Several points need to be made in regard to the publisher's response: (1) The book proposed to the publisher was not even written on an "academic" level, but by an "ordinary housewife" who had come to see the need for Flew's rational apologetic as a result of events in her own life. (2) What about the publishing industry's responsibility to perceive and shape the need and the market? Since when does the medical doctor allow the patient to decide what medicine the patient needs? (3) The simple truth of the matter is that in most—if not all—publishing houses what gets published is what *they* think will sell, will make money. (4) Even then the truth of the matter is that *they* are the ones who put the advertising dollars and "glitzy" ad campaigns behind the fluff they think will sell. It is a perfect example of circular reasoning.[37] It doesn't sell because they don't publish it, and when they do, they don't push it, so of course the market is not "interested." (5) This publisher has an earned doctorate and should know better. I believe any publisher who would make such a statement is removed from the need and the people. In light of Flew's challenge, these facts are indeed relevant and need to be known.

But the fact remains that Flew's challenge is an important one that every generation must meet. A rational apologetic "beginning from the beginning" is very much needed. Such a project would result in an encyclopedic work (which I have had on the drawing boards for years, I might add). Perhaps this book, this debate, can be a new beginning and spur on the great task of building such a thorough systematic and progressive apologetic—*that is if the publishing industry can be convinced.*

Much of Flew's argument through Hume (Flew often has been humorously referred to "as the twentieth-century reincarnation of David Hume") is against a very old form of the theological argument. It is, however, very interesting to note that the argument from design has very recently gained acceptance among many scientists who are fairly new converts to Christianity.[38] One could profit by looking at Hubert P. Yockey's work on information theory (1977; 1981) or Robert Gange's *Origins and Destiny* (1986). This being the case (if Flew is going to raise the issue), it should at least be looked at within a more modern context than that of David Hume (1711–1776).

Flew quotes Hume: "Why then do you refuse to admit the same method of reasoning with regard to the order of nature?" Then Flew says: "This was indeed the sixty-four-thousand-guinea question. Hume has allowed, would indeed insist, that experience must be 'the only standard of our judgment concerning this, and all other questions of fact'" (I. p. 23). The question is exactly what does constitute "experience." Can you rule out court experience that another has had just because you have not had it or cannot have it? Again, perhaps we need a more rigorous empiricism than that of Hume's. Also, as many other critiques of Hume have indicated, we need not accept, carte blanche as it were, Hume's presuppositions and assumptions.

Flew goes on quoting Hume: "If experience and observation and analogy be, indeed, the only guides which we can reasonably follow in inferences of this nature; both the effect and cause must bear a similarity . . . to other effects and causes" (I, p. 24).[39] Flew goes on to say: "The conclusion, which I believe but cannot prove that Hume himself eventually drew, is that we should take the Universe itself and whatever our scientists discover to be its most fundamental laws as the ultimates in explanation" (I, p. 25). This raises some interesting questions. What if—as I will argue—an examination of the foundational issues in metaphysics strongly points to a conclusion that our experience of the "physical" world is not irreducibly mechanical or "physical"? In other words, what if Hume was wrong about some of his basic presuppositions regarding the nature of the physical universe?

Flew seems to say he is willing to let modern—in this context, "current"—science settle the question.[40] But what if modern science strongly points away from Flew's opinions and presuppositions? Will he change his view? Modern science seems to be quite open to the possibility of a created Universe, of an intelligent Creator, and the implications of an open Universe (as opposed to a closed mechanical one) to the question of the existence of God.

4. "Other Evidencing Reasons, and Motivating"—Response

i. Flew, still again, quotes Hume and then writes: ". . . it is also impossible similarly to know that everything or anything must have any cause at all. This subversive implication is by Hume . . . presented as falsifying the 'impious maxim' that from nothing nothing comes" (I, pp. 27). What a ridiculous statement. If this were true, it would destroy the very basis for doing the empirical science Flew prizes so highly and the empiricist (mis)uses to exclude God from the physical Universe. Flew quotes Hume as follows:

> That impious maxim of the ancient philosophy, Ex nihilo, nihil fit, by which the creation of matter was excluded, ceases to be a maxim, according to this philosophy. Not only the will of the supreme Being

may create matter; but, for aught we know *a priori*, the will of any other being might create it, or any other cause, that the most whimisical imagination can assign.

But the famous skeptic David Hume also said: "I never asserted *so absurd* a proposition as *that anything might arise without a cause:* I only maintained, that our certainty of the falsehood of that proposition proceeded neither from intuition nor demonstration; but from another source" [emphasis added].[41] Something cannot come from nothing! Historically, this has been a philosophical truth about reality (also a scientific truth) as universally accepted as any. "From nothing nothing comes," the old philosophical dictum, *ex nihilo nihil fit*, is as valid today as it was in Hume's day.[42]

As we have indicated, the idea that something can come from nothing has been totally rejected in the history of philosophy, for it is clearly self-contradictory and irrational. "Nothing," by definition, does not exist. The dictionary says of "nothing": "not any thing: no thing." It is absurd to assert that "something," a thing that exists, can have as its cause no thing, that which does not exist.

It has also been widely accepted in philosophy that when it comes to accounting for the present existence of something there are only three possibilities. Present existence refers to a thing's conservation in existence rather than its origination. A cause of present existence is a cause of *being* not merely the cause of becoming. My father and mother were the cause of my becoming but they are not now the cause of my being.

The existence of something is either (1) caused by itself, (2) caused by another, or (3) uncaused. In the history of philosophy, the idea of self-causation *(causa sui)* has been considered by most as existentially impossible. The argument goes: "To cause existence, one must exist. But to need one's existence caused, one would have to not exist. Hence, to cause one's present existence, one would have to both exist and not exist at the same time, which is impossible."[43] (2) When caused by another, the present existent is dependent on another for its actual existence. The "thing" is contingent in its act of existing, that is, it is possible for it to exist or not to exist. In which case it needs a cause to account for its present existence. (3) If the present existent is uncaused, it is independent, eternal existence. Again, there are only two possibilities: either the universe is eternal, independent existence, or God is. The question is: "Does the evidence indicate that the universe is eternal?" I think not.

"Can something come from nothing?" You can say yes all you like, but there is still no evidence for this—that the laws of causality are invalid. In fact just the opposite is true. Modern science can only operate on this "assumption" and still continues to support it experimentally. (The very kind of evidence Flew claims is necessary and adequate to prove any proposition!) This idea (that something can come from nothing) is philosophically self-contradictory and irrational, and as far as we know the same is true scientifically. Certainly, there is no proof that something can come from nothing. But—as absurd as it may indeed be—Hume and Flew want us to believe that "the will of any other being might create" matter.

ii. Next Flew goes to Pascal's "wager argument" (I, pp. 28–29). First he admits that Hume "never attended to" this argument. About Pascal's argument, Flew writes: "Given all the assumptions as stated, Pascal is absolutely right. It would indeed be madly imprudent not to place your bet on Roman Catholicism" (p. 28). Of course, Flew then shows that there are many more options than Pascal admitted that render the argument ineffective (p. 28–29). But, interestingly, he does not stop there.

While I am certainly not interested in debating Pascal's wager argument, I am very intrigued by an admission that Flew makes in this regard:

> Once, however, we have appreciated that and why the wager argument, as presented by Pascal, cannot go through, *it becomes possible to point to the sort of predicament in which such an argument might reasonably be accepted as decisive.* Suppose that you had *good reason to believe that only one* of all the infinity of heaven-promising and hell-threatening *systems possessed any degree of plausibility.* Then, surely, the path of prudence would be, for Pascalian reasons, to set yourself to satisfy the requirements of that particular conceivable heaven-promising and hell-threatening Creator. (I, pp. 29)[44]

I think (though I cannot argue definitively here) that precisely such a case can be made for Christianity. *But remember, Flew only demands a "degree of plausibility" before "an argument might reasonably be accepted as decisive."* Surely, it is possible to argue thus effectively. I know several books I think together do the trick: Ramm 1953, Pinnock 1967 and 1980, Gerstner 1967, Green 1968, Purtill 1974, Chapman 1981, Craig 1984, and Moreland 1987, among others. *Surely* Christianity thus has more than a "degree of plausibility." Tony, please check into these!

iii. There is much I would like to say regarding Flew's argument here (I, pp. 29–33), but alas no space. It is also true that most of this material has no bearing on an argument for the existence of God, except (again) in the most secondary way. Most of what Flew writes here could be handled quite effectively with a simple understanding of the implications of the freedom of the human will (see Miethe 1987, pp. 42–48; Thompson 1955, pp. 178–89, 501–3; Trueblood 1957, pp. 275–90).

Flew says: "The least inadequate earthly analogue to the relation between creatures and their ever-sustaining Creator has to be that of puppets to their puppet-master." And later, "The introduction of this unlovely picture is bound to provoke indignation and protest" (I, p. 30–31). Further, Flew writes: "For the contention is not that theists in the Mosaic tradition do always, or even often, think in this way, but that these are in truth, albeit widely unrecognized, necessary consequences of doctrines to which they are as such explicitly and categorically committed" (I, p. 31). Flew writes that protesting this picture by claiming free will misses the point. But he is dead wrong here. I think he misses the point or misunderstands the implications of being created in the image of God and the ramifications of this to personhood and freedom of the human will.

It seems clear here that Flew knows only a Calvinistic or deterministic type of Christianity. This is not the "type" of Christianity to which I subscribe (see the important studies by Pinnock 1975 and 1989; Marshall 1969; Rice 1980; and Craig 1987). I remember very clearly, when I introduced Prof. Flew as he was about to speak to a group of my students in 1985, that he commented to the effect—very matter-of-factly—that all Christians were Calvinists. I replied: "I certainly am not!" To which Tony acted surprised, almost shocked, as if there was no other kind. Evidently, Flew has not heard of the millions of Christians who come from numerous traditions that do not hold to such a determinist view; they do not believe the Bible teaches such or see how ramifications of what they believe necessitate such a view. I am beginning to think I should write my part of this debate under the pseudonym "Servetus."

My friend Flew even quotes Thomas Aquinas (1225–1274) to support these "necessary [deterministic] consequences" (I, p. 31). Yet, this is the same Aquinas who said that "reason in man is rather like God in the world" (Bourke 1960, p. 134).[45] If he is trying to use Aquinas to support the "puppet to puppet-master" theory he mentions above, he is sadly misunderstanding the great *Doctor Angelicus*, for Aquinas also said:

> Were the artist's idea of a house a natural form, he would not be free to design or not to design a house, or to make it in this style or that. . . .
> *But in intellectual natures, where forms are received without matter, the full play of freedom is ensured and with it the ability to will.* To material things, then, natural appetite is attributed; to animals a sensitive appetite; to intellectual substances a rational appetite or will, and the more spiritual

they are the greater the power of will. Since God is at the summit of spirituality, he possesses supremely and most properly the character of will. (Disputations, 23 *De Veritate*, 1 [emphasis added])

Does divine predestination impose necessity on human acts? In this matter we must proceed cautiously so that truth may be strengthened and error avoided. For it is equally false to say that human acts and events do not fall under divine foreknowledge and that foreknowledge and divine predetermination load human acts with necessity, *for that would abolish freedom, the opportunity of giving counsel, the usefulness of laws, the care for acting aright and the fairness of rewards and punishments.* (Opusc. 26, *De Rationibus Fidei ad Cantorem Antiochenum*, 10 [emphasis added])

To be free is not to be obliged to one determinate object: as deriving from the mind's apprehension regarding universal good, the appetite of an intellectual substance is not committed to one determined good. (Opusc. 13, *Compendium Theologiae*, 76)

Free will is not a habit, but a faculty. (*Summa Theologica*, I. a. 83.2)

As understanding and reasoning are from the same faculty of mind, so also are wishing and choosing from the same faculty of will. The will and the free will are not two powers, but one. (*Summa Theologica*, I. a. 83.4)

The judgement of the intellect about what should be done is not committed to any one course. All intellectual natures, therefore, possess free will. (II *Contra Gentes* 48)

Man has free choice, otherwise counsels, exhortations, precepts, prohibitions, rewards, and punishments would all be pointless. . . . Man, however, can act from judgement and adaption in the reason; a free judgement that leaves intact the power of being able to decide otherwise. The reason keeps an open mind, as appears in dialectal proofs and rhetorical persuasions. Particular lines of conduct are contingent. Concerning any one of them the practical reason is not committed beforehand. *A man has free choice to the extent that he is rational. (Summa Theologica, I. a, 83.1* [emphasis added])

There must be a voluntary character in human acts. . . . Therefore, since both factors come from an inner principle, namely, that they act, and that they act for the sake of an end, the movements and actions of these agents are called voluntary. In fact, this is the meaning of the term "voluntary": *that movement and act be from a thing's own inclination.* (*Summa Theologica,* I–II, 6, 1, c)

I could keep quoting, but this will suffice. As Vernon J. Bourke (another of my old philosophy professors) quite correctly points out: "Further analysis suggests to Thomas Aquinas the distinction between the exercise of the act of willing and the specification of the will-act (*exercitium actus . . . specificationem actus*)." A person may decide to will or not to will (simply a question of exercising the will or not); "or having decided to perform a will-act, he may further consider what kind of object he may will" (Bourke 1964, p. 67). Thus, Aquinas, from the point of view of exercising the will, "thinks that no man is necessitated by any object." He can always refrain from thinking of something and consequently from actually willing.

Certainly, this is consistent with the bulk of Catholic tradition. As a modern Catholic dictionary says: "An act of the will is made whenever a man exercises his freedom of choice. The will may either act alone, as in an act of love or of hatred, or it may call upon other faculties, such as the intellect" (Attwater 1958, p. 526). Flew then goes on to quote Jonathan Edwards (a Calvinist indeed) and Luther (I, p. 32). I am certainly no expert on what Luther said (or meant) but it is well known that Erasmus broke with Luther over the issue of the freedom of the will. Erasmus wrote *De Libero arbitrio* in 1527 as an attack on Luther's ideas. He took Luther to task on the thorny issue of predestination and human freedom.

But I am not at all sure what any of this discussion of God and human "determinism" has to do with the question of the existence of God, however important and interesting it certainly is. However, I am sure that what I am about to say is foundational to the question.

5. Foundational Issues in the Philosophy of God

As my much honored philosophy professor Leonard Eslick has said (in the context of the question of whether simple unity is a perfection, but it applies to all metaphysical questions as well): "Questions of this type of thing should be raised at the very outset. It is much too easy to take for granted such attributes of Godhead as absolutely unmoved, not really related to His creatures at all, though they are absolutely dependent upon Him." Yes, it is better—far better—to treat the foundational questions "up front" as it were.[46] It is much better not to assume the hundreds of thousands of years of philosophical and theological baggage any more than one has to, though this is somewhat inevitable. If we don't assume, we may find that much of the disagreement comes from the unquestioned assumptions and preconditions in the history of thought.

i. The Starting Point of Metaphysics. Metaphysics is the science of being *qua* being, that is, the study of existence as such. Such a study of being cannot be limited to a determinate category of existence. Metaphysical being must incorporate all being.

> The very word "metaphysics," therefore, implies a consideration of causes and principles in some way transcending the physical order of explanation. The metaphysician is seeking a more ultimate explanation of real things than can be provided by natural sciences dealing only with material entities in terms of their mobile and sensible being, as subject to becoming and change. (Eslick 1957, p. 247)

Thus a science of metaphysics depends on establishing the existence of a kind of being that is spiritual or immaterial. This has been the problem of all metaphysicians in history. How do you establish a valid science of metaphysics?

There are powerful needs that seem to call for the kind of immaterial being of the metaphysician. For Aristotle and Thomas Aquinas metaphysics was a science in the strictest sense, that is, of that which cannot be other than it is. Most material being (the stars and plants are exceptions in Aristotle and Thomas) seems to be radically contingent, subject to generation and corruption. The essence of material being is that it can be other than it is. There are three canons of maximal intelligibility for metaphysical being: (1) metaphysical being must be first in the order of causality; (2) it must treat of principles that are supremely universal; and (3) metaphysical being is only supremely intelligible if it exists in complete separation from matter. Obviously material beings do not measure up on any of the three counts.

The problem of establishing metaphysical being involves the difficulty in reconciling the demand of maximal universality with the canons of maximal immateriality and primacy in causality.

> In terms of maximal universality, the subject of metaphysics would seem to be *ens commune*, common being distinguished from proper being. . . . But if the subject of metaphysics is to be immaterial, immobile substances, as the other two canons would seem to prescribe, then metaphysics appears to be limited to the consideration of one class of beings to the exclusion of all others. How can we, by treating of principles proper to the being of immaterial substances, attain a knowledge of *ens commune*—of the being common to all beings, both

spiritual and physical? And, indeed, is it even possible for the human mind to achieve a *proper* knowledge of spiritual beings *qua* spiritual . . . ? (Eslick 1957, p. 252)

The history of metaphysics is haunted by this problem. The tension between these metaphysical canons seems to put metaphysics utterly beyond the reach of human natural reason. This is the dilemma that must be honestly confronted and overcome if one is to say that valid metaphysical knowledge exists. This is a crucial issue for this debate!

Aristotle's primacy of Form as the principle of metaphysical being is finally unsatisfactory. Aristotle's being of the separated substances is the being of all things. This kind of predication became known as an analogy of extrinsic attribution. Such a position achieves a reconciliation of the demands of maximal immateriality and universality only at a terrible cost. "If the common being of all things is to be identified with the proper being of any of them, then all save the primary analogate will lose their own proper being" (Eslick 1957, 254–55). Many metaphysicians believe that Aristotle intended such a conclusion.

For Thomas Aquinas what is separated and known as analogically common to all beings is the act of existence itself. This has become known as the negative judgment of separation, that is, that to exist is not the same as to exist in a material way. Metaphysical being is not the result of the abstraction of form from matter. It is achieved by the separation of existence from all material limitations and restrictions. But is it enough to establish the object of metaphysics by seeking arguments within physics, the philosophy of nature, because experience is only physically intelligible according to this view?

Perhaps there is a stronger argument to be advanced by those who think the foundations of metaphysics can be established in physics, which is a valid insight.

Aristotelian and Thomistic philosophy of nature, through the analysis of substantial change, can indeed show that matter, in its primary and ultimate nature, is pure potentiality. As a potential and indeterminate principle, it cannot simultaneously be the intrinsic principle within a being which makes it actually exist. (Eslick 1957, p. 260)

Without this insight substantial change is radically unintelligible and not possible. Yet this is not sufficient to ground the negative judgment of separation.

To fully ground the negative judgment of separation, in order to have a science of metaphysics, compelling evidence must be found in our experience of sensible things.[47] There has to be some basis for a real distinction between essence and existence. This is one possibility for establishing a science of metaphysics, because it cannot be self-engendering. Metaphysics cannot produce its own object by formally "metaphysical processes." Such an argument results in a vicious circle like that of the logical positivists. Any argument to spiritual beings really takes for granted that the object of metaphysics has already been shown via the negative judgment of separation.

Is there compelling evidence in our experience of sensible things to ground the negative judgment of separation?

> If there is to be any valid starting point at all for the journey into metaphysical wisdom, it can only be in our integral experience, perceptual and intellectual, of the world of sensible, material beings and of such massive facts as their existence in modes of formal diversity and numerical distinction. Such experience is charged not only with physical intelligibility, but there is real metaphysical necessity and intelligibility discernible in it. It is structured not only physically but metaphysically as well. There is no other possible source for metaphysical knowledge. (Eslick 1957, p. 263)

Too long we have accepted uncritically the empirical theory that experience is purely physical. It is not purely physical. Physical existence does not exhaust what it is to exist in the world. Humans are not just physical. Humans have *nous*, mind. It is ultimately absurd to deny the existence of the spiritual in the physical world. A narrower type of empiricism cannot account for life, intelligent life, or radical novelty in the world of our experience (II, p. 49–55). We do have direct experience of the spiritual in the real world. A reexamination of the data of experience that is "more searching, more profound, and above all more *empirical* than that which was made by the empiricists of modern philosophy" is called for today. "It is here that we should all begin; and it is only here, if at all, the metaphysical wisdom can have its birth in the human mind." (Eslick 1957, p. 263)

ii. The Empirical Foundations of Metaphysics. It is "incumbent" upon those who would practice metaphysics to ground it in experience. Experience itself must give metaphysics the rationale for the truth of the "negative judgment of separation," that is, that to exist is not the same thing as to exist in a material way. The problem of establishing the objects of metaphysical knowledge is as old as Aristotle. Thus the metaphysician must be able to ground in experience a being that is common to all, "but not univocally distributed in all, and which is not the being proper to physical entities *qua* physical" (Eslick 1966, pp. 1–2).

It is not enough for the negative judgment to point in the direction of "metaphysical knowledge." It must be able to constitute the object of that knowledge for it to be valid.

"One avenue of approach" that should not be neglected is to show there is a great amount of evidence that, because of differentiation and inequality in the physical world, it is incompatible with any materialistic monism; that is, the fact of change and real process in nature in our experience involves both real continuity and discontinuity in beings. The history of philosophy has shown, as in Parmenides, that the logic of materialistic monism must end with a Being from which all differentiation, change, and emergent novelty have been removed. This does real violence to integral experience. This is sufficient to establish the truth that to be material is not the same as to be water, air, or whatever. Thus we have experience of the existence of irreducibly different kinds of physical entities in the physical world (Eslick 1966, pp. 3–4).

Aristotle's negative judgment of separation is not grounded in experience at all. Because physical nature can only give a "science" that is in principle incomplete, one has to affirm by an act of faith that something beyond the physical world must exist. Aristotle is suspect at this point to the Kantian objection that the ideal of such a completion is regulative only and not constitutive of objects of knowledge. According to Kant the idea of being in this metaphysical sense is empty and void of intuitional content. In the twelfth book of the *Metaphysics*, Aristotle tries to go far beyond that which his maxim, there is nothing in the intellect that is not first in sense, will allow. He makes the perfect immanence of vital self-motion that is experienced in thought the grounding of metaphysical knowledge. This is a result of elements in Aristotle's thought inherited from Plato (Eslick 1966, pp. 4–6).

Thomas Aquinas's doctrine of the primacy of *esse* enables him to go beyond his Aristotelian machinery (see Miethe 1976, pp. 85–101, "God in St. Thomas Aquinas"). For Thomas, existence is never the function of the material reception and limitation of forms. Existence is unrestricted, unlimited, and unconfined of itself. This Thomistic insight is unparalleled in any Greek thinker. This insight of Thomas's can only be grounded in experience if our experience includes a mode of existing that is spiritual, that is, nonphysical.

To exist, to experience adventures of becoming (perhaps as well as U-Haul's "adventures in moving"), is to participate in living feeling. The mental pole is conditioned by the physical pole but is not wholly derived from it. The aspect of entities that is physical exists only in the temporal mode of perpetual perishing.

> Properly physical changes are transient, rather than immanent and self-perfecting, terminating always in distinct patients in the future. As a consequence the physical can only exist *in* a subject other than itself, and such an entity which exists in its own right, which perdures dynamically through time as a center of spontaneity and freedom, can be nothing but spirit. (Eslick 1957, p. 10)

The primacy of the living spirit is a metaphysical trait analogically common to all that exists. Existence is to have a mode of duration that involves dynamic and creative selfhood. We can analogically move upon this experience to the Divine Creativity.

"What, precisely, are our empirical contacts with the spiritual?" That question already misunderstands the ultimate nature of our experience. There is no experience of the merely physical as such. All of our experience is of living continuity of memory, that is, a physical encounter with values objectively realized by spiritual agencies in the past and guided by our own spirits for new fulfillment.

> The "physical" aspect of our experience is constituted by those elements in it which derive from the objectified and determined past, and which have a *de facto* or consequent necessity about them. That in this sense the experience of all temporal entities is physically conditioned is surely true. But such experience is not, nor could it be, wholly determined from without, wholly physical. *This would be tantamount to a dead repetition, which could never engender novelty or real difference,* and indeed the utterly homogeneous or spatialized *time* of classical mechanics is not, as Bergson so powerfully pointed out, the real time or duration of which we are actually conscious. . . . [This is very important—T. M.] Matter as such cannot remember, it can only repeat. *The living reflexivity of all knowing is . . . primary evidence of experiential contact with the spiritual.* (Eslick 1957, p. 10 [emphasis added])

The very nature of our experience of time and memory, that is, the living mind reflexively knowing, reveals contact with the spiritual. Flew continually ignores this!

Thus one is able to constitute a metaphysical notion of being that has real content and amplitude. The spiritual creativity in ourselves allows us to also constitute a notion of causality that enables us to come to know *proper* names or attributes of God. To be sure, we do not experience "super or hyper being, life, and goodness" as they are in Divine Infinity, but our experience of them via spiritual creativity allows us to properly apply them in a positive way to ourselves and God. *"To be* is to be free" (Eslick 1957, pp. 11–12).

iii. A Metaphysics of Creation. It is well known that Thomas Aquinas was historically given the task of baptizing Aristotle, that is, of assimilating Aristotelian thought into Christian philosophy. In doing so, Thomas invented a new Aristotle. Thomas differs from Aristotle on many significant points: (1) Freedom is a failure of matter to be assimilated to being. It is a scandal for Aristotle, but not for Thomas. (2) History is without intelligibility in the Aristotelian world, but not for Thomas. (3) There is no personal immortality for the human soul for Aristotle and there certainly is for Thomas. (4) There is in Aristotle no possibility of a "real distinction" between essence and existence, which distinction is fundamental for Thomas. (5) For Thomas there is a proper analogy of being, but there is no possibility of it for Aristotle. "So much by way of certain of the difficulties which, I think, a candid look at Aristotle will disclose. The marvel is, of course, that Thomas Aquinas was able to invent an Aristotle which could be at least partially assimilated to his own central metaphysical insights" (Eslick 1964, pp. 33–35).

The original and central metaphysical insight of Thomas Aquinas was the primacy of existence as compared to essence or form. This insight is compatible with certain doctrines of Plato, Bergson, and Alfred North Whitehead. As Leonard Eslick has said: "I do not think that it is incompatible with certain doctrines originally suggested . . . by Plato, by Bergson and . . . Whitehead—paradoxical as the wedding of the Thomistic natural theology with a reformulated process cosmology might seem" (Eslick 1964, p. 35).

There are no physical substances that endure by virtue of unchanging, substantial formalities such as Aristotle's forms. The timelessness of forms cannot account for individuality or temporal endurance. It cannot account for self-identity of existing individuals or their real agency. Even the perishing cannot be explained by formal contents once shown in the constitutions of actual entities. The perishing is inseparable from physical time and change.

The vital question is, "What is an actual entity?" What unity of being can be said to be in some sense self-existent? These for Leonard Eslick, are souls:

Souls, Plato tells us, are the eldest of all things, prior to bodies, and the self-motions of souls are the ultimate sources of all moved movers or physical motions. This is to assert precisely the primacy of immanent operations over transient, of spiritual motion over physical—a primacy which Aristotle betrayed. (Eslick 1964, p. 36)

Thus it is spiritual motion that exhibits heterogeneous duration. Spiritual motion possesses a history, growth, and a dynamic self-identity. Eslick believes the time that characterizes the duration of the soul, that is, spiritual temporality, is Bergsonian. Eslick feels this to be implicit in what Thomas said, that is, the human body exists because it participates in the existence of the human soul.

Because we are limited by physical existence, our freedom and creativity are always qualified. Thus the mode of our duration is temporal and successive. The subjective aims of bodies are derived from the spiritual entities of which they are adjectival. This is just the opposite of Whitehead. The mental pole has to have priority over the physical pole.

> I would say that in finite spiritual entities it is true that the mental pole is prior to the physical and is not derived from the physical. This is the root, I suggest, of their creative freedom. It also, I think, implies once again that an Aristotelian epistemology of knowledge is unsatisfactory. In some sense the formal principles by which we know, by which we learn, by which we recognize, must be present in us from the beginning. I regard this as return, if you like, to something like the Platonic theory or, perhaps, the Augustinian theory. (Eslick 1964, p. 37)

It is hard to see how one can preserve a vital and continuing selfhood, a continuing and growing self-identity, in terms of a merely static formal content that never changes in which accidental forms come to exist and perish. It would seem that the only temporal entities that can have existence proportioned to enduring and growing selves are these spiritual entities. But even though finite spiritual agencies have a dynamic self-existence, they are not identical with existence itself.

> Their existence is temporal in the mode of Bergsonian duration and entails motion and succession. Their creativity is qualified and subject always to material conditions, so that it cannot be a creativity precisely of existence itself. The ultimate Divine Creator cannot be so restricted. But an absolute creativity can only be found in a being whose very essence is existence and, as such, is unique and transcendent. (Eslick 1964, p. 38)

Thus the perfection of God is not a result of bringing together formal content or of expressing matter-of-fact in eternal objects. A metaphysics based on form as the measure of being has to insist on the finitude of God. If form is the measure of metaphysical being all existence involves a limitation, that is, possibility in some sense is antecedent to actuality, existential act.

The essence of God is existence that is unlimited and unreceived. His perfection is not a matter of a measurement by the finite capacity for forms. Thus the divine creativity of God is not limited. God's life must be beyond physical and spiritual time, indeed all successions. The life of God is eternity in the famous formula of Boethius, "The simultaneous and total possession of life everlasting without beginning or end." Such a life is neither static nor inefficacious. God wills us, his creatures, from eternity and he has known us from eternity. In this sense we make a difference to God, because of God's creative power and not because of ours (Eslick 1964, p. 36). God "takes part" in the Platonic doctrine of *power*, that is, the ability of an existent to make a difference to some other and for that other to make a difference to the first (see Miethe 1976, pp. 36–46, 190–93).

iv. The Real Distinction. The basic questions Thomas's "real distinction" is proposed to answer must be dealt with by metaphysicians in any age. This doctrine of an actual distinction between essence and existence attempts to give one answer to the Parmenidean problem of the One and the Many. Parmenides simply denied the many and opted for a single homogeneous Being. The real question is: "How the many beings of pluralistic theory can be differentiated in their very *existence*." This question divides into two different but related ones:

> First, what is it that distinguishes the existent from the utterly unreal? Is it form, matter, or both together? . . . Or perhaps none of these alternatives can qualify for the function of existential *actuation*. The second form of the question is that of existential *separation*. Could there be a plurality of separately existing entities without *intrinsic* metaphysical composition in each of them—or, at least, all but one? . . . Would the assertion of some completely *extrinsic* principle of limitation suffice. . . . Or, could there be a plurality of existents each metaphysically incomposite and yet not separated in their existence from one another by anything outside of themselves, but each distinct by virtue of their simple being alone? (Eslick 1961, pp. 149–50)

This exhausts the possibilities. It is not meaningful to say that many beings could exist separately from one another with nothing to account for their separate and manifold existence.

In regard to the question, "Does being admit of essential differentiation?" Eslick posits that there are only four main pluralistic alternatives to Eleatic monism. The many, if they exist, will be essentially one differing only by a principle other than essence, or they will have essential differences in their very being. In either case there are two further dialectical alternatives. (1) Any pluralism that holds that essence is unitary for all beings must say that beings differ by something other than essence. This may be denominated "nonbeing." This nonbeing may be either absolute, altogether outside of being, or relative, included within being as a kind of material substrate other than essence. The highest metaphysical principle in either case is that all determination is negation, that is, the Spinozistic maxim. The primary historical example of this first position is the classical atomism of Leucippus and Democritus. (2) The historical examples of the second type of pluralism are Plato and Whitehead. This type bases existential separation of the many on reception "in a material substrate which is internal to being but distinct from essence or form" (Eslick 1961, p. 152).

(3) There are two species of pluralism that propose that being manifests essentially different kinds. The first type holds that there are some entities that are metaphysically incomposite, but differing in their very being itself. "Being in each is simple, subsisting *form*" (p. 152). Plato held something like this in his early dialogues but later abandoned it. Something like this seems to have been held in the materialistic pluralism of Empedocles and Anaxagoras. This idea is found in a much more sophisticated way in Book Lambda of the *Metaphysics* of Aristotle. There are some forty-seven or fifty-five separated substances for Aristotle. The essence of each of the separated substances is pure form alone. They can neither be really related to each other, nor can anything else that exists, as inferior in its mode, be related to them.

(4) The last type of pluralism admits of essential differences among beings, but it does so in regard to metaphysical composition in finite beings of really distinct principles of essence and existence. It is only in this last type of pluralism that an analogical community of being exists. This simultaneously allows both essential variation among existents and the intelligible unity of all being.

> It is important to be able to exhibit the exhaustiveness of this classification of four types of pluralism in order to show that only a real distinction of essence and existence is compatible with an essentially diversified reality which possesses a true analogical unity. That a division between theories denying essential differentiation within being and those which admit it allows of no third alternative seems obvious. Further, the division between our first and second types seems exhaustive. . . . Either such an alien principle of negation will be wholly other than the simple beings separated by it, or it will function as an *internal* principle of otherness in composite beings, as contrary not to *being* but to the essence of beings. Its very contrariety to essence . . .

will make the entities in which it is present deficient *appearances* or images of the Absolute, or the essential reality which beings imperfectly show forth. (Eslick 1961 p. 153)

The metaphysical system described above always causes a schism or fission between appearance and reality. Thus finite existence is always less than fully real in this group of systems.

The type of metaphysical pluralism that posits form as the highest principle can be regarded as eliminated because it destroys all unity of meaning for the concept of "being." Being in that case is either totally univocal with no real differentiation, or it is equivocal. The first type of pluralism is rejected on grounds provided by Plato. Beings cannot be really related by a principle that is the opposite of being. Plato saw that such relations could not relate. "Their very extrinsicism from the being of the terms supposedly related by them logically demanded an infinite regress of relations by which relations are related to their terms" (Eslick 1961, p. 155).

Therefore, the decision is finally between the second and the fourth types of pluralism. Both of these maintain a real distinction within being of metaphysical principles. Thomas Aquinas said that the being of each thing found in a kind or genus is outside the quiddity of the genus. Thus the essential intelligibility between individuals can be abstracted in a single univocal concept, but distinct existences cannot.

The primary difference between the second and the fourth types of pluralism is that actual existence is determined from below essence in Plato and from above in Thomas. Aquina states that being cannot be a genus because the differences in relation to species would fall outside what is understood in the nature of the genus or kind.

> The function of conferring existential actuality upon essence cannot, therefore, be exercised by an indeterminate "material" principle of subjective reception or decision. Even on Platonic or Whiteheadean grounds, conceding for the sake of argument some power of existential actuation to such a cause, it could only confer at best an unreal, appearance type of existence, in contrast with the nonexistential "Reality" of essence. There would always be some failure of embodiment, a degradation into a shadow world, in which a residual irrationality and disorder would be inseparable from concrete existence. (Eslick 1961, pp. 157–58)

Thus real existence is most imperfect in this view because it receives all perfections in the order of forms and essence, but itself lacks in all.

Thomas Aquinas insists that existence is a principle in the order of act, not potency. Existential "actuation" is the function not of essence but of a principle of existing act that is really distinct from essence. It is proportioned as act is to potency. The separation in the world of existence is the result of essence, "either as pure form (in immaterial substances) or as individuated by matter. Neither form nor matter, separately or in conjunction, can exercise the function of existential act" (Eslick 1961, p. 159).

I will end this first engagement by again quoting Hans Küng (who is in part quoting Martin Buber) and rephrasing a question:

> We know all the objections raised by critics of religion from Feuerbach to analytical philosophy, even against the very term "God," which is so often misused. We have tried to take these objections seriously. And yet there is *no alternative to this term*. Despite all its monstrous misuse, it is irreplaceable. "How do you manage time after time to say 'God'? How can you expect your readers to accept the term in the sense in which you want it to be taken? . . . Which term in human language has been so misused, so stained, so desecrated as this?" To this question, Martin Buber, the Jewish philosopher of religion, replies: "Yes, it is the most loaded of all words used by men. None has been so soiled, so mauled. But that is the very reason why I cannot give it up. Generations of men have blamed this word for the burdens of their troubled lives and crushed it to the ground; it lies in the dust, bearing all their burdens. Generations of men with their religious divisions have torn the word apart; they have killed for it and died for it; it bears all their fingerprints and is stained with all their blood. Where would I find a word to equal it, to describe supreme reality? If I were to take the purest, most sparkling term from the innermost treasury of the philosophers, I could capture in it no more than a noncommittal idea, not the presence of what I mean, of what generations of men in the vastness of their living and dying have venerated and degraded. . . . We must respect those who taboo it, since they revolt against the wrong and mischief that were so readily claimed to be authorized in the name of God; but we cannot relinquish it. It is easy to understand why there are some who propose a period of silence about the 'last things,' so that the misused words may be redeemed. But this is not the way to redeem them. We cannot clean up the term 'God' and we cannot make it whole; but, stained and mauled as it is, we can raise it from the ground and set it above an hour of great sorrow." (Küng 1980, p. 508)

Flew quotes John Hick as saying: "The right question is whether it is rational for the religious man himself, given that his religious experience is coherent, persistent, and compelling, to affirm the reality of God"

(I, p. 16). I say: "The right question is whether it is rational for the atheist himself, given his presuppositions, definitional view of reality, and his limited view of experience to say that his 'atheistic' experience is coherent and compelling and thereby to deny the reality of God." On with the debate!

CHAPTER III

A First Rejoinder

Antony G. N. Flew

Introduction

So now I proceed to respond, and to respond as one who certainly is, in the extended sense proposed in "The Presumption of Atheism," a kind of atheist. But then I have at once to protest that I cannot identify myself with or in that specific kind of atheist that Prof. Miethe describes and challenges—in particular in the penultimate sentence of "A First Engagement." To introduce my terminological proposition, I had suggested that "the originally Greek prefix 'a'" should in the future "be read in the same way in 'atheist' as it customarily is read in such other Greco-English words as 'amoral,' 'atypical' and 'asymmetrical'" (I, p. 7). In this broader and more comprehensive sense:

> . . . the term "atheist" becomes correctly applicable to far more people. It applies, immediately, to all those who are atheists in the positive sense, to all those, that is, who "positively disbelieve that there is an object corresponding to what is thus tacitly taken to be a or the concept of God." But then it must also embrace all those who, for whatever reason, would echo Bradlaugh: "I know not what you mean by God, I am without idea of God. . . . I do not deny, because I cannot deny that of which I have no conception." Perhaps too we should include, as a third subclass of negative atheists, those who refuse "to allow the (nevertheless still asserted) existence of God to affect their everyday living." (I, p. 9–10)

Having previously distinguished negative from positive atheists in the terms repeated in the passage just quoted, I ought not to have gone on—or at least not without due warning given—to employ the expression "negative atheists" in a second and quite different way, namely, to embrace all those, even including those previously qualifying as positive atheists, who must be accounted atheists in that broader and more fundamental sense. Perhaps too I should have stated that there is room for a fourth subclass, of those who have never heard or never attended a talk about God. If Prof. Miethe had been confused by such expository deficiencies, then the fault would have been entirely mine.

Yet it appears that he was not. Instead, having earlier given his warm endorsement to the suggested inclusion of a third subclass—"those who refuse 'to allow the (nevertheless still asserted) existence of God to affect their everyday living'"—he quotes the three preceding sentences, adding his own emphasis to the clause "all who are atheists in the positive sense." This quotation is presented as revealing me in my true colors. Miethe's immediate comment reads:

> There goes the "openness," for here we are right back at the "out-dated". . . analytical philosophy/linguistic analysis/British empirical atheism of the first half of this century. (II, p. 59)

1. Theology and Falsification

I am at a loss to understand how any of this, much less all of it, is supposed to be implicit in my specification of the class and subclasses of atheists in the proposed broader and more comprehensive sense. But earlier it has emerged that Miethe believes that my much reprinted note "Theology and Falsification"—first published a month or two before the midpoint of the century—logically presupposed, even if it did not explicitly appeal to, the verification principle, more or less as formulated by the old original logical positivists of the Vienna Circle.

i. The title of Section 1 of "The Presumption of Atheism" was "What Has the Atheist Not to Believe?" Subsection i therefore insisted that we should restrict our attention to a mainstream theism in the Mosaic traditions of Judaism, Christianity, and Islam, dismissing the likes of Tillich as the atheists they truly are, and he was. Subsection ii went on to suggest both that there is something problematic about the concept of God that helps to define these traditions and that it is in the main to this problematic character that we have to look if we are to explain the hardy, perennial difficulties of providing a clear-cut, decisive answer to the question whether in fact it does have application. The subsection begins by contrasting this particular much contested existential question with some others:

> It might at first blush appear that the question of the existence of the God of Abraham, Isaac, and Jacob was on all fours with the question of the existence of Loch Ness monsters, of unicorns, and of Abominable

Snowpersons. In all cases of this sort the difficulty, if there is a difficulty, is the shortage of evidence. (I, p. 3)

Miethe's immediate response is to say that he knows where I am going: "I can see it coming even without reading further . . . ." Flew is going, Miethe is sure, "for the theistic throat by way of his old, old essay 'Theology and Falsification'" (II, p. 44). But although, as Miethe points out, I did refer to that a few pages later my immediate concern was to show that, and why:

> Whereas . . . we have in all these other cases descriptions that would enable us decisively to identify a member of the class hypothesized were we so fortunate as to be confronted with such an actual specimen, this is not true of the present, or perhaps any, concept of God. (I, p. 4)

This is a significantly different problem from the one presented most urgently in that "old, old essay." That was the problem of excogitating an account of God's loving goodness which consists both with some acceptable resolution of the theologian's problem of evil and with something tolerably close to an everyday interpretation of the key terms "love" and "good." To clinch this contention I can scarcely avoid yet another resurrection of at least the final paragraph in that forty-year-old paper:

> Now it often seems to people who are not religious as if there was no conceivable event or series of events the occurrence of which would be admitted by sophisticated religious people to be a sufficient reason for conceding "There wasn't a God after all" or "God does not really love us then." Someone tells us that God loves us as a father loves his children. We are reassured. But then we see a child dying of inoperable cancer of the throat. His earthly father is driven frantic in his efforts to help, but his Heavenly Father reveals no obvious sign of concern. Some qualification is made—God's love is "not merely human love" or it is "an inscrutable love," perhaps—and we realize that such sufferings are quite compatible with the truth of the assertion that "God loves us as a father (but, of course, . . .)." We are assured again. But then perhaps we ask: what is this assurance of God's (appropriately qualified) love worth, what is this apparent guarantee really a guarantee against? Just what would have to happen not merely (morally and wrongly) to tempt but also (logically and rightly) to entitle us to say "God does not love us" or even "God does not exist"? I therefore put to the succeeding symposiasts the simple central questions, "What would have to occur or to have occurred to constitute for you a disproof of the love of, or of the existence of, God?"

ii. Having first satisfied himself that I was about to rest my whole case upon that "old, old essay" when in fact I was not, Miethe then proceeds systematically to misunderstand it. I began there by retelling the Parable of the Gardener, with due acknowledgments to Professor John Wisdom. In response Miethe baldly asserts, without even attempting to show, that in this retelling I made various now unfashionable assumptions, all of which he no doubt rightly reckons that he can dispose of easily and in very short order.

> The parable itself is guilty of making a very big and unprovable assumption—the assumption about "truth" that all analytic philosophers (and British empiricists who stand in that tradition) have made. It assumes (really rather uncritically) that the analytic "principle of verification" is true in an unqualified sense. This principle of verification in analytic philosophy claims we can only know that a thing [proposition?—A.F.] is true if it meets one of two tests. The "thing" [proposition?—A.F.] claimed to be true must be either (a) empirically verifiable or (b) a tautology. (II, p. 45).

But the fact is that at the time of writing that antediluvian essay I did not make, and never since have made, that assumption, nor indeed any of the others Miethe goes on to associate with it. On the contrary, the truth is that the whole object of the exercise was, leaving all that behind us, to put the discussion onto fresh and it was hoped more fruitful lines. Where before the unbelievers had been apt simply to denounce the utterances of believers as being "without literal significance"—upon the authority of *Language, Truth and Logic* (Ayer 1936), no less—I wanted instead to challenge believers to offer their own explanations of what it was they wished to assert. There was no intention to impose any preconditions, whether arbitrary or otherwise, with regard to the content of those explanations. The discussion, it was intended, could and should continue from whatever response each individual respondent saw fit to offer. (For a fuller account of the content of this exercise, compare Flew 1975, *ad init.*)

Miethe, therefore, has contrived to read into "Theology and Falsification" precisely what the writer himself was most concerned neither to say nor even tacitly to assume. So if Miethe still wishes to maintain that the verification principle was nevertheless logically presupposed throughout, then he must now attempt not simply to say but somehow to show that this was the case. He is very welcome to try. But, if he succeeds, I shall be both utterly astonished and profoundly chastened.

The one principle concerning the meanings of assertions and denials to which explicit appeal was indeed made is, surely, self-evident and tautological. It was argued for in the penultimate paragraph:

> Now to assert that such and such is the case is necessarily equivalent to denying that such and such is not the case. Suppose then that we are in doubt as to what someone who gives vent to an utterance is asserting, or suppose that, more radically, we are skeptical as to whether he is really asserting anything at all, one way of trying to understand (or perhaps it will be to expose) his utterance is to attempt to find what he would regard as counting against, or as being incompatible with, its truth. For if the utterance is indeed an assertion, it will necessarily be equivalent to a denial of the negation of that assertion. And anything which would count against the assertion, or which would induce the speaker to withdraw it and to admit that it had been mistaken, must be part of (or the whole of) the meaning of the negation of that assertion. And to know the meaning of the negation of an assertion is, as near as makes no matter, to know the meaning of that assertion.

In the original there are footnotes to both the first and the last sentences just quoted: "For those who prefer symbolism: $p = \tilde{\ }\tilde{\ }p$"; and "For by simply negating $\tilde{\ }p$ we get $p: \tilde{\ }\tilde{\ }p = p$." (These constitute, I think, the only occasions I have ever found to employ the *Principia Mathematica* symbolism in any publication.)

iii. Although Miethe makes no attempt to show that the verification principle was logically presupposed in my retelling of the Parable of the Gardener, he does actually argue for two other conclusions: that I was insisting that "the proposition 'God exists' can only be verified on the basis of a very limited type of evidence" (II, p. 46); and that the way in which I did this was "to limit the evidence and to limit what would be acceptable as evidence to recurring physical phenomena, to things that can be seen (experienced via the five senses) physically" (II, p. 46).

(a) Miethe maintains that this is all implicit in my language in "Theology and Falsification." He asserts:

> Flew's very language already prejudices the case, because it puts the discussion under the limited rules of a strict atheistic empiricism. Such as atheistic empiricism, by arbitrary definition, excludes vast ranges of reality . . . that also cannot be "proven" via the principle of verification. We need to be open to all evidence and not try to arbitrarily rule out of hand any before it is adequately examined, whether the evidence be historical, revelational, or personal. (II, p. 47)

Since what gives rise to the theist theologian's problem of evil is various undeniable and undenied features of the allegedly created Universe, I certainly do have to plead guilty to having taken it for granted that anyone trying to solve the problem of good generated by any of the suggested resolutions of that prime problem of evil would very naturally labor to find and to point to some immanent manifestations of the Creator's omnipotent love and omnipotent goodness. Yet, even after this has been conceded, it remains far from obvious why the introduction of the words "to occur or to have occurred" should be construed as arbitrarily precluding the adequate examination of any sort of evidence—the historical perhaps least of all. After all, for anyone to have any kind of experience is an occurrence.

(b) Wishing to pack as much as possible into my initial contribution, I concluded with an interrogative sentence combining questions about both the existence and the nature of God. Only one of the responses published in *University* was addressed exclusively to the former question. That respondent, Father Thomas Corbishley, S.J., the then master of Campion Hall, Oxford, was not, apparently, inhibited by my employment of the words "occur" and "occurred," for he replied, without hesitation:

> To the question "What would have to occur to or to have occurred to constitute for you a disproof of the love of, or of the existence of, God?" the only thing to be said is, quite literally, "Nothing," . . . the existence of nothing at all, i.e., the nonexistence of anything at all, would constitute for me a disproof of the existence of God.

Without so much as a single word of prefatory protest against his breaking some half-century-old British empirical atheist embargo, my own rejoinder straightway proceeded to point out that, as it stood, without prefix or suffix, Corbishley's response carried an implication he would have had to regard as catastrophic. If in asserting the existence of God he really was denying nothing else but the nonexistence of a Universe, then for him this assertion was formally equivalent to an assertion that there is a Universe; and, when you bring into the reckoning the further consideration that he must allow worthiness to be worshiped to be one of the essential characteristics of God, it seems that Corbishley would thereby become committed to the heretical and hence, to him, unacceptable doctrine of pantheism.

2. God and Metaphysics

Without drastic supplementation Corbishley's response clearly will not do. But something might be made of it by someone who went on to argue that the bare existence of any (logically contingent) being(s) somehow presupposes the existence in addition of a (logically) necessary Being or other putative Ground of all being. If only Miethe had not chosen to devote so much of his space and energy to refuting claims I have not made and would not wish to make, instead of to attempting *either* to refute what I actually said or implied in "The Presumption of Atheism" *or* to defeat the presumption to which that chapter referred, then we might at this moment have been inspecting, rather than just speculating about, a development of this kind. Certainly there are indications that, sometime and somewhere, Miethe would wish to erect such a construction, albeit not, apparently, here and now.

i. Thus he quotes his former professor as saying that "at least traditionally western metaphysics is the study of reality as such, being as such. It must be consummated by some kind of theory of God." Miethe comments: "Without God's existence there is no possibility of 'doing metaphysics'" (II, p. 34).

As one who is himself now very much a former professor I am reluctant to fault such pupil piety. Claims of this kind cannot, however, be accepted on the basis on anyone's unsupported assertion and in default, for instance, of any explanation of how this alleged impossibility is to be reconciled with the actualized possibility of Sir Peter Strawson's *Individuals: An Essay in Descriptive Metaphysics* (1959)—a work in which God appears to be mentioned on only three occasions, and then only as featuring in mistakes made by Leibniz.

Again, Miethe's proposed definition of the word "God," unlike that offered by Swinburne, begins by stipulating that existence is of the essence: "It is enough here to say that I affirm the existence of 'The Supreme Being, or the Ultimate Reality, whose nature is to exist . . .'" (II, p. 39). Since Miethe includes this initial stipulation in his definition, it is not surprising that he proceeds to speak well of the ontological argument; referring, for instance, to "Charles Hartshorne's great modern defense of Anselm's argument in *Proslogium* III" (II, p. 57). What is not only surprising but also unfortunate is that, although Miethe alludes most respectfully here and elsewhere both to this and to other famous arguments, he nevertheless appears to consider it either inappropriate or impossible actually to put forward his own version of any of them, here and now.

Thus he asserts: "Many arguments will need to be seriously examined that cannot be developed in the limited space here, for example, the ontological argument, the moral argument, and the teleological argument (which is becoming very popular again with many scientists), as well as arguments from historical events, revelation, and personal experience" (II, p. 39). Certainly all these arguments do need to be examined; and over the years I have, surely, done rather more than my fair share of such examining. (See, for instance, Flew 1984b.) From the impossibility of doing everything we cannot, however, validly infer the impossibility of doing anything; while if this is not an appropriate place and time for some such examinations or reexaminations whatever is, or would be?

Again, in concluding his reference to Hartshorne's resurrection of the ontological argument Miethe maintains that "modern developments of this grand old argument must be examined carefully and not just dismissed" (II, p. 57). Fair enough.

ii. After presenting his own preferred definition of the word "God," Miethe quotes from one of the passages in which I had myself earlier quoted Tillich and thereupon faults himself for misunderstanding "the Christian concept of God" (II, p. 40). Miethe then reveals that he has "long contended that most of the . . . devastating errors in the history of theology can be traced to an uncritical acceptance of the concept of God from the Neoplatonic philosophy of Plotinus" (II, p. 40). It is, presumably, this same fundamental contention that is expressed again when later Miethe asserts that "Most problems in the history of theology are a result of this adoption of the Greek view of the nature of God" (II, p. 43).

(a) I should like to think, because I am bound to see this suggestion as to Miethe's credit, that he had recognized and was pointing to, and warning against, that ultimately explosive synthesis of incompatibles that results from the melding of Greek and Jewish traditions in Christian theology. The crux is well stated in one of the classics of the history of ideas:

> . . . the God of Aristotle had almost nothing in common with the God of the Sermon on the Mount—though, by one of the strangest and most momentous paradoxes in Western history, the philosophical theology of Christendom identified them, and defined the chief end of men as the imitation of both. (Lovejoy 1936, p. 5)

This synthesis of incompatibles required and requires the identification of the active, living, agent God of Israel, a Being in the succession from the Demiurge of Plato's *Timaeus*, with an altogether abstract, lifeless entity, something from the categorically different tradition of the Form or Idea of the Good/Real in *The Republic*. If anything from the former category is said to be eternal, then the claim is that it is at least everlasting—without end—and (perhaps also) without beginning. But, when the same word is applied to an entity belonging in the latter category, then it has to be construed as meaning that that entity is something of which temporal questions cannot sensibly be asked. Certainly the identification of such incompatibles is a cause of continuing confusion:

> If someone says that God's eternity is something simply out of relation with what occurs in time—that we ought not to say, e.g., that God lived *before* the world came into existence—then his view is probably confused and certainly unscriptural. "Before the mountains were brought forth, or ever thou hadst formed the earth and the world, from everlasting to everlasting thou art God." "Before Abraham was, I am."
>
> I suspect some theologians of wishing to replace this conception of an external God, whose changeless duration co-exists with and overflows the duration of mutable things, with the conception of a God who is changeless because *not actual*. Surely it is for this reason that we hear so much of its being wrong to say God *exists*; for this reason, that Tillich emphatically repudiates the idea of a God who acts—who "brought the universe into existence at a certain moment, governs it according to a plan, directs it to an end." (Geach 1969, p. 74; the Tillich reference is to *Systematic Theology*, vol. 2, p. 6)

(b) The reason for wanting to interpret Miethe as pointing to that sort of synthesis of incompatibles as the source of his "devastating errors in the history of theology" is that it certainly is something to which everyone engaged in philosophical inquiry into the existence and nature of God ought to be alert, and hence something about which a book of the present kind is bound to inform its readers. It is, for instance, essential that all concerned should recognize that the existence of hypothetical entities of these two categorically different kinds has to be argued for in two correspondingly different ways.

Thus, insofar as we are arguing for the existence (or perhaps we should say the subsistence) of some timeless abstract entity, such as the Form or Idea of the Good/Reals, what we need to establish is that this is not a causally but a logically necessary condition of the existence (or subsistence) of something else, the reality of which is not in dispute. That, after all, is how Plato himself argued for the reality of his Forms or Ideas: there necessarily had, he contended, to be a universal, a Form or Idea of Justice if it was to be, as it is, possible truly to characterize several particular performances as just.

But the case is altogether different with a causally shaping Demiurge or with the active, agent God of Israel. To establish the existence of a

Being of that sort what we need is causal arguments. That is why the one and only traditional "proof" of the existence of God for which Hume had either patience or respect was the argument to design.

Unfortunately it is not possible to interpret Miethe's warning in so flattering a way, for his approach to this particular crux is at best inhibited and ambivalent. Certainly his warning against the source of "most of the rather devastating errors in the history of theology" is followed by an excursus on Neoplatonic theological errors. And too this excursus concludes with the Protestant affirmation: "For me, God is the God of the Judeo-Christian Scriptures" (II, p. 44).

But just before launching himself into that excursus, Miethe, rejecting the definition I had quoted from Swinburne, introduces as the first element in his own preferred alternative something of which there is no suggestion at all in Swinburne's definition. Miethe thus begins by stipulating that his God must be: "The Supreme Being, or the Ultimate Reality, whose nature is to exist" (II, p. 39). If this is not the Form or Idea of the Good/Real then you could certainly have had me fooled!

Although Miethe is later prepared to give credit to Plato because in his treatment of that Supreme Idea—the Form of Forms—Plato "never identified this with God" (II, p. 40–41), Miethe, in developing his own definition of the word "God," straightway identifies "the living, personal, loving and merciful Creator and Sustainer of all that exists" with "the Ultimate Reality, *whose nature is to exist*" (II, p. 39 [emphasis added]).

3. Beginning from the Beginning

Earlier in this "First Rejoinder" I reminded readers: first, that I had previously recommended that in the present discussion we should restrict our attention to mainstream theism in the Mosaic traditions of Judaism, Christianity, and Islam (III, p. 85); and, second, that I had then gone on to make two further points I consider to be very important. Those points are that there is much that is problematic about the kind of concept of God that helps to define these traditions and that it is in the main to this problematic character that we have to look if we are to explain the hardy, perennial difficulties of providing a clear-cut, decisive answer to the question whether such a concept does in fact have application.

Carried away by his mistaken conviction that he can see coming—"even without reading further" (II, p. 44)—the assumptions he misreads into "Theology and Falsification," Miethe fails to appreciate the significance of these two points and that I introduced them at the earliest possible moment out of an argued conviction that any systematic theological apologetic, and hence the close critique thereof, ought to begin at the beginning. Now that those distracting misunderstandings have, I hope, been cleared up, we can perhaps most usefully repeat that argument:

> Traditionally, issues that should be seen as concerning the legitimacy or otherwise of a proposed or supposed concept have by philosophical theologians been discussed either as surely disposable difficulties in reconciling one particular feature of the Divine nature with another or else as aspects of an equally surely soluble general problem of saying something about the infinite Creator in language intelligible to finite creatures. . . . All this is, no doubt, all very well when and insofar as the existence of God can be taken for granted. But when, as now, the question before us is whether a or the concept of God does or does not in fact have an object, then any such approach becomes literally preposterous. If we are inquiring whether there in fact is an object corresponding to some putative definite description or whether some supposed class does possess any actual members, then the obvious first steps are, in the one case, to make sure that that description is indeed both coherent and truly definite and, in the other, to ask how any members of that supposed class are to be identified as such. (I, p. 10)

i. It would appear that in Miethe's eyes none of this possesses any force at all. Just as he fails to appreciate that "Theology and Falsification" was an attempt to set the apologetic/counterapologetic debate off on a fresh and it was hoped more fruitful tack, so in practice he refuses to recognize that the present insistence upon beginning from the beginning—demanding that the conceptual problems be tackled first—constitutes a comparably innovative challenge to apologetic. Indeed Miethe, while complaining of space restrictions, even introduces an extended yet doubtfully relevant investigation of perceived problems about the internal unity and external relatedness of a God whose existence is taken for granted (II, p. 40–43).

Miethe summons to his support three paragraphs from Hans Küng. In one of these (II, p. 58), Küng equates the message of "Theology and Falsification" with that of *Language, Truth and Logic* (Ayer 1936). Sincle Küng apparently mistakes the former to have been, like the latter, a whole book rather that a brief note, we may charitably conjecture that he was misinformed about, rather than that unaided he misread and misunderstood, its contents. In another of these paragraphs (II, p. 82) Küng admits that "God" has been one of the most abused of words, but goes on to argue that, for all that, it remains indispensable: "We cannot clean up the term 'God' and we cannot make it whole; but, stained and mauled as it is, we can raise it from the ground and set it above an hour of great sorrow." In the third of the paragraphs quoted, Küng nevertheless manages to find some difficulty in understanding how there can be any confusion or indeterminancy about the putative referent of this (in English) three-letter word:

> After all that we may have heard, it may seem a little odd (not only to theologians) that, up to the present time, in certain philosophical schools and especially in analytical philosophy or linguistic analysis, discussion has centered, with a great display of erudition, not on whether God exists or does not exist but on whether "God" is a meaningful or meaningless term. How is this possible after the great minds of world history have wrestled for a lifetime particularly with the question of God . . . when even today there can be no doubt about the relevance of the term for the greater part of mankind? (II, pp. 57–58)

Küng's own answer comes pat. It is, of course, all to be put down to the infamous Verification Principle. Some no doubt is, or was, but certainly not all. If we are to understand how there can be legitimate doubts about the coherence of some concept of God and about whether that concept is such as conceivably could have actual application, then we need to start by recognizing the irrelevance of the objections deployed here by Küng.

In the first place no one is wanting to maintain that the word "God" is senseless in the way in which the word "gas" was indeed meaningless before it was arbitrarily adopted by chemists to refer—surprise, surprise—to gas. Bradlaugh did not want to maintain that he was as much at a loss to understand what was at issue in contemporary British theological debates as he might have been had they been being conducted in some language that was to him totally unknown. No, philosophical disputes about the meaningfulness of the word "God"—or, much better, about the legitimacy of some specific idea of God—are of another and more sophisticated kind.

For present purposes the most relevant and persuasive example was provided by Leibniz in a short paper of 1684 entitled "Reflections on knowledge, truth and ideas." (I must, and do, apologize for this I hope venially small display of erudition!) Commenting upon the then fairly recent revival by Descartes of the ontological argument, Leibniz contended that this goes through only if it can be shown that the premise concept of God as a logically necessary Being is free from contradiction, which he of course thought that it could be, although in my view it cannot (Flew 1989, chap. 6, sec. 2):

> In truth . . . this argument permits us to conclude only that the existence of God follows if the possibility of God is already proved. For we cannot use a definition in an argument without first making sure that . . . it contains no contradiction. From concepts which contain a contradiction we can draw conclusions contrary to one another, which is absurd.
>
> I used to explain this with the example of the idea of the fastest motion. . . . Let it be assumed that a wheel is turning with the fastest motion. Then it is easy to see that if one of the wheel's spokes were lengthened to extend beyond the rim, its end point would be moving faster than a nail lying on the rim; the motion of which is, therefore, not the fastest: which contradicts the hypothesis. At first blush it might seem that we have the idea of the fastest motion, for we understand what we are saying. Yet the fact is that we cannot have an idea of impossible things.

ii. Immediately after quoting Swinburne's definition of "God" (I, p. 4), I began to take issue with his stipulation that God is to be "a person without a body (i.e., a spirit," as well as with the later claim that "Human persons have bodies: he [God] does not." My objections there extended over six paragraphs (I, pp. 4–6). Certainly the case was and could scarcely fail to be less adequate than the book-length treatment in my Gifford Lectures (Flew 1987). Yet it is scarcely fair for Miethe to complain: first, that I was taking the suggestion of "a person without a body (i.e., a spirit)" as one that "can just be ruled out of court with the wave of a hand or a simple statement in opposition" (II, p. 48); and then that "It is not good enough to dismiss . . . Swinburne's statement simply because you don't like the idea . . ." (II, p. 48).

Resisting the temptation tiresomely to repeat every one of those offended paragraphs complete, I will instead concentrate upon what bears most directly on the crucial identification problem. I argued there that "If persons really were creatures *possessing* bodies, rather than—as in fact we are—creatures who just essentially are members of one special sort of creatures of flesh and blood, then it would make sense to speak of a whole body amputation" (I, p. 5). To this Miethe responded: "Isn't this exactly what Christians and others affirm in believing in life after death, for which there is . . . mounting evidence? (See Kübler-Ross 1969; Moody 1975; Küng 1984 . . . (II, p. 48.)

Well yes, perhaps: put it that way if you like. But if that is how you want to put it, then you must not neglect to notice how utterly different the amputee thus hypothesized is from the Loch Ness monster, from an Abominable Snowperson, or from anything else of the suchlike—from hypothetical entities of the kind, that is, earlier contrasted with the God of "the religious hypothesis" (Hume 1988, XI). And, furthermore, you must also notice that to interpret the sort of materials collected in the works mentioned in Miethe's parenthesis as evidence supporting "the survival hypothesis" presupposes that that hypothesis has already been given sense. That evidence itself, therefore, cannot provide sense. In particular it is presupposed that some account has been given of the kind of entities the survival of which is to hypothesized, and of how members of this kind might be first identified as such and then later—after "the effluxion of time"—reidentified as individually the same.

iii. Any apologists who really have appreciated the need to begin from the beginning will be well advised to bypass the difficulties generated by the first clauses both of Swinburne's definition and of Miethe's preferred alternative. Instead of stipulating that God is to be either "a person without a body (i.e., a spirit)" or "the Supreme Being, or the Ultimate Reality, whose nature is to exist," such apologists will do much better to start by ruling that God is to be understood as being the unitary and creative Cause of the origination, if it had a beginning, and, in any case, of the continuation of the entire Universe. They will, of course, be especially well advised to do this if they intend to go on to make much of the big bang cosmology.

The gambit suggested would provide them with a paradigmatically bare subject of which whatever further attributes they may choose to specify may conveniently be predicated. It is, of course, only after some such further and far more interesting stipulations have been made that it begins even to look as if hypothesizing the existence of God might have substantial explanatory and/or conduct-guiding point. Doubtless it was in the sort of minimal understanding now proposed that in the *Dialogues Concerning Natural Religion*, Pamphilus began by insisting that there is no other "truth so obvious, so certain, as the *being* of a God" (Hume 1947, p. 128).

Even so extremely modest an existential assertion is by no means wholly uncontroversial. Some will wish to dispute whether the Universe needs to have an unsustained sustaining Cause, and others to challenge the very idea of any external initiation, whether by a supposedly uncaused first Cause or whatever else (Grunbaum 1989). Yet it remains true that the most formidable objections arise only after something interesting has been alleged "concerning the *nature* of that divine Being; his attributes, his decrees, his plan of providence" (Hume, p. 128).

If and insofar as our aims are explanatory, then Occamite principles of intellectual economy forbid us to attribute to our hypothesized entity either powers stronger or properties more splendid than those strictly requisite to account for whatever it is we are proposing to explain by reference to it. Certainly in that context Swinburne's "able to do anything, knows everything" (quoted in I, p. 4) is going far too far.

Notoriously such postulational extravagance, once it is supplemented by the reckless addition of the further attributive clause "is perfectly good," generates the traditional theist's problem of evil. Such an addition, presumably implying that the Creator is a partisan within the creation, is understandably attractive to all those whose religious quest is to search for "something, not ourselves, which makes for righteousness." Yet it surely is—revelation apart—not merely unwarranted but positively contraindicated? For, as was argued earlier:

> No one . . . who was approaching the suggestion of an infinite creator God without any prior commitment . . . would be tempted to attribute such partisan interventions . . . to a Being stipulated to be an omniscient and omnipotent Creator? . . . A priori the reasonable assumption must be—as, I am told, some Indian thinkers have maintained—that such a Creator would be "beyond good and evil." (I, pp. 8–9).

Like so much else of importance in the history of ideas this notion that the Supreme Being is or must be perfectly good can be traced back to its ultimate source in Plato. As we have already had occasion to notice, the supreme Form, that is to say the Form or Idea of the Good, is in *The Republic* equated with the Form or Idea of the Real. If "goodness" and "reality" are thus taken to be synonymous, then it would seem to follow that evil must be essentially negative, and hence in some way unreal. About all this it must here suffice to say that, when atheists challenge theists to show how the actualities of evil can conceivably coexist with the existence of an omnipotent yet perfectly good Creator, then it is certainly not the atheists who construe the word "good" in accordance with this peculiar, not to say perverse, metaphysical usage (but see Flew 1984b, secs. 4.6 and 4.7; and compare 2.45ff).

4. Human Choice and God's Responsibility

One sort of response to the challenge of this surely insoluble "problem of evil" has been dubbed the "free will defense" (Flew 1955). Its tactic is to argue that, since human beings and perhaps some other creatures too are divinely endowed with free will, it is not the Creator but these creatures who are properly to be held accountable, even by their Creator, for all the evil consequences of their conduct.

Almost everyone, including at one time the present writer, has insisted on speaking here of free will. This is misleading, for the crux is not whether we ever act of our own free will rather than under compulsion, but whether we ever act at all. Manifestly, however, the true answers to both questions are categorical affirmatives, for an utterly familiar fact about people, and the most important difference between us and the rest of the furniture of the Universe, is that we are agents as well as patients. When agents act it must be true, in a profound and crucial sense, that they always could do other than they do do. Agents as such can, and cannot but, make choices. These choices are sometimes free and sometimes not. But, whether free or under some constraint, agents acting are always and necessarily making their choices between alternatives, the alternatives that have to be open to them precisely insofar as and because they are agents.

i. In order both to bring out the true implications of agency and to show how we can know that as agents we cannot in fact be being necessitated to act in whatever ways we in the event do actually act, let us contemplate two seminal passages from Locke's great chapter "Of Power":

> Every one, I think, finds in himself a *Power* to begin or forbear, continue or put an end to several Actions in himself. From the consideration of this power . . . over the actions, which everyone finds in himself, arise the *Ideas* of *Liberty* and *Necessity*. (Locke 1975, II (xxi) 7 p. 237)

In the second passage Locke mistakes himself to be explaining not action but free action and exploits his medical experience by referring to St. Vitus' Dance:

> We have instances enough, and ofter more than enough in our own bodies. A Man's Heart beats, and the Blood circulates, which 'tis not in his Power . . . to stop; and therefore in respect of these Motions, where rest depends not on his choice . . . he is not a *free Agent*. Convulsive Motions agitate his Legs, so that though he *wills* it never so much, he cannot . . . stop their Motion (as in that odd Disease called *Chorea Sancti Viti*), but he is perpetually dancing. He is . . . under as much Necessity of moving, as a Stone that falls or a Tennis-ball struck with a Racket. On the other side, a Palsie or the Stocks hinder his Legs . . . (Locke 1975, II (xxi) 11 p. 239)

Suppose now that, taking our cue from Locke, we distinguish two categories of bodily movements. Going with rather than against the grain of common usage, let us call those in which persons are agents (doing) movings and those in which they are patients (suffering) motion. On the one hand we have the movings, the doings of people as agents; on the other, the necessitated motions of people as patients—people, that is, in and to which things without their own control just happen.

By making this absolutely fundamental and crucial distinction in this particular way we at the same time indicate how we can, and should, provide ostensive definitions of the terms employed to mark the differences between the members of two radically different categories of bodily movements. In and by doing this we take up a position impregnable to all necessitarian determinist onslaughts, for an ostensive definition just is a definition given by showing, or pointing to, specimens of whatever it is to which the word or expression thus defined is defined as correctly applying. (If, for instance, the word "phlogiston" had been ostensively definable, then it would have been simply incoherent to maintain that, nevertheless, there neither was nor ever had been any such stuff.)

ii. What has been said in Subsection 4, i, immediately above, is relevant to the disposal of Miethe's comments (II, pp. 68ff) on Subsection 4, iii of my first contribution. He begins by suggesting that that subsection itself "has no bearing on an argument for the existence of God except (again) in the most secondary way" (II, p. 68). He thus overlooks that what presents itself to the theist as the (presumably in God's good time) ultimately soluble problem of evil is proffered by the atheist as a refutation of the contention that there exists an omnipotent Creator who is, by definition (and in an ordinary and not in some way-out metaphysical understanding), perfectly good.

I cannot myself now recall ever having said, whether matter-of-factly or otherwise, that all Christians are Calvinists. But, since my memory is just as likely to lapse as Miethe's, I will press no protests here. What I certainly have said often and now happily say again is that Augustine and Aquinas saw, just as clearly as Luther and Calvin, that the agreed and undisputed doctrine that God is the creative and sustaining Cause of the entire Universe and of everything that is in it inescapably implies that God must be the ultimate author and manipulator of—among all other things—all our behavior. This of course includes, in terms of the distinction drawn just now, not only our motions but also our movings. As Aquinas put it at the end of the first of my quotations from the theological giants: "Every operation, therefore, of anything is traced back to him as its cause."

So it is altogether beside the point for Miethe to cite other passages in which the Angelic Doctor asserted the freedom of the will, for none of these contradicts what was said, either by him or by Luther, in my own quotation. To enforce this claim there is, it would seem, no alternative to repeating Luther's words:

> I did not say 'of compulsion'. . . . a man without the Spirit of God does not do evil against his will, under pressure, as though he were taken by the scruff of his neck and dragged into it, like a thief or a footpad being dragged off against his will to punishment; but he does it spontaneously and voluntarily.

When earlier I introduced the image of the relations between puppets and their puppet-master I offered it as "the least inadequate earthly analogue to *the relation between creatures and their ever-sustaining Creator*" (I, p. 30; emphasis added). This it surely is; although because we are and know that we are living, conscious agents and not ordinary, this-worldly puppets, we find it hard to accept this analogy even in the extraordinary, partly out-of-this-world context to which it applies. It does apply there, in as much as, on the view that that analogy is offered to illustrate, God makes each one of us the particular individual person who freely chooses to do or not to do whatever God decides we will do or not do.

5. Explaining and Reducing

Miethe has a fair amount to say about what he believes that atheistical scientists cannot explain. His paper is also full of complaints against people who, by attempting to explain the development of this out of that are supposed to be trying to reduce this to that, or even trying to explain it away. This, surely, is all wrong. In explaining how something comes to be, you do not demonstrate that it is not. On the contrary, you presuppose that it is, or what would there be for you to explain? By explaining, for instance, how acorns evolve or grow into oak trees you neither reduce oaks to acorns nor—even more drastically—explain away oak trees and, hence, presumably, demonstrate their always illusory character.

i. In my younger days a favorite phrase among members of the Student Christian Movement was "a God of the gaps"; and those who employed it would usually issue some warning against the imprudence of pointing to gaps in scientific account of things as sites for—to borrow an expression from the terminology of the KGB—"special measures."

Those who appeal to such putative ad hoc creations as supports for their faith have always to await the latest communiques from the science front with trepidation, for every fresh communique may contain the disturbing news that yet another gap has now been filled. It would, surely, be wiser, wouldn't it, to try to develop a natural theology from the regularities and the wonders that scientists have discovered, rather than from some scratch collection of problems that, you believe, they never will or can solve?

It also occurs to me—though this is scarcely a point to press—that, by emphasizing so many gaps supposedly unfillable by science, Miethe is sketching a picture of a curiously improvident and unsystematic God. If the materials of the actual Universe are in fact such as cannot possibly give rise unaided to all the sophisticated furnishings its Creator wishes it to contain, then why did that Creator not begin by creating different materials that would be more adequate to his purpose?

ii. Objecting to my objection to talk of "a person without a body (i.e., a spirit)," Miethe asks whether "is it really any more obvious to talk as if a person is reducible to 'flesh and blood,' to a psychochemical machine" (II, p. 55).

Where, please, have I talked or written in these terms? Certainly I did employ the phrase quoted within that quotation, twice. The first occasion was when I argued that "If persons really were creatures *possessing* bodies, rather than—as in fact we are—creatures who just essentially *are* members of one special sort of creatures of flesh and blood, then it would make sense to speak of a whole body amputation" (I, p. 5). The second occasion was when I asserted that "in their ordinary everyday understanding, person words—the personal pronouns, personal names, words for persons playing particular roles (such as 'spokesperson,' 'official,' 'premier,' 'aviator,' etc.), and so on—are all employed to name or otherwise to refer to members of a very special class of creatures of flesh and blood" (I, p. 5).

The only clue I can find to suggest why Miethe believes that these two sentences constitute specimens of talking "as if a person is reducible to 'flesh and blood,' to a psychochemical machine" is his statement that I was here "*assuming* that there is nothing more to a human being than flesh and blood, that the human body—and hence thought and all that constitutes a human being—is reducible to a psychochemical machine" (II, p. 49).

But now, to maintain that person words "are words employed to name or otherwise to refer to members of a very special class of creatures of flesh and blood" is not even, necessarily and as such, to rule out of court any suggestion that these peculiar creatures may somewhere contain an unfleshly component or even several unfleshly components. If any prove able both to give *positive* sense to the idea of components of this kind and to explain how specimens might be identified and reidentified, then it remains open to them to make their suggestion and to deploy evidence in its support. (It is necessary to emphasize that "positive," for the adjectives "incorporeal," "immaterial," "unfleshly," and "nonphysical" are all wholly negative, telling us only what the referents of the nouns they qualify are not and nothing at all of what they are.) What and all that here is ruled out by my semantic assertion is saying that persons just essentially *are* these hypothetical, unfleshly components.

Suppose that we now put aside that suggestion that people contain some unfleshly component. Then the remaining content of the claim that "a person is reducible to 'flesh and blood'" amounts to no more than—is itself truly reducible to—the claim that there is nothing to be said about people that cannot be said about flesh and blood. But no one, surely, wants to say anything so silly and so obviously untrue. Certainly if people are so unfortunate as to be run over by steamrollers, then they are indeed reduced to a pulp of flesh and blood and crushed bones. But those remains would simply not be persons, not because persons "just essentially *are*" unfleshly creatures immune to any purely physical destruction, but because such fleshly residues would not and could not possess the distinctive and peculiar properties of persons.

CHAPTER IV

A Second Engagement

Terry L. Miethe

Introduction

In Chapter II, I do indeed "accuse" Antony Flew of "going for the theistic throat" (Miethe, II, p. 44; Flew III, p. 86)! In his second contribution to this debate, I now see that Flew very selectively narrows his assault and goes directly for my particular "theistic throat." I would have expected nothing less from my friend. Flew admits he is "a kind of atheist" (III, p. 84). He is indeed a *kind* atheist personally. As I have implied earlier (II, notes 3 and 4—and elsewhere in print), Tony Flew is the kindest atheist I have ever had the privilege to know.

In regard to Flew's "astounding" admission to be "a kind of atheist," I am reminded of a statement by former president Reagan, which I quote in rough form: "If it waddles like a duck and quacks like a duck, then it must be a duck." I realize this is not the most scholarly analysis of what exactly does constitute "duckness," but (most unfortunately) this is as "scholarly" as the former president ever was. And yet, there is something about this "definition" that does "ring true." Though it lacks scholarly erudition as a definition, it certainly meets the empirical criteria that Flew requires of all those things he judges to be real entities![1]

In Chapter I, Flew gives us this "nice," in his words "more comprehensive meaning" for the term "atheist" (pp. 7–8) that really tells us nothing. The "nice language" aside, Flew has already (I, p. 2) told us that:

> In the present context of discussion in the United States or Britain, the
> atheist will presumably be required either to outright deny or at least

not to positively believe that the conception of God shared by the
"peoples of the Book" . . . possesses or corresponds to some actually
existing object.

And "define" as Flew will—and want to call himself a "negative atheist"
(I, p. 7–8)—he *still* does not believe there is an "actual existing object"
that is called "God." Thus, whether Flew wants to call himself a
"positive atheist" or a "negative atheist," he ends up just like President
Reagan's "duck."

In Chapter I, "A First Engagement," I maintained that Flew's
position lacks (perhaps as much as Reagan's) real scholarly erudition and
empirical insight, that, in fact, he needs to be more empirical, not less. Is
it a reference to this argument that I make throughout my first
contribution (is this what Flew means) when he says: ". . . I have at once
to protest that I cannot identify myself with or in that specific kind of
atheist that Prof. Miethe describes and challenges—in particular in the
penultimate sentence of 'A First Engagement'" (III, p. 84)? I take it that
my (penultimate) sentence to which he refers is: "I say: 'The right
question is whether it is rational for the atheist himself, given his
presuppositions, definitional view of reality, and his limited view of
experience to say that his 'atheistic' experience is coherent and compelling and thereby to deny the reality of God" (II, p. 82–83). I think this is
the right question for any and all atheists. I certainly maintained—and
do maintain—that Flew does have presuppositions, a definitional view
of reality, and a limited view of experience. Most surely, Flew is not
denying in saying that he is "a kind of atheist" that he does *not* think
there is any good or conclusive evidence for the existence of God.

So what kind of "atheist" is Flew? Does he ever really tell us? I
certainly thought so. On page 2 of Chapter I, Flew defines an atheist as
one who "will presumably be required either to outright deny, or at least
not to positively believe that the concept of God shared by the 'peoples
of the Book'. . . possesses or corresponds to some actually existing
object." I also accept this definition of an "atheist" (II, p. 39). What part
of this definition doesn't Flew want to accept? Perhaps, the "to outright
deny" part. If this is the case, I have already said that in private
conversation Flew indicated to me he really was an agnostic (II, note 4).

Now Flew wants to use the term "negative atheist," though he also
admits that he used this term in two ways in his first presentation (III,
p. 84–85). Presumably, Flew wants his definition of "atheist" to be: "all
those who, for whatever reason, would echo Bradlaugh: 'I know not
what you mean by God, I am without idea of God. . . . I do not deny,

because I cannot deny that of which I have no conception.'" I stated in my first presentation (II, p. 58), I liked this definition in that it *appears* on the surface to be more open than what Flew defines as the "positive atheist." Flew writes: "In this interpretation an atheist becomes not someone who positively asserts the nonexistence of God, but someone who is simply not a theist. Let us, for future ready reference, introduce the labels 'positive atheist' for the former and 'negative atheist' for the latter" (I. p. 7–8; II, p. 58).

Again, this so-called "negative atheist" appears *on the surface* to be more open, but in reality is he? I think not! This is seen clearly if we examine Flew's use of "negative atheist" further and the inclusion as part of the definition of "a third subclass," that is, "those who refuse 'to allow the (nevertheless still asserted) existence of God to affect their everyday living.'" I did indeed give this definition my "warm endorsement" (III, p. 85) because I thought Flew, in listing this as a subclass of "negative atheist," understood something very basic to belief. But now I wonder.

If Flew *does* understand why this "third subclass" should be included in the definition "negative atheist," then he must see that, in reality, his supposedly more open definition of "negative atheist," that is, "I cannot deny that of which I have no conception," ends up denying God's existence just as much as the "positive atheist" (remember his admitted second use of the term "negative atheist" includes the "positive atheist") or the "third subclass" of "negative atheist," or for that matter, the "fourth subclass" (III, p. 85). For the believer (and in reality) to deny the *idea* of God is to deny the actual *existence* of God no matter what language game you want to play. Remember, Hans Küng is quite correct in pointing out that there is also an "atheistic language game" that is not self-justified (II, p. 46). Thus, we are right back to President Reagan's duck! (An "atheist" by any other name is still. . . .)

I believe I have shown clearly throughout my "A First Engagement" that Flew is not open to (or at least has not examined) "the evidence in a comprehensive and fair manner" (II, p. 58). What Flew does do, it seems clear to me, is use language very "skillfully" (I would expect this, but I should think we could expect much more) to basically ignore the implications of his statements and position. One of the many dictionaries I own describes Flew as follows: "Flew, Antony (1923–). Twentieth-century philosopher of the analytical school, which maintains that the role of philosophy is to analyze language" (Erickson, 1986). Surely, what we must be about in this debate is much more than just analyzing language.

As I indicated time and again in my "A First Engagement," it is reality itself that we must be careful to analyze. Flew may want to "split hairs" in regard to how one defines an "atheist," but it really all comes back to the same "duck." We must not—cannot—arbitrarily "define" out of existence vast ranges of reality simply because they do not meet our predetermined definition. I think that I have shown that this is exactly what Flew does. It is not good enough to say that I have no idea of God therefore I am denying nothing about "his" actual existence. You must examine all of reality and answer or explain why millions have had what they thought was an adequate idea of or concept of God, from great philosophers to the "common folk." Surely, it is missing the point of our debate to argue on and on over how we define an "atheist." We are not arguing about the definition of an "atheist," but over the question "Does God exist?"

1. "Theology and Falsification"—Response

Flew tells us his "immediate concern" was to show (and here he quotes again from I, p. 4) that:

> We have in these other cases ["Loch Ness monsters and Abominable Snowpersons"] descriptions that would enable us decisively to identify a member of the class hypothesized were we so fortunate as to be confronted with such an actual specimen, this is not true of the present, or perhaps any, concept of God.

Flew then goes on to write: "This is a significantly different problem from the one presented most urgently in that 'old, old essay'" (III, p. 86). But what is Flew arguing here? Certainly, he is trying to say that he is not arguing about the "existence (or more to the point the nonexistence) of God," but about the inadequacy of a meaningful "concept of God." He is talking as if (just as he tried with the term "atheist") he is going to show us a different argument the theist has never answered before and now has to answer.

Flew says that in his "old, old essay" the "problem . . . presented most urgently . . . [was] of excogitating [for the 'uninformed' reader 'excogitating' means 'to think out carefully and fully'] an account of God's loving goodness." To "clinch this contention," Flew quotes again, "yet another resurrection of at least the final paragraph in that forty-year-old paper" (III, p. 86). Flew claims that I have proceeded "systematically to misunderstand" his "old, old essay" and goes on to say "Miethe baldly asserts, without even attempting to show, that in this retelling I made various now unfashionable assumptions . . ."

(III, p. 87). Then Flew writes: "But the fact is that at the time of writing that antediluvian essay I did not make, and never since have made, that assumption [the analytic 'Principle of Verification'], nor indeed any of the others Miethe goes on to associate with it" (III, p. 87).

It seems I need to make three points here:

(1) Flew says he "never [has] made . . . that assumption" (III, p. 87). What assumption—that the analytic principle of verification is true? Flew tells us the "old, old essay's" ("Theology and Falsification") purpose was in "excogitating an account of God's loving goodness," that is, to treat the "problem of evil," and by implication, not the existence of God as such. But what does one find when one looks carefully at Flew's essay. It becomes quite clear that every test the explorers set up to establish the existence of a "gardener" (in this case "God")—they set a watch (sight), set up a barbed-wire fence (again, sight) and electrify it (hearing), and patrol with bloodhounds (smell)—is empirical!

And, when the skeptic despairs because he cannot understand how what the believer calls "an invisible, intangible, eternally elusive gardener differs from an imaginary gardener or even from no gardener at all," *all the evidence* admitted, or allowed, to count for the existence of the "gardener," is without exception, *empirical*. The whole parable is put within a context that clearly allows verification only by way of physical evidence, or empirical sense data, or within the context of the Principle of Verification. The entire argument is indeed empirical. How could this be any clearer?

The argument is unquestionably about the *existence* of the "gardener," and only secondarily, if at all, about the "loving nature" of the gardener (remember in the clearing "were growing many flowers and *many weeds*" [emphasis added]). The "weeds" would have to be equated here with evil and thus there is no explicit denial of the problem of evil by the believer. In fact, there is no mention of them (the weeds) at all. Also, the believer's original assertion is simply about "existence": "Some gardener must tend this plot."

Flew indicates no less than four times (in the remanding two and one-half pages of his essay) that the question *is* the existence of God. In fact, in one place Flew even mentions a "tautology" and twice in his lengthy quote (III, pp. 86) from the "old, old essay," he says essentially the same thing: (a) "as if there was no conceivable event or series of events . . . to be a sufficient reason for conceding 'There wasn't a God after all . . .'" (III, p. 86) and (b) "Just what would have to happen . . . to entitle us to say . . . 'God does not exist'?" (III, p. 86). So what have I misunderstood? It seems quite clear to me that the entire essay does indeed assume the Principle of Verification. I don't see how one could deny it; or, in the context of this argument (even if you are later going to "try" to take the argument to a new level, that of the problem of the "concept of God"), why one would want to deny it?

Flew goes on, (I, p. 27) to quote Hume favorably—indeed Flew tells us he is going to "redeploy Hume's refutation of . . . natural theology" (I, p. 20)—as saying: "The *existence*, therefore, of any being can only be proved by arguments from its cause or its effect; and these arguments are founded entirely on *experience*" [emphasis added]. Hume is further quoted here as relating "experience" to actions like the falling of a pebble and control of the planets in their orbits. Flew writes: "Furthermore, and finally, not only is it impossible to know, antecedent to *empirical enquiry*, that any particular thing or sort of thing either must be or cannot be the cause of any other thing or sort of thing, . . ." (I, p. 27) [emphasis added]).

And, as if the above reference were not enough, Flew again quotes Hume to say he:

> would indeed insist, that experience must be "the only standard of our judgement concerning this, and all other questions of fact." He [Hume] has also urged that "The religious hypothesis . . . must be considered only as a particular method of accounting for the . . . phenomena of the Universe." (I, p. 23)

Flew writes (after a two-page discussion of what he thinks Hume showed so well) that:

> The conclusion, which I believe but cannot prove that Hume himself eventually drew, *is that we should take the Universe itself and whatever our scientists discover to be its most fundamental laws as the ultimates in explanation.* This is a version of what Pierre Bayle taught Hume to call the Stratonician atheism. (I, p. 25) [emphasis added]

If Flew is not advocating "empirical verification" as the test for ultimate reality, I do not know how else to make sense out of these statements. Flew also ignores all the recent science that does indeed point to a cause beyond physical universe (II, pp. 49–54; see also Gange 1986; Wilder-Smith 1981 and 1987). But now, here (III, p. 87) we are told by Flew that empirical verification is not necessary; for he "never . . . made that assumption"? Interesting!

I take it thus that Flew *is* "both utterly astonished and profoundly chastened" (III, p. 87)!

(2) *This* debate is not about the problem of evil per se, though I do state in my first contribution (II, pp. 56–61 and 68–71) both that I think this problem has been adequately addressed and that the answer lies within a defense of the concept of the freedom of the will. I also list several books in the Bibliography treating the problem of evil, for example, Lavelle 1940; Lewis 1962; Sontag 1970; Wenham 1974; Geisler 1978; and Miethe 1984, pp. 127–32. Flew continually ignores the implication of the freedom of the will to this problem.

(3) Flew tells us it was his hope to leave the "old, old essay" "Theology and Falsification" behind and "to put the discussion onto fresh and, it was hoped, more fruitful lines" (III, p. 87). This, of course, I contend is exactly what Flew did not do. Flew basically ignores all that I say in answer to his supposedly new problem of the concept of God (II, pp. 39–44, 56–58). I admit:

> Of course, one would have "difficulties" with the concept of God if the possibility of "extraphysical" reality had already been defined out of court, out of existence, if all human experience—and therefore reality as we know it—had been defined as reducible to a mechanical/physical process. (II, p. 57)

In Chapter II, on pages 39 through 44, I explain why the concept of God has indeed been a problem over the last seventeen hundred plus years since Plotinus. In accepting the idea of Plotinus that the One or the Good was beyond being, essence, and knowledge (that God was totally other) Western theology has played right into the hands of the atheists. As I explained (II, pp. 42–44, 71–83), this definition need not be accepted and we need not play into the hands of the atheists here.

Yes, Flew tells us he wants to raise "difficulties with the concept of God . . ." (I, p. 6) and that he has never "made, that assumption, nor indeed any of the others Miethe goes on to associate with it" (III, p. 87). But Flew quotes John Wisdom as saying: *"The existence of God is not an experimental issue in the way it was"* and "This is due in part, if not wholly, to our betting knowledge of why things happen as they do" (I, p. 6). The clear implication is that these issues (like the existence of God) are no longer "betting issues" because modern science has explained how things happen. This is accepting an outdated view of modern science (and the claims of that science) as I related in "A First Engagement" page 56. And, remember, these quotes of John Wisdom's are in the same paragraph that Flew starts by saying: "Paralleling the recognition of this and similar difficulties with the concept of God."

Thus, I think Flew is faced with a triple failure: First, he is simply wrong that the essay "Theology and Falsification" does not imply the principle of verification and that it is mainly about the problem of evil. Second, he has not "thought out carefully and fully" (to "excogitate") the problem of evil (III, p. 86) in relation to the free will argument[2] in the "old, old essay" (and we do not have space to do that in this particular debate).

Third, Flew tells us: "On the contrary, the truth is that the whole object of the exercise was, leaving all that behind us, to put the discussion onto fresh and, it was hoped, more fruitful lines" (III, p. 87). But has Flew done this? I think not. Flew has not managed to take the argument "onto fresh and". . . "more fruitful lines" vis-à-vis the question of the "concept of God," for even when he claims that he is concerned with the "concept of God" the discussion is limited by a clearly empirical (as atheists would define it) frame. It seems to me that in his first five pages (Chapter III) Flew makes much to-do about nothing. About all we have in the first five pages is the admission by Flew that he is indeed "a kind of atheist."

One very interesting question does come out of the first five pages of Flew's "A First Rejoinder." But before I ask the question, it will be helpful to remember that from the "old, old essay" (written over forty years ago) until at least 1985 in debate Flew has asked the theist for "evidence," for what the theist will allow to count against the theistic hypothesis, that God exists. Therefore, it is only fair, if Flew seriously claims he does not now hold to the Verification Principle or that the "proposition claimed to be true must [not now] be . . . empirically verifiable," that Flew tells us just exactly what he will allow to count *for* the existence of God.

2. "God and Metaphysics"—Response

Flew's main point in this section is basically to chastise me for what I have not *yet* done, while ignoring what I have done, ignoring the important foundation I have laid. He writes:

> If only Miethe had not chosen to devote so much of his space and energy to refuting claims I have not made and would not wish to make, instead of to attempting *either* to refute what I actually said or implied in "The Presumption of Atheism" *or* to defeat the presumption to which that chapter referred, then we might at this moment have been inspecting, rather than just speculating about, a development of this kind." (III, pp. 90)

But I maintain in Chapter II, "A First Engagement," and here in the first nine pages of my "A Second Engagement," that I *have* answered/refuted claims that are both implicit and explicit in Flew's presentation. Ulitmately, the reader must decide.

My first task in Chapter II was to treat Flew's "A Presumption of Atheism" in some sort of systematic manner and to show why much of what he said needed historical perspective or was simply incorrect. This I did. Then, I spent twelve pages introducing those concepts in regard to "God and metaphysics" that are essential in the history of philosophy to building a philosophy of God, for example, "The Starting Point of Metaphysics," "The Empirical Foundations of Metaphysics," "A Metaphysics of Creation," and "The Real Distinction." Flew simply totally ignores this essential metaphysical foundation!

(i) Flew mentions (III, p. 90) that "Miethe proceeds to speak well of the ontological argument. . . ." This is true, but I also said that I would not "in this book be defending" this argument. The ontological argument (from the word *ontos*, "being") is basically the argument that the very concept of an absolutely Perfect Being or Necessary Being demands that such exist. Though he did not consider the proof of Anselm valid, even Aquinas upholds the view that, speaking of God as taken in himself, his existence is evident: "*Nam simpliciter quidem Deum esse per se notum est; cum hoc ipsum quod Deus est, sit suum esse* ("Absolutely speaking, that God exists is self-evidence, since what God is is His own being" (*Summa Contra Gentiles* 1. 11. 1).

The ontological argument is an a priori argument based on pure reason alone. In history, there have been many forms of the ontological argument based for the most part on two distinct arguments, both of which are traced to Anselm (1033–1109), one in the second chapter and a second in the third chapter of the *Proslogium*. A second form of the ontological argument from the one for which Kant's criticism seemed telling was found in Anselm. If one grants the validity of Kant's criticism that "existence is not a predicate" (not everyone does), it affects only the first form of Anselm's argument based on the predicability, not the second form based on the inconceivability of God's nonexistence.

Even though I am not arguing the ontological argument here, perhaps a look at "existence and necessity" would be helpful. The foundation of the attack by logical empiricism upon claims to metaphysical knowledge has been the division of all cognitive propositional statements into analytic and synthetic. In this "synthetic-analytic distinction":

> Analytic propositions are necessary, but void of existential content. In the extreme version, that of Wittgenstein, they are mere tautologies, . . . without extralinguistic reference. Mathematics and logic are divorced from ontology. . . . Synthetic propositions are contingent only, subject to empirical verification or falsification. (Eslick 1968, p. 292)

Thus in the beginning the positivist movement sought certitude via the senses but very quickly settled for probability.

It is obvious that the analytic-synthetic division makes metaphysical statements nonsense. Even Wittgenstein realized at the end of his *Tractatus* that because he was trying to talk about the relations of language to sense, to fact, and because this was not the result of immediate sense perception, what he was saying was unsayable. Metaphysics is an attempt to predicate something necessary about the existential order. But the positivist dichotomy makes the necessary nonfactual and the factual wholly contingent. The claim of the synthetic a priori, even in Kant, is restricted to what he calls the phenomenal, not extending to the noumenal.

The historical roots of this exclusive and exhaustive classification, this dichotomy, can be traced in the thought of Aristotle, Leibniz, Hume, and Kant. Morton G. White is correct in seeing it prefigured in Aristotle (White 1970, pp. 75–91). This is Aristotle's distinction of accidental and essential predication. The difference between Aristotle and modern logical empiricism is that essential predication is existential for Aristotle. The contingency of physical, corruptible existence is not absolute. "X" exists because of essence or form. Thus there is at least a hypothetical necessity involved in the species of animals and plants, even if the existence of particulars in the species is not.

Hartshorne is correct in finding in Aristotle the anticipation of Anselm's ontological argument. Separated substances, that is, pure formal actualities, have actual necessary existence. Thus there are entities necessarily existing that have some contingent proprieties. This is an important notion of Hartshorne's neoclassical metaphysics. Hartshorne thinks that there are things that are both necessary in existence and contingent in respect to the qualities of concrete actuality.

Leibniz's distinction of truths of fact and truths of reason is a version of the synthetic-analytic distinction. For Leibniz truths of fact are contingent. Existence is not a predicate contained in the subjects of such truths. But only in God is existence an analytically contained predicate. Thus the proposition "God exists," for Leibniz, is a truth of reason.

Truths of reason are necessary and undeniable without self-contradiction resulting. In Leibniz what appears to be strongly empirical moves toward a rationalism. Leibniz's analytic-synthetic distinction goes to the opposite extreme as compared to that of logical positivists in our time.

Hume's contribution to this discussion becomes the classical model for logical empiricism in our day. In Hume one has to choose between the necessary truths of mathematics and logic and the contingent truths of the empirical sciences.

> The Humean distinction of "relations of ideas" and of "matters of fact" seemingly answers to the analytic-synthetic disjunction of our positivists, and his consignment of metaphysical tomes to the flames represents the first and definitive appearance of this interpretation of the dualism. (Miethe 1976, p. 175)

Hume never explicitly raised the question as to whether all a priori truths are analytic.

The most important role of Hume in forming the patterns of contemporary logical empiricism grows out of his attack upon the causal principle. This is the idea that whatever begins to exist must have a cause of existence.

> If it be not contradictory to deny this, then a pluralism of only externally related phenomena becomes the model—Hume's sensory atomism and Russell's logical atomism. It is this which is at the heart of the denial of existential necessity by the proponents of the Humean or positivist versions of the analytic-synthetic dualism. (Miethe 1976, p. 175)

At the opposite of this extreme is the assertion that only internal relatedness of appearances is the actual case. If this were true all contingency would be lost and collapse into the unity of the Absolute, that is, into the unqualified existential necessity. If one is to avoid either extreme, both existential necessity and existential contingency must compatibly embrace in modal harmony, which is what Charles Hartshorne indicates.

For Kant knowledge is either pure or empirical. Kant, Hume, and logical empiricists agree that experience cannot disclose necessity and strict universality. Pure or a priori knowledge is necessary and universal, independent of all experience. Empirical or a posteriori knowledge is contingent. For Kant the analytic-synthetic distinction bears upon judgments, depending upon whether the predicate belongs or does not belong to the subject. For Kant the scientifically knowable world depends on the synthetic a priori, the existence of which is denied in logical empiricism.

> At the heart of the matter, however, is a common agreement allowing only sensory intuition, and denying any human intellectual intuition. Existence is not a predicate analytically contained in any subject. The notion of necessary existence has no empirical origin or content, and the movement in thought from contingent existence to necessary existence identified with the *ens realissimum* of God founders in the shipwreck of the ontological argument. Metaphysical ideas cannot constitute positive knowledge, but are only regulative. (Miethe 1976, p. 177)

I hold, along with W. V. Quine, Morton White, and Nelson Goodman, that the two dogmas of empiricism, the analytic-synthetic exclusive distinction and the verification theory of meaning, should be denied. I do not believe that there is a distinction between the empirically verifiable and that which has to do with language alone. Metaphysical statements are not different in kind from those of science. In Quine, metaphysical propositions are readmitted on the same level as scientific propositions, where they now have existential import.

The debate over existence and necessity has taken another "startling and unorthodox turn." This is the neoclassical metaphysics of Charles Hartshorne. Three of Hartshorne's books are fundamental: *The Logic of Perfection* (1962), *Anselm's Discovery* (1965), and *Creative Synthesis and Philosophic Method* (1970). Hartshorne's metaphysics rehabilitates, in modal logic, the ontological argument for God's existence of Anselm of Canterbury (1033–1109).

It is Hartshorne who sees there are two distinct Anselmian arguments, one in *Proslogium* II, which is weakest, and one in *Proslogium* III.

> Almost the whole of Western philosophy, beginning with Anselm's first critic, Gaunilo, seems to be in ignorance of the *Proslogium* III argument, which is the real proof. Anselm's definition of God is the well-known formula: a being than which no greater can be conceived. The first version of the argument hinges upon the superiority of existence to nonexistence, or actual existence to existence in the mind's conception alone. Such an argument is wide open to Gaunilo's "perfect island" objection, since it implies a maximum of perfection inclusive of existence in every genus or kind of thing. (Miethe 1976, p. 178)

Thus for Hartshorne the first form of the argument recorded in *Proslogium* II can be regarded as false. The really surprising thing is that the second version of the argument, which is working on a quite different principle, is almost universally ignored.

The "true Anselmian principle" is "existence without conceivable alternative of not existing is better than to exist with such alternative," so that Greatness that is unsurpassable by others cannot not exist. According to Hartshorne, there are only four alternatives possible for thought in this area, only one of which can be true: (1) positivism—to deny any idea of God answering to the Anselmian definition; (2) such a property is conceivable only as nonexisting; (3) that such a property could be conceived of as both existing and nonexisting; and (4) a priori theism, which holds that the property is conceivable *only* as existing. Hartshorne maintains that if the first three can be eliminated only the fourth can be true.

According to Hartshorne, in God must be found both absolute and relative poles. God is necessary in his existence, but contingent in his concrete actuality. Thus he is surpassable not by others but by himself. Thus the existence of Greatness could not be contingent.

> But in God necessary *existence* itself, as unsurpassable by others in knowledge, goodness, and all un-restricted perfections, is abstract. *That* these perfections will somehow be realized in Divine Actuality is necessary, but *how* remains contingent. Only thus, according to Hartshorne, does one respect the reality of Divine creativity and freedom, and of the participated creativity and freedom of His creatures.
>
> The refutation of the first and the third alternatives can thus be taken as established. (Miethe 1976, p. 179)

If the Anselmian property were conceivable as existing and nonexisting, it would be surpassable. Conceivability of nonexistence would be residual, unaltered by the fact of existing. But according to Hartshorne modal status is independent of facts, thus facts do not determine conceivability.

The second is done away with because an ideal cannot have a clear and consistent meaning and yet be incapable of existing. Thus one is left with the fourth option as the only viable alternative.

> And, indeed, a necessary being is the ground of all possibility. To deny this is to assert universal contingency, itself not a factual or empirical proposition. The two rival propositions "God exists" and "God does not exist" are not two factual hypothesis. (Miethe 1976, p. 180)

They are really two systems of metaphysics for Hartshorne. They are concerned not with facts, but what it is to be a fact. The relation of thought to existence in the ontological argument is to include existence of the universal, unsurpassable individual, whose existence is compatible with any state of affairs.

The "idea" that nothing exists is one relation of thought to existence that is impossible and absurd. The assertion of universal contingency is not possible. It is incoherent. Nonbeing is unthinkable. Heidegger was incorrect in supposing the most important metaphysical question to be why something does exist, rather than why nothing at all exists. Eslick believes this to be only a pseudo-question.

> The genius of Hartshorne's Anselmian strategy stands, I maintain, revealed. It is nothing less than the fulcrum which restores metaphysical intelligibility to experience. Although metaphysical knowledge is non-empirical, it is, in the broad sense experiential. Indeed, Hartshorne is able to go on to show that *to be* is to experience, and, above all, to be included in the contingent experience of the necessary being, God. Like Archimedes, who needed only a lever to move the world while standing outside of it, Hartshorne has performed the same feat in metaphysics. (Miethe 1976, p. 181)

ii. Building a philosophy of God is an important and complex project, a project for which many people, perhaps most, in our comfortable world are not prepared to pay the price. Yet, the world—as you and I experience it—needs such an effort even more than ever before. I believe that we must draw on history (both in a positive and negative sense), philosophical reasoning, claims to revelation, personal experience, and all possible claims to knowledge and truth.

It is clear that the nature of God that originated in Greek philosophical thought is not sufficient. Certainly, the Christian concept of God is much richer than the Greek view. If one views God as utter and simple unity, that which does not admit to degrees, this makes the problem of how the many physical things can participate in that which is without parts. The identification of God with the One of Plato, as interpreted by Plotinus, gives birth to negative theology in the history of Western Christian thought. The traditional theory of the nature of God has always strongly emphasized the utter simplicity and the utter transcendence of God. Thus God is indivisible and transcendent of everything beneath him. Yet, it is clear this is not the God of the Christian revelation.

Plato was not thinking about divinity in this theological context. For Plato simple unity is the One or the Good of his earlier thought and is a principle of the Forms. Plato does not abandon the idea of the One as a principle of the Forms, but the Forms themselves cannot be simply unities of this sort. Plato saw, in the first hypothesis of the *Parmenides*, that if the one is taken just by itself nothing whatever can be said of it. Many philosophers have echoed this even to this day. The consequences of an utter and simple unity are devastating for Plato. Nothing whatever can be predicated of such a unity. Logically this means that any subject one talks about or ascribes qualities to must be composite (Miethe 1976, pp. 36–46).

Even in an attempt to make the statement "one is one" or "one is" the very notion of "is" or "being" adds something to unity taken just in itself. For any statement about "X" to be true, the "X" has to have some composition, that is, something in "X" itself other than simply "X-ness." Even Thomas Aquinas felt that our way of signifying or understanding always involves composition (Miethe 1976, pp. 85–102). Whenever we judge we compose or divide with respect to our subject or predicate. To compose is to affirm that A is B; to divide is to deny, that is, A is not B. This always presupposes that there is something in the subject that is other than just the "A-ness" of that subject. This is basically Plato's point about unity taken simply. It admits of nothing other than unity. There can be in unity taken simply no plurality, no otherness whatever. Thus nothing can be said of it. There must be some foundation in the subject itself that allows it to be really related to other things.

The Neoplatonists supposed that the One in the first hypothesis of Plato's *Parmenides* was identical with the supreme divine principle or Godhead. It is therefore beyond being, essence, or knowledge (Miethe 1976, pp. 60–69). Orthodox Christian theology has always taken for granted, following the Neoplatonic tradition, that the Godhead is absolutely simple with no composition or real distinction. This is not simply the monotheistic position, but that God himself is absolute simplicity and indivisible. This is not what Plato intended at all. Plato regarded unity of this sort as utterly sterile, incapable of creating anything else or having any kind of emanations flow from it. Thus for Plato the hallmark of existing or being always involves *dynamis* or power, that is, the ability of the existent to make a difference to another and of the other to make a difference to the first. If one strips off all real relatedness from the notion of anything whatever, nothing is left that could possibly exist. Thus what Plato really shows in the first hypothesis is that if simple unity is the case, one can have no knowledge about the Forms of reality itself. In fact, they cannot really exist because they lack the power to stand in relation to other things. Their very absolute character destroys the possibility of their existing at all.

Not only will later Christian theological tradition, under the influence of a Neoplatonic interpretation of Plato, think of God as utter and simple oneness, it will also think of God as not really related to the world at all. This will be regarded as part of the divine perfection. Creatures, for Thomas Aquinas, must stand in a real relation to God as being dependent upon him for their very existence. This is well and good. But the orthodox supposition is that God himself is not really related to his creatures because a real relatedness would involve some kind of dependence and God's divinity demands that he be absolutely independent. Whether or not there is a created world would make no difference to the Being of God. The world can produce no effect upon God. This notion of divinity clearly has a Greek philosophical origin and is untenable.

Simple unity is not a perfection at all:

> Questions of this type of thing should be raised at the very outset. It is much too easy to take for granted such attributes of Godhead as absolutely unmoved, not really related to His creatures at all, though they are absolutely dependent upon Him. What for example is so perfect about the utterly simple? Why is the simple better, more perfect, than the complex? This question is never really answered. Why is an absolute mode of existence which is exclusive of relativity to the world better than a mode of divine existence which would combine both? (Miethe 1976, p. 185)

The true nature of God is such that he must have both an absolute character and be the prime example of perfect relativity. God must be in perfect relatedness to everything else. God must exist both in himself as indivisibly and incommunicably one and also must have the power to make a difference to other things and other things must have the power to make a difference to him.

iii. Let us look at the meanings of power. Perhaps the traditional doctrine of the divine omnipotence should be looked at with a view to important revision and qualification. The traditional doctrine comes directly from Greek metaphysics, that is, with an equation of the intelligible with the necessary, of being with form. In the Greek view, divine omnipotence "is thought of as the imposition of the necessity of remorseless reason, resulting in the iron determinism of essentially subordinated causal series, or of a descending syllogism" (Eslick 1968, p. 289). This view is at the root of the problem in historical theology of reconciling the freedom of the creatures of God with his omnipotence. I do hold that God's creativity is unlimited and unconditioned by the dispositions of preexisting material in some way.

The metaphysical problem one faces is how to establish a viable meaning of "power" that allows for God to be unlimited creativity and for his creatures to have true freedom. There are at least two ways this is not possible in relation to the standard doctrine of divine omnipotence. (1) True power cannot be the kind of power of the oriental despot who has the life and death of his subjects at his command. This is arbitrary "power" and is a debased and dishonorable weakness according to Plato. This is related by Plato in a classic text in the *Gorgias*:

> Imagine that I'm in the crowded marketplace with a dagger concealed under my arm and I say to you "Polus, I have just acquired an amazing sort of tyrannic power. If I think that anyone of these men who you see ought to die this very instant, die he shall, whomever I choose! And if I think that any of their heads should be bashed in, bashed it shall be right on the spot! Or, if a coat should be slit, slit it shall be! That's the sort of power I hold in this city!" Then if you didn't believe me and I showed you my dagger, you might look at it and say, "Why Socrates, everybody can have that sort of power. In this way you might burn down any house you pleased, and even the Athenian dockyards and the man-of-war and all the ships, both public and private." But surely this is not what one means by having great power: to do anything one pleases. (Plato 1952, pp. 466–70)

For Plato genuine power is seen in goodness and the knowledge of it. Power alone is *free* and it gives the gift of freedom to others. In this case God in his goodness gives his freedom and allows creatures to participate in and have creativity.

(2) True power cannot be manifested in the imposition of mechanical determinism. The Greeks valued the regularity of motions too highly. Because nature was regular in its normal functioning, events were predetermined. Even Plato failed to realize that such laws

> . . . far from expressing the fullness of divine power, may only be the averagings of dead and habitual repetitions in nature, so that the power of the past, imposed upon the present, evokes only conformity without novel creative response. The forms of "necessary" relatedness expressed in laws may therefore exhibit only the weakness of matter unable to create or innovate, rather than the power of creative spirit. (Eslick 1968, p. 291)

Thus true power, as in Plato's *Sophist*, must be *dynamis*, that is, the power of acting and of being acted upon in relation to others. This is the ability of one existent to make a difference to another and of that other to make a difference to the original existent. Eslick does not think that this formula has ever been improved upon as a metaphysical definition of power. The fact that we affect others is not as important as how we do. It is this *kind* of difference made to others that is most important:

> To the extent to which the power exerted attains its effect by force imposing conformity, that effect has a diminished ontological status and value, proportioned to the inferior metaphysical level of the agent. Slavery begets slavery; freedom begets freedom. The creativity of violence and compulsion is minimal; it is weakness engendering weakness. (Eslick 1968, p. 291)

iv. Surely, Flew will admit that there are many issues based around the arguments for the existence of God (as well as many arguments for the existence of God) that cannot be developed in this book (II, p. 39). One can only do so much in one chapter of one book, especially when much of the space must be given to explaining and answering the errors of "The Presumption of Atheism." On the other hand, it seems clear to me that Flew could have given much more space to adequately addressing—even *addressing at all*—the foundational issues I present regarding building a philosophy of God.

Finally, in the section "God and Metaphysics," Flew faults me (III, p. 93) for stipulating that God must be "The Supreme Being, or the Ultimate Reality, whose nature it is to exist." Flew says: "If this is not the Form or Idea of the Good/Real then you could certainly have had me fooled!" First, Flew seems to be completely oblivious here of my whole discussion of the fact that the Greek errors that were accepted rather uncritically into the history of theology came from Plotinus, not a proper understanding of Plato (II, pp. 40–44) though he alludes to this in the next paragraph.

Second, to say that Plotinus is the root of much error is not to say there is no connection between Greek and Christian thought. Obviously, many great Christian thinkers thought there was (including the apostle Paul, Augustine, and Aquinas). Certainly, the Bible tells us of a God whose nature it is to exist, who is eternal (without beginning or end; cf. Exod. 3:14; Ps. 48:14; John 5:26). As J. I. Packer says:

> God is self-existent, self-sufficient and self-sustaining. God does not have it in him, either in purpose or in power, to stop existing; he exists *necessarily*, with no need of help and support from us (cf. Acts 17:23–25). This is his *aseity*, the quality of having life in and from himself. (Ferguson, Wright, and Packer 1988, p. 276)

My identifications of God as "the living, personal, loving and merciful Creator and Sustainer of all that exists" and as "the Ultimate Reality, *whose nature it is to exist"* are both presented in the Bible and have been argued throughout the history of philosophical thought. These are not at all contradictory as Flew seems to think!

It was my intent from the beginning of this debate to put forth an argument for God's existence at the end of this chapter, "A Second Engagement." This I shall do. It is, however, most unfortunate that Flew proceeds to simply dismiss the material in Chapter I, "A First Engagement," where I build an important foundation by way of issues surrounding the question of the existence of God. In my first engagement, I spent twenty-five pages (II, pp. 40–44, 49–55, 71–83) developing a metaphysics, a philosophy of God, which Flew dismisses in less than seven pages.

3. "Beginning from the Beginning"—Response

Flew tells us we should begin at the beginning; that, in fact, this is what he himself has done. But surely this is exactly what Flew has *not* done. I have already indicated why his attempt to attack the concept of God is not new (II, pp. 39–45, 57–58) and why it is not sufficient (56–58, 71–83). Flew's protests to the contrary, Hans Küng's statement is quite correct that "in analytical philosophy or linguistic analysis, discussion has centered, with a great display of erudition, *not on whether God exists or does not exist but on whether 'God' is a meaningless term* (III, p. 95; II, p. 57 [emphasis added]). If Küng's statement shows nothing else, it correctly stresses that this argument is not new.

But if we look closer, we will also see that this argument regarding the "concept of God" is not the beginning. I have tried to show extensively in "A First Engagement" both why Flew and the analytical philosophy school have a problem with the "concept of God" and that they are the ones who have arbitrarily defined "existence" to be reducible to what they think is "physical" reality. Instead of looking at the nature of reality as we experience it (without the presupposition that it is the result of a physical chemical machine), and without looking at all the evidence from experience (revelation, miracles, etc.) for the existence of God, they simply argue—based on the fact that the evidence does not meet their prescribed tests for reality or view of language—that God cannot exist either because the evidence for his existence is not "empirical" or the language is "meaningless," or *both*. Isn't this really what Flew is doing in his argument that the "concept of God" is such that it does not have an object?

Further, it is one thing to say, as Flew does, that "there is much that is problematic about the kind of concept of God that helps to define these [the Mosaic] traditions [of Judaism, Christianity and Islam]" (III, p. 93) and to move to the statement that therefore the concept of God "does not in fact have an object." Flew never shows the latter in his (soon to be famous) six paragraphs (or in all of his published work). And still further, Flew has not shown—certainly not to my satisfaction—that the description of God is incoherent and truly indefinite. I *do* refuse "to recognize that the present insistence upon beginning from the beginning—demanding that the conceptual problems be tackled first—constitutes a comparably innovative challenge to apologetic" (III, p. 94). I refuse because I do not believe it has been shown that this is indeed beginning from the beginning, that the "conceptual problems [must] be tackled first," or that this approach "constitutes a comparably innovative challenge to apologetic."

   i. Then we find in Flew's Chapter III that Hans Küng is also wrong (along with me) and has misunderstood (according to Flew, "was misinformed about") Flew's "Theology and Falsification." But in Küng's case, unlike in mine, Flew puts this "error" off not to misunderstanding the text, but Flew presumes "Küng apparently mistakes the former ("Theology and Falsification") to have been, like the latter (*Language, Truth and Logic*), a whole book rather than a brief note." (I am not sure what length has to do with it.) Flew, therefore, magnanimously says "we may charitably conjecture that he [Küng] was misinformed about, rather than that unaided he misread and misunderstood, its contents" (III, p. 94). It is not possible, of course, (in Flew's view) that both Küng and Miethe have seen the errors inherent in Flew's "old, old essay."

   After simply dismissing Küng's analysis (a tactic that Flew uses repeatedly and masterfully), he goes on to say:

> For present purposes the most relevant and persuasive example (about the legitimacy of some specific idea of God) was provided by Leibniz. . . . Commenting upon the then fairly recent revival by Descartes of the ontological argument, Leibniz contended that this goes through [is valid?—TM] only if it can be shown that the premise concept of God as a logically necessary Being is free from contradiction, which he [Leibniz] thought that it could be, although in my view it cannot." (III, p. 95–96)

Flew further quotes (presumably Leibniz, though he doesn't really tell us who he is quoting): "For we cannot use a definition in an argument without first making sure that . . . it contains no contradiction."

   The relevant question is: "How do we know it contains no contradiction?" Can we decide simply on the basis of examining the language of the definition? If the "definition" refers to a proposition like "God exists" or "there is a God," then surely we must discuss the actual evidence for the proposition before we simply decide that there can be no actual object because someone believes our definition to be contradictory. How could we possibly know that our definition is contradictory if we have not looked at all the evidence for the actual existence of the proposed object and then—and only then—at how the specific aspects of the definition fit actual reality or the actual entity? But how does one decide (again I assume Flew is quoting Leibniz, not Flew) that his definition is contradictory. In his (here either Leibniz *or* Flew) quoted example (that of the idea of the fastest motion, III, p. 96), the fallacy in the "definition" is not ascertained by examining the definition alone, but by going to a specific example (that of a wheel's spokes lengthened to extend beyond the rim) in reality itself. Certainly, this "contradiction" in the definition can be *asserted* linguistically, but to be *actually* shown as a contradiction we must conduct the actual experiment in reality!

But, perhaps, the operative idea here is expressed in the last sentence quoted (from Leibniz or Flew): "Yet the fact is that we cannot have an idea of impossible things." Again, our response must be: "How do we know the 'things' [propositions, entities?—T.M.] are impossible?" The quoted example, when examined in reality itself, tells us that we could always have (or create) a larger wheel and that the object on the edge of the larger wheel, or longer spoke, would always be traveling faster that the object on the smaller circle. From this, I assume that atheists, like Flew, would want to move to the conclusion that there must be some contradictory idea in the definition or concept of God, for example, that he is in every way that he exists without limit. But this is only a contradiction if we *must* define reality as a closed physical, mechanical machine or system. I have argued throughout "A First Engagement" that a more careful examination of even empirical reality points to an existence that is not irreducibly "physical" and, therefore, not limited by aspects of physical existence. But, Flew has to this point in our discussion largely ignored my argument!

ii. Again, Flew raises his objection to Swinburne that God is "a person without a body (i.e., a spirit)" (III, p. 96). But, again, he virtually ignores all that I have to say in "A First Engagement," pages 48–49, where I explain why we cannot assume reality—or for that matter the human "body"—is reducible to purely physical, mechanical machines; and pages 71–83, where I discuss issues that are foundational for a philosophy of God/metaphysics, for example, "The Starting Point of Metaphysics," "The Empirical Foundations of Metaphysics," and so on. On the other hand, I have hardly dismissed or ignored his "objections," which were "extended over six paragraphs (I, pp. 5–6)," that is, two pages of Flew's text.

Flew does ask an interesting question in his original discussion (I, p. 5): "How is a . . . person to be identified . . . save by reference to the living organism that he or she actually is?" Of course, given Flew's assumptions, such a problem could never arise because persons are nothing but "creatures of flesh and blood." Yet, I have tried to show that Flew's assumption is not so easily made. Nevertheless, the answer in Christian teaching is clear. Each human being has an individual spirit— that part that is not irreducibly "physical"—created in the image of God. So the essence of what makes a person a person—and the part that would (according to Christian teaching) never *not* exist after God creates it—is the spirit, which is consciousness and is tied to the brain.

Flew says: "It should certainly be seen as at least very far from obvious that talk of 'a person without a body (i.e., a spirit)' is coherent and intelligible" (I, p. 5). And, I ask him—*after* seven pages of text on the existence of life, or intelligent life, and of creativity" (II, pp. 48–55)— "is it really any more obvious to talk as if a person is reducible to 'flesh and blood,' to a psychochemical machine, as if *this* were obviously coherent and intelligible. I think not!" (II, p. 55). Again, no reply from Flew!

Next, in regard to Flew's claim that humans are "creatures . . . essentially . . . of flesh and blood" and to my nineteen pages of argument that they are not just flesh and blood (II, p. 48–55, 71–83), Flew quotes me as saying: "Isn't this exactly what Christians and others affirm in believing in life after death, for which there is . . . mounting evidence?" (II, p. 48; III, p. 96). Flew responds: "Well yes, perhaps: put it that way if you like. But if that is how you do want to put it, then you must not neglect to notice how utterly different the amputee . . . is from [here we go again] the Loch Ness monster, from an Abominable Snowperson . . ." (III, p. 96–97). Flew has continually ignored the *content* of my presentation; and, again, he is simply assuming "we are creatures who just essentially are . . . flesh and blood" in spite of evidence that a person is not irreducibly "flesh and blood." Flew requires "empirical" data/evidence while simply ignoring my claim that if he were more empirical, not less, that is, if he would look more carefully at "empirical experience," he would see that this is not "irreducibly physical."

iii. Flew tells us: "Any apologists who really have appreciated the need to begin from the beginning will be well advised to bypass the difficulties generated by the first clauses both of Swinburne's definition and of Miethe's preferred alternative." He then writes: ". . . such apologists will do much better to start by ruling that God is to be understood as being the . . . creative Cause of origination, . . . and . . . of the continuation of the entire Universe" (III, p. 97). While I do not agree that the "first clauses" of the definitions of Swinburne or myself should be "bypassed," I do agree most heartily with Flew's second statement.

This is exactly what I will do in the last section of this chapter. I intend to argue there is a God who is the "creative Cause of origination" and "continuation of the entire Universe." Further, I contend that I have (to some extent) already stipulated/argued this: (1) in my definition of "God," I say (in part) that "God is the living, personal, loving, and merciful *Creator and Sustainer of all that exists*" (II, p. 39) [emphasis added]; (2) in my discussion of the nature of the physical universe (II, pp. 49–55, 65).

On page 98 of Chapter III, "A First Rejoinder," Flew says: "Like so much else of importance in the history of ideas this notion that the Supreme Being is or must be perfectly good can be tracked back to its ultimate source in Plato." But, surely, Flew knows that this claim is also made of God in the Bible (cf. Ps. 5:4; Hab. 1:13; Isa. 40:25, I John 4:8, etc.). It is also important to note here that there is absolutely no historical indication that Plato had any firsthand knowledge of (or for that matter *any* knowledge of) the Old Testament Scriptures.[3]

4. "Explaining and Reducing"—Response

Here Flew tells us: "Those who appeal to such putative ad hoc creations as supports for their *faith* have always to await the latest communiques from the science front with trepidation, for every fresh communique may contain the disturbing news that yet another gap has now been filled" (III, p. 102) [emphasis added—in this sense surely atheists are just as guilty of a "faith" stance].[4] What Flew fails to mention is that this "trepidation" should be equally true of the atheist in reverse, though (to my knowledge) the atheist is hardly ever the first to admit or acknowledge the implications when new scientific information "seems" to support the theist! (See Gange 1986; Wilder-Smith 1981 and 1987.) After all, Flew tells us that he is willing to "take the Universe itself and whatever our scientists discover to be its most fundamental laws as the ultimates in explanation" (I, p. 25). This being the case, given his admissions in this debate, it seems that Flew should be feeling his atheistic foundations slipping out from under him more and more!

On page 102–3 of Chapter III, Flew seems to say that he does not want "to rule out of court any suggestion that these peculiar creatures may somewhere contain an unfleshly component or even several unfleshly components." He then writes: "If any prove able both to give *positive* sense to the idea [of unfleshly] components . . . then it remains open to them to make their suggestion and to deploy evidence in its support." This is what I did in Chapter II, pages 49–55; and pages 72–74, "The Starting Point of Metaphysics"; and 74–76, "The Empirical Foundations of Metaphysics."

Flew suggests: "Suppose that we now put aside that suggestion that people contain some fleshly component" (III, p. 103). But, Prof. Flew, this is precisely what we cannot do! This is exactly (as I argued in "A First Engagement") what a closer examination of the empirical world around us will not allow us to do. Flew goes on to say that if we do this (put aside the suggestion of unfleshly component(s)): "Then the remaining content of the claim that 'a person is reducible to "flesh and blood"' amounts to no more than—itself truly reducible to—the claim that there is nothing to be *said* about people that cannot be said about flesh and blood" [emphasis added].

Then, Flew writes: "But no one, surely, wants to say anything [affirm a proposition?—T.M.] so silly and so obviously untrue?" Now, Prof. Flew, I know you are going to tell us that you are not "talking out of both sides of your mouth" again, aren't you? If people are indeed so "unfortunate as to be run over by steam-rollers" and thus to be "reduced to a pulp of flesh and blood and crushed bones," you tell us that "those remains would simply not be persons. . . ." I could not agree more. But, then, Prof. Flew, on your atheistic theory, exactly what is missing? What makes these former "persons" (now "fleshly residues") residues? It seems to me that in your last paragraph (III, p. 103) you have again admitted both far too much and said (explained) far too little!

I have been *almost* amazed at times in this debate by what Prof. Flew seems to feel compelled to tell us that he has *not* maintained without his feeling as equally "compelled" to tell us what it is that he does maintain, for example, he is not asking for empirically verifiable evidence via a statement like that of the Verification Principle (III, p. 87) when it comes to the existence of God; and, now, he is not denying (it would seem) that a person may contain an unfleshly component or components (III, p. 103). Pray tell us, Prof. Flew: (1) What evidence will you allow to count for God's existence? And (2) what it is that (in part) constitutes a "flesh and blood" person that is not reducible to or does not originate from the "flesh and blood" of a person *in your view*?

5. Argument for the Existence of God

Flew is quite correct—in part—that to "establish the existence of a Being of that sort [of "the active, agent God of Israel"] what we need is causal arguments" (III, p. 92–93). But, as has been indicated/admitted—by both myself and Flew—in the context of this debate, there are many important arguments for the existence of God that need to be carefully examined, for example, the teleological argument, the ontological argument, the moral argument, and the cosmological argument (the standard arguments of a more philosophical nature), as well as arguments from revelation (interesting that Flew always says "revelation apart"), miracles, the resurrection in particular, religious or Christian experience, and so on.[5]

One very important reason for stressing the need to examine each argument for the existence of God carefully is that all truth claims must "make sense" in the context of an examination of how they "fit" with regard to a "worldview." A worldview must be built out of our experience of reality as such. We cannot set predefined and arbitrary limits *before* we examine reality itself in the context of a verifiable worldview. We may indeed find that the claims of different arguments "come together" when we look at the "picture as a whole." Certainly, as has already been seen, it is never valid to rule out of court vast ranges of reality simply because they do not meet preconceived criteria of judgment. When we do not do such prejudging and when we are more empirical than atheistic empiricists, the very aspects of reality they deny not only "make sense" but have a firm basis in our everyday experience that must involve both the "five senses" and the "thought" process necessary to analyze correctly what is observed.

Nor is it sufficient to examine just one form of a particular argument, for in the history of ideas many different forms of one basic type of argument have been given, some of which hold more promise than others. For example, there are many forms of the—as Flew calls it—"argument to design," or teleological argument. As I have mentioned (in this chapter, pp. 109, 123–24), recent developments in science have brought back this argument with new force. Issues such as the new science, the radiation echo, information theory and the gene code, and the nature of the brain and of thought need to be carefully examined, not as a "God of the gaps" argument (as Flew claims to have known in his student days from members of the Student Christian Movement), but because these new arguments stem—precisely as Flew thinks necessary—"from the regularities and the wonders that scientists have discovered . . ." (III, p. 102). And, we have already seen that the ontological argument has two distinct forms historically, though the second form was not "discovered" until this century (Miethe 1977).

i. The Importance of the Question. The ultimate question in regard to the nature of the universe is: "Is the physical universe eternal?" "Can the physical universe as we know it account for itself?" The argument that maintains it *cannot* is known as the cosmological argument (Miethe 1978). Though I should point out it has been argued that one does not have to grant that the physical universe *as a whole* is not eternal for the cosmological argument to prove its case. Aquinas held that reason could prove neither that the world is everlasting nor that it has a beginning in time. Thomas accepted the temporal beginning of creation from revelation, not from rational necessity. Some supporters of the cosmological argument say you only need to grant that some things, even "one blade of grass" is finite, contingent, limited for the argument to be valid.

The cosmological argument (from *cosmos*, "world") usually begins with the existence of the finite world or "some condition within the cosmos, such as change," and argues "that there must be a behind-the-world Cause . . . to explain the existence of this kind of world." "It" is really a family of arguments. There are basically three "families" of cosmological argument: (1) the twelfth- and thirteenth-century form based on *existential causality* as in Aquinas,[6] (2) the seventeenth- and eighteenth-century form based on the *Principle of Sufficient Reason* as discussed in Gottfried Wilhelm von Leibniz (1646–1716) and Samuel Clark (1675–1729),[7] and (3) what is called the Kalam (from the word referring to Arabic philosophy or theology) cosmological argument, which was popular among Arabic philosophers in the late Middle Ages. Historically, the Kalam argument was rejected by most Christian philosophers. Thomas Aquinas, who followed Aristotle, rejected it, though Bonaventure (1221–1274), a contemporary and colleague of Aquinas, argued the Kalam argument was valid (Bonansea 1974). Just recently a very small group of philosophers (Miller 1984) and even some evangelical philosophers and theologians have defended this argument (see Craig 1979, 1980a, 1980b, 1985, etc.).

Many philosophers over the centuries have come to believe that one or more of Aquinas's forms of the argument can be reformulated to overcome the weaknesses originally found in it. Bruce Reichenbach (though his reformulation of the argument is on the basis of "principles of causation and sufficient reason") makes the following important statement in regard to the cosmological argument and metaphysics in general:

> The time has arrived for a reassessment of both the truth and validity of what is to me the most interesting and exciting of the theistic arguments. . . . The era is past when all metaphysical statements or arguments can simply be dismissed as silly or senseless, since they do not meet a preestablished criterion of verifiability. (Reichenbach 1972, pp. viii–ix)

In this context, I will look at only two forms of the cosmological argument that are historically found in Aquinas.

ii. Thomas Aquinas's Argument. Thomas considered himself to be a faithful follower of Augustine. Many philosophers maintain that the basic difference between them is that Augustine used the terminology and (epistemological) frame of Plato, while Aquinas put Christian truth in the terminology and frame of Aristotle. Thomas certainly thought reason could prove the existence of God (Miethe 1976, pp. 85–101, 194–196). Aquinas is famous for his "Five Ways to God." Here I want to look at the Second Way and the Third Way of Aquinas.

It is important to realize that Thomas is not arguing on the bases of "physical causality," which must be temporal and subject to an infinite regress (Brown 1966). Contemporary physics, especially in relativity theory and quantum physics, seems to require that there be a time lag between cause and effect. This seems to destroy the possibility of an essentially subordinated causal series in which agent and patient exist, act, and are acted upon simultaneously.

The Second Way of Thomas, the argument from efficient causality, can be put thus:

1. There are efficient causes in the world (i.e., producing causes).
2. Nothing can be the efficient cause of itself (for it would have to be prior to itself in order to cause itself).
3. There cannot be an infinite regress of (essentially related) efficient causes, for unless there is a first cause of the series there would be no causality in the series.
4. Therefore, there must be a first uncaused efficient Cause of all efficient causality in the world.
5. Everyone gives to this the name of God.[8]

In this "Second Way," Thomas is talking about God in terms of a utterly unique kind of causation, that is, a causation of existence itself. If there is a cause of that sort, it cannot be involved in any kind of subordinated series. It would have to be immediate and direct. This would be "efficient causality" of existence itself, that is, a cause of *being*, not a cause of becoming in the physical sense. I believe that Thomas employs efficient causality itself in every one of the "Five Ways," but it is explicit only in the Second. The sculptor who makes a statue is the efficient cause of the statue.

It is radically impossible, according to Thomas Aquinas, that anything should be the cause of itself (*causa sui*).[9] To cause itself it would have to preexist itself, which is an impossibility. Without a first cause there would be no terminal effect, intermediate causes, or any efficient cause anywhere. Here, Thomas appeals to a type of causality unknown to Aristotle where existence itself is the effect, a type of causality where the effect is a finite efficient cause. This would be a metaphysical kind of causality rather than a physical one.

Samuel Thompson says:

If we are told that there is no scientific evidence which supports the view that there are causes operative in nature we must reply that the question of whether or not there are causes is not a scientific problem. The causal principle can be neither established nor shown to be false by any special science. The findings of the special sciences may support or refute the belief that this or that cause is operative in a given situation, but the question of whether there are causes or not is beyond their reach. This is not in question; it is presupposed by the sciences. We do not expect the sciences to establish the existence of things they investigate; they assume the existence of the things they investigate; they assume the existence of those things, and their investigations could not get under way unless they did make such assumptions. (Thompson 1955, pp. 332–33)

And as Eric L. Mascall further says:

The method of investigation of the world which physical science adopts—observation of measurable phenomena and their correlation and prediction by general statements—is such as to exclude efficient causality from its purview, and hence renders it quite incompetent to decide whether there is efficient causality or not. Efficient causality is not a physical concept but a metaphysical one, and it is only because the physical scientists of the eighteenth and nineteenth centuries insisted on illicitly talking physics in terms of efficient causality that their successors, having discovered that efficient causality is not what physics is as a matter of fact concerned with, have only too often assumed that it is nonexistent. (Mascall 1948, p. 45)

In his Wade Memorial Lecture, Leonard Eslick admits:

It would be *meta*-physical precisely in the sense of transcending the physical and its material conditions. The latter may turn out to be historical and contingent, as relativity theory and quantum physics suggest, but the former, the causality of existence itself, as distinct from qualified existence, could be the work of a divine creative agent. It may even be suggested that this is the meaning of so-called creation *ex nihilo*, so significantly absent from the Greeks, and even from Genesis. (Eslick 1983, pp. 156–57)

But if what Eslick says about the Second Way eliminating "from the divine effects any real contingency and freedom" then there is in it a much more serious problem.

The Third Way of Thomas, the argument from possibility and necessity, can be put thus:

1. There are beings that begin to exist and cease to exist (i.e., possible beings).
2. But not all beings can be possible beings, because what comes to exist does so only through what already exists (nothing cannot cause something).
3. Therefore, there must be a Being whose existence is necessary (i.e., one that never came into being and will never cease to be).
4. There cannot be an infinite regress of necessary beings each of which has its necessity dependent on another because:
   (a) An infinite regress of dependent causes is impossible.
   (b) A Necessary Being cannot be a dependent being.
5. Therefore, there must be a first Being which is necessary in itself (and not dependent on another for its existence).[10]

According to many Christian philosophers, the Third Way of Thomas is the most impressive of the five; it is more fully developed. In the Third Way the nominal definition that is the function of the middle term in the argument becomes God as the Uncaused Necessary Being who causes contingent beings and caused necessary beings.[11] The fact from the world of our experience that one starts with in this argument is the existence of contingent beings, that is, ourselves.

Contingent beings are defined as those that are possible to be and not to be. This is a remarkable starting point (Eslick 1983, p. 156). A contingent being comes into being by generation and passes out of being by perishing. Such beings cannot have the reason for their existence in themselves. They must be caused to be by another. They do not exist by their very essence. That which exists by its very essence is necessary.

The question is whether there must be some Necessary Being or beings. Thomas tries to show the assumption that there are no necessary beings whatever involves self-contradiction. To be contingent is to have the possibility of nonexistence. Thomas says that if universal nonexistence were possible it would still be the case. Even now nothing would exist whatever. This is counterfactual to the admission that there are existing things. It might be objected to this argument that all things indeed are possible to be and not to be but they exercise their existence successively without any radical beginning or end of existence. Out of nothing nothing comes. If everything were simultaneously nonexistent there would indeed be nothing in existence now. This contradicts fact.

Eslick correctly says: "The argument has two movements, the first seeking to establish that *some* necessary being must exist as a cause of the evident existence of contingent things *here* and *now*, and the second that an infinite causal regress of *caused* necessary beings is impossible." The first movement to the Third Way is in the logical form of a *reductio ad absurdum* type of argument. Given the relations of contradictories on the square of opposition, if one is true the other is false, *and* if one is false the other must be true. "Indeed, it is an article of faith of contemporary empiricism, in the spirit of Hume, that *all* actually existing things, all matters of fact, are contingent" (Eslick 1983, pp. 156–57).

"To say that all things without exception are possible to be and not to be is to say that *all* things 'at some time' are nonexistent, which implies the counter-factual conclusion that *right now* nothing exists" (Eslick 1983, p. 157).

It can be summed up well:

This is, I think, the point of absurdity and contradiction. Universal contingency can admit of no exception, and certainly not of the universe itself, whose possible nonexistence, to be meaningful, must be actualized. It must, therefore, have come into existence from antecedent nothingness, but this is impossible, for *right now* nothing would exist.

Thus,

The Third Way is a *tour de force* which struggles to move from the contingent features of the world to the necessary existence of God, not directly but indirectly. I think the struggle succeeds. But it could have been achieved more expeditiously by the ontological argument of St. Anselm, at least as rehabilitated and reformed in our own day by Charles Hartshorne. I think the absurdity of universal contingency is not merely counter-factual (and in this sense the argument is empirical and cosmological) but *a priori*. (Eslick 1983, pp. 157–58)

iii. The Argument Today. Prominent philosophers have reformulated the argument to present what they believe is a true and valid cosmological argument.[12] For example, Bruce Reichenbach in his

The Cosmological Argument: A Reassessment (1972)[13] states the argument as follows:

(S_1) A contingent being exists.
  a. This contingent being is caused either (1) by itself, or (2) by another.
  b. If it were caused by itself, it would have to precede itself in existence, which is impossible.

(S_2) Therefore, this contingent being (2) is caused by another, i.e., depends on something else for its existence.

(S_3) That which causes (provides the sufficient reason for) the existence of any contingent being must be either (3) another contingent being, or (4) a noncontingent (necessary) being.
  c. If 3, then this contingent cause must itself be caused by another, and so on to infinity.

(S_4) Therefore, that which causes (provides the sufficient reason for) the existence of any contingent being must be either (5) an infinite series of contingent beings, or (4) a necessary being.

(S_5) An infinite series of contingent beings (5) is incapable of yielding a sufficient reason for the existence of any being.

(S_6) Therefore, a necessary being (4) exists.

Reichenbach's argument is based on the relationship of causality and sufficient reason (Reichenbach 1972, pp. 19–20). His book is well worth reading.

Other present-day philosophers have restated the cosmological argument thus:

1. Some limited, changing being(s) exist.
2. The present existence of every limited, changing being is caused by another.
3. There cannot be an infinite regress of causes of being.
4. Therefore, there is a first Cause of the present existence of these beings.
5. This first Cause must be infinite, necessary, eternal, and one.
6. This first uncaused Cause is identical with the God of the Judeo-Christian tradition.

This argument is *not* based on the principle of sufficient reason but on the principle of existential causality. The former calls only for an explanation in the realm of reason; the latter demands a ground in reality. I base my argument on existential undeniability.

For the sake of space, we will briefly summarize only the argument based on existential undeniability.

(1) *Some limited, changing being(s) exist.* This premise is *undeniably* true of experience. The necessity of this affirmation is not logical but existential. That is, the nonexistence of everything is not *inconceivable.* (This is granted here only for the sake of argument.) Yet, the fact of the matter is that I do (or in the case of the reader, you do) exist. It is quite clear that I am limited in every way I exist. It is possible for me to be or not to be (contingent being). I am limited to a spatio-temporal continuum. It is also very clear that we experience the world as limited and changing.

But you say, "I may be deluded. Reality may be an illusion." "The fact of illusion *in* the world demonstrates that we have no total illusion *of* the world." Total illusion is impossible. Even the concept presupposes a "backdrop of reality." If this were not true we would not, could not, know anything of "illusion." To deny this first premise involves one in an *actual* (i.e., about physical reality) contradiction.

(2) *The present existence of every limited, changing being is caused by another.* (a) Every limited changing being is composed of both an actuality (its existence) and a potentiality (its essence). (b) But no potentiality can actualize itself. (c) Therefore, there must be some actuality outside of every composed being to account for the fact that it actually exists, as opposed to its not existing but merely having the potential for existence. The question, "Why is it that what can exist but need not exist actually does exist?" is not a meaningless question. Answer: "It is because its potential for existence was actualized or caused by some existence beyond it."

(3) *There cannot be an infinite regress of causes of being.* We are not here talking about a linear series of historical causes of becoming, but a vertical series of causes of *being*, for existence itself. Existential causality refers to the cause of the *being* of entities and not the cause of their becoming. This argument is talking about a cause for the very being of a thing, not its coming into existence (its becoming) or the changes it may undergo. It is impossible to have an infinite regress (go backward to infinity, has no first or beginning cause) of *existent-dependent* causes. An infinite regress of finite beings would not *cause* the existence of anything. At best, this is only sidestepping the issue of causality.

Yet, it is impossible to deny that there is causality within the series. When you simply add another dependent being to a chain of such beings, it does not *ground* the existence of the chain. To say that it does is like saying one could get an avocado by adding an infinite number of pineapples to a basket of pineapples. Adding pineapples to pineapples does not yield an avocado; adding dependent beings to other such beings does not yield a cause or ground for their *dependent* existence. One contingent being cannot ground another such being. No caused being can be an intermediary in a chain of existential causality. Thus it follows that the very first cause of a caused being must be an uncaused Being. A regress of existent causes cannot even get started, let alone be infinite in extension.

(4) *Therefore, there is a first Cause of the present existence of these beings.* This conclusion follows logically from the first three premises. We have established that some limited, changing beings exist. Their present existence is caused by another being. An infinite regress of causes of being is impossible. Thus, it follows necessarily that there must be a *first* Cause of the existence of changing beings. "Indeed, if the last argument against an infinite regress is correct, then this first Cause must be the very first Cause beyond the changing beings, with no intermediary causes in between" (Geisler 1974, p. 201).

(5) *This first Cause must be infinite, necessary, eternal, and one.* Again, this follows logically. If this Cause is the first cause of all dependent, caused being, then it must itself be unlimited in every way it exists (be infinite) or it could not account for limited existence; it *must* be (it is necessary); if it must be then it has always been (it is eternal), and so on. There can be only one such Being. First, an uncaused being is pure actuality and it follows that there cannot be two such beings. Second, this uncaused Being is by its very nature *unlimited*. Many things may *have* existence, but only one thing can *be* existence. Third, pure actuality cannot be divided or multiplied *in Being*. But the force of the argument is that such a Being cannot *not* exist, for finite limited beings exist.

(6) *This first uncaused Cause is identical with the God of the Judeo-Christian tradition.* It has often been said: "All right you have proven the necessity of a First Uncaused Cause of all that exists, but how do you know this God is the Christian God?" If you understand the argument, this conclusion is rather simple. First, as seen above there can only be one such Being. Second, when you have described the attributes of this Being, you have precisely defined what the Bible and the Christians call God; in other words, this uncaused Cause has all the essential metaphysical attributes of God in the Judeo-Christian tradition. He is creator (Gen. 1:1; Heb. 11:3), sustainer of all things (Ps. 36:6; Col. 1:17), one and supreme (Deut. 6:4; Exod. 20:3), infinite and eternal (Ps. 147:5; 41:13), changeless in nature (Ps. 102:27; Mal. 3:16; James 1:17), absolutely perfect and loving (Matt. 5:48; 1 John 4:16), and so on.

Also, a very important point/implication of the argument is some-times missed: God must be able to account for all the positive attributes (he is in fact responsible for) in his creation. He must be personal, or he could not have produced persons. He must be intelligent, creative, loving, and so on. "Pure actuality possesses all the perfections or characteristics of being in the highest and most eminent way possible (viz., infinitely)." "There are not different Gods but only two different approaches to one and the same God: divine declaration and philosophi-cal inference. It should not seem strange to those who believe [by way of divine revelation—which Flew always wants to leave aside] in God's manifestation in His creation (Rom. 1:19, 20; Ps. 19:1) that it is possible to arrive at a knowledge of God by inference through these manifestations" (Geisler 1974, p. 208).

Thomas Aquinas was correct in positing that physical existence cannot account for itself. We know too much about the matter to be materialists. Physically existing things are clearly limited, changing, finite. The idea of universal contingency is not merely counterfactual but ultimately absurd. Contingent existence cannot account for itself. Clearly, that which is itself an effect cannot be the cause of all things. This is not a "very different kettle of fish" (I, p. 6; II, p. 55), Prof. Flew. It is the only "kettle" we have!

CHAPTER V

A Time for Reviewing

Antony G. N. Flew

1. The Variety of Gods

At the very beginning of our discussion, before proceeding to distinguish different senses of "atheism," I observed that "disbelief and nonbelief are necessarily relative to belief" (I, p. 2). For us this is important, because there are many different notions that, whether rightly or wrongly, are in fact accounted to be notions of God.

Some of these are very full and determinate. Others are in the last degree tenuous and vague. Prof. Miethe recalls (II, note 36) how one of his publishers asserted, presumably upon opinion poll evidence, that 95 percent of Americans believe that there is a Supreme Being. Remembering a statement plausibly attributed to the well-loved President Eisenhower—"Everyone must have a religion, and I don't care what it is"—I should conjecture that, if there was any substantial (as opposed to merely verbal) common content to the beliefs of that 95 percent, it was that the cosmological big bang somehow presupposes a Big Detonator and that the consensus extends no further beyond this.

If this conjecture is correct, then the near unanimous agreement concerns only—as Hume's Philo would have put it—"the *being*" and "not the *nature* of *God*" (quoted in I, p. 21). It follows that that publisher was doubly wrong to consider Prof. Miethe's work superfluous—wrong not only in holding that, given some approved belief, there is no need for evidencing reasons in its support, but wrong too in assuming that the more particular and far, far richer belief Prof. Miethe is propounding and commending is almost universal.

i. That there are so many different notions that, whether rightly or wrongly, are in fact accounted to be notions of God is the truth Hans

Küng was pondering in that most eloquent paragraph (quoted in II, pp. 82) that took as its text Martin Buber's rhetorical question: "Which term in human language has been so misused, so stained, so desecrated as this?" But it seems that neither Küng nor Buber recognized this as a reason for urging—as I did, and do—that any truly systematic rational apologetic must begin by sorting out and settling fundamental conceptual questions. Thus, if we are:

> inquiring whether there in fact is an object corresponding to some putative definite description of whether some supposed class does possess any actual members, then the obvious first steps are, in the one case, to make sure that that description is indeed both coherent and truly definite and, in the other, to ask how any members of that supposed class are to be decisively identified as such. It is only when, and if, and insofar as such logically prior conceptual problems have been satisfactorily solved that it can become sensible to move on to the substantial and much more exciting but logically secondary question or questions of fact. (I, pp. 10).

This passage is worth repeating both for what it says and still more for what it does not say. Miethe is all the time complaining about my alleged verificationist presuppositions, my supposedly definitional view of reality, and what he believes to be my scandalously limited view of experience: "Of course, one would have "difficulties" with the concept of God if the possibility of "extraphysical" reality had already been defined out of court, out of existence . . ." (II, p. 57).

Certainly the examples I offered earlier in the same chapter in order to show how there may be reasonable disagreement as to whether some entirely proper concept has any actual application were about as physical as they could have been: "Loch Ness monsters . . . unicorns . . . Abominable Snowpersons" (I, p. 3). But, in trying to make something clear, one is bound to select studiously undisputatious illustrations. So it is hard indeed when that careful choice is mistaken to imply or presuppose a refusal to admit the legitimacy of any concepts of which the objects are or would be of some totally different and acceptably nonphysical kind.

ii. Another consequence of there being many different notions that are generally accounted to be notions of God is that one and the same person may at one and the same time be some sort of atheist or agnostic with regard to one such notion of God, but with regard to another a firm believer. This has implications for our understanding of what I distinguished as a third kind of atheist:

Perhaps too we should include, as a third subclass of negative atheists, those who refuse "to allow the (nevertheless still asserted) existence of God to affect their everyday living," for, when the God thus still persistently asserted is stipulated to be the supreme partisan within the creation, then it becomes very hard to accept such assertions as sincere. (I, p. 10)

What, of course, is so "very hard to accept" is that such a person believes in a God "stipulated to be the supreme partisan within the creation." Surely, any halfway competent defense attorney would put in an insanity plea on behalf of a client who, while aware at the time of his offense that he was in full view of an Authority able and inflexibly resolved to punish all offenders, nevertheless offended? (This is, by the way, a point that needs to be considered by those laboring, with Milton, "to justify the ways of [such a] God to man.") But in all actual cases the chances are that an atheist of this sort is an atheist only with respect to a God "stipulated to be the supreme partisan within the creation" and that what he claims to believe in, no doubt sincerely, is an unintrusive Big Detonator of some kind. Since the atheism I profess is an atheism with respect to the God of Mosaic theism, I should not necessarily be being inconsistent if I were to be inclined to a more inhibited agnosticism with regard to many Gods more limited and less intrusive (II, note 4).

At the beginning of Chapter IV Miethe makes a great song and dance about his difficulties in determining what sort of atheist I am. Apparently these difficulties were caused by the second sentence of Chapter III: "I have at once to protest that I cannot identify myself with or in that specific kind of atheist that Prof. Miethe describes and challenges—in particular in the penultimate sentence of 'A First Engagement.'" That in its turn reads: "I say 'The right question is whether it is rational for the atheist himself, given his presuppositions, definitional view of reality, and his limited view of experience to say that his 'atheistic' experience is coherent and compelling and thereby to deny the reality of God.'"

So whatever is the problem? Have I still failed to make it manifest that, however mistakenly, I do not agree that I am presupposing what Miethe maintains that I am presupposing, that I do rule out realities by definition as he seems to think that I do, or that I insist upon some similarly blinkered conception of experience? And furthermore, for good measure, I would not want to ground my rejection of the reality of God upon some subjectivistic and autobiographical claim about the coherent and compelling character of my "'atheistic' experience."

2. Arguments to Design

That "there are many different notions that, whether rightly or wrongly, are in fact accounted to be notions of God" is something we need to remember whenever we come to consider what are presented as arguments for the existence of God. An argument that, whether probative or not, may at least be of the correct kind to support a claim that one particular concept of God does indeed have application may not be even relevant to discussion about the existence of a Being of some categorically different kind. Again, an argument that might be allowed to constitute a proof of a Being endowed with comparatively modest defining characteristics would have to be put down as altogether insufficient to prove, or even as actually contraindicative of, the existence of a God whose nature had been stipulated more lavishly.

i. At one point Miethe quotes himself as saying that "traditionally western metaphysics is the study of reality as such, being as such. It must be consummated by some kind of theory of God" (II, p. 34). But the sort of concept of God that would be appropriate in and to such an abstract study of the essential nature of being as such, and the existence or subsistence of the object of which might conceivably be demonstrated by that study, are about as far removed as could be from the concept the existence of whose object Miethe wants to prove (cf, again, III, 2, ii).

When, for instance, a God of metaphysics is said to be perfectly good, neither the goodness nor the perfection are those attributable to a moral agent. Rather the perfection is that of an ideal circle, and the goodness is somehow to be identified with existence. Aquinas, surely, somewhere remarks that "good" and "real" are convertible terms? It is this identification that I suggested "can be traced back to its ultimate source in Plato" (III, p. 98). So my suggestion cannot be falsified by citing earlier biblical sources for the contention that an altogether different Supreme Being is in correspondingly different senses both perfect and good.

An analogous ambiguity afflicts the word "necessity," for when, for employment in an ontological argument, the word "God" is defined as referring to a logically necessary Being, the required necessity is logical and carries the implication that to deny the existence of such a God would be to contradict yourself (IV, pp. 112ff.). But if and when the biblical Jahweh is said to be a necessary Being, then his nonexistence is, presumably, being asserted to be not inconceivable but, in some more practical way, simply and sheerly impossible (IV, p. 121).

ii. It is by considering arguments to design that we can best come to appreciate that and how what might be allowed to constitute proof of a "Being endowed with comparatively modest defining characteristics would have to be put down as altogether insufficient to prove, or even as actually contraindicative of, the existence of a God whose nature had been stipulated more lavishly." Much has been said about this already (I, 1, iii, a, and pp. 24), albeit, it would appear, not to much effect. More needs to be said now, if only to ensure that the new third form of argument to design gets a mention in the present book.

(a) The first and most familiar form takes off from particular features of our Universe that look as if they must have been designed, but that are known not in fact to have been the work of any natural designer.[1] It is then argued that these features must be the results of interventions by a Supernatural Designer. It is arguments of this subsort, the premises of which are apt to be undermined by progress in the sciences, showing that certain of those features "that look as if they must have been designed" would and presumably do result from the operation of causes neither conscious nor intelligent (Dawkins 1986).

Miethe makes much of the unsolved problems of evolutionary biology: the origin of life, the "thousands upon thousands of missing links," and so on (II, pp. 49ff.). Fair enough; far be it from me to minimize the inadequacies of the "Darwin-Oparin-Haldane 'warm little pond' concept." But Miethe must in his turn recognize the embarrassing implications if this problem or any of the other problems turns out to be not just still unsolved but forever insoluble. To present your postulated Creator as having made, and apparently having had to make, such crucial ad hoc interventions leaves you wide open to objections of the kind that Leibniz brought against Newton. A Creator both omniscient and omnipotent could and surely would ensure that the development of his creation in and toward the fulfillment of his intentions was perfectly smooth and did not have to be kept on course by frequent timely adjustments to the steering.

(b) The second sort of argument to design takes as its premise the general order of nature, so it is not threatened by any particular possible scientific advance. Indeed, if anything, every such advance strengthens that premise. The contention derived therefrom is that that order cannot be intrinsic to the Universe but must be imposed upon it by an external and Supernatural Orderer. The contrary position is the Stratonician atheism: "The conclusion . . . is that we should take the Universe itself and whatever our scientists discover to be its most fundamental laws as the ultimates in explanation" (I, p. 25).

This is the passage, duly emphasized, that provoked Miethe's triumphant response: "If Flew is not advocating 'empirical verification' as the test for ultimate reality, I do not know how else to make sense out of these statements" (IV, p. 109). But thus to reach the Stratonician atheism as a conclusion is precisely not, in an arbitrary and blinkered way, to presuppose it from the beginning. What truly would be arbitrary and blinkered would be to insist that order, which to all appearance is intrinsic to the Universe, nevertheless cannot but be externally imposed by a Supernatural Orderer postulated for the purpose.

(c) The third and most powerful form of argument to design is a recent development. Indeed it was developed most satisfactorily in a book published only late last year (Leslie 1989). Its premises are drawn from contemporary scientific cosmology. Taking as given exactly those same laws and principles the scientific cosmologists themselves employ in their calculations, it can be shown that, were not various quantitative relationships in physics exactly what they are, then the circumstances in which the evolution of intelligent organisms becomes even possible could never have occurred, circumstances that, even as it is, seem to be excessively rare. That evolution was and remains, as the great Duke said of the decisive Battle of Waterloo, "a damned nice, close-run thing."

This conclusion Leslie describes as showing that "our universe is spectacularly 'fine tuned for Life.'" This expression, he is careful at once to explain, is to "mean *only* that it looks as if small changes in this universe's basic features would have made life's evolution impossible. Thus talk of 'fine tuning' does not presuppose that a divine Fine Tuner . . . must be responsible" (Leslie 1989, pp. 2–3). His argument, like the others, is therefore not *from* but *to* design. (If we already knew that the Universe is designed, then the inference to a Designer would be immediate and deductive.) It is, as he insists, *"an argument from probabilities. . . .* The conclusion to this argument from probabilities could be that it is altogether likely that *either* there exist many universes *or* that God has ensured that our universe is just right for Life, or *both*" (Leslie 1989, p. 155).

In two early chapters Leslie presents several cases in which the precision of the fine tuning and consequent improbability of any alternative to design seem to be of an inconceivably high order. He concludes:

[There] is no excuse for yawning at . . . an apparent discovery that Life depended on fine tuning of the earlier cosmic density to one part in ten followed by fifty-four zeros . . . or that changing the balance between

gravity and electromagnetism by one part in ten followed by thirty-nine
zeros would have made the stars burn too fast or too slowly. . . . Many
such findings may be mistaken; but it can seem altogether unlikely that
all of them are when they form a list as long as . . . Chapter 2 gave.
(Leslie 1989, p. 201)

To make the sum of all these many items of fine tuning comfortably
unremarkable we should need to postulate the actual existence of some
even more fabulous number of additional universes. That, as Leslie
modestly refrains from pointing out, must be accounted a heroic saving
hypothesis to end all heroic saving hypotheses! So suppose we reject it
as a truly desperate alternative and instead ask ourselves how much the
fine-tuning argument can probabilify. Like other arguments to design it
provides support for conclusions that, while they can certainly be
reconciled with, equally certainly do not themselves support, the
contention that our Universe is the creation of an omnipotent, omniscient, and otherwise perfect God. Quite the contrary: for, as was urged
earlier, a striving to exploit and overcome limitations is implicit in the
very idea of design (I, 3, i, a). Thus this Fine Tuner would appear (not to
have been the Prescriber of but) to have been constrained by all the laws
of nature and to have been able to fulfill the intentions we have
hypothesized and attributed (to him? her? it?) only by determining the
values of various crucial physical constraints. Contrast this labored,
protracted, indirect, one is almost inclined to say devious approach with
the forthright, immediate, and meansless methods of Jahweh as
recorded in Genesis 1 and 2!

3. The Significance of Choice

There is in Chapter IV a short paragraph rounded off with an assertion
that took my breath away. Miethe first points out that, although "*This*
debate is not about the problem of evil per se*," he did in Chapter II state
"both that I think this problem has been adequately addressed and that
the answer lies within a defense of the concept of the freedom of the
will. I also list several important books in the bibliography treating the
problem of evil. . . ." Miethe then concludes: "Flew continually ignores
the implications of the freedom of the will to this problem" (IV, p. 110).

Of course, all previous publications by either protagonist are in the
present context so much water under the bridge. But I may be permitted—and it will, I think, be positively helpful—to make brief mentions
of two or three of mine before going on to review the treatment, in the
final pages of Chapter I, of the "implications of the freedom of the will to
this problem."

It was way back early in 1955, in an abbreviated version of the "Divine Omnipotence and Human Freedom" later reprinted in *New Essays in Philosophical Theology* (Flew and MacIntyre 1955), that I began to treat what Miethe now so curiously berates me for continually ignoring. It was indeed that paper that, I believe, first introduced the since widely adopted label "free will defense" for the tactic of those who attempt to resolve the apparent contradiction between the manifest abundance of evils within the Universe and the alleged existence and activity of an omnipotent and (morally) perfect Creator with the help of "a simple understanding of the implications of the freedom of the human will" (II, p. 69).

But my contention was not and is not that there is no such thing. Very far from it. Instead I want with all possible emphasis to insist that we humans are—and, if you like, essentially are—creatures of a kind that can and cannot but make choices, creatures that, as agents, always could do other than we do do.[2]

Since experience of choice and agency may well be an important part of what Miethe is forever accusing me of ignoring, abolishing by definition, or otherwise ruling out from consideration, it remains perhaps barely worthwhile just to mention also two of many comparatively recent publications in which I have striven to demonstrate the enormous importance of what this sort of experience is experience of. Thus in Flew 1978 (chap. 7) I argued vehemently against the leading behaviorist author of a best-seller with the sinister and menacing title *Beyond Freedom and Dignity*, that it is perverse and preposterous to attempt to erect a science of human psychology upon a denial of this most peculiar fact of our nature. Flew 1985 insists upon the same truth in a different academic context, arguing that anything that is to merit the diploma title "social science" must recognize and never forget this most fundamental fact about its human subject matter.

What I actually did maintain, first thirty-five years ago in "Divine Omnipotence and Human Freedom" and now again in the final pages of Chapter I (4, iii, b), is that an omnipotent and omniscient Creator cannot by any means be relieved of responsibility for either the right or the wrong choices made by that Creator's human creatures. It must therefore be, and most manifestly, unjust for their Creator to reward or to punish those creatures for any of their behavior—even deeds their Creator must, *ex hypothesi*, somehow have ensured that they chose to do freely.

It is, I think, as obvious as it should be unsurprising that this contention had Miethe rattled. Certainly his response is all over the place. Thus he claims that it "is really not so much an argument against the existence of God as it is against the possibility of 'free will' given the existence of God" (II, p. 59) and, then again later in the same chapter, that "most of this material has no bearing on an argument for the existence of God . . ." (II, p. 68). But if you have defined your God as (morally) perfect and if some of your other stipulations entail that the God so conceived would be a monster of injustice, then your proposed concept is incoherent and hence not merely does not but could not have a fully corresponding object.

Again, the first sentence of one paragraph of his commentary upon this material reads: "It seems clear here that . . . Flew knows only a Calvinistic or deterministic type of Christianity" (II, p. 69). Yet the very first sentence of the paragraph immediately following notes that "Flew even quotes Aquinas to support these 'necessary [deterministic] consequences'" (II, p. 69). Indeed I did; and Luther and the apostle Paul, for seeing that these predestinarian consequences do indeed follow necessarily from agreed premises is not an intellectual achievement compassed only by Calvin and his followers. It is, for instance, hard to find any substantial disagreement—as opposed to differences of phrasing, emphasis, and authorial reaction—between the teachings of Augustine's *De Libero Arbitrio* and those of the *De Servo Arbitrio* of the Augustinian Luther.

Miethe concludes this particular piece of commentary by quoting several other passages from Aquinas (II, pp. 69–71), all of which, I presume, he somehow contrives to construe as contradicting my own citation from the *Summa Contra Gentiles*. I am surprised that Miethe should think it so easy to discover a radical inconsistency in the teachings of the Angelic Doctor, an inconsistency which, here at any rate, I am myself at a loss to discover. It seems that Miethe, like so many others, simply takes it for granted as an obvious truth that anyone who employs the word "predestination" must necessarily be contradicting anyone asserting the freedom of the will. To help him to emancipate himself from this inhibiting prejudice I recommend Question 23 in the first part of the *Summa Theologica*. There in eight articles *de praedestinatione* Aquinas develops and defends a position apparently different in no relevant way from that which Calvin was to take in the *Institutes*.

4. Persons and Spiritual Substances

Back in Chapter III (p. 103), I argued that, if people were so "unfortunate as to be run over by steamrollers" and thus to be "reduced to a pulp of flesh and blood and crushed bones," then "those remains would simply not be persons." As we would expect, Miethe agrees wholeheartedly.

But then he makes his challenges: ". . . on your atheistic theory, exactly what is it that is missing? What makes these former 'persons' (now 'fleshly residues') residues? . . . What it is that (in part) constitutes a 'flesh and blood' person that is not reducible to or does not originate from the 'flesh and blood' of a person *in your view?"* (IV, p. 127).

i. To which the short straight answer is that, in my view, all the characteristics of a person are the characteristics of, and in that understanding may be truly said to originate from, the particular organism that that particular person essentially is. So what "makes these former 'persons' (now 'fleshly residues') residues" and no longer persons is that "a pulp of flesh and blood and crushed bones" is no longer a living organism of any kind at all, and hence, *a fortiori*, no longer a living organism of that very special kind which may have characteristics of the sorts peculiar to and distinctive of persons.

(a) This answer will not, I fear, satisfy Miethe. In the first place, he apparently takes the expressions "reducible to" and "orginating from" to be virtually equivalent. And, furthermore, he seems to be assuming also that to say that whatsitsnames evolved or originated from thingamabobs licenses inferences to the conclusion that whatsitsnames are reducible to, are themselves merely, or are themselves nothing whatsoever but thingamabobs. But, if oak trees are reducible to acorns, then it is certainly not in the depreciatory understanding in which this statement would imply that oak trees are merely or are nothing whatsoever but the acorns out of which they grew. Again, people develop or originate from fertilized human ova. But that does not imply either that fertilized human ova (already) are people or that people are merely, or are no more than, or are nothing whatsoever but fertilized human ova.

(b) In the second place, and more important, it is clear that Miethe wants the something more, the what it is "that is missing," the "What makes these former 'persons'. . . . residues," to be a crucial component that now is lacking. Confronted by the "pulp of flesh and blood and crushed bones" he asks me to tell him what it is that constitutes a "flesh and blood" person that is missing in and from that pulp.

But the assumption that the decisive difference has to be of this substantial kind remains unwarranted. It might even be put down as superstitious, since the demand is that the behavior of a person be explained as the behavior of a sort of person within that person.[3]

ii. What Miethe believes to be the true answer to his challenging question, and hence the answer he would ideally wish me to give, is that what is missing from the wretched residues is the immaterial substances that are the proper subjects of all peculiarly and distinctively personal predicates and that persons really and truly are, not organisms of the very special sort that we are first taught to identify as such, but the immaterial substances thus hypothesized.

(a) Miethe complains that I am "simply assuming 'we are creatures who just essentially are . . . flesh and blood' in spite of evidence that a human being is not irreducibly 'flesh and blood.'" (IV, p. 125). But my contention was about the meaning of person words, and to support this contention I deployed evidence of the appropriate linguistic kind (I, pp. 4–5). Against this Miethe offered arguments that were entirely beside the point, for they would show, if they showed anything, that creatures of the sort correctly described as persons contain an immaterial component essential for the production of most or all the phenomena peculiar to and distinctive of persons.

But to show all this, even if it had been shown, would not be even to begin to show that people just are their immaterial components, rather than the organisms of that special kind of which these things have supposedly been shown to be the most essential components. No doubt the operations of a brain are causally necessary to the production of the phenomena peculiar to and distinctive of persons, but that is not to say that people *are* their brains. As Plato's Socrates remarked, to conclude a famous argument: "Fancy being unable to distinguish between . . . the cause of a thing and the condition without which it could not be a cause" (*Phaedo* 99B).

In my attempt to meet Miethe's objections I was, as I like to think, characteristically conciliatory and open-minded! To say what I was saying about the meaning of person words, I conceded, "is not even, necessarily and as such, to rule out of court any suggestion that these peculiar creatures may somewhere contain an unfleshly component or even several unfleshly components" (III, p. 102–3). But anyone wishing to press that suggestion has got to meet and overcome certain difficulties, difficulties Miethe has certainly not attempted to surmount and seems not even to have recognized:

> If any prove able both to give *positive* sense to the idea of components of this kind and to explain how specimens might be identified and reidentified, then it remains open to them to make their suggestion and to deploy evidence in its support. It is necessary to emphasize the "positive," for the adjectives "incorporeal," "immaterial," "unfleshly," and "nonphysical" are all wholly negative, telling us only what the referents of the nouns they qualify are not and nothing at all of what they are. (III, pp. 103)

It might be thought that at least the difficulty about essential negativity, if not the difficulties of identification and reidentification, could be met by stressing that the incorporeal entities to be hypothesized are stipulated to be spiritual substances. (A substance here is something that, unlike a grin or a temper, can significantly be said to exist independently and in its own right; it makes no sense, for example, to suggest that, if someone loses her temper and departs in a huff, her lost temper might yet be found where she had lost it.) If, however, we are proposing to try to explain what we choose to call spiritual phenomena as being produced by the operation of spiritual substances, then we cannot afford to define spiritual substance as the we-know-not-what that produces spiritual phenomena.

(b) Miethe picks out some, perhaps all, of the phenomena that are in our experience distinctive of and peculiar to persons and labels these "spiritual." He then proceeds to argue that they could not be produced by or be characteristics of anything purely material. Hence they must be attributed to spirits. This, surely, is what misleads him to believe that I, who do not agree with that conclusion, am committed to a "limited view of experience" (II, p. 83)—the limitation being, presumably, a refusal to admit experience of any of the phenomena Miethe likes to call spiritual. But there never has been and is not now any such refusal on my part. The difference between us is that he sees these phenomena as the work of spirits, whereas I also see them but as the activities of persons.

Since persons as organisms can scarcely fail to be accounted material things, albeit of the most special of all sorts, it should give us at least an initial shock of surprise to hear it maintained that phenomena that are distinctive of and, in our experience, peculiar to such persons necessarily cannot be characteristic of anything material. Compare here both my earlier protest against the suggestion "that we could, and even do, learn to apply the word 'person' to 'various individuals around us' by first learning how to pick out certain peculiarly personal characteristics and then identifying persons as creatures of the kind that possess these characteristics" (I, p. 5) and my later objection to the "arbitrary and blinkered" insistence that "order, which to all appearance is intrinsic to the Universe, nevertheless cannot but be externally imposed by a Supernatural Orderer postulated for the purpose" (V, p. 143).

Certainly the characteristics Miethe calls spiritual are quite radically different from and hence not, in his depreciative understanding of reducibility, reducible to characteristics either from the exceedingly narrow range of those truly attributable to elementary particles or from the vastly richer but still boringly suborganic range similarly attributable to manageably sized pure specimens of all the chemical elements. And so on. But none of this constitutes a reason for insisting that the newly emerging characteristics in any of these successive ranges cannot be the properties of anything that is through and through material.

5. The Ontological Argument

In Chapter II Miethe says: "Though I will not in this book be defending the ontological argument per se, modern developments of this grand old argument must be examined carefully and not just dismissed" (p. 57). I had hoped that that was the last we were going to hear of it here, since I do not share Miethe's affectionate respect for "this grand old argument," an argument purporting to conjure an existential conclusion "than which no greater can be conceived" out of a most penurious and purely definitional premise. But Chapter IV dashed these hopes (pp. 112–17). Miethe commends to our acceptance the version developed by Charles Hartshorne: "The 'true Anselmian principle' is 'existence without conceivable alternative of not existing is better than to exist with such alternative,' so that Greatness that is unsurpassable by others cannot not exist" (IV, p. 116).

Since the only candidates qualified for membership of the class existent "without conceivable alternative of not existing" would appear to be the subjects of existence theorems in mathematics, what this argument would prove, if it proved anything, would be: not "the active, living, agent of God of Israel, a Being in the succession from the Demiurge of Plato's *Timaeus*," but "an altogether abstract, lifeless entity, something from the categorically different tradition of the Form or Idea of the Good/Real in *The Republic*" (III, p. 91). But the more devastating objection is to the unsupported and—in any but the most factitious understanding of "better than"—flagrantly false assumption that what is better than must exist.

Although, as will be obvious, something well short of enthralled by Hartshorne's development of the ontological argument, I was much intrigued to be told that "Hartshorne is able to go on to show that *to be* is to experience . . ." (IV, p. 117), for this would seem to be a form of metaphysical idealism more total even than that of Berkeley. Whereas he maintained that to be is *either* to perceive (experience) *or* to be perceived (experienced), Hartshorne is here said to have held that "*to be* simply and solely is to experience." Is this really intended to imply that Hartshorne's experience has no subject or, more likely, no subject other than Hartshorne's God?

6. The Ultimates and Limits of Explanation

The original game plan for the present work provided that both of the two members of every pair of chapters should be of roughly equal length and that these lengths in every successive pair should be substantially shorter than in its predecessor. Only the most indulgent of judges would allow that the first of these two provisos has so far been satisfied. I am now myself in train to violate the second. My only excuse, if excuse is needed, is that Miethe chose to defer his "Argument for the Existence of God" till the end of Chapter IV (pp. 127–37), rather than to deploy it at the beginning of Chapter II.

i. It will, I think, be most helpful to our readers if in my response I focus on questions about what can and cannot be explained, and how and on what the conditions are under which we are entitled to assume that there must be explanations and of what sort. In the nature of the case not everything can be explained, while, even where there are explanations to be discovered, we are not entitled to assume that they will be of the kind we find most satisfying.

(a) To enforce the first of these two points I cannot do better than to quote what I said in Chapter I (p. 25–26) in support of the contention that the Stratonician atheism possesses the comparative advantage of postulational economy:

> Every system of explanation must include at least some fundamentals that are not themselves explained. However far you rise in a hierarchy of explanations—particular events in terms of general laws, laws in terms of theories, theories in terms of wider and more comprehensive theories, and maybe even further—still there has to be at every stage, including the last stage, some element or elements in terms of which whatever is explained at that stage is explained. Nor is this inevitability of logic escaped by theists, for whatever else they may think to explain by reference to the existence and nature of their God, they cannot thereby avoid taking that existence and that nature as itself ultimate and beyond explanation.
>
> This necessity is common to all systems. It is no fault in any and certainly not a competitive weakness of one as against another. The principle of sufficient reason—that there has to be a sufficient reason for anything and everything being as it is and will be—is not, as has often been thought, necessarily true. It is instead demonstrably false (Penelhum 1960).

(b) "Perhaps the simplest and most psychologically satisfying explanation of any observed phenomenon is that it happened that way because someone wanted it to happen that way" (Sowell 1980, p. 97). It will be immediately obvious both that this is true and that we can hope to find a true explanation of this most satisfying kind only for relatively few observed phenomena. What is very much less obvious is that many social institutions that look as if they must have been the planned products of superhumanly brilliant design have instead evolved over time as the unintended products of intended and all too human actions and interactions. The discovery in the eighteenth century of this enormously important truth was the great achievement of the Scottish founding fathers of social science, and its significance—both practical and theoretical—is to this day widely overlooked (Hayek 1967 and 1973).

ii. Miethe writes of Hume's "attack upon the causal principle. This is the idea that whatever begins to exist must have a cause of existence" (IV, p. 114). It is important to appreciate exactly what Hume was attacking and what are the implications of the success of that attack. He always insisted, and most emphatically in a letter, that he "never asserted so absurd a proposition as that anything might arise without a cause" (Hume 1932, vol. 1, p. 187). The relevant section in *A Treatise of Human Nature* is entitled, significantly, "Why a cause is always necessary" (I, iii, 3). Hume begins:

> . . . with the first question concerning the necessity of a cause: 'Tis a general maxim in philosophy, that *whatever begins to exist, must have a cause of existence*. This is commonly taken for granted in all reasonings, without any proof given or demanded. 'Tis suppos'd to be founded on intuition, and to be one of those maxims, which tho' they may be deny'd with the lips, 'tis impossible for men in their hearts really to doubt of. But if we examine this maxim . . . we shall discover in it no mark of any such intuitive certainty; but on the contrary shall find, that 'tis of a nature quite foreign to that species of conviction.

What Hume's examination discovered was that this "general maxim in philosophy" is not a logically necessary truth: its denial is certainly not self-contradictory or otherwise incoherent. A further and supplementary examination revealed that it is impossible to know a priori that any particular occurrence or sort of occurrences either cannot be or must be the cause of any other particular occurrence or sort of occurrences. As Hume was to say later, "Not only the will of the Supreme Being may create matter, but, for aught we know a priori, the will of any other being might create it, or any other cause that the most whimsical imagination can assign" (Hume 1988, p. 164). Or indeed it could, equally conceivably, occur uncaused—like hydrogen atoms in the long since falsified but always fully intelligible so-called continuous creation theory of Hoyle and Bondi.

So what Hume was arguing and surely showed is that all our causal knowledge must be empirical knowledge. About the status of and warrant for the "general maxim" itself he adds, in the final paragraph of that section of the *Treatise*, that ". . . the opinion of the necessity of cause to every new production must necessarily arise from observation and experience. The next question, then, shou'd naturally be, *how experience gives rise to such a principle?*" It emerges at once, however, that "it will be more convenient to sink this question" in another: "'Twill, perhaps, be found in the end, that the same answer will serve for both questions." So any mention of possible implications is deferred. When it occurs, in a passage already quoted (I, pp. 24–25), it is presented as a hesitant afterthought:

> . . . a difficulty, which I shall just propose to you without insisting on it; lest it lead into reasonings of too nice and delicate a nature. In a word, I much doubt whether it be possible for a cause to be known only by its effect . . . or to be of so singular and particular a nature as to have no parallel and no similarity with any other cause of object, that has ever fallen under our observation. (Hume 1988, p. 180)

iii. In the light of these Humean insights it is hard to see much force in any of the putative existential proofs in the Thomist tradition: the Five Ways thus appear to be revealed as dead ends. Miethe begins: "The ultimate question in regard to the nature of the universe is. . . ." But his sentence goes straight on to provide us not with one but with two supposedly ultimate questions: "Is the physical universe eternal?" and "Can the physical universe as we know it account for itself?" The second he glosses over by saying: "The argument that maintains it *cannot* is known as the cosmological argument." He then adds: ". . . one does not have to grant that the physical universe . . . is not eternal for the cosmological argument to prove its case" (IV, p. 129).

(a) This is a most important addition. One could wish that all those—starting with Aquinas himself—who have wanted their arguments to be construed in this way had taken care from the beginning to make that clear, for it means that the various series of the various versions—series of causes or of movers or whatever—are not to be conceived as temporally successive. Hence the hypothetical entities of the conclusions—the entities to which "Everyone gives . . . the name of God"—must, at least in the present context, be Sustainers rather than Initiators.

To say this is not, of course, to say that they could not also in truth be both. Whereas, however, it is easy to persuade the public that the original big bang required some kind of First (initiating) Cause, it is much more difficult to carry conviction with the contention that it is the mere continuing existence of the physical universe that requires some external explanation, for construed thus correctly the Way which Aquinas believed "more manifest" is closed by modern (as opposed to Aristotelian) physics. Like everyone else in that older (Aristotelian) tradition, Aquinas was assuming that not only the initiation but also the continuation of motion required explanation. Appropriately enough, his favorite illustration was that of a man brandishing a stick.

(b) Himself insisting that we are not to think here of temporal succession, Miethe represents the Second Way as involving five steps. Step three runs: "There cannot be an infinite regress of . . . efficient causes, for unless there is a first cause of the series there would be no causality in the series" (IV, p. 130). But now, given that this is not a series stretching back in time, what is the need for or possibility of generating any series at all? Instead of concluding—step four—"Therefore, there must be a first uncaused efficient Cause of all efficient causality in the world," why not, following soundly Ockhamite principles of postulational economy, simply accept that what to all appearance are the efficient causes within the universe indeed are, so to speak, efficacious in their own right? Nor will it do to pretend a general disrespect for such principles, for how else than by appealing to them is the conclusion that there can be only one uncaused efficient cause to be justified?

(c) Miethe represents the Third Way as again involving five steps. But if we are supposed to think of the series of possible beings as not in temporal succession, then the whole presentation becomes unintelligible. For consider step two: "But not all beings can be possible beings, because what comes to exist does so only through what already exists (nothing cannot cause something)" (IV, p. 132). But now, suppose that we generously waive an objection that surely ought to be sufficiently decisive and read the argument as presupposing temporal succession. It still remains open to a different but equally decisive objection, for it is obvious that in step two possible beings are being contrasted with actual beings. But in step one possible beings were defined, quite differently, as "beings that begin to exist and cease to exist."

(d) There follow in Chapter IV two eyebrow-raising statements, with which Miethe may or may not be wishing to associate himself, but which I want to query briefly. First, Miethe quotes Eslick as asserting: "To say that all things without exception are possible to be and not to be is to say that *all* things 'at some time' are nonexistent, . . ." (IV, p. 133). But, most manifestly, it is not to *say* anything of the such, and the desired conclusion will follow only on the grotesque assumption that all possibilities are realized "at some time."

Second, Miethe quotes Bruce Reichenbach as maintaining that "An infinite series of contingent beings is incapable of yielding a sufficient reason for the existence of any being" (IV, p. 134). But what warrant can Reichenbach have for thus insisting that there must be and is an explanation of some kind that would satisfy him for the here admittedly conceivable existence of an infinite series of contingent beings? And, furthermore, the principle of sufficient reason, as formulated by Leibniz, is not merely not necessarily true. It is necessarily false (I, 3, ii).

(e) At the very end of Chapter IV Miethe develops an argument he insists "is *not* based on the principle of sufficient reason but on the principle of existential causality" (p. 135). Equally clearly the First Cause to which it is directed is not the first in a temporal series, for the third step in this argument reads:

> *There cannot be an infinite regress of causes of being.* We are not here talking about a linear series of historical causes of becoming, but a vertical series of causes of *being*, for existence itself. Existential causality refers to the cause of the *being* of entities and not the cause of their becoming. This argument is talking about a cause for the very being of a thing, not its coming into existence (its becoming) or the changes it may undergo. (IV, p. 135)

To this or any other such attempt to distinguish and to demand different causes for the *being* and for the *becoming* of existent entities, my response has once again to draw upon the incorrigible Monster of Malmesbury. In chapter 46 of his *Leviathan* I find a curt, characteristic, crushing comment: "This is vain philosophy. A man might as well say, that one man maketh both a straight line and crooked, and another maketh their incongruity."

CHAPTER VI

A Third Engagement

Terry L. Miethe

Introduction

I started Chapter IV by commenting that Prof. Flew had very selectively narrowed his assault and had gone "directly for my particular 'theistic throat.'" Unlike in Chapter III, my friend Tony Flew starts Chapter V by complimenting me. He writes:

> It follows that that publisher was doubly wrong to consider Miethe's work superfluous—wrong not only in holding that, given some approved belief, there is no need for evidencing reasons in its support, but wrong too in assuming that the more particular and *far, far richer belief Prof. Miethe is propounding and commending* is almost universal." (V, p. 2 [emphasis added])

Now I *am* worried. Thank you—I think—Prof. Flew!

At any rate, I could not agree more with Prof. Flew here (regarding the double error of the Christian publisher) both that (1) "evidencing reasons" are needed to defend the question at hand and the Christian faith and that (2) the Christian publisher in question was wrong and more than a little naive to believe that the poll the publisher referred to (mentioned in Chapter II, note 37, and in V, p. 138) should be regarded as proving anything. To the extent this publisher (and the second publisher who told my author friend, "Our market simply does not seem to be interested in books defending the rationality of the Christian faith") is (or are) correct, it is indeed a very sad state of affairs. In any case, this "state of affairs" must change if the church is ever to be healthy *or* if Prof. Flew is (or other atheists are) to have, as he (they) deserves to have, this much needed "systematic and progressive apologetic, . . . a rational apologetic" (I, p. 19) with "evidencing reasons" (V, p. 138).

1. "The Variety of Gods"—Response

I agree that the supposed 95 percent of Americans who responded positively to an opinion poll that a Supreme Being exists is almost meaningless in regard to practical considerations (as regards the nature of the Supreme Being or personal actions on the part of the "believers" as a result of this belief), but this fact may not be meaningless in theory. One could argue—I think effectively—that the very fact that such a large percentage of people believe in the existence of such a Being is an important indication of (or pointer to) such a Being's existence (see Trueblood 1957, pp. 177–88; Geisler 1974, pp. 13–83).

After all, many thinkers, such as Otto, Kierkegaard, Tillich, and Koëstenbaum, have acknowledged the reality of the Transcendent while identifying it with realities both personal and impersonal, pantheistic, deistic, or theistic. Others, such as James, Jung, Feuerbach, Sartre, Freud, Fromm, and Dewey, while arguing against the objective reality of a Supreme Being, have acknowledged the importance of religious belief (or experience) and the need of the Transcendent. If such a need is admitted and it is valid to try and argue that this "need" is nothing more than "wish fulfillment," it is equally valid to try to explain this need/experience by an innate awareness in a person of the existence of God.

Flew again refers to David Hume here (V, p. 138) and even says: "If this conjecture is correct [that 95 percent or a very substantial percentage of people believe in a Supreme Being], then the near unanimous agreement concerns only—as Hume's Philo would have put it—'the *being*' and 'not the *nature* of God.'" Though I doubt if he realizes it, Flew has (again) either said much too much or much too little here, for I must remind Flew that this is precisely what this debate is all about—the *"being"* or existence of God.

i. I agree with Flew "that any truly systematic rational apologetic must . . . [sort] out and [settle] fundamental conceptual questions." I do not, however, agree that these "conceptual questions" are logically prior to questions of fact or to the question of God's existence. As I have indicated (see Chapter IV), I think Flew is simply wrongheaded in claiming that the conceptual problems are "logically prior." Flew quotes (V, pp. 139) from Chapter I, pp. 10: "It is only when, and if, and insofar as such logically prior conceptual problems have been satisfactorily solved that it can become sensible to move on to the *substantial and much*

more exciting but logically secondary question or questions of fact"
[emphasis added]. I remember in his "A First Rejoinder" (Chapter II)
Flew chides me a little for giving so much space, paying so much
attention, to his new (so he claims) argument rather than putting forth a
positive argument for the existence of God, which is interestingly (by
Flew's own admission) now referred to as "the substantial, and much
more exciting . . . question . . . of fact."

Flew comments: "Miethe is all the time complaining about my
alleged verificationist presuppositions, my supposedly definitional view
of reality, and what he [Miethe] believes to be my [Flew's] scandalously
limited view of experience" (V, p. 158). My [Miethe's] first comment here
is to affirm that I have shown in Chapter II, and certainly in Chapter
IV, that Flew's "verificationist presuppositions" are *real* not alleged and
that his view of reality is *indeed* definitional. While I would not go quite
so far as to call his "limited view of reality" "scandalous," it certainly *is*
limited! Flew then admits that the examples he offered in Chapter I
"were about as physical as they could have been." No disagreement
here.

But I have a strong sense that Flew does not realize (because of his
really *pleasant* wrongheadedness—and I sincerely mean this, for it is as
pleasant as any wrongheadedness could be) what he is saying or really
admitting here. He repeatedly gives "physical" examples because he
believes there are no other kind, that he has never experienced any other
kind. Yet Flew systematically ignores the "more rigorous empiricism"
that very strongly argues that even "physical" existence is not irreducibly physical.

There is no question that Flew's position represents a "naturalistic
bias" (a mental leaning or inclination, partiality, prejudice, bent) both
against the possibility of a supernatural event (miracles) and the existence of a Supernatural Agent (God). As my good friend Gary Habermas
says:

> First, most of these philosophical objections are attempts to mount up
> the data against miracles [or God's existence] in an a priori manner (that
> is, *before or in spite of the factual evidence*) so that no facts could actually
> establish their occurrence [or God's existence because according to Flew
> "conceptual problems" are logically prior to questions of fact—T. M.].
> For instance, it is an unjustified assumption that whatever occurs in the
> world must automatically be a natural event having a natural cause.
> Such an assumption ignores the fact that if a historical miracle [indicat-
> ing the existence of a miracle Maker] occurred it would have to occur in

nature. Therefore, to always expand the laws of nature belies a naturalistic prejudice. [emphasis added]

Habermas further says—which also applies to evidence for the existence of God as well as for miracles—". . . the statement that we must always assume a naturalistic explanation is, once again, an a priori assumption against miracles. . . . We can describe a natural process but when we attempt to naturalistically predetermine the cause of all events, we beg the very question that we seek to answer." Habermas, then, quotes a theistic philosopher: "Flew's argument is an almost classic case of an unfalsifiable position which in the process of justification begs the whole question in favor of naturalism" (Miethe, Habermas, and Flew 1987, p. 16).

Flew says: "So it is hard indeed when that careful choice is mistaken to imply or presuppose a refusal to admit the legitimacy of any concepts of which the objects are or would be of some totally different and acceptably nonphysical kind" (V, p. 139). There has been no "mistake" here. Nowhere to this point in Flew's argument is there any admission of even the possibility of such "totally different and acceptably nonphysical kind" of being. In fact, just the opposite is true! Nowhere has Flew even admitted the possibility that human beings are not irreducibly physical, except to say that a person who has been rolled over by a steamroller—"reduced to a pulp of flesh and blood and crushed bones"—is admittedly not the same! Flew says:

> But those remains would simply not be persons, not because persons "just essentially *are*"unfleshly creatures immune to any purely physical destruction, but because such fleshly residues would not and could not possess the distinctive and peculiar properties of persons. (III, p. 103).

If this is not begging the question again, I don't know what would be. No one in this debate is saying that persons are not at least in part fleshly, physical. But a further and more important point is that I am arguing there is a basis in *existing "physical beings"*—in part of what constitutes a "person" as such—for nonphysical reality. In other words, there is in our experience of reality as such reason to believe that a "totally different and acceptably nonphysical kind" of Being exists.

Now—all of a sudden as it were—I am supposed to believe that I have been "mistaken," that Flew has been misunderstood, simply because of his claim to "careful choice." I think not. Flew repeatedly holds (and not only by implication) that such a being that is not irreducibly "physical" is "a very different kettle of fish." He repeatedly is willing to accept proof *only* for the "physical" objects that his criteria for "evidence" (which is always empirical) will allow. But most importantly, when I give him reason—based on a more rigorous empiricism—to think of the nonphysical as an inseparable part of the physical, he ignores both the claim and the implications.

The implication of my argument that human beings are not irreducibly "physical" is that we have an example even in the "physical world" of what Flew insists on calling a "different kettle of fish," objects that are seen, . . . which would give us reason to believe that those that are "not seen" (by us) may in fact exist, and hence, . . . that there may be "some . . . different and acceptably nonphysical kind" of being. Notice, I took out the word "totally" (from Flew's wording) in regard to "different," because I do not believe the Christian concept of God is *totally* different in "being." This is the error that Plotinus made. Aquinas was quite correct regarding the "analogy of being." The Christian concept is that *we* are created in his image (God's) and therefore share much with him. This is what, in part, makes—according to Flew's own admission—the "belief" that "Miethe is propounding and commending . . . far, far richer"! It is also—if true—what makes Flew's "verificationist presuppositions, . . . definitional view of reality, and . . . limited view of experience" factually (and ultimately) morally and "spiritually" bankrupt.

ii. Here Flew starts talking (again) about how it "is so 'very hard to accept'" or believe "in a God 'stipulated to be the supreme partisan within the creation'" (V, p. 140). But what Flew cannot seem to grasp is that the "God" he repeatedly wants to paint as "inflexibly resolved to punish all offenders," is not the God I worship, nor is he—I would argue—the God the majority of Christians believe is revealed in the Bible! My definition of God states that he is the "*merciful* Creator and Sustainer of all that exists" (II, p. 39) [emphasis added]).

It can be effectively argued that Flew's "concept of God" represents a rather significant *misunderstanding* of what a majority of Christians believe about the concept/character/nature of God. As interesting as it would be to argue about God's character or nature *as if he already existed*—for this is what Flew really would have to do—or (as Flew would want to say) about the concept of God (all to be used by Flew to deny the *fact* of God's existence) is to get the "cart before the horse." Further, this is *not* the real subject of this debate as much as Flew may want to make it so. As for myself, I certainly believe in a God who is much "richer" in concept/character and has a much richer relationship to his creation (we humans) than either a "God" who is "inflexibly resolved to punish all offenders" or who "is an unintrusive Big Detonator of some kind." This is not the "God" of Christian theism, nor is it—I believe—the God of "Mosaic theism" (to use Flew's term).

Now Flew says—rather amazingly to me—that: "Since the atheism I profess is an atheism with respect to the God of Mosaic theism, I should not necessarily be being inconsistent if I were to be inclined to a more inhibited agnosticism with regard to many Gods more limited and less intrusive" (V, p. 140). Very interesting! Oh, really. Again, Prof. Flew, pray tell us *if* this is so, just what you can about the "nature" or "concept" of this "more limited and less intrusive" "God"? You cannot have it both ways, can you? Either you are arguing against what is by your admission a "far, far richer belief Prof. Miethe is propounding and commending" (V, p. 138) or you are opening up the possibility that you might accept (presumably) a less rich concept of God, but a "God" nevertheless, and that this would "not be inconsistent." It would definitely be inconsistent, *if* anyone reads carefully the implications of your argument in this debate.

Yes, Prof. Flew, you *have* made it clear (V, p. 140). You have "[made] it manifest that, however mistakenly, [you] do not agree" that the God of "Mosaic theism" exists. What you have not done is enlighten us either to (1) "what you would allow to count for God's existence" or (2), really, what is so terribly contradictory about the Christian concept of God. You *have* stated (or presupposed) some very old (definitional) arguments and *have* more than indicated that you misunderstand what I think a majority of Christians call God.[1] And, while you here claim that you do not "rule out realities by definition" and do not "insist upon some similarly blinkered concept of experience," you have not told us one thing about or given us one reason why I am wrong in what I argue about "a more rigorous empiricism" in Chapters II and IV. You say: "I would not want to ground my rejection of the reality of God upon some subjectivistic and autobiographical claim about the coherent and compelling character of my 'atheistic' experience" (V, p. 140), but that is exactly what you do.

2. "Arguments to Design"—Response

Flew starts this section by reminding us again that "there are many different notions that, whether rightly or wrongly, are in fact accounted to be notions of God" (V, p. 141). This is undoubtedly true, but it does not have the force of argument against the existence of God that Flew thinks it has for two reasons: (1) The fact that many people have a belief in God—though the "concept" is different—can just as well be used to argue *for* the existence (being) of God as against. And (2), as I have pointed out and as Flew has also admitted, we are arguing here for (or against) the God of "Christian theism" or "Mosaic theism" (to use Flew's own term), which is a "much richer" concept. I have defined the concept of God for which I am arguing by saying:

> Many concepts could be used in definition or characteristics given to describe this "actually existing object." It is enough here to say that I affirm the existence of "the Supreme Being, or the Ultimate Reality, whose nature is to exist. God is the living, personal, loving, and merciful Creator and Sustainer of all that exists. In every way that He exists, He exists in perfection, without limit." . . . God is "spirit," does not have a physical body, and that there can be only one such Being. He is the only proper object of worship. (II, p. 39)

Thus Flew's supposedly important insight (there are many different notions of God) is in a very important sense irrelevant to this debate. It is up to Flew to treat specifically the concept of God we have both agreed to argue for or against, the God of "Mosaic theism," and not the "many different notions" possibilities.

i. Flew writes: "At one point Miethe quotes himself [it is clear in the text that I am quoting Leonard J. Eslick—T. M.] as saying that 'traditionally' western metaphysics is the study of reality as such, being as such. It must be consummated by some kind of theory of God" (II, p. 34). Flew then goes on to comment:

> The sort of concept of God . . . appropriate . . . to such an abstract study of the essential nature of being as such [metaphysics], and the existence or subsistence of the object of which might conceivably be demonstrated by that study, are about as far removed as could be from the concept of the existence of whose object Miethe wants to prove." (V, p. 141)

It is certainly one thing for Flew to simply assert this and quite another to support or prove the assertion. First, this completely ignores the argument of the "analogy of being" of Aquinas, which is where I find my metaphysical roots, *not* in Plotinus's misunderstanding of Plato or in Greek thought as such. Second, it completely ignores my argument for the existence of God in Chapter IV, pp. 135–37. There I argue that only one Being of the nature of which I am arguing can exist and that "This first uncaused Cause is identical with the God of the Judeo-Christian tradition." Flew has simply made a statement here (V, p. 141) and nothing more.

ii. I must point out here (again) that I am not formally arguing for (or to) a design argument. Flew certainly hits the standard criticism of "arguments to design." Basically (it has been long argued in the history of philosophy), if such arguments prove anything, they prove only a limited designer or architect, not a Supreme Being. This may indeed be so. And this is certainly not the kind of "designer" for which I am arguing. But, interestingly, this is not the kind of being the scientists who use recent findings from information theory, the gene code, and other areas are trying to support. In fact, when a colleague of mine and I attended a week-long series of debates between theists and atheists (in which Tony Flew was also a participant), we asked several of the scientists who were fairly recent converts to theism (and specifically to Christian theism) why they were now Christians. They told us that the newest scientific evidence regarding the complexity and nature of the universe and of life pointed very strongly to a personal God, not just some impersonal force.

Flew has said that he is willing to accept the evidence of science and suggests that it "would, surely, be wiser" for theists "to develop a natural theology from the regularities and the wonders that scientists have discovered" (III, p. 102). I am reminded of what Benjamin Constant said in regard to his *History of Polytheism* in a letter to his friend Claude Hochet (dated 11 October 1811): "My work is a singular proof of the truth of Bacon's saying, that a little science leads to atheism and more science to religion." Constant started his work "certain that there is nothing after this world," but ended it with his "whole plan . . . recast." I pointed out this is exactly why some scientists (many of whom are now Christians) are arguing for a theistic universe over against an atheistic one. But Flew pays practically no attention to this. Eventually, one has to ask oneself just how far one is willing to go in denying—how much sense it makes to continually ignore—all the "pointers" that seem to be coming from all aspects of thought and/or reality and pointing to the existence of God.[2]

Flew writes that I [Miethe] make "much of the unsolved problems of evolutionary biology" and says, "Fair enough; far be it from me [Flew] to minimize the inadequacies of the "Darwin-Oparin-Haldane 'warm little pond' concept" (V, p. 142). All right, Prof. Flew, from your perspective what are the inadequacies as they relate to the question of origins? Then Flew goes on: "But Miethe must in his turn recognize the embarrassing implications if this problem or any of the other problems turns out to be not just still unsolved for forever insoluble." I do not understand what the "embarrassing implications" are of which Flew speaks. I assume that

I should find it "embarrassing" if creation "was [not] perfectly smooth" because God had to keep it "on course by frequent timely adjustments to the steering." I cannot help but see a couple of big assumptions here. Far be it for me to say what "a Creator both omniscient and omnipotent" would have to do or not do, or what in his mind constituted "perfectly smooth," and so on.

Just what are these "frequent timely adjustments"? Is Flew referring to the "thousands upon thousands of missing links"? Surely, the "thousands . . . of missing links" are not a problem for the believer, for they do not even exist on the creation model. Yes, both the atheist and the theist must hold strongly to belief in an orderly universe,[3] but the theist has never maintained that just because there are "laws of nature" God cannot ultimately still be in control of, and involved in, the workings of the universe. Quite the contrary, the Christian *is the one* who holds precisely this.

Flew defines "Stratonician atheism" as: "The conclusion . . . is that we should take the Universe itself and whatever our scientists discover to be its most fundamental laws as the ultimates in explanation" (I, p. 25; V, p. 142). If this is how one is going to define "Stratonician," then in light of all the information currently available in science (which is leading many scientists to argue that such information points "to a personal God, not just some impersonal force") perhaps we should be talking—as strange as it might sound—of a "Stratonician theism."

Next, Flew states that it "truly would be arbitrary and blinkered . . . to insist that order, which *to all appearance is intrinsic to the Universe,* nevertheless cannot but be externally imposed by a Supernatural Orderer postulated for the purpose" (V, p. 143 [emphasis added]). But, again, isn't Flew's phrase "to all appearance is intrinsic to the Universe" exactly the point at issue here? Is it so clear—"to all appearance"—that order is intrinsic to the Universe? (I am so tempted to say once again, "Come on, Prof. Flew, you are again just begging the question here.")

In the third "type" of Flew's proposed three-part arrangement of "arguments to design," he says:

> The . . . most powerful form of argument to design is a recent development. . . . Taking as given exactly those same laws and principles the scientific cosmologists themselves employ in their calculations, it can be shown that, were not various quantitative relationships in physics exactly what they are, then the circumstances in which the evolution of intelligent organisms becomes even possible could never have occurred, circumstances that even as it is, seem to be excessively rare. (V, p. 143)

I think Flew has missed the point here (has misunderstood what is at issue). First, the argument is clearly and strongly *against* chance evolution. If any evolution is acceptable, it would have to be *theistic* evolution.

What Flew is referring to here is known as the anthropic [from the Greek *anthropos*, meaning "man"] principle. It accounts for a number of nice "coincidences." Among the coincidences (for example) mentioned in regard to the anthropic principle is the structure of the atomic nuclei. The nuclei are held together by a highly balanced force. If the force were reduced by only a few percentage points, it would cause the simplest composite nucleus, that of deuterium, which contains one proton and one neutron, to fly apart. If this happened, all the stars, including our sun, would be in "severe difficulties" since they use deuterium in their fuel chain. But if the nuclear force were very slightly stronger an even worse event would occur; two protons could possibly stick together (the force is not actually strong enough for this to occur). If this were possible, at the big bang all the free protons would have matched up. There would have been no single protons left to make hydrogen, the building block for stars.

Another delicate balance is between electromagnetism and gravity. Electromagnetism provides the support that keeps a star from collapsing on itself from its own gravity. A minute shift in the balance would cause all stars to become either blue giants or red dwarfs. The point the anthropic principle makes is that the universe is full of these very important "coincidences." This leads to the (anthropic) principle, the idea that life will arise only in those universes in which conditions are suitable and it is only in these universes that anything can be contemplated.

But the contemplations will be limited by the fact that the existence of the contemplators places constraints on what sort of world they can perceive. This "observer-oriented" approach to the basic cosmological questions is quite different from the traditional scientific approach. Traditionally the observer plays no part, but in today's new physics the human plays "an essential role in determining the nature of the world he observes with increasing amazement" (Davies 1983, p. 24). It is this increasing amazement that has led many astronomers and physicists to change the anthropic principle somewhat and announce with Sir Fred Hoyle that "there must be a God" (Varghese 1984, pp. viii, 23–37).

It has only been in the last hundred years (really less) that scientists have been talking about scientific cosmology.[4] Of recent developments, Stanley L. Jaki says:

Is it reasonable to assume that an intelligence which produced a universe, a totality of consistently interacting things, is not consistent to the point of acting for a purpose? To speak of purpose may seem, since Darwin, the most reprehensible procedure before the tribunal of science. *Bafflingly enough, it is science in its most advanced and comprehensive form—scientific cosmology—which reinstates today references to purpose into scientific discourse.* Shortly after the discovery of the 2.7° K radiation cosmologists began to wonder at the extremely narrow margin allowed for cosmic evolution. The universe began to appear to them more and more as if placed on an extremely narrow track, a track laid down so that ultimately man may appear on the scene. (Varghese 1984, p. 71 [emphasis added])

Thus, it is "no wonder that in view of this quite a few cosmologists, who are unwilling to sacrifice forever at the altar of blind chance, began to speak of the Anthropic Principle." They seemingly were forced by their own findings to formulate this "principle of man." This is because it seems more and more like the universe "may have after all been specifically tailored for the sake of man" (Varghese 1984, p. 72). In reality, this is a very old philosophical view. In fact, a central tenet of Thomas Aquinas's philosophy is that the universe was created for the sake of humankind.[5] But as Jaki reminds us: "It must not, however, be forgotten that such a tenet, or the Anthropic Principle, can never be a part of scientific cosmology. Science is about quantitative correlations, not about purpose" (Varghese 1984, p. 72).

Second, Flew is incorrect that his third "type" of argument to Design—the anthropic principle *as he relates it*—"is the most powerful form." The arguments from science to which I referred in Chapter IV are not just from an external "anthropic principle," but from a much stronger "internal" one that unites both the principles of physics ("external") and the complexity of life and intelligent life ("internal") to argue from a worldview based on an incredibly complicated (to say it mildly) universe in every part of it to the existence of a personal God.

Third, given these various quantitative relationships in physics and intelligent life, for example, from information theory, enzymes, and so on, that indeed drawn "exactly" from the "same laws and principles" (at least as argued by the scientists to which I have referred), the force of the argument is that evolution is *not* possible! Flew even admits that the "circumstances" that favor evolution "even as it is, seem to be excessively rare" (V, p. 143). He says that Leslie's conclusion is that "our universe is spectacularly 'fine tuned for Life.'" I certainly agree! Also, Flew writes, with regard to the possibility of making "all these many items of fine tuning comfortably unremarkable we should need to postulate the actual existence of some even more fabulous number of additional universes." And then Flew says: "That, as Leslie modestly refrains from pointing out, must be accounted a heroic saving hypothesis to end all heroic saving hypotheses!" (V, p. 144). This is an important admission! When will Flew recognize this to be also true of his own continual arguing for atheism against the opposing evidence?

Flew ends this section of his argument with the following comment: "Like other arguments to design . . . [they] certainly do not themselves support the contention that our Universe is the creation of an omnipotent, omniscient, and otherwise perfect God" (V, p. 144); that is, the God for which I [Miethe] am arguing. Perhaps not, but they raise (at the very least) a very strong "pointing finger" to where the other arguments *do* take us. And, they may well take us to God himself (as many modern scientists now think). This remains to be seen, as the logical implications of the real complexity of the universe and of life are now beginning to be fully understood. But at the very least, we have here not a "God of the gaps" argument, but the kind of scientific argument Flew has indicated it "would, surely, be wiser" for theists "to develop [that is] a natural theology from the regularities and the wonders that scientists have discovered."

3. "The Significance of Choice"—Response

Flew starts this section by admitting (that in "a short paragraph" in Chapter IV) I took his "breath away" (V, p. 144). I am glad I finally had at least some small effect on him in the context of this debate, for Flew seems (up to this point) to have largely ignored *my arguments*. This fact remains: this debate *is not* about the problem of evil. Flew repeatedly misses the point. It is not that I do not think this issue is (or other issues he raises are) important. I do! But this book is not, cannot be, about it (them)! This debate is (supposed) to be about the question of the *being* or existence of God.

I will readily admit—and have said so repeatedly to my students— that the problem of evil is the most difficult problem for the Christian to answer. This admission, though, does not mean that I do not think it has been answered. In fact, I think Augustine, when he "established the main lines of thought that were followed by the majority of Christian thinkers" regarding the problem of evil over 1,560 years ago, actually did a rather good job of it (Miethe 1984, p. 127–32).

But my point is that *this* debate is about the existence of God. And, if this issue—the existence of God—is going to be effectively treated we must set (1) the foundation by addressing the problems raised historically in the discipline of metaphysics, for example, the starting point of metaphysics, the empirical foundations of metaphysics, a metaphysics of creation, the real distinction, the meaning of power, and so on. These I have presented (II, pp. 71–83; IV, pp. 117–22) while Flew has yet to even really address them, let alone answer them in this debate. We must recognize as well and (2) see there are limits to what can be effectively covered in one debate. Flew repeatedly tries to "water down" our debate by raising "most every problem" in the history of philosophy of religion, issues that are not directly relevant to the topic of this debate, or by "attacking" issues I am not arguing. Flew knows better than this! This is at best a diversionary tactic. Flew knows we cannot treat in any fashion (let alone adequately) all the issues that might *relate* to the existence of God in one book. I must admit, however, that throughout the course of this debate I have probably been too lax in allowing these diversionary tactics. But I have allowed them to show that I have tried (1) to take Flew's arguments seriously and (2) to show, however briefly, that there are answers to *his* arguments.

Interestingly enough, much of what Flew seems to want to argue is at issue really *only after* the existence of God has been established. After all, the "problem of evil" is not really a problem—protest as Flew may—unless we have an objective standard of goodness. This is ultimately true practically and logically. If there is no God then what is "evil"? Who, then, is to say which individual interpretation—everything is relative if there is no Absolute to inform the system—is "good" or "evil" or that "might does not make right!"

When I say "Flew continually ignores the implications of the freedom of the will to this problem [the problem of evil]" (IV, p. 110), I mean in *this* debate. Flew continually raises the issue/problem when it is not the subject of this debate, then acts as if no one had ever seriously addressed the implications of the problem of evil. He remind us of "two or three" of his previous publications. Flew writes: "Since experience of choice and agency may well be an important part of what Miethe is forever accusing me of ignoring, . . . it remains perhaps barely worthwhile just to mention . . ." what he argues in his publications: *A Rational Animal and Other Philosophical Essays on the Nature of Man* (Flew 1978) and *Agency and Necessity* (Flew 1987, with Godfrey Vesey). But I have never accused Flew of denying "experience of choice and agency," but rather of not realizing the *implications* of freedom of the will and the Christian claim that we are created in the image of God to the problem of evil. Does Flew treat in either of these publications mentioned the issue of the freedom of choice (or the Christian defense of free will as an answer) to the problem of evil? Does he treat (even acknowledge) the implications of free will to being created in the image of God? I have both of these books by Flew. He does not!

I remind you of what Flew has written: "The least inadequate earthly analogue to the relation between creatures and their ever-sustaining Creator has to be that of puppets to their puppet-master." And later, "The introduction of this unlovely picture is bound to provoke indignation and protest" (I, p. 31). Further, Flew writes: "For the contention is not that theists in the Mosaic tradition do always, or even often, think in this way, but that these are in truth, albeit widely unrecognized, *necessary consequences of doctrines to which they are as such explicitly and categorically committed*" (I, p. 31 [emphasis added]). Flew says that protesting this picture by claiming free will misses the point. But—as I have said—he is dead wrong here. I think he misses the point or misunderstands the implications of being created in the image of God and the ramifications of this to personhood and freedom of the human will.

Flew tells us that "way back early in 1955" he believes he "first introduced the since widely adopted label 'free will defense'. . ." (V, p. 145). Now, in Chapter I (p. 30–31) Flew tells us "that . . . puppets to their puppet-master" is the contention he thinks is "in truth . . . [the] necessary consequence" of doctrines to which Christians "are as such explicitly and categorically committed." Then, he tells us in Chapter V (p. 145) that "my contention was not and is not that there is no such thing [as freedom of the human will]." Which is it, Prof. Flew? You cannot have it both ways. Surely, "puppets to their puppet-master" does not represent *any* possible concept of freedom of the will.

"What I actually did maintain, first thirty-five years ago . . . is that an omnipotent and omniscient Creator cannot by any means be relieved of responsibility for either the right or the wrong choices made by that Creator's human creatures" (V, p. 145), writes Flew. I obviously disagree. But, first, notice that we are again talking about "an omnipotent and omniscient Creator" as if he existed. This—again—completely misunderstands the implications of being created in the image of God and the implications of the freedom of the will to the nature of human beings.

What are the implications of being created in God's image? It should be obvious from the beginning that God is the rational being. Humankind's creation in the image of God (Gen. 1:27) carries with it the particular ability of rationality or thought. The human person, commonly defined as a rational animal, is responsible only because of the mind and what that entails: a capacity for knowing and discerning. The statement "God made man in his own image" logically implies that humankind's very nature is such as to be rational.

A very important part of being created in God's image, and therefore being rational, is free will. For God to create us in his image, to delegate rationality to us of necessity, entails that God has also delegated sovereignty to us, that is, the freedom to act and to be responsible for our actions. It is not uncommon for some philosophers to define freedom out of existence. Some use symbolic or modal logic to prove humans are determined and therefore not free. But such could hardly be the case. Just because the physicist has to stop motion to measure it does not mean there is no such thing as motion, any more than just because the philosopher defines freedom out of existence, it means there is no such thing as freedom.

What is needed is a more rigorous empiricism, for it is obvious that we all experience reality as though we do indeed have free choice. The ability to know is itself evidence of freedom. As Samuel M. Thompson has said so well:

> That man is free we may be confident, as confident as we are that man is capable of knowing. For unless man is free, capable of some kind of genuine creative act [this certainly would not be true of Flew's puppets—T. M.], then he cannot know. He can only react [could Flew's puppets even "react"?—T. M.], and his supposed awareness that he can react is only another reaction, and so on endlessly. . . . Determinism is not, and never was, a working philosophy of life. One can conceivably die but it; no one ever consistently lived by it. If people would reflect more simply and sincerely on their actual experience of living they would be less vulnerable to a great deal of academic nonsense, and philosophy would be the gainer. In essence determinism is one of those theories which, as Professor Broad said of behaviorism, 'are so preposterously silly that only very learned men could have thought of them.'" Whether or not we are in fact free is a question only for those who wish to play games with concepts [Prof. Flew]. Once we see what the question is we see that the very possibility of considering it *as a question to which true or false answers may be given* presupposes the fact of freedom. (Thompson 1955, pp. 178–79).

Trueblood quotes Lewis Mumford in this regard: "If man were 'just an animal' he would never have found that fact out" (Trueblood 1957).

It has been said many times, by many different people, that the human is the only animal who laughs, the only one who weeps, the only one who prays, the only one who walks fully erect, the only one who makes fires, the only one who can invent, the only one with a written language, the only one who is proud, the only one who can make progress, the only one who guides his own destiny, the only one who is penitent, and the only one who needs to be. Humans are unique by virtue of the very fact that they puzzle about their uniqueness. They are part of nature, but they are also more than nature. Yes, we have appetites, but we can deny their satisfaction by conscious purpose to the extent that a human being can actually willfully starve to death.

Freedom, then, is crucial.[6] The gift of freedom enters into almost every distinct human experience. "It bears, for example, upon the reality of sin, because the fact that man *can* sin represents a remarkable ability. [If we were only the puppets Flew mentions we would not have the ability to sin, nor would the problem of evil be a problem.—T. M.] No other creature known to us can sin at all. . . . The heart of positive freedom is the twin experience of *deliberation* and *decision*" (Trueblood 1957, pp. 277–79). As one systematic theologian has said: "To say that the stronger motive always prevails is an empty tautology, since the test by which a motive is proved stronger is simply that it prevails" (Tillich 1951, p. 184).

As Thompson writes: "Knowledge is a guide, but not, in its role as knowledge, a cause" (1955, p. 184). The example has been given of a music score. It may guide the musician's performance, but it does not cause his performance.

> He may follow it or not, as his ability permits and as he pleases. It makes no difference to the score whether he plays the music or not, and it makes no difference to the musical meaning of the score. The score is not itself a part of the performance. It is only a guide which the player may follow. If a music score caused the player to follow it then to learn to play a musical instrument would be an easy matter. (Thompson 1955, p. 184)

Insofar as humans are free, they can act in a way that is considered appropriate to the occasion or in a way that is not, but obviously they can choose. Thompson goes on to say:

> The confusion concerning causes and occasions is a part of the same misunderstanding which enables some philosophers to consider cognition as itself only one among man's many reactions to stimuli. Knowledge, on this view, is just another effect of causes operating on the organism, and it in turn is the cause of other effects. Knowledge, in short, is considered simply one of the connecting links in the casual chain of human behavior. This is only one more way in which

philosophical naturalism commits its characteristic fallacy, the fallacy of
mistaking essence for existence. (Thompson 1955, p. 185)

There are many obvious difficulties with determinism. It is faced
with two "tremendous contradictions." (1) The contradiction concerning
truth. If we are to take determinism seriously, it would necessitate the
idea that all intellectual judgment is itself determined. This would have
to apply even to the judgment that determinism is true. "The damning
fact about mechanistic determinism is that it undermines the possibility
of truth and yet claims to be true" (Trueblood 1957, p. 281). Trueblood
goes on to write:

> The climax of this criticism is that determinism provides no intelligible
> theory of error. It holds that error occurs and is, indeed, extremely
> common, inasmuch as so many people have not become convinced
> determinists, but it does not tell us how error is possible, how error can
> be detected, or even what error is. (Trueblood 1957, p. 281)

(2) Causal determinism destroys "the very planning on which so much
store is set." The determinist does not like the fact that freedom to
decide "brings in an incalculable element that the planner seeks to
avoid." Yet if complete determinism is true, the very idea of planning is
itself undermined.

> The paradox which the planner must face, however, if he is intellec-
> tually alert, *is that in the terms of his philosophy his very effort to plan was
> itself also determined by prior conditions.* Therefore, he does not actually
> plan at all, but is merely the helpless and passive performer of deeds
> which are materially necessitated. It is generally supposed that, by
> taking careful thought, we can make a better world, but men and
> women who are truly convinced of the determinist creed cannot be
> influenced by such foolishness. (Trueblood 1957, p. 282)

Human freedom is no restriction upon God's power. Exactly the
opposite is in fact true: "If God had to negate man's freedom and force
him to choose in the proper way, then His omnipotence truly would be
compromised." Freedom, again, in humans is delegated sovereignty
freely given by God to us because we are created in his image.

> Perhaps the basic error in the notion that there is an inconsistency in
> asserting both human freedom and divine omnipotence is the idea that
> God's power is a kind of compulsion, exerted upon and against other
> things. It should be plain to us, even from our own limited experience
> [Prof. Flew], that external coercion is the very feeblest of all forces when
> used against another's will. You may force another to act in a certain

way, but you cannot by force bring him to desire to do what you have determined he shall do, or to mean what you compel him to say. The stronger his will the further does your compulsion alienate him from your purposes. You may break his will, but then his acquiescence is not truly his act. If God is truly omnipotent He does not force man's will; rather He enlists it. Even when man's will remains defiant, God turns that defiance to His own purpose. (Thompson 1955, p. 503)

As one philosopher of history has put it: "Man's freedom, his capacity for genuine decision, is taken as fundamental, for without it there could be neither religion nor ethics" (Herberg 1951, p. 92; also quoted in Trueblood 1957, p. 289). And, as Trueblood has said: "Without the recognition of freedom we should have a woefully inadequate conception, not only of man, but likewise of God" (Trueblood 1957, p. 289).

Freedom is only meaningful in the light of the being and nature of God. We are free only because our freedom is derived from being created in the image of God. God is certainly free in ways that we are not. "The crucial difference is revealed in the observation that *man makes nothing that is free*. . . . The omnipotence of God is shown in the fact that He alone has made free beings" (Trueblood 1957, p. 290). Yet, though our freedom is different, limited as compared to God's, to *be* (in the sense of created in God's image) is to be free and to be free is to be able to create, both for God and for us.

God is a personal being. Much of the biblical language about God uses personal categories. R. T. France describes what it means to be personal:

A person is a conscious being, one who thinks, feels, and purposes, and carries these purposes into action, one who has active relationships with others—you can talk to a person, and get a response; you can share feelings and ideas with him, argue with him, love him, hate him; you can *know* him, in a way which can only be described as "personal"! (France 1970, pp. 19–20)

Creation in God's image carries with it all the responsibilities of personhood described above.

God is a living being. He is actively present here and now. This is seen in the very name of God (Exod. 3:14, 15). The Hebrew word "to be" signifies a dynamic, active presence. God is actively related to humans; and humans, by being created in God's image, are actively related to God. Thus, being created in God's image enables humans to embrace *God's* rationality and *his* freedom and *his* personality and to have a capacity for a relationship with God.

Flew "argues": "But if you have defined your God as (morally) perfect and if *some of your other stipulations entail that the God so conceived would be a monster of injustice,* then your proposed concept is incoherent and hence not merely does not but could not have a fully corresponding object" (V, p. 146 [emphasis added]). It is precisely here that Flew is so wrong, makes his biggest mistake! It is based on his definition (understanding) that "the God so conceived would be a monster of injustice," not on mine. The God I am defending is *not* "a monster of injustice." This is exactly where Flew misunderstands the implications of free will and being created in God's image. It is humans who freely sin and humans who freely condemn themselves, not God.

Flew concludes this section with the statement that he is: "surprised that Miethe should think it so easy to discover a radical inconsistency in the teaching of the Angelic Doctor [Thomas Aquinas] . . ." (V, p. 146). It is not my intent to say that I had (nor do I think I have) discovered "a radical inconsistency" in Aquinas. In fact, I quoted Aquinas as saying: "In this matter [of predestination and human freedom] we must proceed cautiously so that truth may be strengthened and error avoided" (II, p. 70). I was pointing out that Aquinas should not be *used* to support the "other stipulations" Flew thinks both make God "a monster of injustice" and "an incoherent concept."

Then Flew says: "It seems that Miethe . . . simply takes it for granted as an obvious truth that anyone who employs the word 'predestination' must necessarily be contradicting anyone asserting the freedom of the will." Where does Flew get this? I have *never* said I think the word 'predestination' must necessarily be contradicting anyone asserting the freedom of the will." I have not even said here that I do not believe in some form of predestination. How ridiculous! I *have* consistently maintained that the "neo-Calvinistic double predestinarian" God is not the God of the Bible or the "morally perfect" God I worship! In another place, I have argued—in part—that the radical "deterministic type of Christianity" is the "Calvinistic Christianity" of neo-Calvinists, not of Calvin himself (Miethe 1989, pp. 71–96). Therefore, I will not "fight" with Flew—at least in this debate—if he thinks that Thomas and Calvin are not "different in [any] relevant way" in this regard.

4. "Persons and Spiritual Substances"—Response

I am glad to see that Flew is finally taking up some of my arguments/ questions (V, pp. 146–50)! Flew answers my question exactly the way I knew he would have to answer it. But, again, in so doing it seems he admits far more than he realizes.

i. My point is that Flew is here only playing "word" or "language games" based on his naturalistic bias. I have good reason to *fear* that Flew will never admit—realize—that the language games he insists on playing will never adequately account for reality as we experience it! But again I must try to help him to see. I have argued that there is more to a person than simply "flesh and blood" (II, pp. 52–55, 74–83; IV, pp. 124–25, 126–27). Flew simply refuses to acknowledge the evidence.

(a) Flew correctly asserts that his answer he "fears" "will not satisfy Miethe"; but not because of the explanation he gives (V, p. 147). I am not arguing what he thinks, nor making the assumption he relates. No, again, Flew misses the point. The question is: "On a naturalistic, mechanistic scheme where (how) do the 'thingamabobs' (living and intelligent beings) get (develop) properties, for example, life, intelligence, and creativity, that the 'whatsitsname' (*materialistic, mechanistic* Universe) does not have?" Again, we know much too much about matter to be materialists.

What precisely is the matter with "matter"? Matter has a past. Clearly, that which is itself an effect cannot be the cause of all things. But how do we know that matter is an effect and not the first cause? For this to be true, matter would have to be the author of life (as well as other aspects of reality we have mentioned). But how can it be? Matter itself has no life. For matter (the physical universe) to account for life, either matter would have to be animated by a "vital energy" and this would be distinct from matter (thus it would still not be matter that lives, but the "spirit" of matter) or, of course, we must posit spontaneous generation. If we did, we would have something without any cause coming out of nothing from which nothing comes (a scientific and logical "scandal" and impossibility to me, but—evidently—not to Flew).

What of the immaterial for the role of "creator," for example, a "force" or "energy" that brought all things out of nothing? First off, we must say that such a "force" or "energy" would have to be "self-existent." If it were not self-existent it would not be the ultimate source. It must be "external." "It" had to always have been there or one had to bring it into existence. It must be "personal." If it were impersonal how could it have produced persons? When you have said all these things you have described some of the (very essential) attributes of God!

There is yet another way in which effort has been made to avoid the causal argument: "being by evolution." It should be pointed out though, that most evolutionists have not appealed to it. Darwin, for example, believed that God made the original "gemmules" from which the world evolved. Nevertheless some have still professed to believe in "causal evolution." What are the position's "intrinsic merits"? If all evolved from evolution, from what did evolution evolve? We recognize ourselves again in the coils of the infinite regress. How can there be an evolution that does not evolve? Some would say that it does not "produce" this evolving world, it *is* this evolving world. This, however, is begging the question.

The legitimate question arises: "May not the Ultimate Cause have been the source of all mere existence and these "mere existences" have simply developed, under necessity, their own purposiveness?" (As I have indicated, this is the *minimum conclusion* of the anthropic principle, i.e., theistic evolution.) But, of course, stating it this way makes the question appear absurd. Perhaps no more absurd than it really is. It is also interesting to consider that for nonpurposive agents to develop purpose, which they did not have to begin with, would be self-contradictory. But will someone say that things may have developed purposiveness unpurposefully or accidentally? That is, we are thinking of nonpurposive agents developing purposeful actions that suit them for survival? This is the same as saying that unpurposing agents develop purposive action for the purpose of surviving (a double contradiction). So then, we know that this Ultimate Cause is a purposive cause.

(b) In Chapter V, note 3, Flew says: ". . . whereas machines must be nonliving and at least ultimately man-made, *organisms 'just growed' and are necessarily alive*. This is why I am myself uneasy about being described (II, p. 55) as one who talks "as if a person is . . . a psycho-chemical machine" (emphasis added). Nice language here, "organisms 'just growed' and are necessarily alive. . . ." But that is precisely the question, Prof. Flew! Come on now, do you really expect us to believe this? Protest as you may (undoubtedly will), but you have to explain both why (how) persons have life, intelligence, and creativity as resulting from lifeless matter and why they are not (of course, I argue that they are not) just "psychochemical machines" given the atheistic naturalistic view—your view. It is *your* view—atheistic naturalism—that really does not even allow for "human" puppets!

ii. (a) Certainly, we know that Flew likes to play language games. His "contention was about the meaning of person words . . ." (V, p. 148). Flew writes: "Against this Miethe offered arguments which were entirely beside the point, for they would show . . . that creatures of the sort correctly described as persons contain an immaterial component essential . . . to and distinctive of persons." Hardly beside the point! Why cannot Flew see that "evidence of the appropriate linguistic kind" is not entirely good enough when talking about an examination of reality as such! Because of his naturalistic (blinders) bias! The language must conform to reality, not the other way around.

In the next paragraph Flew says: "But to show all this, even if it had been shown, would not be even to begin to show that people *just are their immaterial components*" (V, p. 148 [emphasis added]). I am not trying to show that people "just are their immaterial components." I would be quite happy to show that what it is to be a "person" in the Christian view—and in reality as such—is to be a unity of body (material) and spirit ("life force" if you like; see II, pp. 48–55, 71–76; IV, pp. 126–27). As I have mentioned in Chapters II and IV, there is very good reason to believe—a great deal of evidence to support—that persons are not reducible to just "flesh and blood."

Flew tells us that he "was . . . characteristically conciliatory and open-minded!" (V, p. 148); that, he raised "certain difficulties" that must be "overcome, . . . difficulties Miethe has certainly not attempted to surmount and seems not even to have recognized" (V, p. 148). He then quotes from Chapter III, pages 103, basically saying that one would need to give a "*positive* sense to the idea of" an unfleshly component(s). To do this Flew says we would have "to explain how specimens might be identified." He tells us that: "the adjectives 'incorporeal,' 'immaterial,' 'unfleshly,' and 'nonphysical' are wholly negative." Again, I think Flew is dead wrong here. I have given both the positive sense he calls for, by which this component can be identified, and described the component in terms that are not negative in the sections of Chapter II (pages 49–55, 71–83).

Flew writes: "It might be thought that at least the difficulty about essential negativity, if not the difficulties of identification . . . could be met by stressing that the incorporeal entities are . . . spiritual substances (V, p. 149). Correct, Prof. Flew. If we define this "unfleshly" component (Flew's word choice, which is indeed negative and based on his naturalistic bias) as "spirit," surely we have something that meets his requirements, that is, it can be "identified" and is not "wholly negative." When I look in my Webster's dictionary, I read of "spirit": "1. a) *the life principle*, esp. in man, orig. regarded as inherent in the breath or as infused by a deity. . . . 2. the *thinking, motivating, feeling part of man*, often as distinguished from the body; *mind; intelligence.* . . . 3. . . . *life, will, consciousness, thought*, etc., regarded as separate from matter . . . [emphasis added]." Precisely, Prof. Flew, *exactly* what I have been talking about all along. I do not think it is hard to identify these "qualities." And, they certainly are not negative. You, on the other hand, are the one who has to maintain—and do in fact maintain—that all of these "qualities" are reducible to lifeless physical matter!

(b) Flew writes: "The difference between us is that he [Miethe] sees these phenomena as the work of spirits, whereas I also see them but as the activities of persons" (V, p. 149). I see them as activities of persons as well. No, Prof. Flew, the difference between us is that I explain them (these "unfleshly" qualities) *consistently* and *causally* as resulting from a cause in kind (God) where you (and other naturalistic, materialistic atheists who must assume that our experience is only of "person words" reducible to matter and chemicals) want us to believe that they (qualities like *the life principle;* the *thinking, motivating, feeling part of man; mind; intelligence; will; consciousness; thought*) just happen (by mere chance) or are the result of (come from) the evolution of lifeless matter into living beings (again by mere chance).

Further, Flew wants us to *accept* science when he thinks it supports atheism's "evolution of the gaps" theory,[7] but to *ignore* it or *deny* that the laws of causation apply to the questions of origin or "contemporary scientific cosmology" when the evidence is against his position. Even though he admits problems with, does not want "to minimize the inadequacies of the Darwin-Oparin-Haldane 'warm little pond' concept," he wants to totally ignore the implications of the recent positive evidence of science regarding the complexity of the Universe *and* of life. It is the theist who accepts *consistently* the principle of causality on which all of science is based, not the atheist who wants to plead an exception— a very big exception—when it comes to questions of origin!

In fact, Flew ends Chapter V (p. 149) by admitting that: "Certainly the characteristics Miethe calls spiritual are quite radically different from and hence not . . . reducible to . . . elementary particles or [the] . . . boringly suborganic range." And, then Flew writes: "But none of this constitutes a reason for insisting that the newly emerging characteristics in any of these successive ranges cannot be the properties of anything that is through and through material." Now, I—with this assertion by Flew—feel as if it "took my breath away"!

5. "The Ontological Argument"—Response

Here we are told that Flew does not have "affectionate respect" for "this grand old argument" (V, p. 150). I can certainly understand why, because if the argument is correct (valid), then it clearly does away with the language game Flew so enjoys playing (see IV, pp. 112–17). Flew has already told us that: "An analogous ambiguity afflicts the word 'necessity,' for when, for employment in an ontological argument, the word

'God' is defined as referring to a logical necessary Being, the required necessity is logical and carries the implication that to deny the existence of such a God would be to contradict yourself" (V, p. 141). Flew writes: "But if and when the biblical Jahweh is said to be a necessary Being, then his nonexistence is, presumably, being asserted to be not inconceivable but, in some more practical way, simply and sheerly impossible."

Though I am not arguing for the existence of God—in this debate— by way of an ontological argument, it seems important to point out here that Flew is oversimplifying this at best. What is really at issue in such an argument is the relationship of logic to reality and vice versa. If logic and reality are inseparably tied together, then to deny the existence of God proved by a valid ontological argument would be not just to "contradict yourself" or involve yourself in a "logical" contradiction but would involve a much more basic error. This is, of course, the force—if valid— that the second form of the ontological argument in Anselm (and in Hartshorne) carries.

Thus the question is: "Is the rationally inescapable the real?" By rationally inescapable is meant a noncontradictory view the only possible alternatives to which are contradictory. Of course, what is rationally inescapable is not necessarily psychologically or volitionally coercive, for one may believe or affirm a position that is really logically contradictory. A rationally inescapable position is coercive only if one wishes to make peace with the principle (or law) of noncontradiction. It is the only possible position one can hold *if* one wishes to be logical.

So then, the basis of rational inescapability is the law of noncontradiction. And, in order to prove that the rationally inescapable is really true one must show that the principle of noncontradiction must apply to reality; that is, it must be shown that the principle of noncontradiction must be true apart from our knowledge about it. This view is called cognitive independence. To say as A. J. Ayer (following Wittgenstein) that ". . . our justification for holding that the world could not conceivably disobey the laws of logic is simply that we could not say of an unlogical world how it would look" is insufficient, for this is only to say that the law of noncontradiction is *linguistically* necessary but not that it is *ontologically* so. Whereas if it is to be contended that the rationally inescapable is real, then it must be shown what is rationally inescapable is also *ontologically* necessary.

Furthermore, it will not suffice to argue (some maintain) that the law of noncontradiction must apply to reality because there is no way to deny the principle of noncontradiction without using it in the very denial, for all that this argument proves is that the principle is rationally undeniable or inescapable. It does not show that it is ontologically necessary. That is to say, something might possibly *be* unreal even though it is not possible to *think* of it as unreal. For example, one might agree that the ontological argument shows that it is rationally necessary to posit an Absolutely Perfect Being without agreeing that this being really exists. So then, in order to show that the rationally inescapable is real, one must prove that it is not possible that something that can really *be* false when we must inescapably *think* of it as true.

It will not help to say that this denial of the applicability of the principle of noncontradiction is contradictory, for this would amount to saying no more than the denial is not true because it is contradictory. And, this would be arguing in a circle: it would be using the law of noncontradiction to prove the law of noncontradiction. This is another way of saying that no *reductio ad absurdum* arguments can be used to prove the law of noncontradiction, for to say that the denial of the law of noncontradiction is absurd is to say that it is contradictory, and this is assuming the law of noncontradiction to prove the law of noncontradiction.

Is there any way out of this impasse? Is there any way to prove that the principle of noncontradiction must apply to reality and, therefore, that the rationally inescapable must be real? That is, is there any way to prove that the rationally inescapable is real without using the law of noncontradiction in the proof? The answer seems to be that there is no direct way to do so, for every rational proof would have to use the law of rationality (i.e., the law of noncontradiction) in the very proof of it, otherwise the proof would not be a rational proof. And what other kinds of proofs are there but rational ones?

But if there are no direct proofs of the law of noncontradiction, are there any indirect proofs? Certainly there are no valid indirect proofs of the law of noncontradiction of the *reductio ad absurdum* variety, for as has been shown, this is arguing in a circle. However, perhaps all is not lost. There is yet another indirect way to substantiate the ontological validity of the law of noncontradiction. Francis Parker (1967), for example, argues that any denial of the reality of the rationally inescapable is self-defeating, for to deny its independent reality is to affirm it in the same breath in which it is denied by implying that the principle of noncontradiction is true independently of our knowledge of it. That is, in order to deny its reality one must assume that one's denial is true of reality. But the only way one's denial of the law of noncontradiction could be true of reality is on the condition that the law of noncontradiction cannot be denied of reality, otherwise the very denial would make no sense.

Of course, this does not prove that the principle of noncontradiction is true of reality but only that it cannot be consistently or meaningfully denied of reality. There could still be some strange sense (some would argue) in which the rationally inescapable might *be* unreal even though it cannot be *thought* or *asserted* to be unreal. But arguments from silence cannot be used as "proof" in philosophy. The reason there is no way for anyone to either think or say that the principle of noncontradiction does not apply to reality is that the very act of thinking, of affirming, implies that the principle is really true apart from our thought about it. In other words, there is no way for anyone to think or state a consistent position apart from the principle of noncontradiction. And, if the denial of the principle is *no position at all*, then the skeptic has, as Aristotle pointed out, reduced himself to a vegetable—he is not really saying anything at all.

In brief, the bases for believing that the law of noncontradiction does apply to reality and, therefore, that the rationally inescapable is real are that this position is literally undeniable and its opposite is unthinkable. One may affirm its validity consistently but one cannot deny it consistently. The law of noncontradiction is not only used when one affirms it but it is used when one denies it. It is inescapable. In other words, in the very act of denying it the principle of noncontradiction affirms itself. It is affirmable but it is not deniable. And, there is no way for one to *think* otherwise than that the principle does apply to reality. The very "question" as to whether noncontradiction applies to reality is no question. It has no meaning, unless the law of noncontradiction does apply to reality. It is impossible to even think or question the position that noncontradiction does apply to reality.

6. "The Ultimates and Limits of Explanation"—Response

Previously, Flew chastised me (III, p. 89–90) for not putting forth my positive argument for the existence of God earlier in this debate. I answered (in part) that in Chapter II (pp. 71–83, for example) had been building the philosophical foundation for a causal argument and then—after repeatedly responding to Flew's arguments—I presented my causal argument in Chapter IV (pp. 127–37) as I had planned. Now (V, p. 151), Flew recalls the "original game plan" for our book, tells us he is about to violate the second of its "provisos" [each chapter should be substantially shorter than its predecessor], and then says his: "only excuse . . . is that Miethe chose to defer his 'Argument for the Existence of God' till the end of Chapter IV (pp. 127–37) rather than to deploy it at the beginning of Chapter II."

It was also agreed in the "original game plan" that Flew would start by presenting *his positive case for atheism* and I would respond to his arguments and then build my case. Now, Flew has spent—at his own discretion—thirteen pages (and five sections of his seventeen pages) in Chapter V (with many of these pages arguing *against* what I am not primarily arguing *for* in this book) and he has yet to mention my causal argument.

i. Flew starts this section by telling us it will be "most helpful" if he focuses "on questions about what can and cannot be explained" and "on what the conditions are under which we are entitled to assume that there must be explanations, and of what sort. In the nature of the case not everything can be explained" (V, p. 151). Very interesting. Again, Flew has made an important claim and/or admission. Again, it is quite clear that Flew is content to play language games and to believe that it is valid to ask us to accept the "big exception" previously referred to (VI, pp. 177–78), which the atheist *must* assume to avoid the implications regarding the nature of reality that are jumping out at him from all directions today.

Flew reminds us that: "every system of explanation must include at least some fundamentals that are not themselves explained" (V, p. 151). Here he refers to "general laws, laws in terms of theories, theories in terms of wider and more comprehensive theories, and maybe even further. . ." (V, p. 151). Surely Prof. Flew is not talking about "theorems" here? A "theorem" being "a proposition that is not self-evident but that can be proved from accepted premises and so is established as a law or principle." He calls these "fundamentals that are not themselves explained" "*laws*," and so on. Is he talking about an "axiom," which is defined as: "(1) a statement universally accepted as true, maxim (2) an established principle or law of a science, art, etc. (3) *Logic, Math*, a statement that needs no proof because its truth is obvious; self-evident proposition?" Whatever Flew is talking about here I must remind him that even these must make sense in the context of a noncontradictory worldview or else they are discarded—in logic, in philosophy, in science—for others that do make sense (fit) in the context of the worldview.

Flew tells us that this "inevitability of logic [is not] escaped by theists" (V, p. 151), "for whatever else they may think to explain by reference to the existence and nature of their God, they cannot thereby avoid taking that existence and that nature as itself ultimate and beyond explanation." I am indeed surprised by this sentence. This statement makes me wonder if Flew understands the causal principle or the cosmological argument as I am defending them. To be "ultimate" is not to be beyond "explanation."

I am reminded of a particular class session at McCormick Theological Seminary nearly twenty years ago.[8] The professor brought into our class a group of Chicago inner-city high-school students to "confront" us seminarians with the "real world." One of the high-school students—who was even more brash than we seminarians were—told the story of how he had recently "dumbfounded" a minister in his area. He walked into the minister's office and said: "You believe in God, don't you?" Minister: "Yes." Student: "You believe that everything has a cause, don't you?" Minister: "Yes." Student: "You believe that God caused everything, don't you? O.K., then *who* caused God?" According to the student, the minister had no answer.[9] The student's eyes gleamed with joy as he related to us how he had stumped the minister. Possibly, this student had been reading Antony G. N. Flew?

ii. The answer that should have been given to the high-school student is really rather simply (not to be confused with being simplistic). The cosmological argument is not arguing that "everything" needs a cause, only that "limited, finite, contingent" things (beings) need a cause. It is also essential to the argument to understand that such existence *cannot* account for itself—the causal principle. God's existence is not "beyond explanation." He is eternal! Surely, even the atheist understands and accepts this "category" of [eternal] existence, for either "God is eternal" or the "physical Universe as we know it is eternal"—unless, of course, atheists (and Flew) want to say that something *can* come from nothing, which Flew admits is not what Hume said. Actually, I first called our attention to this fact in Hume in Chapter II (p. 67)!

"Granting Hume's epistemological atomism—that all empirical impressions are 'entirely loose and separate'—there is no empirical way to establish a necessary causal connection for sensible experience" (Geisler 1974, p. 209). But, as we have seen, Hume's distinction of "relations of ideas" and of "matters of fact," his sensory (or epistemological) atomism, is by no means certain, nor is Hume's analysis of causality. But even if it were, my argument is based on existential causality, not empirical causality. This is where the fact that Hume himself never denied that things have a cause for their existence (referred to by me in Chapter II, p. 66, and admitted by Flew in Chapter V, p. 152) becomes very important. "Indeed, it would be ontologically absurd to suppose that something could arise from nothing."

As I have said, the principle of existential causality is that "every limited being has a cause for its existence."

> This principle is not based in any mere conceptional or definitional necessity but in the fundamental reality that nonexistence does not cause existence. Our knowledge of the fact of existential causality arises out of an analysis of finite being. The analysis may be summarized thus: (1) Existence as such is unlimited; (2) all limited existence is being limited by something distinct from existence itself (this limiting factor will be called essence); (3) whatever is being limited is being caused (for to be limited in being is to be caused to be in a certain finite way; a limited existence is a caused existence); (4) therefore, all limited beings are caused beings. (Geisler 1974, p. 210)

Thus the principle of causality is established by an analysis of what finite being actually is. Finite being is seen to be caused being, and caused being must have a cause of its being or existence.

Subjectivism has a long history and has had stout defenders. The weakness of the subjectivists' position is that they say, in effect, that we have to distrust and nullify a certain basic kind of experience which all people seem to have and all people seem ready to trust until they are convinced it is false. It is a basic judgment of experience that perception is the direct awareness of some real things that exist in their own right, independent of our awareness of them. Perhaps the most serious error subjectivists make is their neglect of experience itself, their failure to take account of our direct and immediate differentiation of perception from imagery. Subjectivists need to realize that our recognition of the difference between image and percept is so obvious and so fundamental to all our judgment that we cannot make sense of the attempt to deny it. The answer to subjectivism is that any theory that impeaches any basic mental act impeaches in principle the whole range of mental activity. It impeaches eventually reason itself, and thus it impeaches its own impeachment.

"Those who go so far as to deny, as did David Hume, that there is any difference at all [between image and percept] except a difference of degree of vividness and steadiness, also find it impossible, as did Hume, to put their theory into practice" (Thompson 1955, pp. 293–300). Thompson goes on to say quite accurately of Hume:

> In Hume's hands both the real world of nature and the minds which pretend to know it dissolve into series of bits of awareness which mean nothing beyond themselves except other bits and which have no relations among themselves except psychological relations. Hume's

honesty extended to the admission that he could not believe his own philosophy, by which he meant that philosophy fails in its attempt to make experience intelligible. What Hume did not understand is that the real failure lay in the basic presuppositions of the whole line of thought which he had brought to its conclusion. (Thompson 1955, p. 300)

Flew tells us "that it is impossible to know a priori that any particular occurrence or sort of occurrences either cannot be or must be the cause of any other particular occurrence or sort of occurrences" (V, p. 152). But, of course, this is exactly what the cosmological argument is *not* doing. The argument to the existence of God from existential causality is not a priori (nor, for that matter, is the Kalam cosmological argument), but argues that on the basis of an examination of reality itself we must draw a very important factual conclusion (see IV, pp. 136–37).

iii. It is quite correct, as Flew points out, that I am arguing a cosmological argument on the basis of existential causality. Flew writes: "Hence the hypothetical entities of the conclusions . . . must, at least in the present context, be Sustainers rather than Initiators" (V, p. 153). But there exists no necessary contradiction between these two, as Flew also correctly admits: "To say this is not, of course, to say that they could not also in truth be both." Certainly, the Christian God is both!

Yet, Flew tries to make it sound like an argument from existential causality is somehow deficient when compared to an argument from initiating Cause: "it is much more difficult to carry conviction with the contention that it is the mere continuing existence of the physical universe that requires some external explanation." To say that the argument from existential causality does not include initial causality amounts to no more than a very simplistic understanding of the argument and, in fact, misses both the import of the causal principle and the conclusion of the argument. It is simply not correct that my argument—or Aquinas's—is tied to Aristotelian physics. In fact, my argument is, if anything, more relevant given Einsteinian physics.

Flew moves "faster than the speed of light" from his assumption that "it is hard to see much force in any . . . putative existential proofs in the Thomist tradition"—based on what he thinks is the unassailable wisdom of David Hume—to simply dismiss Aquinas's Five Ways with the statement: "the Five Ways thus appear to be revealed as dead ends" (V, p. 153). Then, Flew, in an equally simple manner, proceeds to dismiss my cosmological argument (as he has largely dismissed the foundation I have laid) with three-fourths of a page—and half of that space is taken up by a quote from me; then Flew ends with a quote from the "Monster of Malmesbury." Unbelievable!

Obviously, not all philosophers are as sure as Flew that the cosmological argument reaches nothing but a "dead end," because each of the three historic forms of the argument are still defended today and deserve serious analysis: (1) the form of the argument based on existential causality as in Aquinas (e.g., Geisler 1974), (2) the form based on the principle of sufficient reason (Reichenbach 1972), and (3) the Kalam cosmological argument (Miller 1984; Craig 1979, 1980a, 1980b, 1985, etc.). This Flew certainly has not done! He could have used most—if not all—of the first twenty-seven pages of Chapter V much more effectively if he had given the cosmological argument this detailed critical analysis. I am reminded of a statement by Thomas B. Warren, a philosopher who debated Flew on the existence of God some fourteen years ago:

> And what attention has Dr. Flew given to those arguments? Has he taken them up and declared the validity or invalidity? Has he considered each and every *premise*, declared them true or false and shown you why? You know, as well as I, that he has not. My arguments stand clearly unassailed. (Flew and Warren 1977, p. 231)

I must admit that I feel much the same in this debate.

CHAPTER VII

My Last Word: "Enough"

Antony G. N. Flew

It is now high time, and overtime, for protagonist and deuteragonist to give place to tritagonist and tetragonist, and perhaps for others, although the ruins of my knowledge of classical Greek provide insufficient materials for the construction of their corresponding titles. So it is fortunate that I have precious little more to say that would not be a reiteration of things already said. Such mere repetition would be a scandalous waste of paper, since it is a quick and easy matter for any readers wishing either to reconsider or to refresh their memories to turn back the pages to earlier chapters.

I shall, therefore, confine myself to a scrappy series of brief, possibly abrupt remarks. First, Prof. Miethe asks the question: "What it is that (in part) constitutes a . . . person that is not reducible to or does not originate from the 'flesh and blood of a person . . . ?" Since I have insisted *ad nauseam* and beyond that people are members of a (very special) class of corporeal creatures, it should, surely, be obvious that I am maintaining that the characteristics of people are characteristics of— or, if you like, "originate from"—such corporeal creatures.

Second, Miethe asked: "What evidence will you allow to count for God's existence?" (IV, p. 127). This I shall not answer, because I have tried to show that it is the duty of proposers rather than of opposers of existential hypothesis to indicate, at least in principle, how the entities hypothesized might be identified. That this essential preliminary is here never satisfactory completed is, I believe, a main reason why questions about the existence of various Gods remain perennially disputatious.

Third, Miethe insists: "this debate *is not* about the problem of evil," but about the "existence of God" (VI, p. 167). Because he believes that this problem is soluble it is Miethe who misses the point. What he sees as an important but here irrelevant problem I introduced as a refutation, a refutation not of the claim that there exists a God of some sort, but of the particular God thesis presently under debate. Miethe then goes on to complain that I have never discussed "the Christian defense of free will as an answer . . . to the problem of evil" (VI, p. 168) and, in particular, not in Flew 1978 or Flew and Vesey 1987. Certainly, if I had wanted to refer back to an earlier treatment of that, then I should have cited (as in fact I also did) "Divine Omnipotence and Human Freedom" in Flew and MacIntyre 1955 or "The Freewill Defence" in Flew 1984a rather than either of those. But there was and is no call here for any reference further back than to Chapter I, 3, iii, and Chapter III, 4, in both of which places that is exactly what I did discuss.

Fourth, Miethe maintains that "if this issue—the existence of God—is going to be effectively treated we must set . . . the foundation by addressing the problems raised historically in the discipline of metaphysics . . . ," and complains that I do not even really address them, let alone answer them (VI, p. 168). Certainly it is true that I have refused to address these issues in detail and one by one. But that was because it seems to me that they are relevant, if at all, only to the question of the existence of a God of altogether the wrong kind. See Chapter III, 2, especially ii.

Fifth, Miethe reminds readers that I wrote: "The least inadequate earthly analogue *to the relation between creatures and their ever-sustaining Creator* has to be that of puppets to their puppet-master" (VI, p. 169 [emphasis added]). Miethe then goes on and on about human distinctiveness—as if I had said either that we are not, or that Christians believe that we are not, in any important way different from such this-worldly puppets. Most of his contentions under this head are such as I myself am not just reluctantly prepared to concede, but positively eager to assert and emphasize (compare, for instance Flew 1978 or Flew 1985). All these contentions are, however, equally irrelevant to the proposition actually in dispute, as the addition of emphasis will, I hope, now make clear. See again, Chapter I, 3, iii; and especially the final, shattering quotation, Rom. 9:18–24.

Sixth, it is perhaps worth giving one illustration of the extent of my agreement with Miethe's here irrelevant contentions. He quotes Samuel Thompson as saying: "Whether or not we are in fact free is a question only for one of those who wish to play games with concepts [Prof. Flew]. Once we see what the question is we see that the very possibility of considering it . . . presupposes the fact of freedom" (VI, p. 170). Those prepared to look back to Chapter III, 4, i may remind themselves that there—wishing, as it might be said, "to play games with concepts"—I argued that the crucial concept of necessitating determination could not even be acquired and understood save by creatures in a position to know that the thesis of such an universal determinism is in fact false.

Seventh, Miethe asks, "What precisely is the matter with 'matter'?" (VI, p. 175) and proceeds to provide many answers. Let us consider one of these: "that for nonpurposive agents to develop purpose . . . would be self-contradictory" (VI, p. 176). Presumably the point is that it would indeed be self-contradictory to say that something nonpurposive formed the purpose of developing purpose. But to point this out is not even to begin to counter the suggestion that the purposive might have evolved nonpurposively from the nonpurposive.

Again, Miethe has much to say about what, he supposes, matter cannot cause or must be caused by. All these arguments assume what Hume showed to be false, that we can know a priori that certain things or sorts of things either must be or cannot be the causes of other things or sorts of things. See, again, Chapter I, 4, i and compare Chapter V, 6, ii and iii.

I presume that the reason why Miethe persists in offering arguments of this kind as if they were possessed of real force is that he believes that, if he can dismiss "Hume's [positive] analysis of causality" (VI, p. 183), then he can by the same token dismiss Hume's great negative thesis. But the latter is certainly not logically dependent upon the former. Nor have I anywhere in the present debate assumed that that analysis is correct or, indeed, anywhere near correct. (It was in fact in 1954 that I first began to challenge it in print, a challenge later developed in both Flew 1961 and Flew 1986b.)

Eighth, Miethe believes that he solves the problem of identifying spiritual substances by triumphantly referring me to "Webster's dictionary" (VI, p. 177). Oh dear! Please remember what the problem was. It was not to tell us which human characteristics may be picked out as spiritual. It was to provide for the identification of spirits conceived as substances, as subjects of discourse, that is, which—unlike grins or tempers (V, p. 149)—can significantly be said to exist separately, apart from the subjects of which they may be predicated. The most that Webster or any of his competitors does for us is to answer the first of these two questions. Compare, again, Chapter V, 4, ii.

Ninth, Miethe quotes from the prepenultimate sentence of Chapter V, 4: "Certainly the characteristics Miethe calls spiritual are quite radically different from and hence not, *in his depreciative understanding of reducibility*, reducible to *characteristics either from the exceedingly narrow range of those truly attributable* to elementary particles or *from the vastly richer but still boringly suborganic range similarly attributable to manageably sized pure specimens of all the chemical elements"* (VI, p. 178). It is, however, only by omitting all the words here underlined that Miethe contrives to present that statement as inconsistent with my conclusion that "none of this constitutes a reason for insisting that the newly emerging characteristics in any of these successive ranges cannot be the properties of anything that is through and through material."

Tenth, Miethe maintains: "God's existence is not 'beyond explanation.' He is eternal! Surely even the atheist understands and accepts this 'category' of [eternal] existence?" (VI, p. 183). Understand, yes, but accepts that it is uniquely self-explanatory, no. Since what I said that I was arguing was that all explanation must end with ultimates that are not themselves explained, I in my turn am surprised to find that Miethe expects me to agree that "[eternal] existence" is, exceptionally, self-explanatory. And of course I was arguing what I was arguing not because I was ignorant of, but because I wanted outright to challenge, a fundamental assumption of the cosmological argument. It was because I believed—and do believe—that this fundamental assumption is false that I refused, as I see it, to waste space by examining any particular current version in detail.

President Wilson famously propounded fourteen points. Moses brought down Ten Commandments from Mount Sinai. Miethe at least will not fault me because, following the higher authority, I stop now at ten.

CHAPTER VIII

A Few
Final Words

Terry L. Miethe

Introduction

Antony Flew is certainly correct about one thing: it is high time that this Great Debate be brought to an end. Therefore, I will make only a few comments about Prof. Flew's "My Last Word." It is also time for our debate to be flung open to the floor. In my last section, "Open to the Floor," I will issue an important challenge to carry on the debate on the question of the existence of God into all the relevant and important areas Prof. Flew and I could only touch on or mention.

1. A Brief Response to Flew's "Decalogue"

In his second point, Flew tells us he will not answer my question: "What evidence will you allow to count for God's existence?" (VII, p. 187) Interesting indeed! It is entirely proper to ask the atheist this question just as it is to ask the theist its reverse. If *either* is going to be honest, then it can certainly be expected that *each* would have thought about what counts *against* his respective position as well as for it. I remember all too well, after I had already spent a couple of hours defending my master's thesis, I was then asked by one examiner: "You have written critiquing and criticizing Nietzsche's thought. Now show us that you really understand it by defending him." This is good scholarly practice. Intellectual honesty demands such! But Flew will not answer.

As to Flew's third point, it really amazed me that (1) Flew cannot see (as C. S. Lewis, a former Oxford atheist, showed) that for atheism the problem of evil is really circular (Lewis 1960, p. 45–46). The atheist is actually arguing that God does not exist because of all the injustice in the world. But how can there be "injustice" unless we assume a standard of justice? Gilson says:

> Even what is considered the most formidable objection to the existence of God, namely, the presence of evil in the world, in no way affects what has just been said about the presence of the idea of God in us. On the contrary, it rather strengthens the significance of that fact. If it is absurd that there should be evil in a God-created universe, the omni-presence of evil, since it is felt and experienced by all men with an overwhelming evidence, should make it impossible for human minds to form a notion of God. (Gilson 1969, p. 187–88)

(2) How can there be an *ultimate* standard of injustice unless we have an ultimate standard of justice? An ultimate standard of justice is precisely what the theist believes God to be. Clearly, the problem of evil is less so (for *who* is to say just what *is* evil) in a real sense if—as the atheist claims—God does not exist!

(3) For atheists' argument against God on the basis of evil to succeed they must assume the theistic equivalent of God. This is self-defeating. As has been correctly pointed out: "The dilemma of the atheist can be put this way. Either he stands inside a theistic position to criticize it as inconsistent or else he moves outside of it and finds his own grounds to stand on. But if he stands inside there is always an answer to his choice" (Varghese 1984, p. 132). (4) The atheist is constantly raising the problem of evil but never gives a solution. It is high time the theist called: "Foul!" I defy *the atheist to give an answer* to the problem of evil. It is Flew who has missed the point. The "problem of evil" is hardly a refutation of the Christian God as Flew claims (VII, p. 187–88). On the contrary, it is Christianity that has an answer.

In Flew's point four, he *admits*—"Certainly it is true that I have refused to address these issues . . ." (VII, p. 188)—that he does not treat the foundational metaphysical issues I raise (build) in Chapter II! Flew thinks it is enough simply to ignore them *because he believes* they are irrelevant to the Christian God even when I have argued the opposite in Chapter IV. I wish I would have known in advance that it was enough for one side in this debate simply to ignore what the other side thought was important. If I had (and if I believed this was intellectually honest), I certainly could have shortened my responses to Flew, which would have allowed me more space to build my case! Flew says he can ignore my metaphysical foundations because he believes "they are relevant . . . only to the question of the existence of a God of altogether the wrong kind." And, yet, Flew *repeatedly* (as I have pointed out) argues that the fact that there are many concepts of "various Gods" [his words] is an issue in this debate. Amazing!

In point five I am further truly amazed. Flew says: "Most of his [Miethe's] contentions under this head are such as I myself am not just reluctantly prepared to concede, but positively eager to assert and to emphasize" (VII, p. 188). In other words, Flew eagerly agrees with me in "most" of what I say about free will. Yet, Flew cannot see what I clearly show: (1) the implications of free will to being created in the image of God, (2) that creatures with such ability are not the puppets he postulates, (3) that a God who created such free creatures cannot be the kind of God Flew repeatedly wants to push upon us as the Christian concept, and (4) the importance of the freedom of the will to the problem of evil (which he steadfastly refuses to admit). Further, these contentions are hardly "irrelevant to the proposition actually in dispute" (VII, p. 188). Remember, it is Flew who repeatedly raises the issue. Also, it is important to remember that it is very difficult to understand how these free creatures, which Flew and I agree exist, could have evolved from lifeless matter and then developed purposiveness.

When I first read my friend Tony's point eight—especially the "Oh dear!"—I laughed out loud! This strikes me as a tactic I have seen sophomore college debaters employ to get the other side and the audience off the facts being presented. I quoted Webster's simply to show that it is not nearly as hard to come up with *positive* language for what constitutes "spirit" as Flew seems to feel it is, nor does it appear that a majority of people find it hard to define "spirit." The dictionary records the definition quite matter-of-factly, that is, as commonly understood usage. Flew goes on to say that the real problem "was to provide for the indentification of spirits conceived as substances . . ." (VII, p. 189). But this I did both earlier in Chapter II and also in building my metaphysical foundations, for example, "The Empirical Foundations of Metaphysics," pp. 74–76, "The Real Distinction," pp. 79–83, and so on, which Flew has already admitted he chose to ignore! Oh my! (Sorry, Tony, being equally "sophomoric—or at least having a "fun-loving nature" just as you do—I couldn't resist.)

Then, in point ten, Flew says that an atheist: "Understands [the category of eternal existence], yes, but accepts that it is uniquely self-explanatory, no" (VII, p. 190). Interesting statement when you consider the atheistic alternatives. I have argued there is an Uncaused—that is, eternal—Cause, God. An Uncaused Being is not a contradiction. If an Uncaused Being is a contradiction, then so is the atheist's uncaused universe. "Conversely, if it is meaningful and non-contradictory to speak of an *uncaused universe*, then it is also meaningful and non-contradictory to speak of an *uncaused* God" (Varghese 1984, p. 130). Further, I argued that only limited or caused existence (effects) need a cause. I grant that something must exist that *is* eternal. Remember, it is not the theist who wants to beg a very big exception, that causality is not relevant to questions of origin.

Again, you cannot have it both ways. Either you grant spontaneous generation (which is philosophically and scientifically contradictory—and I don't hear Flew loudly championing this) or that something is eternal. If something is eternal, then—clearly—that *is* its "explanation," is all the explanation it needs. The question is: What does the evidence indicate is eternal—the physical universe or God? In regard to this business of "spontaneous generation" I cannot help being reminded again of what George Wald, Harvard professor and believer in evolution, said as long ago as 1955: "One has only to contemplate the magnitude of this task of bringing together complex organisms in this manner to concede that spontaneous generation of a living organism is impossible. Yet, here we are—as a result, I believe, of spontaneous generation." Talk about a "leap of faith"!

Flew *again* pulls his "if I don't agree with it, I am entitled to ignore it" form of "argumentation." He says of the cosmological argument: "It is because I believed—and do believe—that this fundamental assumption is false that I refused . . . *to waste space* by examining any particular current versions in detail" (VII, p. 190 [emphasis added]). If I didn't know Tony better, I would say that such a statement "smacks" of real arrogance or intellectual dishonesty. Again, Flew can *ipso facto* decide that it is a "waste [of] space" to examine my argument and we [I, the theist, and you, the reader] are simply to accept his view. Yet, I have answered his (by agreement in the "original game plan" it was supposed to be) "positive" argument for atheism point by point.

Finally, with regard to Flew's Chapter VII, what a "cute" (clever) ending. Flew, having in his chapter ten points, makes reference to the Ten Commandments in the Old Testament. It is indeed interesting that Flew makes so many references to the Bible, but at other times in this debate wants to insist "revelation apart" (see I, pp. 8–9, 30; III, p. 98). Perhaps these Bible quotes are a vestige left over from his "preacher father." I kept waiting for Flew to present us with the gospel. Well, this philosopher, for one, is "not ashamed of the gospel, for it is the power of God for salvation to every one who believes." (Rom. 1:16). What is the "gospel"? I am reminded of that most beautiful scripture:

For God so loved the world, that He gave His only begotten Son that,
whoever believes in Him should not perish, but have eternal life. For
God did not send the Son into the world to judge the world; but that the
world should be saved through Him." (John 3:16–17, NASV)

This most certainly does not present the picture of the terrible, vengeful
God Flew paints whenever he refers to Christian tradition (I, p. 30).

Yet, in all honesty, I must quickly add that I very much agree with
Maritain when he said: "If books were judged by the bad uses man can
put them to, what book has been more misused than the Bible?" Clearly,
truth is the first casualty of a fundamentalist mentality. This mentality is
nothing short of bigotry, that is, "Don't confuse me with the facts, my
mind is already made up!" And bigotry is the antithesis of Christianity!
That is most clearly manifest when people preach and teach as if *only one*
interpretation to any given Bible text exists—*their own*! All you have to
do to see a picture of this phenomena is to turn on your television set to
practically any one of the many "televangelists." I have seen—and
experienced—this far too often myself!

2. Open to the Floor

I opened my first contribution to this debate (Chapter II) by recounting
that in the whole history of thought the question "Does God exist?" is
the most important a person can ask. I think we can now clearly see why
this is so. I quoted Trueblood that being an atheist very seldom makes
a person happy or popular. I agreed we should do all we can to
change this situation. Much later, Flew called our attention to the
"original game plan" for our book (V, p. 151). I remind Flew that the
"original game plan" we had agreed on was that Tony would start by
presenting *his positive case for atheism*. Yet, very few atheists have
presented a *positive* argument for atheism. Ultimately, it will be up to
you—the reader—to decide if Prof. Flew has done so here. Gilson
rightly says:

Atheists like to denounce the shortcomings of the proofs of God's
existence [at least when they don't think it a waste of space], and many
of the proofs are inadequate, but some of them appear convincing to
trained metaphysical minds, while there has never been a convincing
metaphysical proof that there is no God." (Gilson 1969, p. 197)

It is important to point out: "To reject that affirmation [that God exists] as
metaphysical is a great naivete. Of course it is metaphysical to say there
is a God, but it is equally metaphysical to say there is no God" (Gilson

1969, p. 198). Yet, Flew has not dealt with my sections on metaphysics or my argument for God's existence.

I also said we should "respect, even admire," (II, p. 38) a good person who is an *honest* atheist. But eventually we have to ask ourselves just what constitutes "honesty" (all "good" people are at times dishonest) in the face of the facts. Many philosophers are today talking about the collapse of modern atheism—not necessarily that there are less atheists, but that there is less reason for being one. The claim is that "there is a *collapse* of the *intellectual grounds* for *holding* an *atheist* position" (Varghese 1984, p. 128) because of the philosophical, scientific, and ethical evidence *for* the existence of God. Even the editors of *Philosophy Today* have said: "No responsible philosopher can escape reflecting upon the unique character and problems of contemporary atheism."[1] And, I add no responsible philosophers can simply accept their past assumptions, play word games, and ignore "particular current versions" of arguments because they "believe" them to be "false" or examining them to be a "waste of space." Such is neither good philosophy nor is it really even intellectually honest!

I believe Prof. Flew and I agree that how an individual answers the question "Does God exist?" is indeed most important and should affect his or her entire life. In fact, we can thank Prof. Flew for so correctly identifying as a third subclass "negative atheists," "those who refuse 'to allow the (nevertheless still asserted) existence of God to affect their everyday living'" (I, p. 10). Yes, this is quite correct. One cannot answer this question by stating a simple "Yes, I believe" or "No, I don't." The question has undeniable practical (affecting daily life) implications! Those who claim to believe in God and do not practice what they say they believe are just as much atheists as any.

In today's world it is the atheist who insists on an irrational leap of "faith," not the theist. Permit me to quote Antony G. N. Flew again: "Faith, as my preacher father used sometimes to proclaim in sermons, should be not a leap in the dark but a leap toward the light" (I, p. 13). When we look at the evidence from history, science, and philosophy it is the atheist who is leaping headlong into the dark, who is running away from reality. "Escapism" is running away from reality. It is the atheist who is the escapist, the one who refuses to look at the evidence and face up to the facts.

It is important here to point out that Tony Flew and I have agreed on several things, but the most important is that this debate is about the existence of the God of the Judeo-Christian tradition[2] (see I, pp. 2, 3, 8; III, pp. 85–86, 92–93; V, pp. 140, 141, 144). This fact makes it ultimately

important that alongside the philosophical arguments for God's existence many other claims need to be examined, for example, the whole
area called "Christain evidences," which includes evidence for the
historicity of revelation (and the inspiration of the Bible), the resurrection of Jesus (see Miethe, Habermas, and Flew 1987), and so on.[3]

You will remember I mentioned a recent opinion poll according to
which 95 percent of the people in the United States believe in "God."
Tony Flew and I both commented on the relative importance of this
poll—or lack of it. Well, to polls there seems to be a long history, and
unfortunately, no end.[4] In response to such a poll in Great Britain in the
mid-sixties, 94 percent of the people claimed they believed in a personal
God. Ultimately, the real question, then or now is: "But how many of
them do anything about him?" British theologian Michael Green admits
that: "The church has gone a long way to make Christianity incredible. It
is the church, not Jesus Christ, that is the main stumbling-block for
ordinary people."

"A great many people who are all too ready to dismiss religion with a
wave of the hand are themselves unwilling to face up to the challenge of
Jesus Christ." Green goes on to say:

> If Christianity is wrong about our origin or destiny, the purpose and the
> meaning of life, the value of persons and the secret of living together in
> community, then get up and say so! Say it violently, agressively if you
> like: but say it *after you have personally examined the evidence.* Yet this is
> precisely what so many are apparently too afraid or too lazy to do. On
> matters of such vital importance they are content to be guided by scraps
> of information gleaned long ago in the Sunday school, by the latest
> newspaper attack on the faith, or by the voice and visiting habits of the
> local clergy!

What is the challenge of Christianity? "People are afraid of facing up to
the challenge of Christian standards of behaviour and Christian disci-
pleship" (Green 1968, p. 117–18). I, too, am convinced that a large part of
modern apathy about God, and Christianity, is a result of nothing less
than ignorance, fear, personal hurt (many have been terribly hurt by
"Christians" and by churches), and general escapism.

It is interesting, too, to remember what Prof. Flew tells us in Chapter
I on page 11, when he says—in effect—that he is not "demanding that
the debate should proceed on either a positive or a negative atheistic
assumption. That would indeed preclude a theistic conclusion." This is
exactly what I think Prof. Flew has done, that is, proceeded on an
atheistic ("positive" or "negative" makes no difference) assumption that

does—given his position—preclude a theistic conclusion! Note that while Flew wants to tell us that his "presumption of atheism is as much impartial between rival disputants as the presumption of innocence," his very next words after that comma are: "it is fair and proper for me to state now and in so many words that I do nevertheless believe that, in the fresh perspective proved by this proposed presumption, the whole enterprise of theism appears even more difficult and precarious than it did before" (I, p. 12). But I *must* ask, "What "fresh perspective"?—and "proved," hardly! At the very least, I think you will agree that this is a most interesting statement when you examine it in the light of Flew's total argument.

Finally, I too want to issue a challenge to *you*, the reader, atheist or theist: spend the rest of your life examining the evidence for the position you hold. As Gilson (himself acknowledged as a great philosopher) said about the question of the existence of God: "one hardly needs a Gallup Poll among professors of philosophy in order to determine the correct answer, the more so inasmuch as the professors of philosophy might happen not to be the best possible judges of the question" (Gilson 1969, p. 182). What I think—or what Prof. Flew thinks—does not absolve you of the responsibility of answering the question for yourself!

My good friend William F. Luck[5] has pointed out that we need to expose "atheism for the sterile philosophy it is." Prof. Flew wants us to believe he has presented us with a "new" argument while he feels it is sufficient to ignore "particular current versions" of arguments I have presented. "The idea that the contemporary [atheistic] position on the question is new is an illusion. There is nothing new about materialism" (Gilson 1969, p. 200). And atheism—by definition—is always fundamentally materialism!

Is atheism a philosophy you can live with intellectually and practically? I challenge you to examine all the arguments, to build a consistent worldview that you *can live with*, and then to try to live consistently by what you claim to believe. This debate has (in the sense of this one book) ended for Tony Flew and myself, but perhaps it is just beginning for you. No matter where you are "on the road" to truth, I challenge you to keep moving ahead because *veritas vos liberabit* (the truth shall make you free)![6]

The Claims of Theology

A. J. Ayer

A. The Existence of God

In W. H. Mallock's satire "The New Republic," which was first published in the 1870s, at a time when the conflict between science and religion was at its height, a character representing Dr. Jowett is made to admit that an atheist opponent can disprove the existence of God as he would define him. "All atheists can do that." This does not, however, disturb the doctor's faith. "For," he says, "the world has at present no adequate definition of God; and I think we should be able to define a thing before we can satisfactorily disprove it."[1]

I said this was a satire, but the words which are put into Jowett's mouth represent a point of view which is still not uncommon. People who try to justify their belief in the existence of God by saying that it rests on faith are sometimes maintaining no more than that the proposition that God exists is one which they have the right to accept in default of sufficient evidence; but sometimes they look to faith for the assurance that the words "God exists" express some true proposition, though they do not know what this proposition is; it is one that surpasses human understanding. The first of these positions is discussable, though I think it misguided, but the second is merely disingenuous. Until we have an intelligible proposition before us, there is nothing for faith to get to work on. It can be an article of faith that beings of superhuman intelligence, if there are any, entertain propositions that we cannot grasp. This requires only that we can make sense of the expression "beings with superhuman intelligence." But if we really cannot grasp these propositions, if the sentences which purport to express them have no meaning for us, then the fact, if it were a fact, that they did have meaning for some other beings would be of little interest to us, for this meaning might be anything whatsoever. The truth is, however, that those who take this

Originally published as Chapter Ten in *The Central Questions of Philosophy* by Sir Alfred Ayer. London: George Weidenfeld & Nicolson, Limited, 1973. Reprinted with permission.

position do understand, or think they understand, something by the words "God exists." It is only when the account they give of what they understand appears unworthy of credence that they take refuge in saying that it falls short of what the words really mean. But words have no meaning beyond the meaning that is given them, and a proposition is not made the more credible by being treated as an approximation to something that we do not find intelligible.

In fact, the world is not without descriptions of gods, whether or not they severally or collectively count as adequate definitions. Until we are provided with a criterion of adequacy, this is a detail that need not detain us. Thus, those who believe in many gods tend to ascribe properties to them which fit the human activities over which they are thought to preside. The god of war is martial, the god of love amorous. In some, though not in all cases, these gods are at least intermittently corporeal and they operate in space and time. Those who believe that there is just one God are in general agreement that he is an intelligent person, or something like one, that he feels emotions such as love or moral indignation, that he is incorporeal, except in the case of the Christian God, when, for a period of about thirty years, if one assumes the identity of the Son and the Father, he had what are ordinarily supposed to be the incompatible properties of being both corporeal and incorporeal, that, again with this exception, he is not located in space, though capable of acting in space, that he is either eternal or with the same exception not located in time, though capable of acting in time, that he created the world and continues to oversee it, that he is not subject to change, that he is all-powerful and all-knowing, that he is morally perfect and consequently supremely benevolent, and that he necessarily exists.

There may be some doubt whether the predicates that are ascribed to this one God are all of them meaningful or mutually consistent. For instance, we have found reason to think that if the notion of disembodied persons is intelligible at all, they must at least be located in time. Neither is it clear how a being that feels emotions can fail to be subject to change, unless we suppose that he feels the same emotions with the same intensity all the time, in which case there must be some danger of their sometimes lacking their appropriate objects. What is anyhow obvious is that these different predicates are for the most part not logically connected. We shall have to consider later on whether it is possible to make sense of the idea that the world was created. If this is a significant proposition, it may be taken to entail that the creator was intelligent. It may also be taken to entail that he was incorporeal, on the ground that the existence of a physical body could not precede the existence of the universe, though then it is not clear why the same should not apply to the existence of a mind. It surely does not entail that the creator is eternal; he might have come into existence at any time before he created the world or ceased to exist at any time after. Neither does it entail that he is all-powerful. He might have wished but been unable to create a different world, and having created the world that he did, he might subsequently have found that it escaped wholly or partly from his control. It might also develop in ways that he was unable to foresee. Clearly also, there is no logical connection between having any degree of power, including the power to create the universe, and being morally good. Indeed, if one thought of the world's history as having been planned by its creator, a strong case could be made for inferring that he was malevolent. Finally, even if the creator could consistently possess all these other properties, it would not follow that he necessarily existed. If he was thought to be a God, his possession of them might be necessary, in the sense that they were ascribed to any God by definition, but this would not entail that it was not a contingent proposition that the definition was actually satisfied.

The idea that God necessarily exists is worth pursuing, since it is involved in two of the best-known attempts to prove that there is a God. The first of these is originally due to St. Anselm and has come to be known as the ontological argument.[2] A version of it, not significantly different from St. Anselm's, was also advanced by Descartes.[3] The first premise of the argument is that God is perfect, in a sense which implies that no greater being is imaginable. This is taken to be true by definition. We are not told exactly what is comprised in perfection or greatness, but this does not matter to the argument, so long as it can proceed to its second premise, which is that a merely imaginary being is not so great as a real one. This also is taken to be true by definition. It is then argued that if God did not exist, he would not be the greatest being imaginable. But since by definition he is the greatest being imaginable, it follows that he exists. To say that he exists necessarily is, in this context, just to say that his existence follows from his essence or, in other words, from the way he has been defined.

Though some philosophers, even in our own day, have been convinced by this argument, it is surely fallacious. The most common way of rebutting it, which was suggested by Kant,[4] is to deny that anything can include existence in its definition. To define an object is to list the predicates which it has to satisfy, and existence, it is said, is not a predicate. For example, one may define a centaur as a creature with the head, trunk, and arms of a man joined to the body and legs of a horse. If one then goes on to say that centaurs exist, one is not adding another property to the definition, or predicating anything of the objects to which it applies, as one would be if one said that centaurs were bellicose. One is making a statement of a different order, namely the false statement that the definition is satisfied. In the same way, one may enumerate the properties which constitute a God's perfection as consisting in omnipotence, omniscience, supreme benevolence, or whatever, but in adding existence one is not listing a further property; one is saying, truly or falsely, that there is something to which they belong.

I think that this answer is along the right lines, but it is not entirely satisfactory because it places too much emphasis on a rule for framing definitions which one might think could be broken. For instance, if one looks up the word "centaur" in a dictionary one will find that centaurs are credited not only with the properties that I listed but also with being fabulous. If this were taken seriously as part of the definition, then in the improbable event that anything was found to answer to the other specifications of a centaur, it could not properly be called one: some other term would have to be found to designate this creature which differed from a centaur just in not being fabulous. In the same way, I suppose that someone could insist on making it part of the sense of the term "God," or indeed of any other term, that it carried an assumption of existence. For such a person, to say "God does not exist" would be a misuse of language, because the attribute of nonexistence would deny what the use of the subject-term had presupposed. But now it becomes clear that nothing is gained by this maneuver, since it remains an open question whether the subject-term has any use. Let it be written into the definition of a perfect being that he is not imaginary. The question whether there is anything that has all the other properties of a perfect being and is also not imaginary can still significantly be answered "no." Thus, even if we allow to St. Anselm that to conceive of a greatest imaginable being is to conceive of him as existing, it will not follow that there actually is anything to which this concept applies.

Does it make any difference if God is defined as a necessary being? There is some difficulty in understanding what this could mean, but I suppose it might be taken to mean that whatever predicates he satisfied, he satisfied necessarily. In this respect, though presumably not in others, he would be assimilated to a number. This is not, indeed, true of all the predicates which numbers satisfy, but it is true of some of them, and these would furnish the analogy. In fact, I think it very doubtful whether the comparison is tenable, but there is no need to press the point, as this move does nothing to save the argument. For even if it be granted that if the predicates in question are satisfied at all, they are satisfied necessarily, it remains a mere assumption that they are satisfied at all.

Sometimes when it is said that God is a necessary being, what is meant is that he is a being, and indeed the only being, that contains in itself the reason for its own existence. This was the position, or one of the positions taken by St. Thomas Aquinas,[5] who did not believe that the ontological argument was valid but thought that there had to be a necessary being in the foregoing sense. This definition of God was accepted by Spinoza and, as we have seen,[6] it led, in his case, to the identification of God with nature. The difficulty, as we then remarked, is to understand how such a definition could possibly be satisifed. If what is meant by a reason is a logical ground, the implication would be that God's existence follows from his essence, and we are back with the ontological argument. If what is meant is a cause, it is hard to see what sense can be attached to the proposition that something causes itself. What is the difference, one may ask, between saying that something causes itself and saying that it has no cause?

In St. Thomas's case, the fundamental idea appears to have been that the world cannot just happen to exist in the way that it does. We have theories which account more or less successfully for the observable facts, but the propositions which figure in these theories are themselves contingent, or if the theories take the form of deductive systems, it is a contingent matter that their axioms are satisfied. To bring the facts under laws is not to show that they could not have been otherwise but only to fit them into general patterns. We seek to simplify these patterns by developing more far-reaching theories, but however far we go, we always end in the position that this is how things generally are. The question why they are so is answered only by the production of another theory which leaves us with the same question to be asked again. The answer that we need is one that assures us not just that this is how things are but that this is how they must be. But such an answer can be forthcoming only if the final explanation is found in the existence of a deity whose actions proceed from his nature and whose nature could not be different from what it is.

There is an echo of this reasoning in the writings of modern existentialists, who conclude that the world is absurd just because everything in it might have been otherwise. Those who take this position do not see any reason to believe that there is a God, but they imply that if only there were a God, the world would have a significance which it tragically lacks.

In this, they are mistaken. The search for an ultimate reason is emotionally understandable but it is not intellectually coherent. To begin with, the recourse to a deity will not explain anything, unless it yields hypotheses which we can successfully project, and we shall see presently that it is doubtful whether this is so. Let us suppose, however, that this condition can be satisfied. Let us suppose that we can attribute purposes to God which account for the way in which the world is organized. Would it not be a contingent fact that he has these purposes? No, it is said, because they will be in accordance with his nature. Being what he is, he is bound to have these purposes. But then is it not a contingent fact that he has this nature, that he is, for example, benevolent rather than malevolent? No, it is said again, because his nature is included in his definition. But then we return to the fallacy of the ontological argument.

Not only that, but the necessity which is attributed to God's actions and the explanatory role which they are supposed to play are incompatible. From necessary propositions only necessary propositions follow. Their content is wholly abstract. They are consistent with everything that might actually happen. But an explanation derives its power from not being consistent with everything that might actually happen; it favors one actual pattern in contrast to others which are logically possible. So, if one could think of the history of the world as being regulated by a God's decisions, one would have to allow both that its history could conceivably have been different, and that the God's decisions could also have been different, if they were themselves to be explicable. Here too there would have to be a point at which the explanations stopped. No further reason would be given why God's nature was what it was, or, if this were made a matter of necessity, why there was a being with such a nature. If it were rational to settle for an explanation of this sort, the reason would not be that it did away with contingency, but that it made sense of our experiences in a way that scientific theories did not. But then it would have to be shown that this was so. It would not be enough to say that there was some explanation of this kind which we had not fathomed. This would be permissible only if the existence of God had been independently established. If the positing of a deity is to be justified by its explanatory value, the explanation has actually to be given.

B. The Argument from Design

Can it be given? Only, it would seem, if we are able to detect a pattern in the course of events which can be held to support the hypothesis that they are planned. We may then be able to develop a theory about the intentions of the planner which can be empirically tested. Again, it will not be enough to say that there is some plan or other. It has to be a system that we can successfully project.

The belief that the world affords sufficient evidence of an ulterior plan is responsible for the argument in favor of the existence of a God, which is commonly known as the argument from design. The proponents of this argument do not take it to show that there necessarily is a God, but only that the assumption of his existence is a reasonable hypothesis. Their position is elegantly and fairly stated by one of the participants in Hume's *Dialogues Concerning Natural Religion*. "Look round the world: Contemplate the whole and every part of it: You will find it to be nothing but one great machine, subdivided into an infinite number of lesser machines, which again admit of subdivisions, to a degree beyond what human senses and faculties can trace and explain. All these various machines and even their most minute parts, are adjusted to each other with an accuracy, which ravishes into admiration all men, who have ever contemplated them. The curious adapting of means to ends, throughout all nature, resembles exactly, though it much exceeds, the productions of human contrivance; of human design, thought, wisdom, and intelligence. Since therefore the effects resemble each other, we are led to infer, by all the rules of analogy, that the causes also resemble: and that the Author of nature is somewhat similar to the mind of man: though possessed of much larger faculties, proportioned to the grandeur of the work, which he has executed."[7]

Before we try to evaluate this argument, let us take a closer look at the conclusion. What properties is the author of nature supposed to have, and how is he related to the world for which he is made responsible? In the first place, as one of the other participants in Hume's dialogue remarks, there is nothing in the analogy to favor the assumption of a single author, rather than a multiplicity. There is nothing to favor the assumption that the world as we find it is the fruit of his only attempt to make a world, rather than the outcome of previous experiments on his own part or on that of others; if anything the analogy would point the other way. There is nothing either to license the inference that he is eternal or indeed that he is incorporeal; since all the

designers that we have actually observed have been mortal and embodied, the analogy, if it were to be pressed, would again point the other
way. It would suggest that his faculties are larger than ours, but not that
he is omnipotent, nor yet that he is benevolent. The ascription of
benevolence to him would require us to find empirical evidence not
merely that the world had an author but that it had an author who meant
well by the creatures whom he had put into it.

What now of the designer's relation to the world? If one supposes
there to have been an act of creation, I do not see how one can avoid the
conclusion that it took place at some time. If one supposes this to be the
first instant in time, one will find it difficult to say in what sense the
author of nature existed antecedently to its creation. The idea that he
existed outside time is one to which it is difficult to attach any meaning.
It is true that abstract entities can be said to exist outside time, if they can
be said to exist at all, but the activities which are attributed to the deity
are hardly such as are consistent with his existing after the fashion of an
abstract entity. A more intelligible theory would be that events in his
history temporally preceded the act of creation. This would be, in a way,
to include him in the universe, but on the assumption of his existence,
he would anyhow have to be included, if the universe was taken to
comprehend everything that there is. The creation of the world as we
know it would then appear more as a transformation, a radical change in
the total course of events, though not necessarily as a transformation of
preexisting matter. It is, however, to be noted that the analogy with the
makers of human artifacts is still further weakened if we suppose the
material world to have been created out of nothing at all.

In view of these difficulties, the proponents of this argument might
be better advised to lay more stress upon the metaphor of the *author* of
nature. Instead of comparing the world to a machine, which needed to
be designed and built, they could compare it to a play, which needed to
be written and directed. Among other things, this accords better with
the ordinary concept of creation. The author, who would also be
spectator and critic, would exist in time, but the time in which he existed
would be incommensurable with that of the incidents in the play, which
would have its own spatio-temporal structure. The participants in the
play would not be able to verify the existence of its author, except on the
dubious assumption that when they had played their parts they were
somehow translated into his world, but it might be maintained that they
could attach sense to the hypothesis that he existed, as the fundamental
principle of a secondary system which they could use to account for the
proceedings on their stage.

But now the question arises whether the character of the world as we know it gives any support to these analogies. The fact that regularities are detectable in it is not sufficient, for we have seen that no describable world can fail to exhibit some regularity. Neither is it sufficient that some processes within it are goal-directed, for the fact that ends are pursued and sometimes attained within a system is not a proof that the system as a whole is directed toward any end. What needs to be shown is that the entire universe presents the appearance of a teleological system. If one prefers the dramatic analogy, the play has to have a moral or at least some discernible plot. Can this requirement be met? It does not seem that it can. None of those who have compared the world to a vast machine has ever made any serious attempt to say what the machine could be for. They have spoken of there being an overall purpose, but have not said what it was. Again it will not do to say that there is a plan, but one too intricate for us to fathom. This answer might pass muster if the existence of a deity had been independently established, but if the sole reason given for believing in his existence is that the book of nature must have had an author, then the grounds for taking this metaphor seriously have to be produced.

Insofar as theists have held any view at all about the purpose for which the world was created, they have generally assumed that it had something to do with the emergence of man. This is a view which it is perhaps natural for men to take but hardly one that would be supported by a dispassionate consideration of the scientific evidence. Not only did man make a very late appearance upon the scene in a very small corner of the universe, but it is not even probable that, having made his appearance, he is there to stay. As Russell put it, "The second law of thermodynamics makes it scarcely possible to doubt that the universe is running down, and that ultimately nothing of the slightest interest will be possible anywhere. Of course, it is open to us to say that when that time comes God will wind up the machinery again: but if we do say this, we can base our assertion only upon faith, not upon one shred of scientific evidence. So far as scientific evidence goes, the universe has crawled by slow stages to a somewhat pitiful result on this earth, and is going to crawl by still more pitiful stages to a condition of universal death. If this is to be taken as evidence of purpose, I can only say that the purpose is one that does not appeal to me. I see no reason therefore to believe in any sort of God, however vague and however attenuated."[8]

C. Religious Hypotheses

At this point it may be objected that it is not fair to assess religious hypotheses in terms of scientific theory. We have seen that our reason for accepting the scientific picture of the world is that it accounts for the primary facts of observation in a way that we find satisfactory. At the same time we allowed that other methods of accounting for these facts might be conceivable. Instead, therefore, of trying to give a religious flavor to a scientific system which it does not suit, ought we not to consider the hypothesis of God's existence as the basis of a rival system which applies directly to the primary facts?

This indeed was the position taken by Berkeley,[9] though he did not put it in quite those terms. Conceiving of percepts as ideas in the mind of their perceiver, for which the perceiver's own volitions were not causally responsible, he argued that they must have some external cause. He rejected the theory that they were caused by material objects, on the ground that the belief in the existence of such objects, beyond the reach of our perception, was not only unverifiable but incoherent, and maintained instead that our ideas were directly supplied to us by God. He did not, indeed, suppose that God was any more perceptible than matter, but he thought that whereas we could have no notion of matter, we did have a notion of spirit, and he argued, invalidly, that because ideas were spiritual, as being in the mind, they had to have a spiritual cause. As I remarked earlier,[10] he also looked to God to keep things in being. Though he sometimes wrote as if he were prepared to conceive of the physical objects of common sense in phenomenalist fashion as permanent possibilities of sensation, his main view was that if they continued to exist at times when they were not otherwise being perceived it was as ideas in the mind of God.

Is such a position tenable? It is certainly not forced upon us in the way that Berkeley claimed. Though I think that he was very largely justified in his attack on the Lockean form of the causal theory of perception,[11] we have seen that it is possible to arrive at physical objects as abstractions out of percepts, and that once a primary physical system has been developed in this way, it may be legitimate to admit physical entities of an unobservable sort, if they figure in theories which have an explanatory value. We have also seen that it is a mistake to start by treating percepts as private entities, and there is nothing in their character to suggest that they must have a spiritual cause. Nevertheless, none of this debars the Berkeleyan system from being an alternative option. If anyone were inclined to take it, he would need to be clearer than Berkeley seems to have been about the nature of the ideas which he attributed to God. For instance, when God keeps things in being, is it through having tactual sensations of all of them simultaneously? If his ideas are visual, from what point of view are they obtained? To avoid such awkward questions, the best course would probably be to represent God just as thinking continuously of perceptible objects as having such and such properties and standing in such and such relations to one another, and as being constantly disposed to supply us with sensations that match these thoughts.

Such a theory, if it is allowed to be intelligible, cannot be directly tested. No experiments could be devised which would decide between it and a materialistic theory. The only reason there can be for accepting it is that it yields a fruitful arrangement of the facts of our experience. Does it do so? Does it yield any hypotheses that we can successfully project? The answer plainly is that it does not. To obtain a theory which had some explanatory value, one would have to make various assumptions about the tenor of God's thoughts and derive conclusions from them which our observations would confirm or refute. This is not, however, what Berkeley does. On the contrary, the ideas which he ascribes to God are simply a reflection of the commonsense picture of the world which we elaborate out of our sensations. So far from employing any assumptions about God's thoughts to forecast changes in our experience, he has to wait upon the course of experience in order to discover what God thinks. But this means that the part played by God is theoretically idle. Neither is it easy to see how this could be otherwise. Unless we simply have God thinking in current scientific terms, in which case his introduction is superfluous, it is not easy to see what assumptions could be made about his thoughts that would yield a genuinely explanatory theory.

But is this not to take too narrow a view of our experience? No doubt it can be left to science to order the phenomena which sustain our conception of the material world. But our lives are not wholly spent in the exercise of sense perception or the reasoning which arises out of it. We also have moral sentiments. Some of us have distinctively religious experiences. There are those who have claimed a direct awareness of God. To account for this range of facts, may not the adoption of a religious hypothesis be not only fruitful but necessary?

So far as religious experience is concerned, we have already answered this question in dealing earlier with mysticism.[12] The problem, as we then saw, is to determine whether and, if so, in what way such experience is cognitive. Again, I do not want to argue that it is impossible for it to be so. If experiences of this kind were widespread, and those who had them agreed in the accounts which they gave of them, I see no decisive reason why they should not be credited with an object. If it is conceivable for there to be mental states which are not associated with a body in the normal way, as we have seen that it may be,[13] this object might even be represented as a person. We should still have the option of accounting for the experiences in question in terms of the physiological and psychological states of those who had them, without allowing them any object, but we might think it unreasonable to follow this course if the accepted criteria of objectivity were very largely satisfied. The consequence, however, of allowing them an object would again be only that we should take a more liberal view of what the world contains. There could be nothing in the character of these experiences to justify any attempt to locate their object outside the world, nor could they sustain any such proposition as that the world had a creator. They might possibly confirm such a proposition if it had been independently established, but this has not been achieved. Accordingly, the answer to the claim that to have an experience of this kind is to be aware of God is that the most that it can come to is that the experience, or its object, if it is thought capable of having one, is endowed with a numinous quality.

D. Religion and Morality

Is there any support for religious belief in the fact that men have moral sentiments to which their actions sometimes answer? The view that there is has been quite widely held. The main arguments which have been advanced in its favor are, first, that only the agency of God can account for the existence of morality, and, secondly, that God's authority is needed to give our moral standards some objective validity.

The first of these arguments seems very weak. The assumption which underlies it is that it is natural for men to behave only in a purely selfish manner. Consequently, if they sometimes forgo their interests, or what they believe to be their interests, in order to serve others, or because they think that the action which promotes their interests is wrong, or that some other course of action is morally binding on them, the ability to behave in this unnatural way must have been given to them by a higher power. Even if the starting point of this argument were true, the reasoning would not be cogent, since it ignores the possibility that moral behavior can be adequately explained in terms of social conditioning, but in fact it is not true. Antecedently to any actual observations that are made of human behavior, there is no reason to expect it either to be selfish or to be unselfish; there is no reason to expect it either to conform or not to conform to any particular moral code. If it seems to us more natural for men to pursue their individual interests, this is only because they most commonly do so, at any rate in our own form of society. I believe that there are, or have been, societies in which it is more common for men to pursue the interest of some group of which they are members, their family or clan or tribe. But even if the prevalent tendency in all societies were for men to behave selfishly, it would not follow that unselfish behavior was unnatural, in the sense of being contrary to nature. Nothing that actually happens is contrary to nature, though there are some actions that we misleadingly call unnatural as a way of expressing our disapproval of them. In fact, I think that a good case can be made for saying that altruistic impulses are innate, though they may be initially weaker in small children than the self-regarding or aggressive impulses. If they are not innate, at least the evidence shows that we have the capacity to acquire them. But how did we obtain this capacity? This question is on a level with any other question about the causes of human behavior. It is no more and no less difficult than the question how we obtain our capacity to injure one another. If there were any good reason to believe that men were the outcome of a God's creation, their creator would be equally responsible for all their characteristics, however much or little we esteem them. Conversely, if there is otherwise no good reason to believe than men were so created, the fact that they behave unselfishly as well as selfishly to each other does not provide one.

In dealing with the argument that a God is required to ensure the objectivity of moral standards, we need to distinguish carefully between the motives for morality and its possible grounds. There is no doubt that belief in a God has frequently been the source of moral incentives. Sometimes the motive has been the altruistic one of love for a deity or a saint whose wishes one believes oneself to be carrying out or love for other human beings on the ground that they are equally the children of God. Perhaps more frequently it has been the prudential motive of fear of future punishment or hope of future reward. It was the belief that men were not generally capable of behaving decently without this prudential motive that led Voltaire to say that if God did not exist it would be necessary to invent him.[14] This is a good epigram, but like many good epigrams, it probably distorts the truth. I do not know that a scientific study has ever been made of this question, but if one were to be made I doubt if it would reveal any strong correlation either of morally admirable behavior with religious belief or of morally reprehensible behavior with its absence. Much good has been done in the name of religion but also very much evil. When the long history of religious intolerance and persecution is taken into account, together with the tendency of religious hierarchies to side with the oppressors rather than the oppressed, it is arguable that the evil has outweighed the good.

Many bad men have indeed been irreligious, but many agnostics and atheists have led very decent lives. Neither do those who are sincerely religious always live up to their good principles. My own conjecture is that the factors which make for the observance or disregard of morality are mainly psychological and social, and that religious belief has had a smaller influence either way than is commonly supposed. However this may be, it is clear that to show that belief in God had had a predominantly good effect would not be to show that the belief was true, any more than showing that it had had a predominantly bad effect would be to show that it was false.

I suspect that the widespread assumption that religious belief is necessary for the maintenance of moral standards arises not so much from any assessment of the empirical evidence as from a tacit or explicit acceptance of the proposition that if there is no God there is no reason to be moral. What is meant is that there is then no justification for morality, but because of the ambiguity of the word "reason," the fallacious inference is drawn that there is neither any ground nor any motive. The conclusion sought is that since there is reason to be moral, there is a God. This is the obverse of the Nietzschean idea that since God is dead, everything is permitted.

Whichever way it is taken, this proposition contains two serious errors, apart from the fallacy of thinking that the absence of grounds for morality entails the absence of motives. The first error is to suppose that morality needs an ulterior justification. The second error is to suppose that a God could supply it. The fallacy which is involved in thinking that morals could be founded on divine authority has been exposed by many philosophers, but perhaps most clearly and succinctly by Russell. "Theologians have always taught that God's decrees are good, and that this is not a mere tautology: it follows that goodness is logically independent of God's decrees."[15] The point is that moral standards can never be justified merely by an appeal to authority, whether the authority is taken to be human or divine. There has to be the additional premise that the person whose dictates we are to follow is good, or that what he commands is right, and this cannot be the mere tautology that he is what he is, or that he commands what he commands. This does not mean that we cannot look for guidance in conduct to those whom we judge to be better or wiser or more experienced than ourselves. To a greater or lesser extent, we can and do take our morals on trust but in so doing we are making a moral decision. We are at least implicitly judging that the rules which we have been brought up to respect or the verdicts of our mentor are morally right: and again this is not the mere tautology that these rules and verdicts just are what they are.

But if a moral code cannot be founded on authority, neither can it be founded on metaphysics or on science or on empirical matters of fact. Scientific and factual considerations are indeed relevant to morals, because of the bearing which they have upon the application of our moral principles. We have to know what the situation is in which we are placed and what the consequences of different actions are likely to be. If, for example, we think it right to try to maximize human happiness, a scientific approach to the practical problems may instruct us how best to set about it. The adoption of such a principle is, however, something which is not dictated to us by the facts. It is a decision for which it may be that we are not able to give any further reason, just as we may not be able to give any further reason for the value that we attach to justice or to liberty. In the end, it is a matter of finding principles which one is prepared to stand by and when they conflict, as for most of us they sometimes will, of giving more weight to one or another according to the circumstances of the particular case.

This does not mean that we have to regard every moral standpoint as equally correct. In holding a moral principle, one regards it as valid for others beside oneself, whether they think so or not. In cases where they do not think so, it will depend on their circumstances whether one judges that they are unenlightened or morally at fault. What has to be admitted is that there is no way of proving that they are mistaken. The most that one can do is argue *ad hominem*. One may be able to show that their principles are inconsistent, or that they are based on factual assumptions which are false, or that they are the product of bad reasoning, or that they lead to consequences which their advocates are not prepared to stand by. Even if we are successful in this, we may not persuade them to change their principles, but at least we shall have advanced some reason why they should. It may be, however, that we cannot find any such flaws in their position and still want to regard it as morally untenable. In that case discussion can go no further. This stage is seldom reached because it is nearly always possible to find a sufficient basis of moral agreement for the argument to proceed, but it has to be accepted as a possibility. Neither is this just the outcome of a subjective attitude to morals. The position is no different for one who believes that value predicates stand for objective, unanalyzable ethical properties. In the case where his intuitions of what is good or right conflict with those of some other moralist he has no means of proving that they are correct.

The difference between him and the subjectivist is that whereas the subjectivist is content to say that these are his principles and leave it at that, the believer in absolute values wants to say that his moral judgments are objectively true. Since, however, his only criterion of their truth is his own intuition, the difference is negligible. The merit of this sort of objectivism is that it avoids any suggestion of moral nihilism. Its demerit is its implication that value judgments are descriptive of something otherwordly, whereas fundamentally they are not descriptive judgments at all. I say "fundamentally" because they sometimes are descriptive of natural states of affairs; they convey the implication that the objects or actions in question come up to standard or fail to do so. But then the acceptance of these standards is presupposed.

E. The Freedom of the Will

From a logical point of view, the association of religion with morals appears rather arbitrary. Not only can morality not be founded on a God's decrees, but there seems no reason why the belief that the world had an intelligent creator should entail any conclusions about the way in which men ought to behave. If the purposes of the creator were thought to be known, one might derive some conclusions about the ways in which men would in fact behave, but that would be all. In the case of Christianity, however, the association is cemented by the belief that God, in the person of his own son, turned himself temporarily into a man, and underwent torture and a painful death in order to make it possible for sinful men to be redeemed from the punishment which he would otherwise have inflicted. In assessing this belief we have to balance the testimony in favor of such events as the virgin birth and the resurrection not only against their improbability, in the light of the rest of our experience, but also against the strangeness of the motive which is attributed to God. For it is very strange. In the first place, the very notion of vindictive punishment, the idea that if someone does harm to others, or even in certain cases to himself, one is required to do harm to him, is one to which objection may be taken on moral grounds, and it becomes even harder to accept when the suffering is vicarious, where one person is punished on account of what others have done. Neither is the objection removed when the scapegoat himself elects to be sacrificed; for what is objectionable is that there should be need for any scapegoat at all. If God wished to absolve men from their sins, why could he not simply do so, without exacting any price from himself or anyone else? Why indeed, if he was so deeply concerned with men's behavior and had the power to make them as he chose, did he not endow them with a nature and a form of life which would ensure that they always behaved in ways of which he approved?

The usual answer to this question is that to have contrived that men should live in this fashion would have been inconsistent with giving them free will, and that it is better that we should have this freedom, however badly we employ it, than that we should simply be a deity's puppets. This answer is sometimes also given in an attempt to reconcile the suffering that men endure with the supreme benevolence which is ascribed to God, but here it wholly fails, if only for the reason that much of this suffering is due to causes which are beyond our control.

Does it fail also in the other case? It is sometimes argued that the power which is ascribed to God of foreseeing everything that happens is inconsistent with men's freedom, but this is a mistake. There is some difficulty, as we shall see, in understanding what is meant by saying that a man does something of his own free will, but if a proposition of this sort is ever true, it must be consistent with the tautology that his actions will be what they will be. But if the man's actions will be what they will be, whether they are done freely or not, then equally someone who says what they will be predicts them truly whether they are done freely or not. It makes no difference here whether the predictions are lucky guesses or manifestations of knowledge. From the fact that someone knows what I shall do, it does indeed follow that I *shall* do it, for the purely semantic reason that this is part of what is meant by saying that he knows that I shall. It does not follow that I am compelled to do it, that I shall not be free to act otherwise. The most that can be inferred is that if I do have this freedom I shall in fact not exercise it.

The position becomes different, however, when one thinks of a God as having made men what they are. The suggestion is that he endowed them biologically with certain initial dispositions and capacities but left them free within certain limits to choose whether and to what extent the dispositions are realized or the capacities developed. A man's character, from which his actions largely proceed, is thought to be the joint product of his initial equipment, the physical and social stimuli to which he has been subjected, and his own past choices. The formation of his character may narrow his freedom; he may, through physical or social conditioning, or as the consequence of his own free actions, be deprived of the power to make choices that he once was able to make; but except in abnormal circumstances, such as that of extreme senility, when the man ceases to be a responsible agent, his freedom of choice never vanishes altogether.

But now we may ask how it comes about that he chooses to act in this way rather than that. Through the exercise of his will. But what does this mean? The idea of the will as a piece of psychological mechanism which converts intentions into physical movements appears to be mythical. All that seems actually to happen is that we think about the advantages and disadvantages of different courses of action and having come to some conclusion simply act. More often, where the action is part of some habitual routine, we perform it without any prior deliberation. In neither case do we feel that we are prodded into action by what Ryle has called "occult inner thrusts."[16] Perhaps a desire can be represented as such a thrust, but then we do not need another one to enable us to set about fulfilling the desire. We may need to concentrate our attention or to make a physical effort, but that is all. In any case, even if there were a recognizable mechanism with which the will could be identified, we could still ask in any given instance how it came to work as it did. Because that was the way in which its owner chose to operate it. But then we return to the question how he came to make this choice. Was it due to the way God made him, or was it a spontaneous occurrence, a matter of chance? On neither assumption does it seem reasonable for God to hold him responsible for what he did.

But then is it reasonable for us to hold him responsible, whether or not we assign any part to a God? Let us look more closely at this problem. There is no doubt that we think ourselves able to draw a distinction between cases in which someone does something of his own free will and cases in which this is not so. What then does the distinction consist in? I think that the best way to try to answer this question is to approach it from the negative side. Under what conditions is our freedom of action thought to be nonexistent or else so limited as seriously to attenuate our responsibility?

The most obvious class of cases in which our freedom is thought to be nonexistent consists of those in which the prospective action is one which is regarded as being physically impossible for the agent to perform or physically impossible for him to avoid. These conditions obtain when the circumstances are known to be such that in conjunction with accepted physical laws they exclude the agent's performance of the action or his avoidance of it. This is, however, not always enough to exculpate him, since it may be held that he could and should have prevented the circumstances from arising. It may be physically impossible for me to keep an appointment because there is no means by which I can get there in time, but I was perhaps not obliged to let this happen. I may not be able to avoid falling asleep, at a time when wakefulness is demanded of me, because I have taken a drug, but it can be argued that I did not have to take it. One may also be held responsible for one's general loss of some physical capacity, if this is thought to be due to one's own folly or negligence.

A second class of cases where freedom is taken to be lacking consists of those in which some action is thought incapable of being performed by the agent or incapable of being avoided, because of the operation of a psychological law. These cases are more contentious, because of our difficulty in finding psychological laws that are agreed to hold univer- sally. It is, however, generally admitted that one has to acquire skills in order to exercise them: one is not expected to speak a language that one has not learned. There are also thought to be neurotic or psychotic states which affect people in such a way that the performance or the avoidance of certain actions is not within their power. Here again they may sometimes be held responsible, to a greater or lesser degree, for falling into this condition.

The circumstances in which our freedom may be thought to be diminished without being altogether removed are very various. For instance, one may feel oneself bound by a moral or a legal obligation which would be infringed by some action that one would otherwise wish or think it right to perform. One may be subject to emotional pressures which it is thought excusable to give way to even if they are not thought to be irresistible. One may be acting under the influence of some false belief. One may be under the control of another person, as when one has been hypnotized or brainwashed. One may be exposed to blackmail or to torture or to other menaces. Even when one is threatened with death, one is considered free to defy the threat, but in most circumstances this would not be thought reasonable. In all these cases, the idea of what it is reasonable to expect a man to do plays a large part in our assessment of responsibility.

From this it emerges that when one is held responsible for some- thing that one has done or failed to do, there is always the implication that one could reasonably have been expected to act otherwise. There may, indeed, have been very little likelihood that one would act otherwise, but that may be held to be the result of one's past conduct which could reasonably have been expected to be different at some earlier stage. But now we must ask what is meant by saying of someone, in a given situation, that he could have avoided acting as he did. The answer is, I believe, that the fiction that he did act differently is one that we find acceptable. Whether the fictitious action is thought to be reasonable depends partly on what we consider to be normal behavior and partly on our moral standards. What makes it acceptable as a possibility is just that it is not excluded by the conjunction of the attendant circumstances, as they are known to us, with the established hypotheses of our explanatory system.

To say that an occurrence is not ruled out by the explanatory system, which we actually have, is not, however, to say that this will always be so. I think it unlikely that there will ever be a working system which enables us to account for every human action in every detail, but equally I do not think that there is any form of action of which one can be sure that it will never come within the reach of established universal laws. Let us, however, assume that we have to be content with statistical laws. In that case it will be a matter of chance whether or not a particular action conforms to the prevailing frequency, and it is not clear why a man should be held responsible for an action which occurs by chance. The same would apply if the action were of a sort that, so far as we could discover, was not governed even by a statistical law, for then we should have to conclude either that there was some explanation which had so far eluded us or that such actions were entirely fortuitous. It has, indeed, been suggested that these are not the only alternatives. Even if a man's actions are not governed by causal laws, he may still have reasons for doing them and therefore be held responsible. But all that this comes to, as we have seen,[17] is that his actions are explained in terms of generalizations of tendency, with the result that, in default of a stronger explanation, the conformity of a particular action to a recognized tendency remains a matter of chance.

Some philosphers have argued that even if we were able to represent all human actions as causally determined, we should still have a use for the concepts of free will and responsibility. They remark, quite correctly, that we should still be able to distinguish between behavior which occurs independently of the agent's volition and actions which are done deliberately, in the sense that we do not admit the fiction of their occurrence in the actual circumstances without the agent's having chosen to do them. Free actions can then be characterized, in the way that Locke[18] and others have proposed, as those in which the agent is not prevented from doing what he chooses, no matter how his choices are themselves determined, and the justification of reward and punishment will be that they exert a causal influence upon the agent's future choices as well as on the choices of others who may be expected to learn from the example.

This is a tenable position, but I think that its advocates underrate the extent to which it departs from our ordinary way of thinking. It is true that considerations of utility are brought to bear upon the character and extent of the rewards and punishments that we think ourselves justified in giving. Even so, our primary reason for rewarding or punishing anyone is that he deserves it; and it is just this notion of desert that our analysis of the concept of free will has put in question. If our outlook were purely utilitarian, we should take much more kindly than we mostly do to the idea of preventive punishment, and we should be much more ready than we mostly are to allow those who have done wrong to escape any reprisal, when no greater good is likely to result from it.

Not only do we treat freedom of choice as entailing responsibility in a way that seems hardly rational in the light of this analysis, but we also ascribe an intrinsic value to it. We try by various methods of education to impel people along the proper paths, but we dislike the idea of employing means of conditioning, such as the use of drugs, which might effectively ensure this result. We feel that they should be left free to choose what they will do, even if they choose badly: we wish to influence their choice but not wholly to determine it. I admit that I share this feeling, but I do not know how to justify it. So long as we go through the process of choosing, why should it matter to us how our choices are explained? What is the value in their being subject only to statistical laws, let alone in their being totally inexplicable?

F. The Meaning of Life

To say that a God who exacted retribution for men's conduct would not be benevolent or rational is not in itself to say that there is no such God. Even so, the existence of a deity of whatever character would have to have been established on other grounds before we could profitably speculate about his attitude to men, and so far these grounds have not been forthcoming. There are, however, those who would say that in pursuing the question whether there is adequate evidence for a God's existence, we have been approaching the subject of religion in the wrong way. According to them, the question we should have been asking is not whether the proposition that God exists is true as a matter of fact or acceptable as an explanatory hypothesis, but rather what function the belief in God fulfills in the lives of those who hold it. The justification for the belief may then be said to be that it makes the lives of those who hold it appear meaningful to them in a way that they otherwise would not.

This is substantially the position taken by the pragmatist William James. Having spoken in one book of "the craving of our nature for an ultimate peace behind all tempests, a blue zenith above all clouds,"[19] he criticizes in another the attempts of what he calls "systematic theology" to define the attributes of God. "Wherein," he asks, "is such a definition really instructive? It means less than nothing in its pompous robe of adjectives. Pragmatism alone can read a positive meaning into it, and for that she turns her back upon the intellectualist point of view altogether. 'God's in his heaven; all's right with the world.' *That's* the real heart of your theology, and for that you need no rationalist definitions."[20] Similarly, in his Gifford lectures on *The Varieties of Religious Experience* he speaks of his wish to vindicate "the instinctive belief of mankind: God is real since he produces real effects,"[21] and what he takes these real effects to be is no more than the feelings of greater energy, security, and satisfaction which he thinks are enjoyed by those who hold religious beliefs.

As a psychological hypothesis, this could be questioned. For instance, the thesis of eternal damnation which has been a prominent feature of much Christian teaching is not likely to produce a feeling of greater security. On the other hand, there is no doubt that many people derive solace from the idea of their having a spiritual father who watches over them, especially when it is allied to the hope that he will secure to them in a future life the happiness which they may not have found in this one. To infer from this, however, that there is such a father, one needs to accept James's pragmatic theory that, since it is not to be expected of a religious hypothesis that it will either accord or fail to accord with any observable fact, the criterion for its truth is just that the vague assurance which it gives that "all's right with the world" is a source of emotional satisfaction. This is in line with the view of some contemporary theists that the doctrine associated with the religious practices in which they engage is acceptable as a useful myth. This view is so modest that it is hard to take issue with it, unless one wants to argue that the myth is harmful, but it does appear open to the practical objection that the satisfaction which most believers derive from their acceptance of religious doctrine depends upon their not judging it as mythical. A myth which is generally seen to be a myth must be in some danger of losing its utility.

But without the help of such a myth, can life be seen as having any meaning? The simple answer is that it can have just as much meaning as one is able to put into it. There is, indeed, no ground for thinking that human life in general serves any ulterior purpose, but this is no bar to a man's finding satisfaction in many of the activities which make up his life or to his attaching value to the ends which he pursues, including some that he himself will not live to see realized. One may deplore the fact that life is so short, but if it were not independently worth living there would be no good reason to wish it prolonged. Where the discarding of the Christian myth may have a cruel effect is in the denial to those whose lives have not been happy of any serious hope that they will survive to find the balance redressed.

It has sometimes been thought that those who cannot take comfort from religion may find it in philosophy. The idea, which goes back to the Greek and Roman stoics, is that the philosopher, by coming to see things in their proper perspective, is able to detach himself from the vicissitudes of life. Conscious of his own rectitude he remains happy even on the rack. This may be contrasted with the Marxist idea that the business of philosophy is not merely to understand the world but to change it. In fact, not many philosophers have taken either of these positions, nor is there anything in the nature of the subject to make this surprising. A philosopher may become detached from ordinary concerns by being absorbed in his work, but so may an artist or a mathematician. He may think it his duty to engage in public affairs, but the line which he takes need not be connected with his philosophical theories. This is not to say that philosophy is incapable of changing the world. We have seen that the world cannot be prised away from our manner of conceiving it: and our conception of the world is something that philosophy can help to change. Even so this is not the source of its charm for most of those who practice it. For them, its value consists in the interest of the questions which it raises and the success which it achieves in answering them.

What I Saw
When I Was Dead

A. J. Ayer

My first attack of pneumonia occurred in the United States. I was in hospital for ten days in New York, after which the doctors said that I was well enough to leave. A final X-ray, however, which I underwent on the last morning, revealed that one of my lungs was not yet free from infection. This caused the most sympathetic of my doctors to suggest that it would be good for me to spend a few more days in hospital. I respected his opinion but since I was already dressed and psychologically disposed to put my illness behind me, I decided to take the risk. I spent the next few days in my stepdaughter's apartment, and then made arrangements to fly back to England.

When I arrived I believed myself to be cured and incontinently plunged into an even more hectic social round than that to which I had become habituated before I went to America.

Retribution struck me on Sunday, May 30. I had gone out to lunch, had a great deal to eat and drink, and chattered incessantly. That evening I had a relapse. I could eat almost none of the food which a friend had brought to cook in my house.

"Originally published in the *Sunday Telegraph*, 28 August 1988. This article was written while A. J. Ayer was recuperating at 'La Migoua,' his house in France, in the summer of 1988. It has also been reprinted as "That Undiscovered Country" in A. J. Ayer's *The Meaning of Life and Other Essays*, with an Introduction by Ted Honderich (London: Weidenfeld and Nicolson, 1990), pp. 198–204. Also included in *The Meaning of Life* . . . is "Postscript to a Postmortem" (pp. 205–208) written by Sir Alfred and originally appearing in the *Spectator*, 15 October 1988. In this *Spectator* article, Sir Alfred says, in part: "My purpose in writing a postscript to the article about my 'death' is not primarily to retract anything that I wrote or to express my regret that my Shakesperian title for the article, 'That Undiscovered Country', was not retained, but to correct a misunderstanding to which the article appears to have given rise. I say 'not primarily to retract' because one of my sentences was written so carelessly that it is literally false as it stands. In the final paragraph, I wrote: 'My recent experiences have slightly weakend my conviction that my genuine death . . . will be the end of me.' They have not and never did weaken that conviction. What I should have said and would have said, had I not been anxious to appear undogmatic, is that my experiences have weakened, not my belief that there is no life after death, but my inflexible attitude towards that belief." (p. 205)

On the next day, which was a bank holiday, I had a long-standing engagement to lunch at the Savoy with a friend who was very eager for me to meet her son. I would have put them off if I could, but my friend lives in Exeter and I had no idea how to reach her in London. So I took a taxi to the Savoy and just managed to stagger into the lobby. I could eat hardly any of the delicious grilled sole that I ordered but forced myself to keep up my end of the conversation. I left early and took a taxi home.

That evening I felt still worse. Once more I could eat almost none of the dinner that another friend had brought me. Indeed, she was so alarmed by my weakness that she stayed overnight. When I was no better the next morning, she telephoned my general practitioner and my elder son, Julian.

The doctor did little more than promise to try to get in touch with the specialist, but Julian, who is unobtrusively very efficient, immediately rang for an ambulance. The ambulance came very quickly with two strong attendants, and yet another friend, who had called opportunely to pick up a key, accompanied it and me to University College Hospital.

I remember very little of what happened from then on. I was taken to a room in a private wing, which had been reserved for me by the specialist, who had a consulting room on the same floor. After being X-rayed and subjected to a number of tests, which proved beyond question that I was suffering gravely from pneumonia, I was moved into intensive care in the main wing of the hospital.

Fortunately for me, the young doctor who was primarily responsible for me had been an undergraduate at New College, Oxford, while I was a Fellow. This made him extremely anxious to see that I recovered; almost too much so, in fact, for he was so much in awe of me that he forbade me to be disturbed at night, even when the experienced sister and nurse believed it to be necessary.

Under his care and theirs I made such good progress that I expected to be moved out of intensive care and back into the private wing within a week. My disappointment was my own fault. I did not attempt to eat the hospital food. My family and friends supplied all the food I needed. I am particularly fond of smoked salmon, and one evening I carelessly tossed a slice of it into my throat. It went down the wrong way and almost immediately the graph recording my heartbeats plummeted.

The ward sister rushed to the rescue, but she was unable to prevent my heart from stopping. She and the doctor subsequently told me that I died in this sense for four minutes, and I have had no reason to disbelieve them.

The doctor alarmed my son Nicholas, who had flown from New York to be by my bedside, by saying that it was not probable that I should recover, and moreover, that if I did recover physically it was not probable that my mental powers would be restored. The nurses were more optimistic, and Nicholas sensibly chose to believe them.

I have no recollection of anything that was done to me at that time. Friends have told me that I was festooned with tubes, but I never have learned how many of them there were or, with one exception, what purposes they served. I do not remember having a tube inserted in my throat to bring up the quantity of phlegm which had lodged in my lungs. I was not even aware of my numerous visitors, so many of them, in fact, that the sister had to set a quota. I know that the doctors and nurses were surprised by the speed of my recovery and that when I started speaking, the specialist expressed astonishment that anyone with so little oxygen in his lungs should be so lucid.

My first recorded utterance, which convinced those who heard it that I had not lost my wits, was the exclamation: "You are all mad." I am not sure how this should be interpreted. It is possible that I took my audience to be Christians and was telling them that I had not discovered anything "on the other side." It is also possible that I took them to be skeptics and was implying that I had discovered something. I think the former is more probable, as in the latter case I should more properly have exclaimed, "We are all mad." All the same, I cannot be sure.

The earliest remarks of which I have any cognizance, apart from my first exclamation, were made several hours after my return to life. They were addressed to a Frenchwoman with whom I had been friends for over fifteen years. I woke to find her seated by my bedside and started talking to her in French as soon as I recognized her.

My French is fluent and I spoke rapidly, approximately as follows: "Did you know that I was dead? The first time that I tried to cross the river I was frustrated, but my second attempt succeeded. It was most extraordinary. My thoughts became persons."

The content of those remarks suggests that I have not wholly put my classical education behind me. In Greek mythology the souls of the dead, now only shadowly embodied, were obliged to cross the river Styx in order to reach Hades, after paying an obol to the ferryman, Charon.

I may also have been reminded of my favorite philosopher, David Hume, who, during his last illness, "a disorder of the bowels," imagined that Charon, growing impatient, was calling him "a lazy loitering rogue." With his usual politeness, Hume replied that he saw without regret his death approaching and that he was making no effort to postpone it. This is one of the rare occasions on which I have failed to follow Hume. Clearly I had made an effort to prolong my life.

The only memory that I have of an experience closely encompassing my death is very vivid.

I was confronted by a red light, exceedingly bright and also very painful even when I turned away from it. I was aware that this light was responsible for the government of the universe. Among its ministers were two creatures who had been put in charge of space.

These ministers periodically inspected space and had recently carried out such an inspection. They had, however, failed to do their work properly, with the result that space, like a badly fitting jigsaw puzzle, was slightly out of joint.

A further consequence was that the laws of nature had ceased to function as they should. I felt that it was up to me to put things right. I also had the motive of finding a way to extinguish the painful light. I assumed that it was signaling that space was awry and that it would switch itself off when order was restored.

Unfortunately, I had no idea where the guardians of space had gone and feared that even if I found them I should not be able to communicate with them.

It then occurred to me that whereas, until the present century, physicists accepted the Newtonian severance of space and time, it had become customary, since the vindication of Einstein's general theory of relativity, to treat space-time as a single whole. Accordingly, I thought that I could cure space by operating upon time.

I was vaguely aware that the ministers who had been given charge of time were in my neighborhood and I proceeded to hail them. I was again frustrated. Either they did not hear me, or they chose to ignore me, or they did not understand me. I then hit upon the expedient of walking up and down, waving my watch, in the hope of drawing their attention not to my watch itself but to the time which it measured. This elicited no response. I became more and more desperate, until the experience suddenly came to an end.

This experience could well have been delusive. A slight indication that it might have been veridical has been supplied by my French friend, or rather by her mother, who also underwent a heart arrest many years ago. When her daughter asked her what it had been like, she replied that all that she remembered was that she must stay close to the red light.

On the face of it, these experiences, or the assumption that the last one was veridical, are rather strong evidence that death does not put an end to consciousness.

Does it follow that there is a future life? Not necessarily. The trouble is that there are different criteria for being dead, which are indeed logically compatible but may not always be satisfied together.

In this instance, I am given to understand that the arrest of the heart does not entail, either logically or causally, the arrest of the brain. In view of the very strong evidence in favor of the dependence of thoughts upon the brain, the most probable hypothesis is that my brain continued to function although my heart had stopped.

If I had acquired good reason to believe in a future life, it would have applied not only to myself. Admittedly, the philosophical problem of justifying one's confident belief in the existence and contents of other minds has not yet been satisfactorily solved. Even so, with the possible exception of Fichte—who proclaimed that the world was his idea but may not have meant it literally—no philosopher has acquiesced in solipsism. No philosopher has seriously asserted that of all the objects in the universe, he alone was conscious. Moreover it is commonly taken for granted, not only by philosophers, that the minds of others bear a sufficiently close analogy to one's own. Consequently, if I had been vouchsafed a reasonable expectation of a future life, other human beings could expect one too.

Let us grant, for the sake of argument, that we could have future lives. What form would they take?

The easiest answer is that they would consist in the prolongation of our experiences, without any physical attachment. This is the theory that should appeal to radical empiricists. It is, indeed, consistent with the concept of personal identity which was adopted both by Hume and by William James, according to which one's identity consists, not in the possession of an enduring soul, but in the sequence of one's experiences, guaranteed by memory. They did not apply their theory to a future life, in which Hume at any rate disbelieved.

For those who are attracted by this theory, as I am, the main problem, which Hume admitted that he was unable to solve, is to discover the relation, or relations, which have to hold between experiences for them to belong to one and the same self.

William James thought that he had found the answers with his relations of the felt togetherness and continuity of our thoughts and sensations, coupled with memory, in order to unite experiences that are separated in time. But while memory is undoubtedly necessary, it can be shown that it is not wholly sufficient.

I myself carried out a thorough examination and development of the theory in my book *The Origins of Pragmatism*. I was reluctantly forced to conclude that I could not account for personal identity without falling back on the identity, through time, of one or more bodies that the person might successively occupy. Even then, I was unable to give a satisfactory account of the way in which a series of experiences is tied to a particular body at any given time.

The admission that personal identity through time requires the identity of a body is a surprising feature of Christianity. I call it surprising because it seems to me that Christians are apt to forget that the resurrection of the body is an element of their creed. The question of how bodily identity is sustained over intervals of time is not so difficult. The answer might consist in postulating a reunion of the same atoms, perhaps in there being no more than a strong physical resemblance, possibly fortified by a similarity of behavior.

A prevalent fallacy is the assumption that a proof of an afterlife would also be a proof of the existence of a deity. This is far from being the case. If, as I hold, there is no good reason to believe that a god either created or presides over this world, there is equally no good reason to believe that a god created or presides over the next world, on the unlikely supposition that such a thing exists.

It is conceivable that one's experiences in the next world, if there are any, will supply evidence of a god's existence, but we have no right to presume on such evidence, when we have not had the relevant experiences.

It is worth remarking, in this connection, that the two important Cambridge philosophers in this century, J. M. E. McTaggart and C. D. Broad, who have believed, in McTaggart's case that he would certainly survive his death, in Broad's that there was about a 50 percent probability that he would, were both of them atheists.

McTaggart derived his certainty from his metaphysics, which implied that what we confusedly perceive as material objects, in some cases housing minds, are really souls, eternally viewing one another with something of the order of love.

The less fanciful Broad was impressed by the findings of psychical research. He was certainly too intelligent to think that the superior performances of a few persons in the game of guessing unseen cards, which he painstakingly proved to be statistically significant, had any bearing upon the likelihood of a future life. He must therefore have been persuaded by the testimony of mediums. He was surely aware that most mediums have been shown to be frauds, but he was convinced that some have not been.

Not that this made him optimistic. He took the view that this world was very nasty and that there was a fair chance that the next world, if it existed, was even nastier. Consequently, he had no compelling desire to survive. He just thought that there was an even chance of his doing so. One of his better epigrams was that if one went by the reports of mediums, life in the next world was like a perpetual bump supper at a Welsh university.

If Broad was an atheist, my friend Dr. Albert Ewing was not. Ewing, who had considered Broad to be a better philosopher than Wittgenstein, was naïve, unworldly even by academic standards, intellectually shrewd, unswervingly honest, and a devout Christian. Once, to tease him, I said: "Tell me, Alfred, what do you most look forward to in the next world?" He replied immediately: "God will tell me whether there are *a priori* propositions." It is a wry comment on the strange character of our subject that this answer should be so funny.

My excuse for repeating this story is that such philosophical problems as the question of whether the propositions of logic and pure mathematics are deductively analytic or factually synthetic and, if they are analytic, whether they are true by convention, are not to be solved by acquiring more information.

What is needed is that we succeed in obtaining a clearer view of what the problems involve. One might hope to achieve this in a future life, but really we have no good reason to believe that our intellects will be any sharper in the next world, if there is one, than they are in this. A god, if one exists, might make them so, but this is not something that even the most enthusiastic deist can count on.

The only philosophical problem that our finding ourselves landed on a future life might clarify would be that of the relation between mind and body, if our future lives consisted, not in the resurrection of our bodies, but in the prolongation of the series of our present experiences. We should then be witnessing the triumph of dualism, though not the dualism which Descartes thought that he had established. If our lives consisted in an extended series of experiences, we should still have no good reason to regard ourselves as spiritual substances.

So there it is. My recent experiences have slightly weakened my conviction that my genuine death, which is due fairly soon, will be the end of me, though I continue to hope that it will be. They have not weakened my conviction that there is no god. I trust that my remaining an atheist will allay the anxieties of my fellow supporters of the Humanist Association, the Rationalist Press, and the South Place Ethical Society.

Evidence for God

Richard Swinburne

Why believe that there is a God at all? My answer is that to suppose that there is a God explains why there is a world at all; why there are the scientific laws there are; why animals and then human beings have evolved; why humans have the opportunity to mold their characters and those of their fellow humans for good or ill and to change the environment in which we live; why we have the well-authenticated account of Christ's life, death and resurrection; why throughout the centuries men have had the apparent experience of being in touch with and guided by God; and so much else. In fact, the hypothesis of the existence of God makes sense of the whole of our experience, and it does so better than any other explanation which can be put forward, and that is the grounds for believing it to be true. This short pamphlet seeks to justify this answer.

Each of the phenomena (things in need of explanation) which I have mentioned has formed the starting point of a philosophical argument for the existence of God, but all that philosophers have tried to do is to codify in a rigorous form the vague reasons which many ordinary men have had for believing that there is a God. These arguments seem to me to have a common pattern. Some phenomenon E, which we can all observe, is considered. It is claimed that E is puzzling, strange, not to be expected in the ordinary course of things; but that E is to be expected if there is a God; for God has the power to bring about E and he might well choose to do so. Hence the occurrence of E is reason for supposing that there is a God. E may be a large phenomenon, such as the existence of the universe, or something a lot smaller, such as our own individual religious experiences.

The pattern of argument is one much used in science, history, and all other fields of human inquiry. A detective, for example, finds various clues—John's fingerprints on a burgled safe, John having a lot of money

Originally published in England by A. R. Mowbray & Company, Limited, for the Christian Evidence Society, 1986. Reprinted with permission.

hidden in his house, John being seen near the scene of the burglary at the time when it was committed. He then suggests that these various clues, although they just *might* have other explanations, are not in general to be expected unless John had robbed the safe. Each clue is some evidence that he did rob the safe, confirms the hypothesis that John robbed the safe; and the evidence is cumulative—when put together it makes the hypothesis probable.

Let us call arguments of this kind arguments to a good explanation. Scientists use this pattern of argument to argue to the existence of unobservable entities as causes of the phenomena which they observe. For example, at the beginning of the nineteenth century, scientists observed many varied phenomena of chemical interaction, such as that substances combine in fixed ratios by weight to form new substances (e.g., hydrogen and oxygen always form water in a ratio by weight of 1:8). They then claimed that these phenomena would be expected if there existed a hundred or so different kinds of atoms, particles far too small to be seen, which combined and recombined in certain simple ways. In their turn physicists postulated electrons, protons, and neutrons, and other particles in order to account for the behavior of atoms, as well as for large-scale observable phenomena; and they now postulate quarks in order to explain the behavior of protons, neutrons, and most other particles.

To be good arguments (that is, to provide evidence for their hypothesis), arguments of this kind must satisfy three criteria. First, the phenomena which they cite as evidence must not be very likely to occur in the normal course of things. We saw in the burglary example how the various clues, such as John's fingerprints on the safe, were not much to be expected in the normal course of things. Secondly, the phenomena must be much more to be expected if the hypothesis is true. If John did rob the safe it is *quite* likely that his fingerprints would be found on it. Thirdly, the hypothesis must be simple. That is, it must postulate the existence and operation of *few* entities, few *kinds* of entities, with few *easily* describable properties behaving in mathematically *simple* kinds of way. We could always postulate many new entities with complicated properties to explain anything which we find. But our hypothesis will only be supported by the evidence if it postulates few entities, which lead us to expect the diverse phenomena which form the evidence. Thus in the detective story example we could suggest that Brown planted John's fingerprints on the safe, Smith dressed up to look like John at the scene of the crime, and without any collusion with others Robinson hid the money in John's flat. This new hypothesis would lead us to expect the phenomena which we find just as well as does the hypothesis that John robbed the safe. But the latter hypothesis is confirmed by the evidence whereas the former is not. And this is because the hypothesis that John robbed the safe postulates *one* object—John—doing *one* deed—robbing the safe—which leads us to expect the several phenomena which we find. Scientists always postulate as few new entities (e.g., subatomic particles) as are needed to lead us to expect to find the phenomena which we observe; and they postulate that those entities do not behave erratically (behave one way one day and a different way the next day) but that they behave in accordance with as simple and smooth a mathematical law as is compatible with what is observed. There is an old Latin saying, *simplex sigillum veri*, "The simple is the sign of the true." To be rendered probable by evidence, hypothesis must be simple.

The Existence and Order of the Universe

My first phenomenon which provides evidence for the existence of God is the existence of the universe for so long as it has existed (whether a finite time or, if it has no beginning, an infinite time). This is something evidently inexplicable by science. For a scientific explanation as such explains the occurrence of one state of affairs S_1 in terms of a previous state of affairs S_2 ans some law of nature which makes states like S_2 bring about states like S_1. Thus it may explain the planets being in their present position by a previous state of the system (the sun and planets being where they were last year) and the operation of Kepler's law which states that states like the latter are followed a year later by states like the former. *But what science by its very nature cannot explain is why there are any states of affairs at all.*

My next phenomenon is the operation of the most general laws of nature, that is, the orderliness of nature in conforming to very general laws. What exactly these laws are science may not yet have discovered—perhaps they are the field equations of Einstein's general theory of relativity, or perhaps there are some yet more fundamental laws. Now science can explain why one law operates in some narrow area, in terms of the operation of a wider law in the particular conditions of that narrow area. Thus it can explain why Galileo's laws of fall holds—that small objects near the surface of the earth fall with a constant acceleration toward the earth. Galileo's law follow from Newton's laws, given that the earth is a massive body far from other massive bodies and the objects on its surface are close to it and small in mass in comparison. But what science by its very nature cannot explain is why there are the most general laws of nature that there are, for *ex hypothesi*, no wider law can explain their operation.

Scientific and Personal Explanation

That there is a universe and that there are laws of nature are phenomena so general and pervasive that we tend to ignore them. But there might so easily not have been a universe at all, ever. Or the universe might so easily have been a chaotic mess. That there is an *orderly* universe is something very striking, yet beyond the capacity of science ever to explain. Science's inability to explain these things is not a temporary phenomenon, caused by the backwardness of twentieth century science. Rather, because of what a *scientific* explanation is, these things will ever be beyond its capacity to explain. For scientific explanations by their very nature terminate with some ultimate natural law and ultimate arrangements of physical things, and the questions which I am raising are why there are natural laws and physical things at all.

However, there is another kind of explanation of phenomena which we use all the time and which we see as a proper way of explaining phenomena. This is what I shall call *personal explanation*. We often explain some phenomenon E as brought about by a person P in order to achieve some purpose or goal G. The present motion of my hand is explained as brought about by me for the purpose of writing a philosophical paper. The cup being on the table is explained by a man having put it there for the purpose of drinking out of it. Yet this is a different way of explaining things from the scientific. Scientific explanation involves laws of nature and previous states of affairs. Personal explanation involves persons and purposes. If we cannot give a scientific explanation of the existence and orderliness of the universe, perhaps we can give a personal explanation.

The Universe Needs Explaining

But why should we think that the existence and orderliness of the universe has an explanation at all? We seek for an explanation of all things; but we have seen that we have only reason for supposing that we have found one if the purported explanation is simple and leads us to expect what we find when that is otherwise not to be expected. The history of science shows that we judge that the complex, miscellaneous, coincidental, and diverse needs explaining, and that it is to be explained in terms of something simpler. The motions of the planets (subject to Kepler's laws), the mechanical interactions of bodies on earth, the behavior of pendula, the motions of tides, the behavior of comets, etc., formed a pretty miscellaneous set of phenomena. Newton's laws of motion constituted a simple theory which led us to expect these phenomena and so was judged a true explanation of them. The existence of thousands of different chemical substances combining in different ratios to make other substances was complex. The hypothesis that there were only a hundred or so chemical elements of which the thousands of substances were made was a simple hypothesis which led us to expect the complex phenomenon.

Our universe is a complex thing. There are lots and lots of separate chunks of it. The chunks have each a different finite and not very natural volume, shape, mass, etc.—consider the vast diversity of the galaxies, stars, and planets, and the pebbles on the sea shore. Matter is inert and has no powers which it can choose to exert; it does what it has to do. There is a limited amount of it in any region and it has a limited amount of energy and velocity. There is a complexity, particularly, and finitude about the universe.

The conformity of objects throughout endless time and space to simple laws is likewise something which cries out for explanation. For let us consider what this amounts to. Laws are not things, independent of material objects. To say that all objects conform to laws is simply to say that they all behave in exactly the same way. To say, for example, that the planets obey Kepler's laws is just to say that each planet at each moment of time has the property of moving in the ways that Kepler's laws state. There is therefore this vast coincidence in the behavioral properties of objects at all times and in all places. If all the coins of some region have the same markings or all the papers in a room are written in the same handwriting, we seek an explanation in terms of a common source of these coincidences. We should seek a similar explanation of that vast coincidence which we describe as the conformity of objects to laws of nature—e.g., the fact that all electrons are produced, attract and repel other particles, and combine with them in exactly the same way at each point of endless time and space.

God Alone Can Explain It

The hypothesis of theism is that the universe exists because there is a God who keeps it in being and that laws of nature operate because there is a God who brings it about that they do. He brings it about that the laws of nature operate by sustaining in every object in the universe its liability to behave in accord with those laws. He keeps the universe in being by making the laws such as to conserve the matter of the universe, i.e., by making it the case at each moment that what there was before continues to exist. The hypothesis is a hypothesis that a person brings about these things for some purpose. He acts directly on the universe, as we act directly on our brains, guiding them to move our limbs (but the universe is not his body—for he could at any moment destroy it, and act on another universe, or do without a universe). As we have seen, personal explanation and scientific explanation are the two ways we have of explaining the occurrence of phenomena. Since there cannot be a scientific explanation of the existence of the universe, either there is a personal explanation or there is no explanation at all. The hypothesis that there is a God is the hypothesis of the existence of the simplest kind of person which there could be. A person is a being with *power* to bring about effects, *knowledge* of how to do so, and *freedom* to make choices of which effects to bring about. God is by definition an omnipotent (that is, infinitely powerful), omniscient (that is, all-knowing), and perfectly free person; he is a person of infinite power, knowledge, and freedom; a person to whose power, knowledge, and freedom there are no limits except those of logic. The hypothesis that there exists a being with infinite degrees of the qualities essential to a being of that kind is the postulation of a very simple being. The hypothesis that there is *such* a God is a much simpler hypothesis than the hypothesis that there is a god who has such and such a limited power. It is simpler in just the same way that the hypothesis that some particle has zero mass or infinite velocity, is simpler than the hypothesis that it has of 0.32147 of some unit or a velocity of 211,000 km/sec. A finite limitation cries out for an explanation of why there is just that particular limit, in a way that limitlessness does not.

That there should exist anything at all, let alone a universe as complex and as orderly as ours, is exceedingly strange. But if there is a God, it is not vastly unlikely that he should create such a universe. A universe such as ours is a thing of beauty and a theater in which men and other creatures can grow and work out their destiny. The orderliness of the universe makes it a beautiful universe, but, even more importantly, it makes it a universe which men can learn to control and change. For only if there are simple laws of nature can men predict what will follow from what—and unless they can do that, they can never change anything. Only if men know that by sowing certain seeds, and weeding and watering them they will get corn, can they develop an agriculture. And men can only acquire that knowledge if there are easily graspable regularities of behavior in nature. So God has good reason to make an orderly universe and, *ex hypothesi*, being omnipotent, he has the power to do so. So the hypothesis that there is a God makes the existence of the universe much more to be expected than it would otherwise be, and it is a very simple hypothesis. Hence the arguments from the existence of the universe and its conformity to simple natural laws are good arguments to an explanation of the phenomena and provide substantial evidence for the existence of God.

The Evolution of Animals and Man

The other phenomena which I have mentioned are also phenomena best explained by postulating the existence and creative activity of God and so add to the cumulative case for his existence. Consider now the evolution of animals and humans. In the middle of the last century Darwin set out his impressive theory of evolution by natural selection to account for the existence of animals and humans. Animals varied in various ways from their parents (some were taller, some shorter, some fatter, some thinner, some had beginnings of wings, others did not; and so on). Those animals with characteristics which made them best fitted to survive, survived and handed on their characteristics to the next generation. But, although in general resembling their parents, their offspring varied from them, and those variations which best fitted the animal to survive were again the ones most likely to be handed on to another generation. This process went on for millions of years producing the whole range of animals which we have today, each adapted to survive in a different environment. Among the characteristics giving advantage in the struggle for survival was intelligence, and the selections for this characteristic eventually led to the evolution of man. Such is Darwin's account of why we have today animals and men.

As far as it goes, his account is surely right. But there are two crucial matters beyond its scope. First, the evolutionary mechanism which Darwin describes only works because there are certain laws of biochemistry (animals produce many offspring, these vary in various ways from the parents, etc.) and certain features of the environment (there is a limited amount of food, drink, space, and so on). But why are there these laws rather than other laws? Perhaps because they follow from the most fundamental laws of physics. But the question then arises as to why the fundamental laws of physics are such as to give rise to laws of evolution. If we can answer this question we should do so. There is again available the same simpler answer—that there is a God who makes matter behave in accord with such laws in order to produce a world with animals and men. To develop my earlier point—a God has an obvious reason for producing men. He wants there to be creatures who can share in his creative work by making choices which affect the world they live in and the other creatures who live in that world. By the way we treat our environment and our bodies, bring up our children and influence our governments, we can make this world beautiful and its other inhabitants happy and knowledgeable; or we can make it ugly and its other inhabitants miserable and ignorant. A good God will seek other beings with whom to share in his activity of creation, of forming, molding and changing the world. The fact of a mechanism to produce men is evidence of God behind that mechanism.

Secondly, Darwinian theory is concerned only with the physical characteristics of animals and men. Yet men have thoughts and feelings, beliefs and desires, and they make choices. These are events totally different from publicly observable physical events. Physical objects are, physicists tell us, interacting colorless centers of forces; but they act on our senses, which set up electrical circuits in our brains, and these brain events cause us to have sensations (of pain or color, sound or smell), thoughts, desires, and beliefs. Mental events such as these are no doubt largely caused by brain events (and vice-versa), but mental events are distinct from brain events—sensations are quite different from elec-trochemical disturbances. They are in fact so different—private, colored, or noisy, and felt—from public events such as brain events, that it is very very unlikely indeed that science will ever explain how brain events give rise to mental events (why this brain event causes a red sensation and that one a blue sensation). Yet brain events do cause mental events; no doubt there are regular correlations between this type of brain events and that type of mental event, and yet no scientific theory can say why there are the particular correlations there are or indeed any correlations at all (why did not evolution just throw up unfeeling robots?). Yet these correlations which science cannot explain cry out for explanation of another kind. That is available. God brings it about that brain events of certain kinds give rise to mental events of certain kinds in order that animals and men may learn about the physical world, see it as embued with color and smell making it beautiful, and learn to control it. Brain events caused by different sights, sounds, and smells give rise to different and characteristic sensations and beliefs in order that men may have knowledge of a beautiful physical world and thus have power over it. Darwinianism can only explain why some animals are eliminated in the struggle for survival, not why there are animals and men at all, with mental lives of sensation and belief; and insofar as it can explain anything, the question inevitably arises why the laws of evolution are as they are. All this theism can explain.

Miracles

There are many reports of occasional miraculous events, events which violate laws of nature. Some of these reports are no doubt false, spead by unreliable witnesses. No doubt when men have claimed to see others levitate (float on air) or recover instantaneously from some disease, some of these reports are just false. Sometimes, too, when men have reported correctly some very strange event, although it seemed to be a violation of natural law, it was not. Magnetism might once have seemed miraculous to some people, but it is a perfectly orderly scientific phenomenon. But laying aside all such cases, there is a residue of apparently well-authenticated, highly unusual events apparently contrary to laws of nature, but such as a God would have reason for bringing about (e.g., a spontaneous cure of cancer in answer to much prayer). Above all, there is the supreme reported miracle—the resurrection of Jesus from the dead. This booklet cannot discuss the historical evidence for the resurrection, but another booklet in this series (*Evidence for the Resurrection*) will consider it in detail. Insofar as that evidence is good evidence (as I believe it to be), it shows Jesus Christ to have been physically resurrected, an event which quite clearly violates the laws of nature and so calls for an explanation different from the scientific. That is available: God raised Christ from the dead to signify his acceptance of Christ's atoning sacrifice, to give his stamp of approval to his teaching, to take back Christ to heaven where he belongs, and thereby to found a church to draw all men to himself.

Religious Experience

Theism is able to explain the most general phenomena of science and more particular historical facts, but it is also able to explain our own individual religious experiences. To so many men it has seemed at different moments of their lives that they were aware of God and his guidance. It is a basic principle of knowledge, which I have called the principle of credulity, that we ought to believe that things are as they seem to be, until we have evidence that we are mistaken. If it seems to me that I am seeing a table or hearing my friend's voice, I ought to believe this until evidence appears that I have been deceived. If you say the contrary—never trust appearances until it is proved that they were reliable—you will never have any beliefs at all. For what would show that appearances were reliable, except more appearances? And if you can't trust appearances, you can't trust them either. Just as you must trust your five ordinary senses, so it is equally rational to trust your religious sense. An opponent may say, you trust your ordinary senses (e.g., your sense of sight) because it agrees with the senses of other men—what you claim to see they claim to see; but your religious sense does not argue with the senses of other men (they don't always have religious experiences at all, or of the same kind as you do). However, it is important to realize that the rational man applies the principle of credulity before he knows what other men experience. You rightly trust your senses even if there is no other observer to check them. And if there is another observer who reports that he seems to see what you seem to see, you have thereafter to remember that he did so report, and that means relying on your own memory (again, how things seem) without present corroboration. Anyway, religious experiences often do coincide with those of many others in their general awareness of a power beyond ourselves guiding our lives. If some men do not have our experiences, even when our experiences coincide with those of others, that suggests that the former are blind to religious realities—just as a man's inability to see colors does not show that many of us who claim to see them are mistaken, only that he is color-blind. It is basic to human knowledge of the world that we believe things are as they seem to be in the absence of positive evidence to the contrary. Someone who seems to have an experience of God should believe that he does, unless evidence can be produced that he is mistaken. And it is another basic principle of knowledge that those who do not have an experience of a certain type ought to believe many others when they say that they do—again, in the absence of evidence of mass delusion.

Conclusion

The case for the existence of God is a cumulative one. I claim that the existence and continued operation of God (normally through the laws of nature, but sometimes setting them aside) can explain the whole pattern of science and history, and also men's most intimate religious experiences. The case for theism has to be balanced against any arguments against it (e.g., from the fact of evil and suffering in the world, which will be considered in another booklet in this series, *Evidence for the Love of God*). But in the absence of good contrary arguments, there is, I suggest, a strong case for the existence of God. As St. Paul wrote in his Epistle to the Romans (1:20), "the invisible things of God since the creation of the world are clearly seen, being perceived through the things that are made."

Does God Exist?
The Argumentation of Hans Küng

Hermann Häring

Expectation, hope, and longing belong to human nature. From the linear, horizontal level of pure humanity, a real qualitative ascent to a superior dimension of reality would appear impossible. But without the existence of a transcendent dimension, it is impossible to transcend the limitations of human life. Thus the question of religion, more precisely the question of God, presents itself.

The multiple proofs and demonstrations presented by renowned atheists succeed indeed in putting the existence of God into question; but by no means do they render the nonexistence of God indubitable. Neither the philosophical-psychological explanations of belief in God (Feuerbach), nor the social-critical explanations (Marx), nor the psycho-analytical explanations (Freud) are in a position to decide the question of the existence or nonexistence of a reality independent of our thinking, willing, and feeling, independent of psyche and society.

Belief in God cannot simply be asserted; nor can it be proven. It can, however, be shown to rest on truth.

Should God exist, then we would have found a fundamental solution to the riddle of the questionableness of reality itself, a fundamental answer to the perennial question of the origin and destiny of the world and of humankind.

That God exists can only be asserted in an act of trust grounded in reality itself.

Thus there is no ground to speak of a stalemate between affirmation and negation of God. Those who say yes to God know why they can put ultimate trust in the reality surrounding them.

Belief in God can thus be justified before reason. Its rationale manifests itself in the practice of a venturesome trust in reality itself: fundamental trust and trust in God are bound up with each other.

The term "God" is indispensable, though ambiguous. In contrast to the philosophical concept of God, the religious understanding of God is concrete and definite, despite whatever differences the religions may have among themselves.[1]

Introduction: Some Hermeneutical Remarks

In the above text taken from his book *Twenty-Four Theses on the Existence of God* (1979), Hans Küng summarizes briefly the arguments developed at length in his book *Does God Exist?*, published in German the year before and in English a year later (1980). The passage summarized covers thirty-six pages in the original, thirty-one pages in the translation.[2] In accord with numerous contemporary theologians, Küng is convinced that the existence of God cannot be demonstrated directly. In the preceeding chapters of *Does God Exist?*, he has shown in detailed studies of the arguments pro and contra why this is so. Instead of direct proof he offers an indirect demonstration, in which God is shown to be the ultimate, all-determining reality underlying our concrete, day-to-day experience of reality in the cosmos as a whole and in our own lives in particular. The existence of this ultimate reality is thus verified as the ground of our everday experience of reality (S. 605; p. 550).

Before looking at this argument in detail, I should like to make certain important hermeneutical observations. Were it possible to prove the existence of God directly, as it is, for instance, possible to demonstrate the existence of the sun from the effects it produces, the argument could be constructed in the following simple, orderly sequence. First the definition of God as "ultimate, all-determining reality" would be explicated and then the meaning of the assertion "God exists" explained notionally. Therefrom would follow the explanation of the manner of verification, so that the demonstration could follow. Three questions would thus have to be answered: (1) What is meant by the term "God" and what is meant by the proposition "God exists"? (2) In what manner can such a proposition be verified? (3) Does God really exist? (The answer here would be the conclusion of the demonstration.) These three questions articulate the meaning, verificability, and truth value of the existence proposition. Only when all three questions are considered in their interconnection with each other is it possible to hope for a satisfactory answer.

For centuries, philosophy and theology sought to answer the question of God's existence with arguments built along the lines of such a logic: first they defined and explained the notion of "God";[3] then they proceeded directly to the process of verification intended to confirm or refute the existence of God,[4] thus overlooking or ignoring the intermediate significance of the affirmation or negation of God's existence for speaker and hearer.

In fact, however, the situation is far more complicated than this simple logic would suggest. Three grounds account for this greater complexity.

The first lies in the nature of language. Language does not simply represent reality as in a mirror; by reason of the relationship it establishes between speaker/hearer on the one side and the subject of discussion on the other, language not only represents but also creates reality.[5] This reality-creating process is above all to be seen when (a) a language statement goes beyond the function of simply communicating information, and when (b) the object the statement refers to lies beyond the sphere of empirically verifiable reality. This is precisely the case with the proposition "God exists": alongside its objective, ontological reference, it also implies a relationship between the speaker/listener and the reality to which it objectively refers.

The second reason lies in the modal character of the results of the verification process. The proposition "God exists" is either meaningful or meaningless depending upon the ability to verify it or not.[6] In itself, the existence of God shows itself to be impossible, contingently possible, or necessary;[7] E. Jüngel goes so far as to speak of it being "more than necessary." These modal qualifications are themselves only the logical qualifications of a parallel question, whether and to what extent the existence of God is "necessary" for *our own* existence and self-understanding as human beings. At the point where the notion of God enters into the self-definition of a culture, the questions of belief, of the meaning of life, of hope or anxiety find their focus. Thus the apparently objective level of argumentation in answering the God question reveals a reciprocal relationship between the definition of God and our relationship to God's reality.

The third reason lies in the context of argumentation.[8] Only indirectly can we legitimate our speaking about God's existence, and this we do by referring namely to the disclosure situation of God's existence. Here it is important to note that existence propositions as such presuppose the affirmation of a comprehensive frame of reference overshadowing the relationship between object and subject. This holds all the more for propositions about the existence of God when God is described as an "all-determining reality." At this point, at the latest, the classical proof method is broken through. The proposition "God exists" cannot be filled with meaning independent of concrete experience: in itself it is empty, so to speak; its meaning derives entirely from its experientially grounded communicative function.[9] This becomes particularly difficult in a cultural context in which speaking of God is no longer obvious and self-evident. For this reason, the very notion of God viewed in terms of the existence proposition calls for a concrete prior agreement between speaker and listener to clarify the problematic regarding the question of God.

To sum up, we cannot clarify the existence proposition independent of the notion of "God"; conversely, we cannot understand the notion of "God" independently of assertions about his existence. Thus the notion of God and the assertions about his existence are prior to formal arguments aimed at demonstrating this existence.[10] As the above remarks from the field of linguistic logic establish, we cannot conceptually objectify this relationship without previously attempting to illuminate its hermeneutical foundations.[11] Prior to constructing the formal argument for God's existence, it is necessary to reach an accord in detail regarding the significance of the assertion of God's existence for speaker and listener, writer and reader. As the subject-object structure of the proposition shows, the assertion "God exists" cannot be divorced from basic human experience without problems. An authentic and proper decision regarding the truth of propositions about God's existence is only possible when the significance of these propositions for speaker and listener have been clarified. Only then can the discussion focus upon the legitimation procedure itself.

I. Faith and the Critique of Religion at the End of the Modern Age

In the light of these observations we can proceed to examine Hans Küng's argumentation. Far in the "foreground" of the God question, he begins with the questions dealing with the origin, meaning, and destiny of human beings and the cosmos in which they are at home. These questions point to the ultimate question: can we find a foundation for our own and for cosmic reality or can we not find such a foundation, in which case we must concede that for us at least this reality is meaningless in the ultimate analysis. It is in this context that the definition of God as "all-determining, ultimate reality" is rooted. Hermeneutically this definition is meaningless outside of this context. One might object that this context is constructed subjectively and arbitrarily: how do we arrive at this material? Küng does not simply poll individuals or take a consensus of psychology and other empirical sciences. Instead he embarks on a time journey through modern intellectual history. Narrating and analyzing, he reconstructs the modern approaches to the God question as exemplified by the principal spokesmen of modern thought. Their history is turned by Küng into a discovery context: in his hands it becomes a narrative disclosure of the God question. Having identified the specific experiences of the figures investigated, Küng proceeds to synthesize them under headings like "rationality," "the world and its history," "atheism," "nihilism," "fundamental trust and fundamental mistrust."[12] Viewed against the background of modern thought, these notions take on concrete meaning and relevance.

It is impossible here to reproduce the many-sided historical analysis Küng undertakes in the first five hundred pages of his book; a few observations must suffice.

Surprisingly, as Küng shows, the arguments for the existence of God elaborated in the European philosophical and theological tradition from antiquity up to the modern age are reducible to a few basic types. One type is represented by the a priori proof offered by Anselm of Canterbury; according to this argument, the idea of an all-perfect, absolutely necessary being implies that such a reality cannot not exist; existence is part of its essence. Despite the criticism that has dogged this argument from the beginning, questioning its attempt to bridge the gap between being in thought and being in reality, this argument has continued over the centuries to find adherents in a culture in which God's existence in fact is viewed as self-evident. A similar destiny is shared by the so-called Five Ways formulated by Thomas Aquinas as a posteriori arguments with an empirical point of departure in five specific experiences.[13] In these "ways" God is identified with the ultimate ground of possibility, for five specific structural relationships found in experienced reality; that is, God is identified with the first mover in the network of motion and change, the first cause in the network of intercausality, the ultimate necessity in the network of necessary conditions, the ultimate perfection in the network of perfections, and the ultimate end and fulfillment within the network of finality.[14] Important to note, however, is that these arguments are not—in the mind of Thomas Aquinas at least—direct proofs in the strict sense. The existence of the five foundations for specific networks within empirically experienced reality may well be demonstrated, but the identification of these foundations with "God" is a step that supposes the readers' agreement to use the term "God" in this way.[15] At least in their context in Thomas's Summa Theologiae, the purpose of these arguments is not to prove God's existence to unbelievers, but rather to disclose to believers specific aspects of God's relationship to us and thus to show that our belief in God has a reasonable foundation. Thus on the level of hermeneutical explication, these arguments indeed have persuasive character, but their primary purpose is to explain to the believing listener/reader, what believing in God means for understanding the meaningfulness of the world and its order, what it means for our thinking and willing. God is seen here not in abstract isolation, but rather in relation to believing men and women seeking understanding of what they believe.

With the coming of the modern age, a new situation arises that continues to govern thinking about God to this day. Küng's narrative analysis begins therefore with Descartes, the father of modern thought (S. 23–63; pp. 3–41). Descartes' aim was to reconstruct philosophical thinking in a new, methodically exact fashion; in this reconstruction, the idea of God plays a central role as the ultimate guarantee for the intelligibility of the world; thus God's existence must be proven conclusively in order to ground our confidence in the knowledge we gain about the world.[16] With this instrumentalization of the affirmation of God's existence, the questionability of that affirmation becomes a real problem for modern thought. The effect of Descartes' thought revolution was to overrate the capabilities of human reason, which thus more and more came to be viewed exclusively within a paradigm of objectifying calculation.

Blaise Pascal, Descartes' younger contemporary, appears in the next chapter of Küng's narrative (S. 64–118; pp. 42–92) as a quasi-clairvoyant harbinger of modern criticism of the development initiated by Descartes. Pascal calls attention to "reasons of the heart," attacking the dictates of a calculating rationalism with all the deleterious consequences that such an autonomous reason would spawn in the further course of modern thinking—developments Küng analyzes in a separate chapter appended to the treatment of Pascal (S. 119–54; pp. 93–115). Pascal's broadening of the notion of reason narrowed by Descartes will play a critical role in Küng's later argument.

The next figure in the story narrated by Küng should be Immanuel Kant; in fact, however, Küng skips over Kant at this point to pursue the rationalist trend that culminates in G. W. F. Hegel. Only later, in the immediate context of his argument for affirming God's existence, does Küng come back to discuss Kant's contribution (S. 590–606; pp. 536–51) to the debate. For Küng, it is Kant who provides the classical formulation of the question of reason in relationship to "God." Kant views the idea of God, alongside the ideas of human freedom and immortality of the soul, as the third necessary postulate of a "practical" reason. Kant sees "God" as a regulative idea, immanent in all human understanding of self and of the cosmos, as the fundamental ground for the practice of knowing. It is a matter of debate whether Kant here has simply identified a postulated ground of practical thinking and acting or whether he has gone on to discover the dimension of ultimate trust, which underlies all human activity. In any case, not to be questioned is Kant's insight that practical reason is dependent upon a regulative idea that is not reducible to the kind of rational proof procedures of a calculating, objectifying theoretical manner of thinking. Does this mean that the Kantian solution is thereby irrational? On this question controversy would be sparked.

Against the background of Descartes' ideal of reason—a notion that lost some sharpness in the Enlightenment—Kant's fundamental critique would appear to represent an intolerable skepticism and the destruction of metaphysics.[17] In the course of his analysis of the inadequacies of classical philosophy, Kant appeared to tear asunder what belonged together: theoretical and practical reason, things in the world (*Dinge an sich*) and their appearance in the knowing subject, demonstrable insights and the regulative ideas required by the practice of living.

In the next section of his narrative, Küng shows how Hegel attempted to overcome the resulting dualism with a theo-logical synthesis (S. 157–90; pp. 129–88). Hegel attempts to think God radically by identifying the history of the world and of humankind as the process of God's own self-explication. In this monumental vision, history and society and art, religion, and philosophy become the "phenomenology of the spirit." In this process God, it would appear, legitimates himself in such a way that any thinking beings should be able to experience it themselves.

Hegel's monumental claim to understand the whole of reality and its history deductively as the rational expression of God's own being was doomed to failure. Hegel's God, if thinkable at all, is only thinkable radically and as a totality. In such a conception, however, freedom disappears. Hegel's speculative synthesis marks a kind of Copernican revolution for the status of philosophy, and in this Hegel's theological opponent in Berlin, F. Schleiermacher, is of one mind with him:[18] God must either be thought out absolutely and without reservation or he must be repudiated without reservation. The logic of this choice is consistent, but dangerous. Thus with L. Feuerbach an equally radical counterdynamic is set in motion, a movement reflecting a widespread cultural state of mind;[19] with Feuerbach, the modern critique of religion takes its start.

Under the heading "The Challenge of Atheism" (S. 221–380; pp. 189–340), Küng analyzes the three classical expressions of religious criticism, those represented by Feuerbach, Marx, and Freud. Theologically, this line of history is exceedingly important, for it discloses hermeneutically much more about the fate of the God question in the nineteenth and twentieth centuries than the history of the proofs for God's existence during this period alone would lead one to expect. With these criticisms, the discussion of God enters a new dimension. No longer is an abstract theoretical argumentation for or against the existence of God the center of attention. What is at stake here is not a "God per se" but rather God's relationship to us; what matters here is human freedom and righteousness, humankind's own coming of age and its learning to stand up straight. The question of God has become at once the question of humanity: what does God mean for the human person and for society? At stake is the nature of reality itself, its materiality and intelligibility.

L. Feuerbach develops his areligious criticism as an argument about the humanity of humankind. Across the board he raises the question of whether or not "God," instead of being the goal of human longing, does not in fact function primarily as a stopgap measure to compensate for our unfulfilled desires (S. 244–50; pp. 210–16).[20] Feuerbach's critique, as Küng shows, has the effect of coupling once and for all the question of God's existence with the question of the credibility of institutions and persons claiming to represent Christian religion (S. 346f.; pp. 213f.). K. Marx's religious criticism expands this perspective by coupling the critique of religion with the practical verification of belief in human action within society, analyzing the de facto function of religion within the bourgeois, capitalist society of the nineteenth century as a consolation to the disadvantaged for the sake of vested interests (S. 251–98; pp. 217–61). S. Freud, by contrast, turned inward to illuminate the role of religion in the arational realm of the human psyche, calling attention to religiously motivated repression and sublimation at the expense of human health and maturity (S. 299–363; pp. 262–323).

The effect of these critics and their disciples has been to widen the horizon of the argument. They have shown, it must be conceded, that important phenomena of religious belief can indeed be explained on critical anthropological, sociological, and psycho-ideological grounds without invoking God's existence. They further reveal that the atheistic rejection of belief is inseparably rooted in a devastating critique of the de facto functioning of institutional religion. Does this mean, then, that human history can in fact do without God altogether?

Nietzsche it was, as Küng shows in his next chapter (S. 381–470; pp. 341–424),[21] who grasped the implications of the atheist challenge: his answer Küng analyzes under the title "Nihilism—Consequence of Atheism." Nietzsche expands his radical critique of religion to a critique of morality, culture, and reality itself. The "death of God" is for him a wide-reaching cultural event of public significance. His response is a plea for a consistent atheism based not upon an idealistic notion of humanity but rather in an "overcoming of man by man" (S. 417; p. 375). At this point it becomes clear that the question of God's existence implies taking a stance with regard to humanity and the cosmos; the question of fundamental certainty comes here irrevocably to the fore (S. 422–26; pp. 380–84): For Nietzsche—having lost his faith in religion, civilization, culture, and progress—questionability and doubt become hallmarks of reality itself: in place of what is customary and thus, to all appearances, securely existing, it is utter nothingness that makes its appearance with ever-increasing clarity (S. 439; p. 387).

At this point, Küng interrupts his narrative to draw the consequences. With Nietzsche, the line of religious criticism marking modern thinking reaches its ultimate term in "nihilism": the negation of the meaning of reality itself. This is the ultimate counterpole to belief in God: doubt about reality, doubt about humankind and the cosmos. From now on, talk about God must take place "against the background of nihilism" (S. 460; p. 416). In contrast to Hegel, for whom belief is taken up into and thus legitimized by reason, Nietzsche saw clearly that with the demise of the certainty of faith, the certainty of reason itself has dissolved (S. 461; p. 417). Translated back into ontological language, the "fundamental certainty of being itself" (S. 461; p. 417) is put in question. Denial of being itself emerges as a possible option. At this point in the argument about God, the ultimate alternative to religious belief has been reached. Here, Küng insists, the discussion must take its stand. The proposition "God exists" expresses the alternative to nihilism. The question of God has once and for all been withdrawn from the realm of abstract, academic discourse; with nihilism it is our response to reality itself that is at stake.

Nihilism, Küng shows, is thus a fact to be reckoned with; it is, as the discussion with Nietzsche shows, "possible, irrefutable, but unproved!" (S. 468f.; p. 423). At this point, a fundamental question arises. Has the process of questioning, the method of systematic doubt brought us to an irremediable stalemate in which the ultimate choice between belief and nihilism becomes groundless? "To be or not to be—that is the question, that is the *basic question*," Küng writes. "Can nihilism be overcome and, if so, how?" (S. 471; p. 425). This question marks the turning point in Küng's argument. Up to this point, he has narrated the fate of the question of God in modern thought, showing how question has followed question until Nietzsche lay bare the ultimate nihilistic core of a consistent, concretely lived atheism. The ultimate consequence of unbelief is the denial of fundamental trust in reality itself. Against this antipode Küng can now formulate the alternative: fundamental trust in reality is ultimately grounded in belief in God (S. 473; p. 427). With Nietzsche, the real problem latent in the apparently so plausible solution of atheism comes into focus. Nietzsche attempted to think through atheism, not simply on the surface as a critique of the practice of belief, but in depth as a fundamental attitude with all its inherent consequences. This is why Nietzsche is so important, why he is seen as the paramount antitheologian in the history of thought, and why his work constitutes the most important context of discovery for the modern question of God.[22]

The horizon of the God question at the end of the modern era can thus be summarized under three headings, which point in the direction further discussion must take:

1. The abstract arguments for God's existence de facto no longer convince; practically they have lost their demonstrative power. Leaving aside the question whether this loss of convincing power be per se and intrinsic or merely accidental and historical, the fact that they do not convince must be taken into account. When we do this, however, we find that the apparent disadvantage reveals a hitherto hidden advantage. The question of God today can no longer be treated on the abstract theoretical plane; it must be handled in the concrete existential context of our own nature and our relationship to reality as such. We can only treat it on a level at which the truth of existence propositions is correlated with questions of the ethical correctness of human conduct and the religious credibility of those claiming to believe in God. The truth of belief in God's being can only convince our contemporaries when it can be shown to produce convincing values and credible practice. In short, *the arguments for God's being must be formulated in terms of the meaning of God for our own being human and for the concrete reality in which we are destined to live out our humanity.* This is the first component of the hermeneutical horizon.

2. The arguments for the existence of God can only be judged in the context of the question of the meaning or meaningless of the reality we experience. This means that *we must learn to understand this reality in such a way that the God question asserts itself within experienced reality instead of in some putative background dimension.*[23] This means attending to the boundary conditions of human experience as such. As the debate between belief and nihilism has shown, these conditions cannot be objectified in terms of their own inherent foundations or connections. We have to do here with a form of understanding that cannot be proven but that reveals to reflective thought a convincing inner rationality: to grasp this inner rationality is to "think" God.

3. Against this background the apparent stalemate expressed in the predicates "unprovable, irrefutable" can be broken. Faced with the alternative of theistic belief or nihilistic unbelief, fundamental trust in or distrust of reality, we find ourselves imbedded culturally and practically in a network of experiential and thoughtful coordinates long before our reason begins to look at arguments. This means that the ground of truth only reveals itself to us when in our thinking we have reached the goal of the truth is being sought.[24] Does this mean that our thinking is circular, that we must first affirm something before we can begin to know it? No! We have to do here not with a form of circular reasoning but rather with a precondition of the knowing process underlying the distinction between the objective and the subjective components of knowing, not circular reasoning but indeed a hermeneutical circle inherent in the nature of our knowing. *The God question crystalizes with its ultimate binding character within the hermeneutic circle of the nature of human understanding*.

The claim that belief in God is the more meaningful, or indeed the only meaningful, alternative must claim its legitimation before the tribunal constituted by the modern dispute about the sense of reality itself; more particularly, it must assert its claim before a court already committed to the negative alternative. Nietzsche was not interested in contesting a superficial notion of divinity capable of being deciphered as a functional interpretation of humanity, of a technologically or culturally manipulatable aspect of reality. Nietzsche attacks head-on the notion and experience of God as developed in the radically monotheistic culture of Christianity. God so conceived is not reducible to individual aspects of reality or to individual experiences, gaps, or principles, however central; God here means the whole, the all-comprehending transcendence inherent in reality as a whole.

With Nietzsche, Küng brings his narrative to an end. The meaning of the proposition "God exists" has been fathomed; it remains to bring the individual elements gained in this narrative tour de force into synthesis.

II. Yes to Reality

In narrating this history, it is Küng's intention to illuminate the character of the modern question of God and to explicate what it means to understand God as the supreme instance ultimately defining humankind and the world. When the atheistic critique of religion and the nihilistic critique of reality are taken seriously, it becomes clear that the truth of God's existence is intimately and necessarily connected with the truth of the reality to which we have empirical access.[25] The recognition of this connection is the invaluable achievement of nihilism. Nihilism has made clear that the debate about the question of God's existence is preceded by a debate about our own reality. To be sure, this is not an entirely new insight! A God who is thought of as independent of our reality, who is understood undialectically as pure transcendence, but whose immanence in the world is simultaneously ignored—ways of thinking contrary to the best Christian and philosophical traditions—loses his significance for the intrinsic understanding of reality.[26] A God who as ultimate cause and final goal remains external to the world and who in consequence becomes a competitor to human freedom is unworthy of the name "God." When Küng attempts to describe the notion of God with metaphoric nouns like "supreme instance," "ground," "support," and "goal," or with verbs like "defining," "determining," "structuring," and so forth, he intends them to be understood intrinsically, not extrinsically.[27] In Küng's hermeneutical perspective, "God's causality" appears as the working of the things themselves, his "final cause" reveals itself in the dynamic functioning of humans and the world, his "ordering principle" manifests itself in the structure, the life-organization, and the cultural process of reality itself. "Determining" is not to be understood as something coming from without; with this term Küng intends to name a depth dimension of our experience of reality, the discovery namely of an ultimate unity intrinsic to and encompassing all beings, a reality we can perceive but that surpasses the powers at our disposal. This depth dimension is given to us in our experience of reality; it is given to us as the boundary defining our own being and that of reality surrounding us. Here we come up against the limit of analogical discourse, that is, God in himself and through himself eludes the defining power of our knowing. This limit, however, is at the same time an opportunity; it makes it possible for us to conceive God as the supreme instance turned toward us and thus perceptible for us within the horizon of human experience.

God's relationship to the world embraces reality as a whole; it is that reality itself, as a whole and in all its parts. In this sense, God participates in every part of that reality and thus is verifiable in our individual, and thus partial, experiences of the world, of life, and of self. Anyone concerned with the question of God's being is forced to pose the question of the meaning or meaninglessness of this experienced reality. Ever since Nietzsche, it is not only God's being that is in question; the question of reality itself for us takes priority. The debate about nihilism, as Küng has shown, calls our attention to the need to distinguish between these two problem levels. Without losing sight of the implicit theological dimension of reality, it is necessary, as Küng shows, to begin methodically with the question of reality as such.

A further service rendered by the discussion of nihilism has been to show that the position we take with regard to the reality in which we find ourselves is not a matter to be treated on a level of abstract, objectifying reason. No human being would ever think of denying his or her own being, identity, or biography with the kind of distant intellectual act with which the existence of God is commonly denied. Among those who with aplomb regard the question of God as a simple matter to be affirmed or denied, no one would think of denying his or her own existence by an act of pure reason. Whether I like it or not, I am compelled to affirm my own existence and identity. I can indeed put an end to my life physically, but I cannot simply deny its existence intellectually. To take my life or to keep it, to accept my existence or reject it, to give order to my way of living or to refuse to do so, to see meaning in my future or only meaningless chaos, these indeed are real options for me; to deny my existence intellectually, however, is not a real option. Put in other terms, concrete living and acting even in its most negative expression presupposes my taking a stand, be it ever so unreflected and unscientific, in favor of my own existence. The same holds true for the reality surrounding me, for the history of the cultural area and the world in which I live. This is no neutral, Archimedian point at which I can begin to think as though fully divested of previous commitments. However much I may reject and condemn the reality surrounding me and the history that has formed me, I cannot simply negate them or wish them away, as many people think they can simply negate or wish away God.

For us, knowledge comes into being as the result of processes, individual and collective, characterized by acceptance or rejection; thus we have contrasting experiences of what we accept as given and what we refuse acceptance of. Such experiences reveal how much our knowledge is built upon prior decisions. Many people thus find meaning in a life of poverty, pain, and deprivation, because they have accepted life, their own life, in an implicit, prior act of trust. Others, on the contrary, are unable to recognize meaning in a life of opulence, pleasure, and abundance, because they have failed to make such an act of trust. In fact, upon closer examination, even the skeptics' refusal to take a stand, the pathos for objectivity, and the passion for criticism betray their roots in an implicit prior acceptance of reality. Küng calls attention to a "fundamental attitude" with innumerable nuances that manifests itself in the nihilism debate as a proported middle position between a consistent "fundamental distrust" and a "fundamental trust" (S. 485–89; pp. 438–41). However, when this alternative holds, excluding such a middle position, then "fundamental trust" and "fundamental mistrust" are not options on the same par; only those who are prepared to submit themselves positively to reality are capable of recognizing and judging this reality from within. Without a basis of trust, no child can grow up healthy; without trust no life worthy of humanity is possible (S. 502–10; pp. 453–60). Every science, every act of rational thought supposes, as Popper claims, a "belief in reason" (S. 511; pp. 461). Thus there are no grounds for claiming that a stalemate exists between yes and no, between affirmation or denial of reality.

In this distinction and correlation between "reality" and "God" lies, in my opinion, the decisive breakthrough of Küng's approach. The aspect of correlation, however, is as important as that of distinction. Because God reveals himself to us as the inner logic of our reality, we learn to deal with the God question precisely in learning to deal with reality. The way in which we cope with our own life prefigures the way we come to cope with the being of God. Without reference to our own reality, a hermeneutically responsible confrontation with the God question is unthinkable. Just as the material concept "reality" is reduced to an empty shell when abstracted from our concrete experience of dealing with the reality in which we find ourselves, so also an objectifying assertion of God's existence as an "all-determining supreme instance" turns out to be lexically empty when it is abstracted from its correlation to the concrete experience of speaker and hearer. Thus when notions like fundamental cause, fundamental ground, and fundamental goal are to be discussed as the ultimate all-encompassing reality of the cosmos, of humans and the world immediately surrounding them, then it is imperative to refer to the notions of cause, ground, and goal to immediate concrete experience of reality. This means discussing obliquely and indirectly the encompassing reality of God as the basis for the singular, individual meaning found in such experiences.[28] When the question of God's existence is put, then we must refer it to the position we take with regard to reality as such. Thus in the God question as in the question of our dealing with reality as such, a twofold structure of meaning and truth comes into focus. This is the dialectic of object-oriented versus speaker/hearer-oriented perspectives, of hermeneutical disclosure from within and logical deduction from without, of assertively taking a position as opposed to floating with judgment reserved. This tension is part and parcel of the argument.[29] The formal-logical sequence of propositions serves in Küng's argumentation as a simultaneous invitation[30] to listeners/readers to recognize the implications of meaning in their own experience and to interpret these implications in terms of the proposed categories of trustworthiness or untrustworthiness.

With these rather abstract considerations we have jumped ahead of Küng's argument. This is now the place to confront the core of Küng's argument in *Does God Exist?* (S. 607–40; pp. 552–84) or in the passage from the *Twenty-four Theses* cited at the beginning of this article. In the foregoing investigations we have approached this argument from two sides. The one side is represented by what Küng calls "inner reasonableness," exemplified by Pascal's "reasons of the heart." This inner reasonableness is closed against any approach from without; it is open, however, to a hermeneutical approach from within: its truth can be disclosed to reason by the hermeneutical illumination of experiential complexes in human life. On the opposite side, we have seen how Küng appeals to this reasonableness precisely in a communicative situation in which the proposition "God exists" has lost its plausibility. Outwardly, we no longer can rely upon the apparent clarity and self-evidence this proposition once enjoyed in the premodern culture. Thus we are thrown back upon an "inner reasonableness," which must nevertheless be communicable because it is rooted in a shared fundamental experience.

We can thus sum up the results of modern thinking and modern criticism. It is not only the response "God exists" but also the very question of God that, with the advent of atheism, threatened to disappear from sight. We have to thank Nietzsche for the invaluable service he has rendered by explicating the radical questionableness of reality itself resulting from the course taken by modern thought. The question remains, can this questionableness of reality as such manifest itself not only as the result of a historical sociocultural process but also as an immediate result of personal experience within the horizon of such inner reasonableness? For Küng it is evident that all efforts and claims to the contrary notwithstanding, neither humans nor their world can be adequately explained in their own terms. This insight manifests itself precisely by and for those who are prepared to accept reality in an act of fundamental trust. Trust means precisely the waiver of apparent securities and the radical openness to the possibility of disappointment from whatever side it may come. Once again we arrive at the turning point represented by nihilism. In the words of W. Weischedel, "Anyone who proposes to confront the question of God philosophically in our age must take account of the situation in which this question is today located; he must put himself at the zero point, from which alone, in the absence of all securities, truth can emerge in a new mode."[31]

III. Yes to God?

This point-zero situation corresponds to the totalizing of the question, consistently practiced by Küng when he translates the question into the dimension of our contemporary identity, our historical legacy, and our future expectations. One recognizes here the allusion to the three classical questions of philosophy: Who are we? Where do we come from? Where are we going? (S. 619f.; pp. 563f.)[32] When these questions are pursued to their ultimate roots, they reveal dimensions Küng designates with reference to *reality as a whole* by the terms "primal ground," "primal support," "primal goal," in short, the "being itself" of reality as a whole (S. 622; p. 566) and then with reference to *humans' own being* by the terms "primal source," "ultimate meaning," and "all-embracing hope," again in short, the "being itself" of my life in particular (S. 623; p. 567). The terms "ground," "support," and "goal," like the terms "source," "meaning," and "hope," bring to expression the radical contingency of our being in the world; with the term "being itself," borrowed from the metaphysical tradition, Küng designates the existential grounding of this contingency.[33] From a hermeneutical point of view, it is clear that such notions are not capable of being further reduced to some underlying term. Taken together, they articulate specific strains of our experience of reality as a whole and of our own life history, strains of experience in which God can be recognized as all-defining reality. It is thus these strains of experience that give meaning to the otherwise empty formula "all-defining reality." In this connection it should be noted, that thanks to K. Marx, we must view reality in terms of the practical dimension of our action in social context. The question of God thus implies ethical practice as an intrinsic dimension of our way of living.

The product of this complex argument is admittedly not a compelling demonstration but a reasonable account and confirmation.[34] The assent to God's existence remains "problematical," for the process of indirect verification in experience remains open to those experiences that speak against his existence. Prereflexive and prescientific conditioning play a not completely analyzable role in our path to positive acceptance of reality as a whole and our acceptance of our life in particular; thus they also play a role in our process of decision for or against the existence of God. We are stamped by attitudes and predecisions long before we begin to ask questions or formulate arguments. This is why the method of indirect verification cannot compel but only invite; it cannot evoke a situation of confrontation with an irrefutable proof compelling assent but only a situation of being confronted with an unavoidable problem requiring decision.

How then should questioners comport themselves? At this point Küng introduced the notions of "trust," "belief," and "decision," voluntaristic notions that need not be irrational, however, at least not when reasonable grounds can be adduced. More of this later. What interests us here is a different question. How is the relationship between argument and counterargument in this situation to be understood? The verification process proposed by Küng is indirect in a twofold manner: (1) the immediate goal of verification is not the existence of God as such, but only the legitimacy of accepting this existence; (2) the goal of verification is not an irrefutably correct affirmation but rather a decision of acceptance resting on an inner reasonableness and plausible grounds for belief. Küng writes: "Statements on God will be verified and tested against the background of our experience of life: not in conclusive deduction from a supposedly obvious experience that renders unnecessary a decision on man's part, but in a clarifying illumination of the always problematic experience that invites man to a positive decision. Only when talk of God is supported by concrete experience of the world and man, related to this and conveyed together with it, is its credibility established" (S. 605; p. 550). Against this background we have to examine Küng's manner of arguing. Having set forth his reflections about reality as such, he proceeds in three steps.

Step 1: The inescapable question. "Without authentic transcendence, there can be no authentic transcending of de facto reality in the here and now. Thus the question of religion, indeed the question of God impinges itself on us." It is not simply the history of the God question that makes the issue inescapable. On the contrary, it is the uninhibited, honest look at the grave problems addressing people and society that renders the God question unavoidable. The world as such remains confined within its ultimate questionableness. The world as a whole and humans in particular are unable to ground themselves in themselves, unable to achieve a satisfying, coherent self-understanding, unable to provide an ultimate answer to the questions of origin, meaning, and goal for the person as individual, for society in its history, for the world as humankind's horizon. In and from this situation of radical questionableness, we are called to answer the question of whether God really exists.

With these thoughts, Küng has not simply shown that the question of God's being exists de facto as inescapable; rather he points to the field of experience of humankind and the world, where the question emerges necessarily with insistent priority. This field it is that not only calls for an answer but also provides the basis for an answer. The problem is equally inescapable for someone attempting to pursue the negative argument. No one can simply shove the question of God's being aside as irrelevant. In this way the field and the perspective, the speaker/hearer-oriented and the object-oriented dimensions for the indirect verifications are staked out. Simultaneously it is made manifest that and why the argument must be conducted with an eye to the practical consequences of every step; the intimate connection between theory and practice must not be lost sight of.

The question arises prior to all reflective processes or argumentation and all "purely scientific" modes of inquiry. Method is not to be separated from the person! If God is really the "all-determining reality," that is, the all-grounding, the existence-supporting, and the meaning-and-direction-giving reality,[35] then he must be intimately connected with our concrete experience.[36] This is the answer to the objection that with such phrases Küng is juggling meaningless, noncommittal expressions. As definitions of God, these expressions are not the product of abstract reflection or arbitrary postulation; they are evoked by our concrete experience or our own reality as lacking in itself adequate ground, support, and direction to explain its experienced groundedness, supportedness, directedness. The "ultimate" question comes into view because the realities of human existence call for "ultimate," all-determining, meaning-giving answers.

To put the matter in another way, in the context of Küng's argumentation, the assertion "God exists" has meaning only insofar as it establishes meaning within our experience. He is not interested in abstract constructions or demonstrations of God as such. His intention is to offer a rationale for our de facto ability to speak of God's existence in relationship to our own way of life. This is the reason that he does not begin his investigation with a discussion of the concept or definition of God but rather with an analysis of the significance of God's existence for our understanding of ourselves and of the world in which we live as these reveal themselves in our history. This history is thus a constitutive element of the argument; in this sense one may say that he defines God as a function of our reality and our experience, though he is careful to point our that the full reality of God is more than such functional definitions can express.

Step 2: God as hypothesis. Having established this definition of God as "all-determining reality" concretized as hermeneutical illumination of specific strains of human experience, Küng proceeds to construct a conditional connection between, on the one hand, these strains of experienced reality requiring explanation and, on the other hand, the existence of God as a hypothetical resolution of this need for explanation. This preliminary hypothetical formulation of an answer to the questions posed by our experience of reality takes the following form *in relation to reality* as a whole:

> If God exists,
> —Then the grounding reality itself is not ultimately groundless . . . because God is then the primal ground of all reality. . . .
> —Then the supporting reality itself is not ultimately unsupported . . . because God is then the primal support of all reality. . . .
> —Then evolving reality itself is not ultimately without direction . . . because God is then the primal goal of all reality. . . .
> —Then reality suspended between being and nonbeing is not ultimately under suspicion of being a void . . . because God is then the being itself of all reality. (S. 622; p. 566)

And the following form *in relation to our personal reality* as individual human beings, each with his or her own history as part of the overall history of humankind:

> If God exists,
> —Then, despite all the menace of fate and death, I can with good reason confidently affirm the unity and identity of my human existence . . . because God is the primal source also of my life;
> —Then, despite all the menace of emptiness and meaninglessness, I can with good reason confidently affirm the truth and meaningfulness of my existence . . . because God is the ultimate meaning of my life;
> —Then, despite all the menace of sin and damnation, I can with good reason confidently affirm the goodness and value of my existence . . . because God is then the all-embracing hope of my life;
> —Then, against all the menace of nonbeing, I can with good reason confidently affirm the being of my human existence: God is then the being itself in particular also of human life. (S. 623f. p. 567f.)

As these formulas make clear, the counterarguments, that is, the experiences of nothingness, of meaninglessness, of baselessness, of directionlessness in the world as a whole, in the history of humankind, and in my own personal history, are neither ignored nor refuted. Reality remains "questionable"; the counterarguments, however, are not the last word.[37] Despite such counterexperiences, it is possible to affirm the identity, meaning, and value of human existence.

In the context of the preliminary hypothesis, God's existence appears as a sufficient condition for the experiences of identity, meaning, and value: "if God exists, then the condition of the possibility of this uncertain reality also exists" (S. 624; p. 568). Under the supposition of this functional definition of God and its explication in reference to experience, the logical consequence connecting condition (God's existence) and consequent (answer to an ultimate question implicit in experience) is patent and inescapable. But what is gained by this step? Küng himself admits that "we cannot conclude from the hypothesis of God to the reality of God": "we can conclude from reality to possibility, but not conversely"! At this stage, neither side of the argument has been proven conclusively. The reality of experience evokes the question of the reality of its ground (does God exist as the possible ground of being?), but the ambivalence of this reality (precisely its contingency) makes a necessary deduction impossible. The experiences of the dissolution of meaning and of the radical questionableness of being are as evident as those of meaning and certainty. They too, however, are not decisive; atheism cannot be proven, but it cannot be disproven either (S. 625; p. 568). Does this mean that God is and remains merely a hypothesis?

It might appear that with this admission, indeed with the whole hypothetical argument, Küng has done a disservice to his cause, bidding farewell once and for all to the possibility of giving a rational account of belief in God or of speaking of God in the realm of scientific discourse. The answer to this objection is found in the third step.

Step 3: Inner reasonableness of decision. At this point we have reached the core of Küng's argument. The hypothetical construction was designed merely to make clear the consequences of an answer to the God question for us humans and our reality. The truth or falsehood of such an answer has up to this point entered the argument only as a concession that as yet it remained unproven. Despite the urgency of the question, a skeptical wait-and-see remains a legitimate attitude. It is at this point that Küng introduces the key principle of his argument: "The fact that God is, can be affirmed . . . only in a confident trust rooted in reality itself" (S. 626; p. 570). As I see it, this statement has four epistemological implications.

1. Objectifying procedures designed to yield compelling proof are rejected by Küng as inappropriate; that is to say, the classical notion of

verification as practiced in modern science is not applicable to the God question. The demonstration of the truth of God's existence is not to be legitimized by an appeal to logical correctness and stringency.

2. The renunciation of such procedures and standards is not an embarrassment but an opportunity making place for a broadening of perspective. Methodically speaking, as explained above, we have to do here with a hermeneutical procedure aimed at disclosing concrete object- and subject-oriented constellations of meaning within human experience of self and of the world around the self. In such a procedure, "God" manifests himself as a condition, indeed the ultimate condition of being, as being manifests itself within the truth content of a comprehensive understanding of reality. The truth of God's being is not attainable as the correct formal-logical consequence of a chain of individual propositions, but rather as a hermeneutical disclosure of meaning within the context of the comprehensive experience of truth in reality as a whole.

In this light, the reason for the cautious irreal, hypothetical construction "IF God WERE to exist, THEN a fundamental solution WOULD BE GIVEN . . ." becomes apparent. We do not have to do here with a propositional connection in formal logic but rather with an invitation, a challenge, a "wager," if you will, in Pascal's sense. With this construction, readers/listeners are offered a set of instructions setting out how to understand their own existence and that of the world around them in such a way that God's existence provides an answer to the radical questions about the ground, support, and goal of this reality. "God" here is offered so to speak as a working hypothesis in the best sense of the term, a working hypothesis for thinking and acting. The truth of the hypothesis thus discloses itself not to the uncommitted logician checking the formal correctness of its propositions and their sequence, but only to those who have committed themselves to practicing it in life. Unlike a logical hypothesis, a working hypothesis reveals its truth in doing: it only convinces those who see it work in their own life or in the shared experience of another.

3. "Trust" is what Küng calls the willingness to put one's reliance into a constellation of meaning one has recognized without being compellingly objectifiable. This is what Küng has in mind when he asserts that God, more precisely the affirmation of God's existence, can only be accepted in an attitude of trust. The neutrality of questioning reason is not illegitimately violated by this assertion, but it is unmasked as mere appearance when extended to the ultimate questions. In the perspective of a hermeneutical illumination of existential meaning, the purporting neutrality of reason proves to be a lack of willingness to give

assent and thus to be a pretense for disguising one's refusal. It is imperative to attend to the precise meaning of trust in this context. It is not that Küng adds to knowing some new, in principle irrational quality purporting to complete or to direct the knowing process. On the contrary, he recalls our attention to the intrinsic connection between trust and understanding: he shows that "trust" namely is part of the framework of understanding and that understanding is a genuine dimension of trust.[38] Trust and its foundation must be thought of reciprocally; their connection discloses itself to the trusting knower as a unity founded in the object of trust.

For Küng, the readiness to commit oneself is an intrinsic aspect of all forms of understanding. For this reason he can begin by studying the function of trust as an aspect of our encounter with immediately experienced reality in all of its dimensions. In doing so he speaks of "fundamental trust" as a basic universal affirmative commitment to reality as such. Only in a second step does he consider trust in God, using the term "faith" to express the radical fundamental trust that finds its ultimate ground in God. Like fundamental trust in general, faith is not a substitute for or a supplement to cognition but rather a part of the framework of cognition itself.

4. This interconnection makes clear why, for Küng, the yes or no answers to the meaning of reality and to the being of God do not have equal status. In the very process of affirmingly thinking through reality, the reasonableness of such an affirmation makes itself manifest. Conversely, the refusal to practice assenting thought has the effect of calling thinking up short before the critical ground is reached; in this case, one fails to achieve an unprejudiced encounter with meaning of reality.[39] By contrast, in the yes to God, an ultimate foundation for trust in reality is assented to. Thus belief in the existence of God lies along a line consistent with trust in reality itself, for every communication of meaning brings its own ground to light.[40] "As radical fundamental trust, belief in God can suggest the condition of the possibility of uncertain reality" (S. 628; p. 572).

Again it should be emphasized that these explanations cannot be molded into a new compelling demonstration. Prima facie, they simply describe the experience of someone who assents to trust and faith. The relative advantages or disadvantages of an affirmative or a negative response are only indirectly illuminated within an intrinsic context of meaning. This means that alternative positions are as little refutable as they are provable; at best they can be analyzed to reveal their inner consistency. This is what Küng means then in speaking of an "inner rationality or reasonableness."

In the following three propositions I shall attempt to elucidate more clearly the meaning of such an "inner rationality."

1. Fundamental trust must contain its rationale within itself, if it is not to be unmasked as ultimate irrationality. Precisely as fundamental it cannot be the result of a prior justifying act; otherwise it would be caught in a spiral of infinite regress. Trust thus appears as a potential part of the very act of willing to know: readiness to learn necessarily includes a fundamental attitude of openness such that the possibility of disappointment is not a priori excluded but at the same time is also not a priori inevitable.

2. The attitude of trust rests upon experiences and insights that can be pointed to by way of example in connection with the grounding of meaning. The experiences as such, however, remain singular, and biographically unique despite their analogically common structures: in short, they can indeed be communicated and discussed, but they cannot be abstractly universalized without loss of content and persuasive force. For this reason, they cannot serve as premises of a logically compelling argument.[41] This is what Pascal meant in referring to "reasons of the heart" and what Küng means by "inner reasonableness."

3. Such an "inner" rationality resting upon concrete experience overreaches all attempts to confine discussion within the isolating boundaries of purely theoretical discourse. Again, we have to do here with concrete, biographically singular experiences, not with abstractly generalized and thus empty experience schemata. The experiences in question may very well be articulatable only within specific language games related to the concrete practice of living. Transposition into theoretical discourse means loss of meaning. For this reason, the abstract question of truth can only be put when the reports of concrete experiences have been heard. Thus the "inner" rationality remains within the tension of the IF-THEN structure of our thinking; it is not capable of being distilled into compelling, self-evident truths. Faith in God cannot in this life defintively transcend the limits of a living experiment.

These considerations make clear that the notions of "trust" and "fundamental trust," though rooted in empirical psychology,[42] are taken by Küng in a much deeper anthropological and epistemological sense. From the point of view of the philosophy of science, it should be clear that "trust" to be sure is a mode of cognition, but one quite

different from the prevailing ideal of rational scientific discourse with its
norms of direct empirical verifiability, quantifiability, and repeatability.
Trust is the reasonable readiness to put one's confidence in, to commit
oneself to truths neither self-evident, demonstrable, nor scientifically
verifiable, truths attested to by concrete experiences of meaning in
events neither repeatable at will nor capable of generalization (S. 510–25;
pp. 461–73). From the point of view of the nihilist problematic, on the
other hand, it should be clear that what is at stake is a comprehensive
and fundamental heuristic scheme in terms of which we interpret and
react to experiences in positive or negative fashion. Such trust in the
context of the God question signifies the readiness to commit oneself to
an interpretive scheme in which reality and humanity, more specifically
my own being, is shown definitively to be intelligible and affirmable
because rooted in the being of God himself.

At this point it may be objected, what gives us the right to so explain
away the radical questionableness of reality with a hypothesis of God's
existence? Is not such a hypothesis simply a mode of escape for the soft-
minded who are unwilling or unable to live with absolute skepticism,
the negation of intrinsic meaning, the groundlessness of ethical norms?
Protestant theologians tend to leave the discussion at this point, con-
tenting themselves with the assertion that God's existence cannot be
further grounded but only proclaimed as God's own word to humankind.[43] Küng, on the contrary, coming from the Catholic tradition,
insists that believers must face this objection and give it a reasonable
answer. His answer can thus be expressed using the categories of
Dalferth. It is the basic ontic, ontological, and anthropological facts, the
questions of goals and meaning, of rules of conduct and their foundations that compel us to raise the issue of God's existence at least as a
question. To do so is by no means to water down the provocation of the
Christian confession of faith. On the contrary, serious discussion of the
issue at this level reveals the point of intersection at which question and
answer alike have their ultimate context.

We have to do here with a dialectical tension between construction
and reconstruction of our notion of God, a tension between the
designative and the predicative function of God talk. Before talking
about the existence of God we must identify what we mean by "God." A
definition like "all-determining reality" is an initial construction; in the
process of further discussion this notion is hermeneutically recon-
structed, being made precise and filled with meaning by reference to
experience. In this process, one must take utmost care to carry out the
reconstruction in such a way that God is shown to correspond to urgent

needs unveiled by the God question without, however, being made into a utopian product of our own anxieties or fantasies of grandeur and might. God must remain God! This tension between construction and reconstruction in the notion of God guarantees that our speaking of God remains within a context in which the issue of inner reasonableness enters into its own process of verification as a critical element. This means: (1) that question and answer be formulated in a way comprehensible for contemporary men and women; (2) that they be formulated so as not to be confined to a particular system of belief; and (3) that critical questions can be put to historical conceptions of God. The distance between authentic, convincing inner reasonableness and ideological wishful thinking is short. Appropriate discourse about God's existence is only possible when the affirmation of God is continually confronted with the radical questionableness of human life and our reality. Otherwise God would not be God!

IV. "God Exists"

The goal of Küng's argumentation is the affirmation "God exists." What does this statement mean? Rather than repeating Küng's own explanations, I propose at this point to offer my own reflections on this theologically controverted proposition along lines I believe compatible with Küng's thinking.

It should be clear, that the assertion of God's existence is only analogically comparable to assertions about the existence of things in our sphere of reality. Directly comparable is the intention on the part of the speaker: the affirmation of existence puts the talk about God expressly in an ontological context. This intention contradicts any attempt to functionalize or fundamentalize the concepts. To functionalize a concept would be to reduce it to a mere cipher for other meaningful contents that can be explicated on an entirely this-worldly, immanent plane.[44] To fundamentalize a concept would be to exclude it from being located within philosophical reflection about reality as a whole. What is affirmed to exist cannot be reduced to the causality, the value structure, or the reasonable grounds of some other existent entity. Thus the assertion of existence resists any attempt to view God as a mere aspect, an immanent legitimation, or a depth dimension, for example, the "wholeness" character of empirical reality. The real possibility of nihilism shows that our understanding of the existence of the world around us is altered when we affirm the existence of God.

With his affirmation "God exists," Küng takes a step that has hitherto provoked sharp criticism, particularly on the part of Protestant theologians, who object that to reduce the God question to the "abstract" question of God's mere "existence" is to fail to take the divinity of God seriously. In this way, they object, God is reduced to an objectifiable being on the same plane as the world and humankind. Rejecting what they regard as a *Verdinglichung*, that is, "reification," the reduction to the status of a quasi-material thing, they emphatically cite Bonhoeffer's biting observation, *"Ein Gott, den es gibt, gibt es nicht* [a God who is there is not God]. Küng has no trouble accepting this maxim, insofar as it criticizes a practical reduction of God's being to something that is there "like Lake Geneva, the Matterhorn, or the love between two human beings." Against an exaggerated interpretation of this phrase, however, Küng counters with a quotation from Bertolt Brecht in his *Geschichten vom Herrn Keuner*; asked if there is a God, Herr Keuner replies: "I advise you to consider whether your conduct would change in the light of your answer to this question. If it would change, then I can help you at least to this extent, that I say, you have already decided. You need a God" (S. 617; pp. 561f.). On the basis of the preceding discussions of atheism and nihilism, fundamental trust and faith, Küng attempts at this point in the argument to give a threefold positive answer to Herr Keuner's question, what would change in our conduct if God were to exist? (S. 618ff.; pp. 562ff.). Instead of recounting Küng's answer, I propose to take a different rather more abstract track in answering this objection. Thus I would call attention to two questions discussed in the analysis of religious language: (1) How can we identify God when we use the term "God"? and (2) What is the nature of the assertion that God exists?

As a first step we have to ask whether "God" in the context of the existence assertion serves as a "designator" or a "predicator." In the first case, God can appear as the subject of further statements; the term is used as a proper name or as an identifying descriptor. Insofar as "God" is a proper name, I can use this name without having to describe his person any further. In this case, I would appear to know him as I might know Fritz or Barbara; I can point to him to identify him. But then question upon question arises—How do I know him? How have I made his acquaintance? How can I bring my knowledge of him into the discussion with my conversation partner—if all I have is a proper name? Conversely, if I use the term "God" as an identifying description, then I must know enough descriptive characteristics about him to distinguish him clearly from other beings. Here the question is, where did I get this prior descriptive knowledge? In either case, caution is obviously called for. Should some insist on using the term "God" as a proper name or as an identifier grounded in a particular religious tradition, for example, the Christian tradition, they run the risk of breaking off discussion with representatives of other religions, with philosophers, and with many men and women in secular society. Representatives of other religions name their God otherwise; secularized men and women likewise have their own names for the ultimate reality within their own particular experience.

In the second case, the term "God" as predicator, the term is used to designate an identifying quality or characteristic predicated of some grammatical subject: "being God" can be predicated of a subject called by a proper name in a particular religion, for example, "Yahweh is God," "Allah is God." This usage is well grounded, not only in religious traditions but also in the dialogue with nonbelievers, for there too the term "God" can only be introduced in this predicative sense. This may be the case even within the community of convictions within a particular religion; the danger exists that further argumentative discussion may be broken off when the predicative usage is neglected.

The designative and the predicative usage complement each other. The preliminary construction of a predicative concept of "God" is inescapable; without it the designative process of identification cannot get under way. At the same time, the designating name must be continuously filled with meaning predicatively, as a product of the continuing reconstruction on the basis of the meaning experiences, which have the effect of making "God" verifiable.[45] In the end, designative and predicative usage coincide in the insight that "God" can ultimately only be defined by "God" himself: "God" can only be understood as God.

Now to the second question: What is the nature of the assertion that God exists? The analysis of existence propositions with a view to propositions about God's existence leads to a complicated state of affairs. There is widespread agreement, that existence propositions can be meaningful only when they are formulated in terms of singular, identifiable entities. Thus well beyond questions of linguistics, "singular existence propositions" include ontological presuppositions;[46] only in terms of their frame of reference can they be illuminated. Already in his 1981 study, Dalferth concluded: "With the assertion 'God exists' I postulate a connection in reality between God and myself, in which each has his place and stands in a relationship open to explication."[47] Three years later Dalferth took this line of thinking further, ascribing a transcategorical and transcendental function to existence propositions: such a proposition does not add semantically a further element of meaning to the object; instead it connects my thought and my reality with one another. The "existing" object confronts me as an irreducible truth.[48] Thus the speaker and the spoken "are both localized in the context of the existent":[49] they are "both in principle identifiable in the same fashion."[50] In traditional terms, we have to do here with the wonder evoked by the realization, that reality exists, that I am myself, that it is in my power to distinguish between reality and fiction.

Existence propositions of this type are not merely constantly presupposed in our speaking about reality;[51] in fact they transcend, implicitly or explicitly, the propositional dimension itself. Viewed as acts of speech, they presuppose an obligation that touches the speaker himself.[52] In statements about reality as a whole, this obligation is implicitly named. In assertions about God, this obligation is directly thematized. The ontological commitment, which already in ordinary existence propositions comes into play, is made propositionally explicit in assertions about reality as a whole. In assertions about God it is introduced into a tradition of ways of speaking canonized by thousands of years of usage. The leap from uncommitted description to explicit acceptance of the obligation carried out is termed by Küng "trust." The radical quest of this obligating dimension of trust in relationship to God is termed by him "faith."

A careful analysis of Küng's argument could show that here questions about knowledge are not being answered by voluntaristic appeals to trust. The attitude of trust consists in the first place in an openness to binding cognition. Trust is the readiness to give explicit assent to the foundations of cognition implicit in cognition as such; in addition it is the readiness to exploit these foundations to give direction to the cognitive process and to formulate the grounds for its propositional expression. The reference to fundamental trust can thus be understood as pointing to the intrinsic consequence of obligations undertaken implicitly in the act of knowing itself.

It is against this background that I recommend reading Küng's hypothetical argument in the "IF–THEN–WOULD BE" formulation. It would be wrong to ignore the discursive situation of the hearer/reader who is to be convinced by the argument:[53] to do so would be to raise suspicions of indulging in moral reproach or authoritarian commandeering instead of engaging in open dialogue.[54]

The situation is so complex, because a discourse arguing hermeneutically from the discovery context normally presupposes prior agreement about this context. In the case of God talk, such agreement cannot be presupposed but must first be built up in a context of legitimation. Here the question arises, how is the discovery context to be transposed into a context of legitimation and cognitive support? Küng formulates a conditional relationship, the members of which are not related to the hearer/reader in exactly the same manner. The existence of God is the proposition to be grounded. Contrary to expectations, however, it appears in this conditional relationship not as the consequence of some premise but rather as the sufficient ground of a series of consequences pertaining to reality as a whole. God's existence is thus introduced as the answer to all the questionableness of the world as a whole and of humankind in particular. However, the consequences of the condition are not simply verifiable empirically. On the contrary, what is empirically verifiable is precisely the scandalous radical questionability of the world and of humanity.

What then has been gained? Küng turns all the argumentative strategies against his own position and thus brings into focus the mental impasse. He himself has put forward the radical questionableness of reality as the result of the history of thought leading up to our present situation; he himself has demonstrated how helplessly theology has responded to the problem. Thus he has brought himself to a point on the plane of legitimating ratiocination where further rational argument becomes impossible. This, however, was precisely his intention. This is the reason why he desists from developing a strategy of counterargument designed to refute or at least weaken the negative consequences.[55]

The resulting debacle forces the discussants to shift the context of their argumentation. In what way? Recall the observation made earlier, that existence propositions always affect the situation of the speaker. Although we cannot formulate the relationship in singular grounding contexts, we can indeed express it in general propositions. It can be realized in the hermeneutical structure of convincing discovery. This is possible, however, only for those who have openly committed themselves to the situation under discussion. Küng describes this condition with the category of trust: "The fact that God exists can only be affirmed in trust rooted in reality itself" (S. 626; p. 570). Note that he does not speak here of "faith": he does not fall into the tautology of saying, "that God exists must be accepted in faith." Trust, in the sense used, here contains a hermeneutical dimension. In this context, Küng refers trust to God only insofar as he is the ground for reality as a whole.

Thus in this situation Küng reverses the principle-consequence relationship. Nothing is demonstrable in the sense that those not committing themselves to the situation are thereby explicitly and inescapably put in the wrong. Küng claims, however, that the relationship can be disclosed, and explained in a reasonable and positive manner. Anyone who understands the compelling situation of disclosure in terms of an attitude of trust experiences this trust as coming from a faith that contains its reasonableness within itself. Arguments for God's existence are thus invitations to entrust oneself to the binding character of comprehensive thinking that penetrates to its own ground; they are no more than this but also no less.

Conclusion: Crossing the Boundaries

As we have seen, Küng unfolds his argument for the exsistence of God against the background of a long history of problems. One obvious reason for this extensive narrative is that the communication of the experience of others corresponds to the appeal to an inner rationality. A further reason, however, is that Küng explicitly attempts with this argument to cross the three classic boundaries of traditional theological discussion, the boundaries, namely, between philosophy and theology, between Catholic and Protestant theology, and between a "scientific" and a "prescientific" model of thinking. These boundaries have grown up historically, but they are often defended in the name of strict logic and conceptual clarity. Within the rules of such discreet language games, arguments take on the appearance of being strict proofs or rebuttals. It is overlooked that these rules are the product of historically conditioned prejudgments and as such represent arbitrary reductions of the complexity of our experience.

1. Küng aims to cross the border between philosophy and theology. This boundary has been drawn since the Enlightenment by a philosophy that has emancipated itself from theology on the basis of the Cartesian ideal of a rationalistic grounding of our thinking. As we have seen, Küng views trust as a reasonable framework for our approach to reality. As contemporary philosophy of science has come to admit, relationships of trust, interest, and readiness to give assent are integral parts of the knowing act and cannot therefore be de facto ignored or methodically bracketed out.[56] In this perspective, faith, that is, "my trust in God as genuine, radical, fundamental trust" (S. 629; p. 572), can be seen as an act philosophical in character.

2. Küng aims to transgress the boundary between Catholic and Protestant theological traditions, as manifested in their opposite positions with regard to the so-called natural theology.[57] The fact is that in our Western European cultural area we speak of God often unwittingly in a framework laid down by Christian tradition. Faith and trust, however, are also possible outside the Christian system of belief. This

does not mean that the form and contents of faith are reduced to a "Christian philosophy," but rather that the theological reflection must open itself without prior conditions to the philosophical discourse about these realities. There is no regionally localizable storm-free zone of knowledge reserved for the Christian.

3. Küng overcomes the customary boundaries defining a rationalistically arguing science, boundaries that make such science incapable of perceiving trust and faith as legitimate modes of thinking underlying its own activities. Clearly, the call to trust must not be understood as an excuse for sober argumentation; however, the time has come to take account once again of a prescientific, practical dimension of all truth. This dimension is above all important as part of a truth, which implies binding consequences for the person who recognizes it.[58]

Thus Küng understands the proposition "God exists" as a summary statement of a faith in God, a faith that can, but need not, be bound to a specific system of religious belief, and that by the same token is not reducible to an attitude of intellectual distance.[59] On the other hand, he understands the proposition as a summary statement of a problematic that has deeply molded the history of Christian culture. This history of the critique of religion cannot be pushed out of sight or psychologically repressed; too deeply has it influenced the way we perceive the God question. Against this background, Küng's arguments are conceived as a challenge to speaking within the church itself and to a theology that has often failed or refused to take problems seriously. What Küng the theologian is calling for is that the Christian churches learn to proclaim their faith in God in a language understandable to contemporary men and women, to enter into dialogue with believers in the religions other than the Christian, and together with nonbelievers and other-believers to work for a more just and peaceful world. God alone can ultimately provide the grounds for our hope in and our engagement for a better future.

(Translated by Dr. Thomas Riplinger)

Notes

Introduction

1. It ended with Schlick's death in 1936, but its influence did not end then. Among its members were G. Bergmann, R. Carnap, H. Feigl, P. Frank, K. Göbel, H. Hahn, O. Neurath, and F. Waismann.
2. Seen historically, the movement shows influences from: (1) the older empiricism and positivism of especially Hume, Mill, and Mach; (2) the methodology of empirical science as developed about the middle of the nineteenth century; and (3) the symbolic logic and logical analysis of language as developed especially by Frege, Whitehead and Russell, and Wittgenstein.
3. Sir Henry Wotton (1568–1639), an English poet and diplomat who matriculated in New College, Oxford, in 1584, wrote this in *A Panegyric to King Charles*. The Latin should be literally translated: "an itch for disputation is the mange of the churches."

Chapter I: The Presumption of Atheism

1. That reference to the "accidents of bread in cheese" was, of course, an altogether characteristic sideswipe against the peculiarly Roman Catholic doctrine of transubstantiation.
2. At the last count, which was no doubt not completely comprehensive, this short and slight piece, originally commissioned for and first appearing in an ephemeral undergraduate journal, had reappeared no less than thirty-three times, including translations into Welsh, Italian, German, and Danish. For some afterthoughts, compare Flew 1975 and 1984a, chap. 6.
3. It is quite interesting to compare what Flew thinks is "literally preposterous" (here in the last sentence of the former paragraph and the first two sentences of this one) with what Gilson thinks is equally difficult in his "The Idea of God and the Difficulties of Atheism" referenced in the bibliography of this book.—T.M.
4. It is interesting to note here that Flew relegates the use of constitutive miracle being the alleged physical resurrection of Jesus bar Joseph to the United Kingdom of the eighteenth century and completely ignores—"refuses" to mention—his own seminal debate on the resurrection (see Miethe, Habermas, and Flew 1987) and its significance.—T.M.
5. Defoe had published *Robinson Crusoe* first in 1719.

Chapter II: The First Engagement

1. See Paul Johnson, *Intellectuals* (San Francisco: Harper & Row, 1989). Chapter 2 deals with Shelley's "disreputable life" (so called by Antony Flew in correspondence of 3 November 1989).
2. In point of fact, Antony G. N. Flew was an undergraduate member of St. John's College and Shelley was an undergraduate member of University College. At Oxford, on the undergraduate level, one's college affiliation is considered far more important by the individual than simply stating he or she went to the "University of Oxford."

   St. John's College (founded in 1555 by Sir Thomas White, a leading member of the Merchant Taylors' Company and one-time Lord Mayor of London) was named after John the Baptist (who was the patron saint of tailors) and was intended to train orthodox clergymen to combat Protestant heresy. But, interestingly enough, it also "trained" Antony G. N. Flew, who is without a doubt one of the most famous atheist philosophers alive today. Indeed much has happened since the Reformation!

3. In fact, in other published material I have said of Antony G. N. Flew: "Tony is one of the finest, most ethical men I have ever met! He is simply wrong, I believe, in holding that God does not exist."

4. As a point of fact, Tony Flew told me as we were riding around Virginia in my car in May of 1985, that he was really an "agnostic." He has always thought a man should stand up for what he believes, be willing to take a stand. Tony further said during our conversation that because he does not believe there is adequate evidence to prove that God exists, he has taken a stand. He uses the word "atheist" and argues as he does because no one has ever proven otherwise to his satisfaction, but he is really—in a technical sense—an agnostic. "Atheist" or "agnostic," I know him to be a man of character.

5. It should go without saying here (but I will just in case there is any question) that I realize that Christians are not the only people who are monotheistic, who believe in one God.

6. And an arrogant theist—or Christian—may be worse than either of the other two. There is no place for intellectual or academic arrogance in the Christian life!

7. The bibliography at the end of this book will be of great help here.

8. Flew quotes Richard Swinburne's definition and says that Swinburne considers his "an undisputatious definition." I do not use Swinburne's definition for several reasons, but basically because Swinburne uses some language that needs to be explained or is not technically accurate, for example, Swinburne says that God is "able to do anything." In a technical sense this is not true. God is "limited" (this use of the word "limited" does not contradict my definition of God above) by his own nature or character. He cannot do anything that would contradict his nature or character. But, then again, he would never want to do such.

   Etienne Gilson, in his *The Idea of God and the Difficulties of Atheism* (1969), defines God by saying: "The constituent elements of that notion, its *essentialia* as Christian Wolff would say, are three in number: (1) God must be a transcendent being, that is, a being that exists apart from both myself and the world; (2) he likewise must be a necessary being; [and] (3) he must be the cause of whatever else exists."

9. The term "Neoplatonism" dates from the nineteenth century and is considered by many as the last great effort of ancient pagan philosophy. The movement was thought to be a direct continuation of Plato's thought by its exponents. Plotinus is considered the founder of Neoplatonism. But Neoplatonism is not at all Platonic in regard to Plato's own theology. This is true both of pagan and Christian Neoplatonism. See Miethe 1976, pp. 60–70.

10. Plotinus supposedly had a number of mystical experiences. In the last six years of his life, Porphyry reports, Plotinus had four ecstatic experiences of union with the One.

11. In the history of Christian thought, theologians have tried to reconcile the absolute unity of God with three divine personalities, that is, the Trinity, by saying it was a mystery and therefore was above explanation or human reason. We can know *that* it is by revelation, but we may not be able to explain *how* it is so.

12. Here meaning "the worthless residue." The literal meaning of *caput mortuum* is "death's head," a skull. The term was used by the alchemists to designate the residue in a flask after distillation was complete and can now be taken "as any worthless residue, even a worthless person."

13. A "tautology," for example, is "a rose is a rose." In this sentence, no new information is given in the predicate that is not already contained in the subject.

14. See relevant items in the bibliography of this book and in the bibliographies of the books listed.

15. In the article "What I Saw When I Was Dead," written after his near-death experience in June 1988, Sir Alfred Ayer tells us his ward sister "was unable to prevent my heart from stopping. She and the doctor subsequently told me that I died in this sense for four minutes." Whether Sir Alfred had a flat electroencephalogram (EEG) or not we are not told. It is interesting to note that Sir Alfred does tell us the following: "The . . . memory . . . of [the] experience closely encompassing my death is very vivid. I was confronted by a red light, exceedingly bright and also very painful even when I turned away from it. I was aware that this light was responsible for the government of the universe. Among its ministers were two creatures who had been put in charge of space." Sir Alfred ends the article by saying: "My recent experiences have slightly weakened my conviction that my genuine death, which is due fairly soon, will be the end of me, though I continue to hope that it will be. They have not weakened my conviction that there is no god. I trust that my remaining an atheist will allay the anxieties of my fellow supporters of the Humanist Association, the Rationalist Press, and the South Place Ethical Society."

16. See: M. Calvin in T. Dobzhansky, M. K. Hecht, and W. C. Steere, eds., *Evolutionary Biology* vol.1 (New York: Appleton Croft, 1967); J. B. S. Haldane in the *Rationalist Annual* 148 (1928):3; and A. Oparin, *Proiskhozhdenie Zhizni. Izd* (Moskovsky Rabochy, 1924) and *The Origin of Life* (New York: Academic Press, 1957).

17. In ancient Greek and Roman plays, a deity brought in by stage machinery to intervene in the action.

18. Really there are many theories of evolution. In recent years many scientists have quietly changed the theory of general evolution, that is, away from basic origins evolving to man and beyond, and/or rejected a general theory and adopted a much more refined and restricted special theory of evolution involving some form of speciation, that is, change within species, rather than evolution of one species into another.

19. There is a wealth of good material currently available on the problems with evolution. You might wish to start with: Robert T. Clark and James D. Bales, *Why Scientists Accept Evolution* (Grand Rapids, MI: Baker, 1966); Norman Macbeth, *Darwin Retried: An Appeal to Reason* (Ipswich, MA: Gambit, 1971); Henry M. Morris and Gary E. Parker, *What Is Creation Science?* (San Diego, CA: Creation-Life, 1982); Evan Shute, *Flaws in the Theory of Evolution* (Nutley, NJ: Craig, 1961), and A. E. Wilder-Smith, *Man's Origin, Man's Destiny* (Minneapolis, MN: Bethany House, 1968).

20. Another term for this is "abiogensis," which means "the origination of living from lifeless matter."

21. Immediately someone will say, "This is just the old teleological argument." It is very interesting that at a recent national conference where panels of atheists and theists debated (in philosophy, natural science, social sciences, theology, culture, and morality) several of the scientists on the natural science panel defending the theistic position were converts to Christianity within the last few years because of what they thought was the validity of teleological arguments, that is, that the order and complexity of the physical universe supports the existence of God. When I ask them why they thought these teleological arguments supported the Christian God, they answered because the scientific evidence points not only to a "God," but to a Personality, a Personal Being behind the physical universe.

22. Stanley Jaki, professor of history and philosophy of physics, gives a thoroughly documented rebuttal of contemporary claims about the existence of or possibility of man-made minds. His book *Brain, Mind and Computers* (New York: Herder and Herder, 1969), poses a serious challenge to philosophies of physicalistic reductionism. He argues convincingly the conviction that the human person, precisely because of the mind, is not a machine, but a marvel.

23. Some will claim that there are possibilities for recovering energy in the universe as we know it, but there is no evidence for this.

24. Flew is quoting here from his *The Logic of Mortality* (1987), pp. 103–4.

25. Many books in the bibliography of this book show quite well that the scientific worldview has changed drastically. It now generally supports a much more "open universe" view.

26. In fact, he comes closer to doing this in the first part of his essay than in the last, though, as we have shown, what we are given is still a rather tired old argument.

27. Again, this one book or debate will not, cannot provide "a thorough and complete apologetic." This is not a "cop-out" but a fact necessitated by the complexity of the question, the nature of the whole of reality, and of the evidence that must be examined. It is hoped, however, that we at least "open some doors" and begin again this important dialogue.

28. See Flew's "The Presumption of Atheism," I, pp. 13–14.

29. Unless, perhaps, one is a total "presuppositionalist" apologetically.

30. I put this in quotes because as I see it "experience is experience." In large part what I am contending, and will be arguing, is that when experience is properly examined, yes empirically, then one will see that experience as such—experience *qua* experience—is not irreducibly physical/mechanical.

31. For example, Aquinas's twelfth-century argument based on existential causality and Anselm's second argument in *Proslogium* III. I will say more about Hume in my second contribution to this debate.

32. Geisler (1982), chap. 3, "Are Miracles Repeatable?" pp. 35–46, has a critique of Antony Flew.

33. I think many of the books listed in the bibliography of this debate certainly do an "adequate" job.

34. This letter (and other responses written by various publishing houses), along with the author's manuscript, was sent to me to ask me what I thought of the work, if I would write an introduction for the proposed book, and if I could help in getting it published.

35. This letter is held in confidence as I do not want to in any way embarrass my publisher friend.

36. I should also add that I have had very similar responses from publishers other than the one who wrote the letter referred to herein. One Christian publisher told me on the phone (after a contract had been signed and an advance paid) that my book on the existence of God was not needed because a *USA Today* newspaper poll had indicated that 95 percent of Americans believe in a Supreme Being. How naive (foolishly simple)!

37. Or what gets published is another book from someone whose book has "sold." Often these "big-name" authors don't even write their own material (see Terry Miethe's "open letter to the church" entitled *Beware of "One-eyed" Kings!*)

38. One might want to check the work of scientists such as Dean Kenyon, Walter Bradley, Allan Sandage, Roger Olsen, and so on.

39. I will address this more specifically in my second contribution to this debate.

40. It is important here to read my "The Limits of Science" in *A Christian's Guild to Faith and Reason* (1987), pp. 95–111.

41. David Hume, *The Letters of David Hume*, 2 vols., ed. J. Y. T. Greig (Oxford: Oxford University Press, 1932), vol. I, p. 187.

42. Lucretius, the first-century Roman poet, wrote in *De Rerum Natura* of the creation of the world: *Nil posse creari de nilo*, "nothing can be created out of nothing," which is also rendered as *ex nihilo nihil fit*, suggesting that every effect must have a cause. Today the Latin phrase is applied rather broadly to suggest that a dull mind cannot be expected to produce great thoughts, anything worth doing requires hard work, you can't get blood from a stone, and so on—all of which are quite true!

43. But in process philosophy/theology, the idea that self-causation is contradictory is denied. Charles Hartshorne has argued that it is possible. See Charles Hartshorne, "Whitehead on Process: A Reply to Professor Eslick," *Philosophy and Phenomenological Research*, vol. 18, no. 4, pp. 514–22.

44. I do not really like the phrase "heaven-promising and hell-threatening" as *the* defining terms of Christianity. In fact, I think this language prejudices the case somewhat. And I certainly disagree with fundamentalists that a proper method of evangelism is to "scare a person out of hell and into heaven."

45. There is no question in Aquinas but that humans have freedom of choice, though it should be pointed out that Thomas almost never speaks of free will (*libera voluntas*) and practically always discusses human freedom in terms of free choice (*liberum arbitrium*) of means.

46. I realize—unfortunately from personal experience—that those who have the fundamentalist mind-set are always going to condemn questioning assumptions and dogmas (or at the very least caution against it), even though they may indicate something quite different publicly.

47. While I still think there is a real distinction between essence and existence, this may not be the *only* way of constituting metaphysical knowledge. Leonard Eslick moved to a rationalism of the Hartshornian type, where the existence of God is established via the second formulation of Anselm's ontological argument.

Chapter IV: A Second Engagement

1. Or is Flew going to claim again—as he did in his first rejoinder—in his answer to this section that he doesn't require empirical verification in regard to claims about God's existence?

2. See Richard Purtill, "Flew and the Free Will Defence" in *Religious Studies* 13 (1977):477–83.

3. Finally in this section, Flew says: "About all this it must here suffice to say that . . . " (III, p. 98). Why must "it . . . here suffice"? Because of space? While Flew feels it valid to "chastise" me several times for mentioning in my "A First Engagement" that the space restrictions of our topic or of a single book preclude me from going into further detail, evidently it is all right for him to feel such restrictions.

4. I have never maintained "a God of the gaps" position. I certainly agree that it is most dangerous to do so!

5. It is not just "betting a dead horse" to insist both that such arguments need to be examined and that they cannot be examined (at all, let alone adequately) in the context of one book.

6. See Norman L. Geisler, *Philosophy of Religion* (Grand Rapids, MI: Zondervan, 1974), pp. 190–226.

7. Richard Taylor, *Metaphysics* (Englewood Cliffs, NJ: Prentice-Hall, 1974); William L. Rowe, "The Cosmological Argument," *Nous* 5, no. 1 (1971):49–61, and *The Cosmological Argument* (Princeton, NJ: Princeton University Press, 1975); and Bruce R. Reichenbach, *The Cosmological Argument: A Reassessment* (Springfield, IL: Charles C. Thomas, 1972).

8. Geisler, *Philosophy of Religion*, p. 174. See Thomas Aquinas, *Summa Theologica*, I, q. 14, a. 13, "Whether the Knowledge of God Is of Future Contingent Things."

9. Some Christian philosophers now think that Charles Hartshorne is correct that there can be *causa sui*. See Leonard J. Eslick, "Substance, Change, and Causality in Whitehead," *Philosophy and Phenomenological Research* 18 (1958):503–13; and Charles Hartshorne's reply, "Whitehead on Process: A Reply to Professor Eslick," *Philosophy and Phenomenological Research* 18 (1958):514–22. For Thomas, unlike Spinoza, not even God can be *causa sui*.

10. Geisler, *Philosophy of Religion*, pp. 174–75. See Thomas Aquinas, *Summa Theologica*, I, q. 2, a. 2, reply to obj. 2.

11. Angels are for Thomas Aquinas examples of caused necessary beings.

12. Though William L. Rowe argues from "the form the argument takes in the 18th century" (and *not* that of Aquinas, which I argue in this contribution), and while Rowe admits that "it cannot reasonably be maintained to be a *proof* of its conclusion," he does say, however, ". . . it may be a perfectly sound argument." He also says: "For although its premises may be true, we are not in the position of knowing that they are true." See William L. Rowe, "The Cosmological Argument," *Nous* 5, no. 1 (1971): pp. 49–61.

13. Published by Charles C. Thomas, Springfield, Illinois, in three parts: the first establishes what appears to be a true and valid cosmological argument; the second addresses the question of the nature of causation and the causal principle; and in the third objections, both traditionally and more recently, are considered and evaluated.

Chapter V: A Time for Reviewing

1. The supposedly benighted Topsy, for instance, was absolutely right to insist that—at least to every this-worldly appearance—she "just growed."

2. I have, however, in the twenty-five years between become reluctant myself to speak here, as both philosophers and theologians have traditionally done, of the freedom of the will, for both those who act freely and those who act only under compulsion do nevertheless act and hence both necessarily could, in the profoundest sense, do other than they do.

3. By the way, save in the context of Cartesian exegesis, it is best not to apply the Rylean label "ghost in the machine" to such views, for, whereas machines must be nonliving and at least ultimately man-made, organisms "just growed" and are necessarily alive. This is why I am myself uneasy about being described (II, p. 55) as one who talks "as if a person is . . . a psychochemical machine."

Chapter VI: A Third Engagement

1. Flew certainly has aligned himself with a rather rigid Calvinistic concept of God.

2. I understand how the philosophical "purist" wants one argument that can be considered "definitive." I am also quite aware of those who throw out the whole "bucket" because they say that a bunch of weak arguments is like a "leaky bucket," not much help. But, eventually, when one is talking about forming a consistent worldview there has to come a point when it is admitted that—while perhaps not individually definitive—a series of strong arguments adds with such force that they must be considered valid in the context of the worldview. Remember, even Flew acknowledges that: ". . . the word "proof" is not ordinarily restricted in its application to demonstratively valid arguments, arguments, that is, in which the conclusion cannot be denied without thereby contradicting the premises" (I, p. 12).

   Flew goes on to make the *very important* statement: "It is, therefore, worth underlining that when the presumption of atheism is explained as insisting that the onus of proof must be on the theist, the word 'proof' is being used in the ordinary wide sense in which it can embrace any and every variety of sufficient reason." But does Flew allow this kind—or level—of proof? I think it is obvious that he does not! Then Flew makes another important admission/concession when he says: "It must at once be conceded that it is one thing to say that a belief is unfounded or well founded and quite another to say that it is irrational or rational for particular persons, in their own particular times and circumstances and with their particular experience and lack of experience, to hold or to reject that belief" (I, pp. 16–17).

3. As Flew pointed out in his debate with Gary Habermas (Miethe/Habermas/Flew 1987, pp. 4–5).

4. See Stanley L. Jaki, "From Scientific Cosmology to a Created Universe," in *The Intellectuals Speak Out About God*, ed. Roy Abraham Varghese (Chicago: Regnery Gateway, 1984), pp. 61–78.

5. See "Thomism," in Terry L. Miethe, *The Compact Dictionary of Doctrinal Words* (Minneapolis, MN: Bethany House, 1988), pp. 206–7.

6. A much fuller treatment of the issue of free will versus determinism needs to be done than can be handled here. I suggest reading, as a beginning, chap. 11, the section entitled "Man's Freedom," and chap. 28, the section entitled "Human Freedom and God," in Thompson's *A Modern Philosophy of Religion* and chap. 19 in Trueblood's *Philosophy of Religion*.

7. I claim here to have orginated this term, Tony!

8. A great old Presbyterian seminary founded in 1829, for which I have a great deal more admiration now than I had when I was a brash young student there!

9. Having taught for many years now, I am quite aware that a student's view of what has or has not happened is not always the most objective view of a particular happening or event.

Chapter VIII: A Few Final Words

1. Introduction to Etienne Gilson's "The Idea of God and the Difficulties of Atheism," *Philosophy Today* 13 (1969):174.

2. There has been some disagreement on both sides about what constitutes argument for or against the Christian God. It is also true that while I believe there can be only one God, Tony finds it confusing at best that there are so many different concepts of this God.

3. Apologetics and Christian evidences are often viewed as the same discipline. Occasionally, however, a distinction is made between apologetics as a philosophical discipline concerned with refuting non-Christian worldviews and Christian evidences as historical and biblical evidences in favor of Christianity.

4. Gilson, in his article "The Idea of God and the Difficulties of Atheism" (1969), mentions a poll in *Time* in 1965 in which "97% of the U.S. population . . . answered that they believed in God. . . . That impressive figure probably means that, being asked: *Do you think there is a God?*, 97% . . . put a cross in the *yes* column, and only 3% answered *no*." Gilson goes on to say: "The case is different when it comes to the quality of that belief in God and the inquirer observes that of the 97% of those who said they did believe in God, only 27% declared themselves deeply religious. At that point, the inquiry is moving to a different ground. Religion is a moral virtue, and all those who believe in God do not necessarily possess that virtue" (p. 182).

5. If you are interested in a very good monthly apologetics newsletter, send for *The LodeStar Review*, 200 W. Franklin St., Wheaton, Illinois 60187.

6. This is the motto of The Johns Hopkins University, but it is, of course, originally found in John 8:31–32.

Appendix A: The Claims of Theology

1. W. H. Mallock, "The New Republic," p. 231.

2. See Anselm, *Proslogion*, sec. 2.

3. See René Descartes, *Discourse on Method*, part 4 and meditations 3 and 5.

4. See Immanuel Kant, *Critique of Pure Reason*, "The Ideal of Pure Reason."

5. See Thomas Aquinas, *Summa Theologica* Ia, 2, 3.

6. See A. J. Ayer, *The Central Questions of Philosophy* (London: Weidenfeld & Nicholson, 1973), p. 8.

7. David Hume, *Dialogues Concerning Natural Religion*, part 2.

8. Bertrand Russell, *Why I Am Not a Christain*, pp. 24–25.

9. See George Berkeley, the second of the *Three Dialogues of Hylas and Philonous*.

10. See Ayer, *Central Questions of Philosophy*, p. 60.
11. See Ayer, *Central Questions of Philosophy*, pp. 86–88.
12. See Ayer, *Central Questions of Philosophy*, pp. 4–7.
13. See Ayer, *Central Questions of Philosophy*, pp. 124–26.
14. Voltaire, *Epistles*, 96.
15. Bertrand Russell, *Human Society in Ethics and Politics*, p. 48.
16. See Gilbert Ryle, *The Concept of Mind*, p. 67.
17. See Ayer, *Central Questions of Philosophy*, p. 181.
18. See John Locke, *An Essay Concerning Human Understanding*, book 2, chap. 21.
19. William James, *The Will to Believe*, p. 180.
20. William James, *Pragmatism*, pp. 121–22.
21. James, *Pragmatism*, p. 517.

Appendix D: Does God Exist? The Argumentation of Hans Küng

1. Theses 6–13 in Hans Küng, *24 Thesen zur Gottesfrage* (Munich, 1979), pp. 6f., which has unfortunately not been translated into English yet. In this work, Küng summarizes the argument of the principle work, *Does God Exist? An Answer for Today*, in a series of brief "theses." To correctly understand the theses, it is necessary to read the larger book, but as a summary the theses with their brief explanations are well suited to bringing the main thrust of Küng's argument to the fore.

2. Hans Küng, *Existiert Gott? Antwort auf die Gottesfrage der Neuzeit* (Munich: Piper, 1978); English translation under the title *Does God exist? An Answer for Today* (New York; Doubleday, 1980). In the text, references are given in parentheses in the form (S. . . . ; pp. . . .), whereby the first designates the German text and the second the English translation. Occasionally slight modifications have been made in the translation, particularly when German wordplays are involved. It should be noted that the English title is less precise than the German. The German title makes clear that Küng's point of departure is the history of the God question in modern thought beginning with the rationalism of Descartes, culminating in the theo-logic of Hegel, then experiencing the challenge by the atheistic critique of religion represented by Feuerbach, Marx, and Freud, and so coming to the term in the nihilism of Nietzsche. The narration of this history fills the first half of the work (S. 21–470; pp. 1–423), the aim being to establish the perspective in which the question of God's being must be put today. The second half of the book attempts then in three stages to give an answer to the question thus put. These stages are: (1) "Yes to Reality—Alternative to Nihilism" (S. 471–528; pp. 425–78), (2) "Yes to God—Alternative to Atheism" (S. 529–640; pp. 479–584), and (3) "Yes to the Christian God" (S. 641–767; pp. 585–702). The heart of Küng's argument for God's existence is found within the second of these sections under the heading "God Exists" (S. 607–40; pp. 552–83).

3. On this point, H. Albert insists in his *Traktat über die kritische Vernunft*, 3d ed. (Tübingen, 1975).

4. Adherents of this position see the arguments for the existence of God as a clear, unequivocal, objectifiable, logical consequence. This supposition underlies the famous parable of the invisible gardener authored by J. Wisdom and taken over by A. Flew. Here the discussants have failed to put the critical hermeneutical question—whether the quest for a cause to explain the flowering garden is an appropriate analogy to the search for a cause of reality itself.

5. The linguistic theory put forth polemically by Ludwig Wittgenstein in his *Tractatus Logico-philosophicus* was already philosophically outdated by the time of publication. Wittgenstein's greatest contribution to the debate over the function of language is precisely his refutation of this his own original misunderstanding. Thus his *Philosophical Investigations* should be required reading for every serious theologian.

6. This position corresponds to the notion of the verification principle articulated by the Vienna Circle. It is relevant for the God question inasmuch as it compels theologians to reflect more clearly about the meaning of theological statements.

7. This becomes clear, for example, in Kant's critique of the so-called ontological argument first proposed by Anselm of Canterbury in his *Proslogion*. In this attempt to deduce the necessary existence of God from the notion *id quo maius cogitari nequit* (that greater than which cannot be conceived), the existence of God is claimed to be inherent in the notion of God as such. As to the position of E. Jüngel, see his *Gott als Geheimnis der Welt*, 2d ed. (Tübingen, 1977) pp. 1–54.

8. In the positively simplified version, the verification principle is seen as allowing only direct empirical verification. This simplification is understandable in the light of the modern history of the logic of demonstration, in which—apart from the induction problematic—only objectivized, necessarily compelling arguments were admitted as proof. Here I. U. Dalferth (*Religiöse Rede von Gott* [Munich, 1981], pp. 505f.) has shown in connection with Flew's parable that the verification problematic is in fact only the more visible part of a much deeper problem. In question is not the verifiability or falsifiability of individual propositions but rather the much broader question of whether religious speaking is at all rational, whether it can be justified on reasonable grounds.

9. "Before attempting to express existence propositions through existence quantifications, it is necessary to clarify what the term exist means in such propositions and whether this meaning is compatible with what the existence quantor expresses. Thus it is by no means certain that the notion exist in the proposition God exists must or even can be understood in terms of the existence quantor. Simply to transpose the statement into the language of predicate logic does not suffice to answer the question of what this statement means when asserted in the course of Christian speaking about God." (I. U. Dalferth, *Existenz Gottes und christlicher Glaube* [Munich, 1984], pp. 94f.). According to Dalferth (*Religiöse Rede* . . . , p. 631), expressions like "I," "you," "he," "here," "there," "now," "then" represent orientational features of language that are relative to the time and place of their utterance. They can only be correctly understood when one attends to the individual context of the speaker's utterance. That is to say, their concrete meaning can only be grasped by taking into account their pragmatic function as structuring the speaker's field of speech and speaking in an individual constellation of time and place. In a corresponding manner, transcendental terms like "true," "good," "something," "being," and "exist" cannot be fixed abstractly in their meaning but can only be explicated in relationship to their concrete use in a propositional context. Lexically, they are empty, so to speak; their meaning can only be disclosed in context of their pragmatic communicative function in concrete usage. This can be, for instance, the certification of an assertion about an object, a judgment about the characteristics of such an object, or an evaluation of what is asserted about the object, and so on. In contrast to the deictic terms, the use of such terms is not speaker-oriented but rather, one may say, object oriented: their individual concrete meaning is disclosed by their function in relationship to the object in discourse.

10. For the problematic of existence propositions, see Dalferth, *Existenz Gottes*, pp . 94–99.

11. Dalferth, *Religiöse Rede*, p. 633.

12. Küng's argument rests upon his extensive and intensive analysis of the fate of God in modern thought: Descartes' ideal of rationality, Pascal's critique of rationalism, Hegel's coupling of the idea of God with that of history, the atheistic critique of religion represented by Feuerbach, Marx, and Freud, the dead-end of nihilism recognized by Nietzsche. What might appear to be a hermeneutical weakness here is in fact the hermeneutical strength of Küng's argument. This extensive narrative tour through five centuries of Western thought enables readers to recognize their own experience in the

experience of the individual thinkers treated, thus making communication possible. The framework of this communication is the story of the experiencing and the denying of God in the course of modern Western civilization. Whether this framework is equally suited to readers in other cultural and religious contexts is an issue Küng has attempted to face since 1980 in his contributions to the dialogue between Christianity and the world religions.

13. The points of departure for Aquinas are: the phenomenon of motion and change, causal interdependence, the contingency of being, the order of perfection in being, and the fact of finality in things.

14. W. Weischedel, *Der Gott der Philosophen*, vol. 1 (Darmstadt, 1975), pp. 135–41.

15. In Thomas's arguments, the conclusion is not "herewith is proven the existence of God" but rather *et hoc omnes dicunt Deum* ("this is what all men call God"). That is to say, the argument moves into an epideictic linguistic act, pointing to God as a reality already familiar to the reader.

16. Weischedel, *Der Gott der Philosophen*, pp. 165–75.

17. Pascal recognized the problem of radical skepticism with full clarity. Thus he refers constantly and expressedly to Pyrrhonism (the skeptical school in classical antiquity) and to Montaigne (1533–1592), the first skeptic of consequence in the modern period. The skeptical lineage is later represented by P. Bayle (1647–1706), who in turn influenced L. Feuerbach.

18. The theologian Friedrich Schleiermacher was the principal antipode to Hege in Berlin. Unwittingly, as Karl Barth has shown, he was to provide Feuerbach with the categories and the arguments on the basis of which the latter would build his atheistic system to refute the existence of God.

19. It is one of the most remarkable phenomena in the history of atheism that Feuerbach succeeded in convincing so many of his educated contemporaries almost overnight. Karl Marx took Feuerbach's atheism for a proven fact needing no further discussion. Thus in the second half of the nineteenth century, the intensive, critical occupation with the existence or nonexistence of God and the way this question might be resolved by and large disappears, to reappear again only with Friedrich Nietzsche at the end of the century. During this period, theism and atheism harden into ideologies incapable of dialogue.

20. It would be interesting to pursue the history of belief in God as a dialectic of need and desire (*besoin* and *désir*) in contemporary French thinking. Important figures in this story are Ricoeur, Lacan, and Foucault; also important is the renewed interest in Heidegger in contemporary French philosophy.

21. Küng interprets nihilism not so much as a logical consequence of atheism but rather as a historically consequent radicalization of atheism when the ground of being and meaning has been dissolved.

22. In point of fact, the polar opposition between theistic belief and nihilistic unbelief has brought forth virtually no qualitative advances since Nietzsche. Mentionable is Sartre's impressive formulation of the anthropological consequences. Among poststructuralist thinkers one can observe a tendency to fragment or dissolve the question of meaning itself.

23. To introduce his concept of "inner rationality," Küng could well have called attention to the the notion of "experience," which in recent years has increasingly evoked discussion among European theologians (cf. E. Schillebeeckx, *Christ: The Experience of Jesus as Lord* [New York, 1980], pp. 30–64). A useful summary for our purposes is offered by J. Splett, "Über die Möglichkeit Gott heute zu denken," in W. Kern et al., eds., *Traktat Religion, Handbuch der Fundamentologie*, vol. 1, [Freiburg, 1985], pp. 136–55, in particular pp. 140–44.

24. Augustine formulates the relationship between faith and knowledge in terms of the metaphor of the path of knowing. Knowledge is and remains the goal of believing.

Believing goes before knowing not because the believer de facto knows more, but rather because the inner consent of the believer alone makes knowing possible.

25. Classical ontology has formulated this connection between the truth of God's being and the truth of the reality around us in terms of the so-called transcendentals: oneness, truth, goodness, beauty. Nihilism can hardly dispute the raw existence of reality. What it contests, and this with plausible arguments, is that existing reality has a significant foundation, inner consistency, or intrinsic orientation. The question of whether or not the reality we experience exists or not pales before the radical denial of reality in its ontological connectedness.

26. Caution is necessary lest God be reduced to a quasi-physical efficient cause, a quasi-physical or psychological object of desire, a quasi-pedagogical example, a constructor of reality constellations at the service of humans, or as a power intervening in our lives like another human being. God is not a competitor with human agents but rather the ground of human freedom. The major philosophical and theological tradition has always connected the immanence and transcendence of God dialectically. The point here is not to call into question a metaphysical theology but rather to call attention to the need to differentiate its claim to truth.

27. These ideas derive from Artistotle's analysis of causality, which distinguishes two "external" causes, efficient and final causality, from the two "internal" causes, material and formal causality.

28. W. Pannenberg is correct is demanding that God should be verifiable in the framework of our reality (*Systematische Theologie*, vol. 1 [Göttingen, 1988], pp. 175f. et al.). He speaks of "implications of meaning" in our experience that can be thematized explicitly in religious statements.

29. For instance, the thought of an unending chain of causes containing its own refutation belongs to the argument as an immediate logical conclusion in the same degree as the thought that the formal argument only can convince when it takes the form of a generalization of concrete experience.

30. Küng locates his verification procedure between an "empiristic" and a "general hermeneutical" criterion of verification: the first would demand an empirical proof of God's being, the second would content itself with establishing that "God" and "God exists" can be meaningful. Küng seeks a "knowledge of God grounded in experience." What he means by this is not a strict deduction from an absolutely evident experience, but rather a "clarifying illumination of the always problematical experience that invites man to a positive decision" (S. 604f.; pp. 550f.).

31. Weischedel, *Der Gott der Philosophen*, vol. 1, "In this question, the questioner himself comes into play in a special way. He is himself part of the universe of beings, and he is this in a very special sense, inasmuch as he has the possibility of putting this universe into question. When he asks about the whole, he asks at the same time about himself as the questioning member of this whole. For this reason it is of decisive importance for his own self-understanding, whether and how he conceives this whole, in short, whether it is possible to make statements about God as the ground of being as a whole, or whether this is indeed impossible for human thought. Put in other terms, is our human situation irredeemably that of God's absence [*Gottverlassenheit*], a situation we cannot change but only enthusiastically greet, stoically bear or painfully mourn, or is it possible even in today's world to utter the *De profundis*?" (p. xviii).

32. See, for instance, the beginning of the foreword to E. Bloch's *Prinzip Hoffnung* (Eng. *The Principle of Hope* [Cambridge, MA, 1986]): "Who are we? Where do we come from? Where are we going? What do we expect? Many feel themselves confused. The ground under their feet is swaying: they know neither why nor wherefrom. This condition is that of anxiety; when it is concretized, it becomes fear."

33. Before rationalistic critics denounce the manner of speaking as "conceptual salad" (see H. Albert, *Das Elend der Theologie. Kritische Auseinandersetzung mit Hans Küng* [Hamburg, 1979], p. 82), they should take these matters into consideration. Albert has by no means grasped the hermeneutical complexity of a truly adequate definition of the notion of "God."

34. This position can be accepted as well by philosophers who do not conclude thereby that all argumentation for the existence of God is meaningless or impossible. Thus K. Jaspers, in *Der philosophische Glaube* (Munich, 1963), p. 34 (Eng. *Philosophical Faith and Revelation* [New York, 1967]), writes: "The proofs of God's existence have not become superfluous because they have lost their strict demonstrative character. Instead they continue to serve as a certification [*Vergewisserung*] of believing. They represent paths of thinking that, when originally thought out, seize the thinker with the self-conviction of the deepest event of living and that, when reflected upon with understanding, make a repetition of this certification experience possible."

35. "All defining" is likewise—how could it be otherwise—a metaphorical statement that must be filled with meaning according to the concrete conditions of experience.

36. In speaking of "concrete experience" I mean to say that a very definite, spatio-temporally distinct event is the center of such an experience. This means of course that we do not have to do here with a collective experience: no single event can be experienced by all people. The approach of indirect verification points rather to a typical class of experiences that indeed confront every human being, despite the singularity of the particular events involved: experiences of this type are those, for instance, of death, pain, disappointment, but also joy, etc.

37. Unresolved in Küng's argumentation is the precise relationship between argument and counterargument. He emphasizes that the counterarguments against meaningfulness in reality are not once and for all refuted by the positive experiences of meaning and value. What then? Are they merely weakened in their force of conviction or are they in fact taken up into the positive demonstration. The meaning of the issue at stake can be illustrated by the following three questions. (1) Does Küng mean to say that the questionableness of reality forces us to face the question though it gives us no answer, or would he conclude with the transcendental-theological argument that the questionability itself implies the possibility of an answer? (2) Do the negative experiences of death, evil, and so on, simply show that the affirmation of God's existence is forever threatened by the counterassertion, or do these negative experiences themselves call for belief in God's existence as the only possible solution to the problems they pose? (3) Are the counterarguments simply premises for an indirect but inconclusive falsification, or do they serve in an alternative hermeneutical perspective together with the positive experiences as part of the indirect verification of God's existence?

38. Augustine describes believing as "thinking with assent" (*cum assensione cogitare*). The borderline, for him, does not run between believing and thinking but between false thinking on the one side and proper thinking on the other, namely, thinking with belief. A closer analysis of his notion of believing would help make clear that the modern competition between "thinking" and "believing" is by no means the only model suitable to expressing their relationship.

39. In this case it is probable that it does not come to an unreserved perception of the radical questionableness of reality itself. The person who trusts can be more deeply disappointed than one who has called up short in the open field of indecision or skepticism. Thus it is not excluded, that Nietzsche, for instance, may very well in fact have put more trust in reality than some of his opponents. A decision in this matter is not for us to make: only God sees into human hearts! Küng's argument is an appeal for the fundamental connection between the search for meaning and the act of trust; he has no intention of making empirical judgments about belief and unbelief in the individual case.

40. For this reason Küng does not exclude the possibility of an implicit belief in God.
41. The best example for this type of rationality is that of love resting upon the knowledge and conviction that one of my fellow human beings in fact loves me, that he or she wills me well, that he or she indeed wishes to share life with me.
42. Küng has no intention of developing a comprehensive psychology of trust; his excursion into the world of developmental psychology is designed merely to offer some "concretion" (S. 502–10; pp. 453–60).
43. I. U. Dalferth exemplifies this trend. From his highly differentated preliminary considerations he goes on to draw a quite undifferentiated conclusion: "That something exists at all, that more than one thing exists, that this plurality exists as a multitude of objects in space and time, and that among these objects there exist beings who have the ability to know these facts of being—all of these facts have nothing to say about the existence of God or about the truth of the assertion 'God exists.' In short they speak only for themselves. The conviction that God exists, which finds expression in the Christian assertion of God's existence, does not take its origin in the provocation of ontological, ontic, or anthropological primal facts, as though these should compel us to speak of God" (*Existenz Gottes*, p. 169).
44. This is the case, for example, when "God" is interpreted as a cipher for love, humanity, finality, incomparable power, unconditional moral imperative, the experience of ultimate boundaries and contingency, and so on.
45. Dalferth, *Religiöse Rede*, pp. 565–96.
46. Dalferth, *Existenz Gottes*, pp. 100–54.
47. Dalferth, *Religiöse Rede*, p. 591.
48. Dalferth, *Existenz Gottes*, pp. 124–26.
49. Dalferth, *Existenz Gottes*, p. 152.
50. Dalferth, *Existenz Gottes*, p. 154.
51. Dalferth, *Existenz Gottes*, pp. 88f. recounts W. V. O. Quine's thesis concerning "ontological commitment," according to which in all forms of speaking the existence of some object(s) is assumed. "Thus in every speech the speaker commits himself to the existence of precisely those objects, which take the place of the logical variables for which they stand when the statement is translated into the formal logic of value corresponding to the judgment about the truth of the proposition. Thus, when someone asserts that God has created the world, he is saying implicitly that God exists and that the world has been created by him, i.e., that it has not come to be of itself or been created by someone else. In saying this the speaker is thus committing himself to an ontology which reckons with the existence of God."
52. In connection with the theory of speaking acts, it would appear correct to speak of an illocutionary dimension of existence assertions.
53. As examples one might point to the parables of Jesus or to folk tales and poems. Without a preliminary readiness of the listener or reader to be influenced by them, they are incapable of being understood. They evoke discovery contexts into which the hearer is drawn; they intend to evoke networks of foundation that are inseparably connected with being affected by them and giving them one's assent.
54. This is illustrated by the argumentation of K. Barth. His reference to God's unique and true Word may well be understood and grounded in the inner logic of his discourse. But he is incapable of translating the grounding argument into the intersubjective situation in which believer and unbeliever attempt to come together to speak of God. A further authoritarian usage appears when the founding of the assertion of God's existence is reduced to a moralistic command to "think" God. A conscious neglect of the distinction between "thinking" and "grounding" fails to take account of the unique situation of theology: its theme, the existence of God, is such that it can never achieve more than reasonable plausibility, but by the same token it is not reducible to a negligible quantity. Thus in our age there exists no other assertion for which the need

for being grounded has so much been called upon as the assertion of God's existence. On the other hand, leaving aside the field of general plausibility as such, no grounding situation is more complex than that of this assertion.

55. The apologetic procedure is still often used in theology. It goes unnoticed as a rule that such arguments only prove their own weakness, because they reduce the place for experiencing and deriving God's existence to but a narrow segment of reality. As the famous parable of J. Wisdom shows so impressively, in such arguments God dies the death of thousands of distinctions and reservations.

56. In his discussion of natural theology, Küng takes the account of the European discussion since the fifties. In the Protestant realm, this discussion has been dominated above all by the figure of K. Barth. The Catholic side, by contrast, was long identified polemically with a rationalistically narrowed position based upon the definitions of Vatican I.

57. To properly appreciate Küng's argumentation, it is important to recall his reference to the previous book *Being a Christian*, in which he originally developed this argument. There the argument does not stand in the framework of an abstract question of God's being but rather as a preliminary to the concrete question of belief in the Christian God. Like the abstract question, the abstract answer calling attention to a not further specified radical trust and belief can in fact serve only as a preparation for that concrete form of trust and faith identified with a specific religion, be it Jewish, Christian, or other.

58. For the Christian theologian, the act of faith in the existence of God represents the ultimate summing up of his belief in the God of Jesus Christ.

Bibliography

Adams, Robert. 1979. "Moral Arguments for Theistic Belief." In *Rationality and Religious Belief*. Edited by C. F. Delany. Notre Dame, IN: University of Notre Dame Press. Pp. 116–40.

Anderson, J. N. D. 1970. *Christianity: The Witness of History*. Downers Grove, IL: InterVarsity.

Aquinas, Thomas. 1920. *Summa Theologica*. Translated by the Fathers of the English Dominican Province. London: Burns, Oates and Washbourne.

———. 1956–57. *Summa Contra Gentiles*. Translated by Vernon J. Bourke et al. New York: Doubleday.

Attwater, Donald, ed. 1958. *A Catholic Dictionary (The Catholic Encyclopædic Dictionary)*. 3d ed. New York: Macmillian.

Austin, J. L. 1962. *Sense and Sensibilia*. Oxford: Clarendon.

Ayer, A. J. 1936. *Language, Truth and Logic*. London: Gollanoz. 2d ed. 1946.

———. 1973. *The Central Questions of Philosophy*. London: Penguin.

Bado, Walter, S. J. 1964. "What Is God? An Essay in Learned Ignorance." *The Modern Schoolman* 42:3–32.

Barth, Karl. 1962. *Anselm: Fides Quaerens Intellectum (Faith in Search of Understanding)*. English translation by I. W. Robertson. Cleveland, OH: Meridian.

Berman, David. 1988. *A History of Atheism in Britain: From Hobbes to Russell*. London and New York: Croun Helm.

Bethell, Tom. 1976. "Darwin's Mistake." *Harper's Magazine* (February):70–74.

———. 1985. "Agnostic Evolutionists: The Taxonomic Case Against Darwin." *Harper's Magazine* (February):49–61.

Bode, E. L. 1970. *The First Easter Morning*. Rome: Biblical Institute Press.

Bonansea, Bernardino M. 1974. "The Impossibility of Creation from Eternity According to St. Bonaventure." *Proceedings of the American Catholic Philosophical Association* 48:121–35.

Borne, E. 1961. *Atheism*. New York: Hawthorn.

Bourke, Vernon J. 1945. *Augustine's Quest for Wisdom: Life and Philosophy of the Bishop of Hippo*. Milwaukee, WI: Bruce.

———. 1960. *The Pocket Aquinas*. New York: Washington Square.

———. 1964. *Will in Western Thought: An Historico-Critical Survey*. New York: Sheed and Ward.

———. 1965. *Aquinas' Search for Wisdom*. Milwaukee, WI: Bruce.

Brown, Colin. 1969. *Philosophy and the Christian Faith*. Chicago: InterVarsity.

Brown, Patterson. 1966. "Infinite Causal Regression." *The Philosophical Review* 35:510–25. Later published in *Aquinas: A Collection of Critical Essays*. Edited by Anthony Kenny. Notre Dame, IN: University of Notre Dame Press, 1976. Pp. 214–36.

Bruce, F. F. 1960. *The New Testament Documents: Are They Reliable?* 5th rev. ed. Grand Rapids, MI: Eerdmans.

———. 1974. *Jesus and Christian Origins Outside the New Testament*. Grand Rapids, MI: Eerdmans.

Buell, Jon A., and O. Quentin Hyder. 1978. *Jesus: God, Ghost or Guru?* Grand Rapids, MI: Zondervan.

Burrill, Donald R. 1967. *The Cosmological Arguments: A Spectrum of Opinion*. Garden City, NY: Doubleday, Anchor.

Butler, Joseph. 1896. *The Analogy of Religion*, in *The Works of Joseph Butler*. Edited by W. E. Gladstone. Oxford: Clarendon. *The Analogy of Religion* was first published in 1736.

Caldecott, Alfred. 1901. *The Philosophy of Religion in England and American*. London: Methuen.

Campbell, George. 1762. *A Dissertation on Miracles*. London: Tegg. Reprinted in 1834.

Campbell, Keith. 1986. *ANC: A Soviet Task Force?* London: Institute for the Study of Terrorism.

Chapman, Colin. 1981. *The Case for Christianity*. Grand Rapids, MI: Eerdmans.

Chenu, M. D. 1964. *Toward Understanding St. Thomas*. Chicago: Henry Regnery.

Christian, W. A. 1964. *Meaning and Truth in Religion*. Princeton, NJ: Princeton University Press.

Clark, Gordon H. 1964. *The Philosophy of Science and Belief in God*. Nutley, NJ: Craig.

Collins, James. 1954. *A History of Modern European Philosophy*. Milwaukee, WI: Bruce.

———. 1959. *God in Modern Philosophy*. Chicago: Henry Regnery.

———. 1962. "Philosophy and Religion." In *Great Ideas Today*. Edited by Robert Hutchins and Mortimer J. Adler. Chicago: Encyclopaedia Britannica, Inc. Pp. 314–72.

Continuum. 1967. Winter issue, number 5, devoted to the contemporary experience of God.

Copleston, Frederick. 1964. *A History of Philosophy*. Vol. 5: *Modern Philosophy: The British Philosophers, Part II, Berkeley to Hume*. Garden City, NY: Doubleday, Image Books.

Craig, William Lane. 1979. *The Existence of God and the Beginnings of the Universe*. San Bernardino, CA: Here's Life Publishers.

———. 1980a. *The Cosmological Argument: From Plato to Leibniz*. New York: Barnes and Noble.

———. 1980b. "Philosophical and Scientific Pointers to Creation ex Nihilo." *Journal of the American Scientific Affiliation* 32:5–13.

———. 1981. *The Son Rises*. Chicago: Moody.

———. 1984. *Apologletics: An Introduction*. Chicago: Moody.

———. 1985. "Professor Mackie and the Kalam Cosmological Argument." *Religious Studies* 20:367–75.

———. 1987. *The Only Wise God: The Compatibility of Divine Foreknowledge and Human Freedom*. Grand Rapids, MI: Baker.

Daniélou, J. 1957. *God and the Ways of Knowing*. Cleveland, OH: Meridian.

Davies, Brian. 1982. *An Introduction to the Philosophy of Religion*. Oxford: Oxford University Press.

Davies, Paul. 1983. "The Anthropic Principle." *Science Digest* (October).

Dawkins, R. 1986. *The Blind Watchmaker*. New York: Norton.

Denzinger, H. 1953. *Enchiridion Symbolorum*. 29th rev. ed. Freiberg im Breisgau: Herder.

Dietl, Paul J. 1968. "On Miracles." *American Philosophical Quarterly* 5:130–34.

Dirscherl, D., ed. 1967. *Speaking of God*. Milwaukee, WI: Bruce.

Dray, William H. 1964. *Philosophy of History*. Englewood Cliffs, NJ: Prentice-Hall.

Edwards, Jonathan. 1957. *The Freedom of the Will*. Edited by Paul Ramsey. New Haven, CT: Yale University Press. Originally published in 1756.

Ellis, E. Earle. 1980. "Dating the New Testament." *New Testament Studies* 26 (July):487–502.

Empson, William. 1965. *Milton's God*. Rev. ed. London: Chatto and Windus.

Erickson, Millard J. 1986. *Concise Dictionary of Christian Theology*. Grand Rapids, MI: Baker. P. 58.

Eslick, Leonard James. 1957. "What is the Starting Point of Metaphysics?" *The Modern Schoolman* 34 (May):247–63.

———. 1961. "The Real Distinction: Reply to Professor Reese." *The Modern Schoolman* 37:149–60.

————. 1964. "Toward a Metaphysics of Creation." *Metaphysical Investigations: A Selection of Lectures Delivered Before the Philosophers' Club of Saint Louis University.* St. Louis: St. Louis University.

————. 1966. "The Empirical Foundations of Metaphysics." *Proceedings of the Saint Louis University Philosophy Club.* Later published as "The Negative Judgment of Separation: A Reply to Father Burrell." *The Modern Schoolman* 44 (November): 35–46.

————. 1968. "Omnipotence: The Meanings of Power." *The New Scholasticism* 42 (Spring): 289–92.

————. 1983. "From the World to God: The Cosmological Argument." *The Modern Schoolman* 60:153.

Evans, C. Stephen. 1978. *Subjectivity and Religious Belief.* Grand Rapids, MI: Eerdmans.

Ewing, A. C. 1973. *Value and Reality.* London: Allen and Unwin.

Fabro, Cornelio. 1968. *God in Exile: A Study of the Internal Dynamics of Modern Atheism from Its Roots in the Cartesian Cogito to the Present Day.* Westminster and New York: Newman.

Fairbairn, Andrew M. 1902. *The Philosophy of the Christian Religion.* New York: Hodder & Stoughton.

Ferguson, Sinclair B., David F. Wright, and J. I. Packer, eds. 1988. *New Dictionary of Theology.* Leicester, England: InterVarsity. Pp. 274–77.

Ferré, Frederick. 1967. *Basic Modern Philosophy of Religion.* New York: Scribner.

Ferré, Nels F. S. 1946. *Faith and Reason.* New York: Harper & Brothers.

Fischer, David Hackett. 1970. *Historians' Fallacies: Toward a Logic of Historical Thought.* New York: Harper Torchbooks.

Fisher, George Park. 1899. *Manual of Christian Evidences.* New York: Scribner.

Flew, Antony G. N. 1955. "Theology and Falsification" and "Divine Omnipotence and Human Freedom." In *New Essays in Philosophical Theology.* Edited by Antony Flew and Alasdair MacIntyre. New York: Macmillan. Pp. 96–99.

————. 1961. *Hume's Philosophy of Belief.* London: Routledge and Kegan Paul.

————, ed. 1964. *Body, Mind, and Death.* New York: Macmillan.

————. 1966. *God and Philosophy.* New York: Dell.

————. 1975. "'Theology and Falsification' in Retrospect." In *The Logic of God: Theology and Verification.* Edited by M. L. Diamond and T. V. Litzenburg. Indianapolis, IN: Bobbs-Merrill.

————. 1978. *A Rational Animal and Other Philosophical Essays on the Nature of Man.* Oxford: Clarendon.

————. 1984a. *God, Freedom and Immortality.* Buffalo, NY: Prometheus. Reissue of a book first published in 1976 as *The Presumption of Atheism.*

————. 1984b. *God: A Philosophical Critique.* LaSalle, IL: Open Court. Reissue of a book first published in 1966 as *God and Philosophy.*

————. 1985. *Thinking About Social Thinking: The Philosophy of the Social Sciences.* Oxford: Basil Blackwell.

————. 1986a. "Apologia pro Philosophia Mea." In S. G. Shanker, ed. *Philosophy in Britain Today.* London and Sydney: Croum Helm.

————. 1986b. *David Hume: Philosopher of Moral Science.* Oxford: Basil Blackwell.

————. 1987. *The Logic of Morality.* Oxford: Basil Blackwell.

————. 1989. *An Introduction to Western Philosophy.* Rev. ed. London: Thames and Hudson.

————, and Alasdair Macintyre. 1955. *New Essays in Philosophical Theology.* London: SCM.

————, and Thomas B. Warren. 1977. *The Warren-Flew Debate on the Existence of God.* Jonesboro, AR: National Christian Press.

————, and Godfrey Vesey. 1987. *Agency and Necessity.* Great Debates in Philosophy. Oxford: Basil Blackwell.

France, R. T. 1970. *The Living God.* Downers Grove, IL: InterVarsity.

———. 1986. *The Evidence for Jesus.* Downers Grove, IL: InterVarsity.

Gange, Robert A. 1986. *Origins and Destiny.* Waco, TX: Word.

Geach, P. T. 1969. *God and the Soul.* London: Routledge and Kegan Paul.

Geisler, Norman L. 1974. *Philosophy of Religion.* Grand Rapids, MI: Zondervan.

———. 1976. *Christian Apologetics.* Grand Rapids, MI: Baker.

———. 1978. *The Roots of Evil.* Grand Rapids, MI: Zondervan.

———. 1982. *Miracles and Modern Thought.* Grand Rapids, MI: Zondervan.

Gerstner, John H. 1967. *Reasons For Faith.* Grand Rapids, MI: Baker.

Gilby, Thomas. 1951. *St. Thomas Aquinas Philosophical Texts.* London: Oxford University Press.

Gilson, Etienne. 1956. *The Philosophy of St. Thomas Aquinas.* Authorized translation from the 3d rev. and enl. ed. of *Le Thomisme.* New York: Dorset Press. Originally published by Random House.

———. 1969. "The Idea of God and the Difficulties of Atheism." *Philosophy Today* 13 (Fall):174–205. Reprinted from *Great Ideas Today* 1969 by Encyclopædia Britannica, Inc.

Green, Michael. 1968. *Runaway World.* Downers Grove, IL: InterVarsity.

Green, Ronald M. 1978. *Religious Reason: The Rational and Moral Basis of Religious Belief.* New York: Oxford University Press.

Grunbaum, A. 1989. "The Pseudo-problem of Creation in Physical Cosmology." In *Philosophy of Science* 61:373–94.

Habermas, Gary R. 1980. *The Resurrection of Jesus: An Apologetic.* Grand Rapids, MI: Baker.

———. 1988. *The Verdict of History: Conclusive Evidence for the Life of Jesus.* Nashville, TN: Thomas Nelson. Originally published (1985) under the title: *Ancient Evidence for the Life of Jesus: Historical Records of His Death and Resurrection.*

———. 1989a. "Resurrection Claims in Non-Christian Religions." *Religious Studies* 25:167–77.

———. 1989b. "Jesus's Resurrection and Contemporary Criticism: An Apologetic." *Criswell Theological Review* 4.1 (fall):159–74. Part 2 of this article is in vol. 4, no. 2.

Hackett, Stuart C. 1982. *The Resurrection of Theism: Prolegomena to Christian Apology.* 2d ed. Grand Rapids, MI: Baker.

Harris, Samuel. 1883. *The Philosophical Basis of Theism.* New York: Scribner.

Hartshorne, Charles. 1962. *The Logic of Perfection.* LaSalle, IL: Open Court.

———. 1965. *Anselm's Discovery.* LaSalle, IL: Open Court.

———. 1970. *Creative Synthesis and Philosophic Method.* LaSalle, IL: Open Court.

———, and William L. Reese. 1953. *Philosophers Speak of God.* Chicago: University of Chicago Press.

Hayek, F. A. 1967. *Studies in Philosophy, Politics and Economics.* London: Routledge and Kegan Paul.

———. 1973. *Law, Legislation and Liberty. Vol. 1, Rules and Order.* Chicago and London: University of Chicago Press and Routledge and Kegan Paul.

Helm, Paul, ed. 1981. *Divine Commands and Morality.* New York: Oxford University Press.

Herberg, Will. 1951. *Judaism and Modern Man.* New York: Farrar, Straus.

Hick, John, ed. 1964. *The Existence of God.* New York: Macmillan.

———. 1977. *Evil and the God of Love.* Rev. ed. San Francisco: Harper & Row. Originally published in 1966 by Macmillan.

———, and A. C. McGill, eds. 1967. *The Many-faced Argument.* Recent Studies on the Ontological Argument for the Existence of God. New York: Macmillan.

Hobbes, Thomas. 1914. *Leviathan.* Edited by A. D. Lindsay. London and New York: Dent and Sons, and E.P. Dutton.

Holland, R. F. 1965. "The Miraculous," *American Philosophical Quarterly* 2:43–51.

Holmes, Arthur F. 1975. *Philosophy: A Christian Perspective, An Introductory Essay.* Downers Grove, IL: InterVarsity.

Horigan, James E. 1979. *Chance or Design?* New York: Philosophical Library.

Hübner, Kurt. 1983. *Critique of Scientific Reason.* Translated by Paul R. Dixon and Hollis M. Dixon. Chicago: University of Chicago Press.

Hume, David. 1932. *The Letters of David Hume.* Edited by J. Y. T. Greig. 2 vols. Oxford: Oxford University Press.

———. 1947. *Hume's Dialogues Concerning Natural Religion.* 2d ed. Edited by N. Kemp Smith. Edinburgh: Nelson. Originally published in 1779.

———. 1988. *An Enquiry Concerning Human Understanding.* Edited by Antony Flew. LaSalle, IL: Open Court. Originally published in 1748.

Huxley, T. H. 1904. *Collected Essays.* London: Macmillan.

Jaki, Stanley L. 1969. *Brain, Mind and Computers.* New York: Herder and Herder.

———. 1978. *The Road of Science and the Ways to God.* Chicago: University of Chicago Press.

Johnson, O. A. 1965. "God and St. Anselm." *The Journal of Religion* 45:326–34.

Kaufmann, Walter. 1963. *The Faith of a Heretic.* New York: Doubleday, Anchor.

———. 1966. *Nietzsche: Philosopher, Psychologist, Antichrist.* New York: Meridian.

Kerkut, G. A. 1960. "Implications of Evolution." *International Series on Monographs on Pure and Applied Biology.* Vol. 4. New York: Pergamon.

Keyser, Leander S. 1950. *A System of Christian Evidences.* 10th ed., rev. Burlington, IA: Lutheran Literary Board.

Kim, Seyoon. 1982. *The Origin of Paul's Gospel.* Grand Rapids, MI: Eerdmans.

Klubertanz, George P. 1963. *Introduction to The Philosophy of Being.* 2d ed. New York: Appleton-Century-Crofts.

Kübler-Ross, Elisabeth. 1969. *On Death and Dying.* New York: Macmillan.

Küng, Hans. 1980. *Does God Exist? An Answer for Today.* Translated by Edward Quinn. Garden City, NY: Doubleday.

———. 1984. *Eternal Life? Life After Death as a Medical, Philosophical, and Theological Problem.* Translated by Edward Quinn. Garden City, NY: Doubleday.

Ladd, George E. 1975. *I Believe in the Resurrection of Jesus.* Grand Rapids, MI: Eerdmans.

Lacroix, J. 1965. *The Meaning of Atheism.* New York: Macmillan.

Laudan, Larry. 1977. *Progress and Its Problems: Toward a Theory of Scientific Growth.* Berkeley, CA: University of California Press.

Lavelle, Louis. 1940. *Evil and Suffering.* Translated by Bernard Murchland, C.S.C. New York: Macmillan.

LeFevre, Perry. 1968. *Philosophical Resources for Christian Thought.* New York: Abingdon.

Leslie, John. 1989. *Universes.* New York and London: Routledge and Kegan Paul.

Lewis, C. S. 1947a. *The Abolition of Man.* New York: Macmillan.

———. 1947b. *Miracles: A Preliminary Study.* New York: Macmillan.

———. 1955. "On Obstinacy in Belief." In *The World's Last Night and Other Essays.* New York: Harcourt Brace Jovanovich.

———. 1960. *Mere Christianity.* New York: Macmillan.

———. 1962. *The Problem of Pain: The Intellectual Problem Raised by Human Suffering Examined with Sympathy and Realism.* New York: Macmillan.

———. 1970. *God in the Dock: Essays on Theology and Ethics.* Grand Rapids, MI: Eerdmans. Specifically chaps. 2, 8, and 9.

Lewis, H. D. 1982. *The Elusive Self.* Philadelphia: Westminster.

Locke, John. 1975. *An Essay Concerning Human Understanding.* Edited by Peter H. Nidditch. Oxford: Clarendon. Originally published in 1690.

Lonergan, Bernard J. F. 1973. *Philosophy of God, and Theology.* Philadelphia: Westminster.

Lovejoy, A. O. 1936. *The Great Chain of Being: A Study of the History of an Idea.* Cambridge, MA: Harvard University Press.

Lubac, H. de. 1960. *The Discovery of God.* New York: Kennedy.

Lucas, J. R. 1970. *The Freedom of the Will.* Oxford: Clarendon.

Luther, Martin. 1957. *The Bondage of the Will*. Translated by J. I. Packer and O. R. Johnson. London: J. Clarke. Originally published in 1525.

MacKay, Donald M. 1979. *Human Science and Human Dignity*. Downers Grove, IL: InterVarsity.

———. 1982. *Science and the Quest for Meaning*. Grand Rapids, MI: Eerdmans.

McInerny, Ralph M., ed. 1968. *New Themes in Christian Philosophy*. Notre Dame, IN: University of Notre Dame Press.

McIntyre, C. T., ed. 1977. *God, History, and Historians*. New York: Oxford University Press.

McPherson, Thomas. 1972. *The Argument from Design*. London: Macmillan.

Maddell, Geoffrey. 1981. *The Identity of the Self*. Edinburgh: The University Press.

Madden, Edward H., and Peter H. Hare. 1968. *Evil and the Concept of God*. Springfield, IL: Charles C. Thomas.

Magnusson, Magnus, and Hermann Palsson. 1960. *Njal's Saga*. Harmandsworth: Penguin.

Marshall, I. Howard. 1969. *Kept by the Power of God*. Minneapolis, MN: Bethany House.

———. 1977. *I Believe in the Historical Jesus*. In the "I Believe" series. Grand Rapids, MI: Eerdmans.

Mascall, E. L. 1948. *He Who Is*. New York: Longmans, Green.

Matson, W. I. 1965. *The Existence of God*. Ithaca, NY: Cornell University Press.

Miethe, Terry L. 1976. *The Metaphysics of Leonard James Eslick: His Philosophy of God*. Ann Arbor, MI: University Microfilms, Inc.

———. 1977. "The Ontological Argument: A Research Bibliography." *The Modern Schoolman* vol. 54 (2 January):148–66.

———. 1978. "The Cosmological Argument: A Research Bibliography." *The New Scholasticism* vol. 52 (spring):285–305.

———. 1981. "Atheism: Nietzsche." In *Biblical Errancy: An Analysis of its Philosophical Roots*. Grand Rapids, MI: Zondervan. Pp. 130–60.

———. 1982. *Augustinian Bibliography, 1970–1980: With Essays on the Fundamentals of Augustinian Scholarship*. Westport, CT: Greenwood.

———. 1984. *The New Christian's Guide to Following Jesus*. Minneapolis, MN: Bethany House.

———. 1987. *A Christian's Guide to Faith and Reason*. Minneapolis, MN: Bethany House.

———. 1988a. *The Compact Dictionary of Doctrinal Words*. Minneapolis, MN: Bethany House.

———. 1988b. Apologist's Corner: "The Christian and Debate." *The LodeStar Review* (November):2.

———. 1989. "The Universal Power of the Atonement." In *The Grace of God/The Will of Man*. Edited by C. Pinnock. Grand Rapids, MI: Zondervan. Pp. 71–96.

———, and Vernon J. Bourke. 1980. *Thomistic Bibliography, 1940–1978*. Westport, CT: Greenwood.

———, ed., Gary R. Habermas, and Antony G. N. Flew. 1987. *Did Jesus Rise From the Dead? The Resurrection Debate*. San Francisco: Harper & Row.

Mill, John S. 1874. *Three Essays on Religion*. 3d ed. London: Longman, Green, Reader and Dyer.

Miller, E. L. 1984. *Questions That Matter: An Introduction to Philosophy*. New York: McGraw-Hill. Pp. 254–63.

Mitchel, Basil, ed. 1957. *Faith and Logic: Oxford Essays in Philosophical Theology*. London: George Allen & Unwin.

———. 1980. *Morality: Religious and Secular*. Oxford: Clarendon.

Mitton, C. Leslie. 1974. *Jesus: The Fact Behind the Faith*. Grand Rapids, MI: Eerdmans.

Montgomery, John Warwick. 1964. *History and Christianity*. Downers Grove, IL: InterVarsity.

————. 1965. "Inspiration and Inerrancy: A New Departure." *Evangelical Theological Society Bulletin* 8 (Spring):45–75. Also reprinted in *The Suicide of Christian Theology*, pp. 314–55.

————. 1970. *The Suicide of Christian Theology*. Minneapolis, MN: Bethany House.

————. 1972. *Where Is History Going?* Minneapolis, MN: Bethany House.

————. 1975. *The Shape of the Past*. Minneapolis, MN: Bethany House.

————. 1978. *Faith Founded on Fact*. Nashville, TN: Thomas Nelson.

Moody, Raymond A., Jr. 1975. *Life After Life*. New York: Bantam.

Moreland, J. P. 1987. *Scaling the Secular City: A Defense of Christianity*. Grand Rapids, MI: Baker.

Morris, Henry M. 1974. *Scientific Creationism*. El Cajon, CA: Master.

————. 1984. *The Biblical Basis for Modern Science*. Grand Rapids, MI: Baker.

————, and Gary Parker. 1982. *What Is Creation Science?* San Diego, CA: Creation-Life Publishers.

Morrison, A. Cressy. 1944. *Man Does Not Stand Alone*. Rev. ed. New York: Revell.

Mosley, A. W. 1965. "Historical Reporting in the Ancient World." *New Testament Studies* 12 (October):10–26.

Moule, C. F. D. 1967. *The Phenomenon of the New Testament*. London: SCM.

————. 1977. *The Origin of Christology*. Cambridge: Cambridge University Press.

————. 1981. *The Birth of the New Testament*. 3d rev. ed. San Francisco: Harper & Row.

Mullins, E. Y. 1905. *Why Is Christianity True? Christian Evidences*. Philadelphia: American Baptist Publication Society.

Murray, J. C. 1964. *The Problem of God*. New Haven, CT: Yale University Press.

Nash, Ronald H. 1988. *Faith and Reason: Searching for a Rational Faith*. Grand Rapids, MI: Zondervan. Part 5, "Miracles," pp. 225–74; specifically chap. 16, "David Hume's Attack on Miracles," pp. 225–40.

Neville, Robert C. 1968. *God the Creator: On the Transcendence and Presence of God*. Chicago: University of Chicago Press.

Newton-Smith, W. H. 1981. *The Rationality of Science*. International Library of Philosophy. Boston: Routledge and Kegan Paul.

Owen, H. P. 1965. *The Moral Argument for Christian Theism*. London: Allen and Unwin.

Pannenberg, Wolfhart. 1976. *Theology and the Philosophy of Science*. Translated by Francis McDonagh. Philadelphia: Westminster.

————. 1987. "Response to the Debate." In Gary Habermas and Antony Flew, *Did Jesus Rise from the Dead? The Resurrection Debate*. Edited by Terry L. Miethe. San Francisco: Harper & Row. Pp. 125–35.

Parker, Francis H. 1967. "The Realistic Position in Religion." In *Religion in Philosophical and Cultural Perspective*. Edited by Clayton Feaver et al. New York: Van Nostrand.

Pascal, Blaise. 1960. *Pensées*. Arranged by Louis Lafuma and translated by J. Warmington. London: Dent.

Peacocke, A. R. 1979. *Creation and the World of Science*. Oxford: Oxford University Press.

————, ed. 1981. *The Sciences and Theology in the Twentieth Century*. Notre Dame, IN: University of Notre Dame Press.

Peirce, C. S. 1934 onward. *Collected Papers*. Cambridge, MA: Harvard University Press.

Pinnock, Clark H. 1967. *Set Forth Your Case: An Examination of Christianity's Credentials*. Nutley, NJ: Craig.

————, ed. 1975. *Grace Unlimited*. Minneapolis, MN: Bethany House.

————. 1980. *Reason Enough: A Case for the Christian Faith*. Downers Grove, IL: InterVarsity.

————, ed. 1989. *The Grace of God/The Will of Man*. Grand Rapids, MI: Zondervan.

Plantinga, Alvin, ed. 1965. *The Ontological Argument: From St. Anselm to Contemporary Philosophers*. Garden City, NY: Doubleday, Anchor.

————. 1967. *God and Other Minds: A Study of the Rational Justification of Belief in God*. Ithaca, NY: Cornell University Press.

——— . 1974. *God, Freedom, and Evil*. New York: Harper & Row.

Plato. 1952. *Gorgias*. Translated by W. C. Helmhold. Indianapolis, IN: Bobbs-Merrill.

——— . 1961. *Plato: The Collected Dialogues*. Edited by Edith Hamilton and Huntington Cairns. Princeton, NJ: Princeton University Press.

Plotinus. 1956. *Plotinus: The Enneads*. Translated by Stephen MacKenna. London: Faber and Faber.

Purtill, Richard L. 1974. *Reason to Believe*. Grand Rapids, MI: Eerdmans.

——— . 1976. "Proofs of Miracles and Miracles as Proofs." *Christian Scholars Review* 6 (no. 1):39–51.

——— . 1977. "Flew and the Free Will Defence." *Religious Studies* 13:477–83.

——— . 1978. *Thinking About Religion: A Philosophical Introduction to Religion*. Englewood Cliffs, NJ: Prentice-Hall.

——— . 1985. *C. S. Lewis's Case for the Christian Faith*. San Francisco: Harper & Row.

Ramm, Bernard. 1953. *Protestant Christian Evidences*. Chicago: Moody.

——— . 1954. *The Christian View of Science and Scripture*. Grand Rapids, MI: Eerdmans.

Reichenbach, Bruce R. 1972. *The Cosmological Argument: A Reassessment*. Springfield, IL: Charles C. Thomas.

Reid, J. K. S. 1969. *Christian Apologetics*. Grand Rapids, MI: Eerdmans.

Rice, Richard. 1980. *God's Foreknowledge and Man's Free Will*. Minneapolis, MN: Bethany House.

Robinson, John A. T. 1976. *Redating the New Testament*. Philadelphia: Westminster.

——— . 1977. *Can We Trust the New Testament?* Grand Rapids: MI: Eerdmans.

Rowe, William L. 1971. "The Cosmological Argument." *Nous*, vol. 5 (no. 1):49–61.

——— . 1975. *The Cosmological Argument*. Princeton, NJ: Princeton University Press.

Shapiro, Robert. 1986. *Origins*. New York: Summit.

Silvester, Hugh. 1971. *Arguing with God*. Downers Grove, IL: InterVarsity.

Six, J. E. 1967–68. *L'athéisme dans la vie et la culture contemporaines*. 2 vols. Paris: Desclée.

Smart, Ninian. 1964. *Philosophers and Religious Truth*. London: SCM. Specifically chap. 2, which is an answer to the criticism that miracles are unscientific.

Smith, Gerard, and L. H. Kendzierski. 1961. *The Philosophy of Being*. Christian Wisdom Series. New York: Macmillan.

Smith, John E. 1967. *Reason and God: Encounters of Philosophy with Religion*. New Haven, CT: Yale University Press.

——— . 1968. *Experience and God*. New York: Oxford University Press.

Sontag, Frederick. 1970. *God, Why Did You Do That?* Philadelphia: Westminster.

Sowell, Thomas. 1980. *Knowledge and Decisions*. New York: Basic.

Stearns, J. Brenton. 1966. "On the Impossibility of God's Knowing That He Does Not Exist." *The Journal of Religion* 46:1–8.

Stephen, Leslie. 1876. *English Thought in the Eighteenth Century*. 3d ed. London: Murrary.

Strawson, P. F. 1959. *Individuals: An Essay in Descriptive Metaphysics*. London: Methuen.

Swinburne, Richard. 1970. *The Concept of Miracle*. London: Macmillan.

——— . 1977. *The Coherence of Theism*. Clarendon Library of Logic and Philosophy. Oxford: Oxford University Press.

——— . 1979. *The Existence of God*. Oxford: Clarendon.

——— . 1981. *Faith and Reason*. Oxford: Clarendon.

——— . 1986. *The Evolution of the Soul*. Oxford: Clarendon.

Taylor, Richard. 1974. *Metaphysics*. Englewood Cliffs, NJ: Prentice-Hall.

Tennant, F. R. 1925. *Miracle and Its Philosophical Presuppositions*. Cambridge: Cambridge University Press.

——— . 1956. *Philosophical Theology*. Vol. 2, *The World, the Soul, and God*. Cambridge: Cambridge University Press.

Tenney, Merril C. 1963. *The Reality of the Resurrection*. New York: Harper & Row.

Thaxton, Charles B., Walter L. Bradley, and Roger L. Olsen. 1984. *The Mystery of Life's Origin: Reassessing Current Theories.* New York: Philosophical Library.

Thompson, Matthew. 1989. "The Problem of Good in the Problem of Evil." A Thesis submitted to and accepted by the Faculty of Arts of the University of Birmingham, England.

Thompson, Samuel M. 1955. *A Modern Philosophy of Religion.* Chicago: Henry Regnery.

Thurman, L. Duane. 1978. *How to Think About Evolution.* 2d ed. Downers Grove, IL: InterVarsity.

Tillich, Paul. 1948. *The Shaking of the Foundations.* New York: Scribner.

———. 1958. *Dynamics of Faith.* New York: Harper Torchbooks.

———. 1967. *Systematic Theology.* 3 vols. Chicago: University of Chicago Press.

Trueblood, David Elton. 1957. *Philosophy of Religion.* New York: Harper & Row.

Valecky, L. C. 1968. "Flew on Aquinas." *Philosophy* 43:213–30.

van Frassen, Bas C. 1980. *The Scientific Image.* Oxford: Clarendon.

Varghese, Roy Abraham, ed. 1984. *The Intellectuals Speak Out About God.* Chicago: Regnery Gateway.

Wenham, John W. 1974. *The Goodness of God.* Downers Grove, IL: InterVarsity.

———. 1984. *Easter Enigma: Are the Resurrection Accounts in Conflict?* Grand Rapids, MI: Zondervan.

Whately, Richard. 1849. *Historical Doubts Relative to Napoleon Bonaparte.* New York: Robert Caster. Satirizes Hume's attack on miracles, claiming that Hume's views would eliminate historical knowledge of other unique and nonmiraculous events.

White, Morton G. 1970. "The Analytic and the Synthetic: An Untenable Dualism." In *Analyticity.* Edited by J. F. Harris, Jr., and R. H. Severens. Chicago: Quadrangle. Pp. 75–91.

Wilder-Smith, A. E. 1968. *Man's Origin, Man's Destiny.* Wheaton, IL: Harold Shaw. Currently published with Bethany House.

———. 1970. *The Creation of Life.* Wheaton, IL: Harold Shaw.

———. 1981. *The Natural Sciences Know Nothing of Evolution.* Costa Mesa, CA: T.W.F.T.

———. 1987. *The Scientific Alternative to Neo-Darwinian Evolutionary Theory: Information Sources and Structures.* Costa Mesa, CA: T.W.F.T.

Wisdom, John. 1953. *Philosophy and Psychoanalysis.* Oxford: Basil Blackwell.

Wright, Christopher J. 1983. *An Eye for an Eye: The Place of Old Testament Ethics Today.* Downers Grove, IL: InterVarsity.

Yockey, Hubert P. 1977. "A Calculation of the Probability of Spontaneous Biogenesis by Information Theory." *Journal of Theoretical Biology* 67:377–98.

———. 1981. "Self-Organization Origin of Life Scenarios and Information Theory." *Journal of Theoretical Biology* 91:13–31.

Young, Warren C. 1954. *A Christian Approach to Philosophy.* Grand Rapids, MI: Baker.

About the Contributors

TERRY L. MIETHE is Dean of the Oxford Study Centre and is currently a postdoctoral fellow at Christ Church, the University of Oxford, England. Before this Dr. Miethe taught at Saint Louis University and the University of Southern California. He has also been a visiting professor at nine colleges and universities around the world and has lectured at over thirty-five. Dr. Miethe holds the M.A. from Trinity Evangelical Divinity School; the M.Div. from McCormick Theological Seminary; the Ph.D. in philosophy, Phi Beta Kappa, from Saint Louis University; and the A.M. and Ph.D. in social ethics and theology from the University of Southern California. Dr. Miethe has written or edited twelve books, including works on Augustine and Aquinas; *The New Christian's Guide to Following Jesus* (1984), *A Christian's Guide to Faith and Reason* (1987), and *The Compact Dictionary of Doctrinal Words* (1988) (all with Bethany House Publishers); and *Did Jesus Rise From the Dead? The Resurrection Debate* (1987; with Harper & Row). He has also written dozen of articles.

ANTONY G. N. FLEW was for many years Professor of Philosophy at the University of Reading, England. Before this Dr. Flew taught at Christ Church, University of Oxford; King's College, University of Aberdeen; and the University of Keele. He has also been a visiting professor at many universities around the world. For the past several years, Dr. Flew has been a visiting professor at the Social Philosophy and Policy Center at Bowling Green State University in Ohio. Dr. Flew holds the M.A. from St. John's College, University of Oxford and a D. Litt. from the University of Keele. Dr. Flew has written eighteen books. Among the most famous are *God and Philosophy* (1966) and *The Presumption of Atheism* (1984a); among the most recent are *Thinking About Social Thinking: The Philosophy of the Social Sciences* (1985), *David Hume: Philosopher of Moral Science* (1986), *The Logic of Morality* (1987), all with Blackwell's, Oxford. Dr. Flew has also edited nine books and written dozens of articles.

SIR ALFRED AYER was educated as a King's Scholar at Eton and as a classical scholar at Christ Church, Oxford. After spending a short period at the University of Vienna, he became a Lecturer in Philosophy at Christ

Church in 1933 and Research Student in 1935. After World War II, he returned to Oxford as Fellow and Dean of Wadham College, Oxford. From 1946 to 1959 he was Grote Professor of the Philosophy of Mind and Logic at the University of London. He was Wykeham Professor of Logic in the University of Oxford, and was a Fellow of New College, Oxford, from 1959 until 1978. From 1978 to 1983 he was a Fellow of Wolfson College, Oxford. In addition, he was a Fellow of the British Academy and an Honorary Member of the American Academy of Arts and Sciences. His principal publications were *Language, Truth and Logic; The Foundations of Empirical Knowledge; Philosophical Essays; The Problem of Knowledge; The Concept of a Person; The Origins of Pragmatism; Metaphysics and Common Sense; Russell and Moore: The Analytical Heritage; Probability and Evidence: Philosophy in the Twentieth Century; Russell; Hume; Freedom and Morality; Ludwig Wittgenstein;* and *Voltaire.* He also published two volumes of autobiography and contributed articles to philosophical and literary journals. Sir Alfred was knighted in 1970 and was a Chevalier de la Légion d'Honneur.

HANS KÜNG is the most prominent Catholic theologian living today. He studied at the German College in Rome, the Gregorian University, and the Institute Catholique, and the Sorbonne in Paris. Dr. Küng is a professor at the University of Tübingen, in Germany. He is well known around the world and has been a visiting professor at the University of Chicago and the University of Michigan, Ann Arbor. Among his books are *The Church; On Being a Christian; Signposts for the Future; The Christian Challenge; Does God Exist? An Answer for Today; Eternal Life? Life After Death as a Medical, Philosophical, and Theological Problem;* and *Why I Am Still a Christian.*

RICHARD SWINBURNE is a Professor of Philosophy and Philosophy of the Christian Religion at Oriel College, the University of Oxford. Before this, Dr. Swinburne had academic appointments at the universities of Oxford, Leeds, Hull, and Maryland and was Professor of Philosophy at the University of Keele. His published work includes *Space and Time; The Concept of Miracle; An Introduction to Confirmation Theory; The Coherence of Theism; Faith and Reason; The Existence of God;* and *The Evolution of the Soul.*

HERMANN HÄRING is Professor of Theology and Dean of the Theological Faculty at the University of Nijmegen, Netherlands where he is the successor to Edward Schillebeeckx. Dr. Häring is a former colleague and student of Dr. Hans Küng at the University of Tübingen. Prof. Häring holds the degrees of Dr. Theol., with a dissertation entitled: *Das Kirchenbild in der Bultmannschule* (which treats the ecclesiology of R. Bultmann, E. Fuchs, G. Ebeling, G. Bornkamm, E. Käsemann, and H. Conzelmann in ecumenical context) and the degree of Dr. Theol. Habil., with a dissertation entitled: *Problematik und Lehre des Bösen bei Augustinus* both from Tubingen. His published work includes: *Kirche und Kerygma. Das Kirchenbild in der Butlmannschule; Was bedeuted Himmel?; Zum Problem des Bösen in der Theologie; Gegenentwürfe 24 Lebensläufe für eine andere Theologie* (coeditor); and *Wörterbuch des Christentums* (coeditor).